NEW DOCUMENTS
ILLUSTRATING
EARLY CHRISTIANITY

NEW DOCUMENTS
ILLUSTRATING
EARLY CHRISTIANITY

Volume 5
Linguistic Essays

by

G. H. R. Horsley

with cumulative indexes to vols. 1-5
newly prepared by S.P. Swinn

The Ancient History Documentary Research Centre
Macquarie University
1989

The Ancient History Documentary Research Centre (Director: E.A. Judge, Professor of History) has been formed within the School of History, Philosophy & Politics at Macquarie University to focus staff effort in research and professional development and to coordinate it with the work of other organisations interested in the documentation of the ancient world.

Committee for *New Documents Illustrating Early Christianity*
Chairman: P.W. Barnett, Master of Robert Menzies College, Macquarie University.
Members: P. Geidans, D. M. Knox, J. Lawler, J.A. Shepherd.

Editorial Consultants
F.I. Andersen, Professor of Studies in Religion, University of Queensland.
G.W. Clarke, Deputy Director, Humanities Research Centre, Australian National University.
J.A.L. Lee, Senior Lecturer in Greek, University of Sydney.
K.L. McKay, formerly Reader in Classics, Australian National University.
T. Muraoka, Professor of Middle Eastern Studies, University of Melbourne.

This volume has been produced with the support of the Greek Publications Fund, the Macquarie Greek Summer School, the Macquarie University Research Grant, the Society for Early Christianity, and the following individual donors: P. Anstey, P. S. Reay-Young and J.G. Sperling.

Editorial correspondence should be addressed to Professor E.A. Judge, School of History, Philosophy & Politics, Macquarie University, N.S.W. 2109, Australia.
Business address: The Ancient History Documentary Research Centre, Macquarie University, N.S.W. 2109, Australia.

CONTENTS

INTRODUCTION

This volume in the *New Docs* series is rather different in conception from its predecessors. When the first volume was produced at the beginning of this decade the primary purpose was to review the Greek documentary publications to discover how much new material was appearing annually which might be felt worth the attention in particular of those whose focus was the NT. By the time the fourth volume appeared (1987), this comprehensive testing had demonstrated conclusively that MM ought to be replaced, not merely revised. The frequency with which MM is reprinted shows that there is a continuing demand for such a tool.

When the decision was taken in late 1980 at Macquarie University to publish a bulletin to evaluate the need for a new MM, the project committee determined that there should be a commitment initially to produce five numbers. This fifth volume offers a stocktaking for the series. The linguistic essays it contains attempt to deal more fully than was possible in the preceding volumes with a range of questions adumbrated there. There is no suggestion that what is presented here is the 'last word' in comprehensiveness. Some of the essays draw upon the potential of certain aspects of General Linguistics for the study of ancient languages. An appendix surveys, in somewhat random fashion, what impact Linguistics is having on the study of Ancient Greek. Other essays evaluate selected books published on NT syntax and lexicography over the last generation. The fourth chapter, on lexicography, includes some detailed analysis of MM itself; this material serves as part of our rationale for planning a new dictionary to replace it. The final chapter, which most obviously partakes of the character of a 'typical' *New Docs* entry, is relevant to the present volume's linguistic focus since it deals in part with the neglect of onomastics in NT research.

With the exception of this last-mentioned essay, readers who are familiar with the previous volumes will find here a change of tone. It must be said that portions of this book have not been as congenial to write as were its predecessors: iconoclasm is not really to my taste. Yet over the several years' gestation which most of these essays have had and, indeed, during several years prior to that, I have come to feel that I should lay out more fully what is at stake in the debate on the existence of Jewish Greek, or what may be the effect on NT philology of neglecting non-literary evidence for the situation of Greek at the turn of the era.

Furthermore, the reader of these essays should note that they contain a degree (small, I hope) of exaggeration of my own position. That these pages — taken as a whole; the final chapter provides the contrast — should lack that evenhandedness which was largely present in the preceding volumes has been a decision consciously made, after weighing the risk it involved. The intention is to provoke a rethinking of the questions raised here on the part of those who immerse themselves in the Greek NT. This book is written from the standpoint of how the non-literary Greek sources may enrich and inform our appreciation of the context of early Christianity and the phenomenon of the NT books, but it will rightly be countered that this is not the whole story. The point being urged here, however, is that this is a part of the story that is too often neglected. The multiplicity and diversity of the new texts presented in the previous volumes of *New Docs* has been designed to test the assumption commonly made over the last 50 years that the vocabulary and institutions of the NT were sufficiently documented in principle from non-literary sources by the work of Deissmann, Moulton and Milligan, and other contemporaries. The tacit consensus appears to be that the beneficial yield from these data has been largely exhausted, and that there is little need to examine 'more of the same'. Yet on the basis of this sample drawn from publications appearing in the years 1976-79, the conclusion is inescapable that the volume and character of the new material published since the first two or three decades of this century is such that NT and early Christian studies have lost both linguistic and historical opportunities of importance from the neglect of continuing research of the Deissmann type.

In earlier and different forms the material included here has been circulated to a rather larger circle of colleagues than to the consulting editors alone. I am glad to place on record here my personal appreciation to the following who have read part or the whole of the manuscript at one time or another, and helped me to guard my flank: E.L. Bavin, D.A. Carson, F.W. Danker, G.D. Fee, F.T. Gignac, R. Hasan, C.J. Hemer (†), B.M. Metzger, G. Mussies, M. Silva, R.S. Stroud, E. Tov. It should not be misconstrued from my naming them that they therefore agree with everything written here.

Abbreviations

Abbreviations follow standard conventions, except where altered for clarity.

Journals — as in *L'Année philologique*.

Papyrological works — as in S.R. Pickering, *Papyrus Editions* (North Ryde, N.S.W., 1984).

Epigraphical works (for which no standard guide exists) — according to generally used conventions (see LSJ), preceded where necessary by *I* (e.g., *I.Apollonia*). See also the very useful *Guide de l'épigraphiste*, edd. F. Bérard et al. (Paris, 1986).

Ancient authors, biblical and patristic works — generally as in LSJ, BAGD, and Lampe (see below).

Some other abbreviations used, occasionally frequently, in this and preceding volumes:

Aland, *Repertorium*	— K. Aland, *Repertorium der griechischen christlichen Papyri* I. *Biblische Papyri* (Berlin, 1976)
BAGD	— Bauer/Arndt/Gingrich/Danker, *A Greek-English Lexicon of the New Testament and other Early Christian Literature* (Chicago, 1979²)
BDF	— Blass/Debrunner/Funk, *A Greek Grammar of the New Testament and other Early Christian Literature* (Chicago, 1961)
BDR	— Blass/Debrunner/Rehkopf, *Grammatik des neutestamentlichen Griechisch* (Göttingen, 1979¹⁵)
Bib.Pat.	— *Biblia Patristica. Index des citations et allusions bibliques dans la littérature patristique* (Centre d'analyse et de documentation patristiques; 4 vols; Paris, 1975-87)
CIJ	— J.B. Frey, *Corpus Inscriptionum Judaicarum* (2 vols; Rome, 1936, 1952); vol. 1 repr. with Prolegomenon by B. Lifshitz (New York, 1975)
CPJ	— V.A. Tcherikover, A. Fuks, et al., *Corpus Papyrorum Judaicarum* (3 vols; Cambridge [Mass.], 1957-64)
DACL	— Cabrol/Leclercq, et al., *Dictionnaire d'archéologie chrétienne et de liturgie* (15 vols; Paris, 1907-1953)
Deissmann, *Bible Studies*	— G.A. Deissmann, *Bible Studies* (ET: Edinburgh, 1923; repr. Winona Lake, 1979)
Deissmann, *LAE*	— G.A. Deissmann, *Light from the Ancient East* (Grand Rapids, 1980⁴)
ECL	— Early Christian Literature

Foraboschi	— D. Foraboschi, *Onomasticon Alterum Papyrologicum* (4 vols; Milan, 1966-71)
Gignac, I/II	— F.T. Gignac, *A Grammar of the Greek Papyri of the Roman and Byzantine periods* I. *Phonology*; II. *Morphology* (Milan, 1976, 1982)
Hatch and Redpath	— Hatch and Redpath, *A Concordance to the Septuagint and other Greek Versions of the Old Testament* (Oxford, 1897; 2 vols repr. Graz, 1954)
Lampe	— Lampe, *A Patristic Greek Lexicon* (Oxford, 1961, repr.)
LSJ/LSJ Suppl.	— Liddell/Scott/Jones, *A Greek-English Lexicon* (Oxford, 1940⁹, repr. with supplement ed. E.A. Barber, 1968)
LXX	— Septuagint (Rahlfs' edition)
Migne, *PG/PL*	— Migne, *Patrologia Graeca/Patrologia Latina* (Paris, 1857-87/1844-64)
MM	— Moulton and Milligan, *The Vocabulary of the Greek Testament* (London, 1930; repr.)
Naldini	— M. Naldini, *Il Cristianesimo in Egitto. Lettere private nei papiri dei secoli II-IV* (Florence, 1968)
N/A²⁶	— Nestle/Aland, *Novum Testamentum Graece* (Stuttgart, 1979²⁶)
NB	— F. Preisigke, *Namenbuch . . . enthaltend alle . . . Menschennamen . . . in griechischen Urkunden . . . Ägyptens . . .* (Heidelberg, 1922)
Peek, *GVI*	— W. Peek, *Griechische Vers-Inschriften* I (Berlin, 1955)
Solin, *GPR*	— H. Solin, *Die griechischen Personennamen in Rom. Ein Namenbuch* (3 vols; Berlin, 1982)
Spicq, *NLNT* I/III	— C. Spicq, *Notes de lexicographie néo-testamentaire* (2 vols, plus Suppl. vol.; *Orbis Biblicus et Orientalis* 22.1-3; Göttingen, 1978-1982)
Spoglio	— S. Daris, *Spoglio lessicale papirologico* (3 vols; Milan, 1968)
UBS³	— *The Greek New Testament* (New York; United Bible Societies, 1975³)
Turner, *Typology*	— E.G. Turner, *The Typology of the Early Codex* (Pennsylvania, 1977)
van Haelst	— J. van Haelst, *Catalogue des papyrus littéraires juifs et chrétiens* (Paris, 1976)
WB	— F. Preisigke, et al., *Wörterbuch der griechischen Papyrusurkunden* (Heidelberg, et alibi, 1924-)

Dates are AD unless otherwise marked. IV¹ = 'first half IVth century', IV² = 'second half IVth century'; etc.

Item numbers are in bold type throughout the Review, for cross-referencing.

For those wishing to refer to this volume, the **abbreviation** *New Docs* vol.5 is suggested.

Textual sigla used are as follows:—

αβ̣	— letters not completely legible
. . . .	— 4 letters missing
‾ ‾ ‾ ‾	— indeterminate number of letters missing
[αβ]	— letters lost from document and restored by editor
[±8]	— about 8 letters lost
<αβ>	— letters omitted by scribe and added by editor
≪αβ≫	— editorial correction of wrong letters in the text
(αβ)	— editor has resolved an abbreviation in the text
{αβ}	— letters wrongly added by scribe and cancelled by editor
[[αβ]]	— a (still legible) erasure made by scribe
`αβ´	— letters written above the line
α´ or ᾱ	— letter stands for a numerical equivalent
v., vv., vac.	— one, two, several letter spaces left blank (*vacat*) on document
m.1, m.2	— first hand (*manus*), second hand
front/back	— writing along the fibres/across the fibres of a papyrus sheet.

In each of the previous volumes the **indexes** were quite extensive. As part of the stocktaking which this present book constitutes, it was decided that a set of cumulative indexes should be devised *de novo* to allow users to search more efficiently for material scattered through the series. These indexes have been compiled by S.P. Swinn. Not only have the customary five indexes been produced with all references reverified and omissions rectified, but also a new one for those wanting to find where grammatical questions are dealt with. Moreover, the indexes are now far more specific in their reference to actual pages rather than to an entry in general. Bibliographical details of all the documentary volumes culled in *New Docs 1976-1979* are also listed. An introductory statement to each index indicates what is and is not included.

A further difference from *New Docs 1976-1979* is that a bibliography of secondary literature — apart from items dealt with only in Appendix B — has been included. The main reason for this decision is that quite a number of works from Linguistics are mentioned, in addition to literature from Biblical and Classical Studies.

This fifth volume of *New Docs* is my swansong as regards the series. This decision had already been made well before I left Macquarie University during 1988, and was determined by the realisation of our project team (P.W. Barnett, E.A. Judge, J.A.L. Lee and myself) that we, i.e., Lee and I as the designated Chief Investigators, must concentrate our attention more single-mindedly on work for the new Dictionary to ensure that we finish it. At the time of writing this, some three dozen volunteers in seven countries are helping as readers of documentary texts, and producing slips. For those concerned that this volume should not mark the end of *New Docs*, it may be mentioned that the committee at Macquarie responsible for the series has determined to proceed to vols 6-10, with another author appointed and adopting a more concise format. *New Docs* has come to have a life of its own apart from being a vehicle to test the need for a new MM, and for that I am glad. Scope was allowed in these volumes to explore historical questions, as well as more strictly philological matters. The diverse socio-historical facets of the subject which emerge from scrutiny of inscriptions and papyri show the same complex web of relationships by which Jews and Christians were bound to their hellenistic environment as does the linguistic analysis. They fortify the conclusion that NT scholarship has generally settled for an over-simplified understanding of these relationships.

Acknowledgements

This book, begun in one congenial environment, has been brought to completion in another. Library staff at both Macquarie and La Trobe have demonstrated much goodwill in locating needed items. The editors of *Biblica* granted permission for material to be included here from an article which has appeared in that journal (65 [1984] 393-403). C. Duim gave considerable time to go through several Dutch works with me. At Macquarie, R.R.E. Cook and P. Geidans have helped in numerous ways to ensure that the process of publication did not lag. The typing of this book was undertaken at different stages by E. Lewis, S. James, and A.C. Walker. Considerable help with proof-reading was provided by J.M. Holmes, T.L. Pert, and A.C. Walker.

The *New Docs* series has been greatly fortified by the involvement of the consulting editors and the Centre's Director, each of whom has set aside considerable amounts of time to read and comment on draft material for each volume. Their contribution is not always readily apparent in the book, but let no one doubt that the volumes would have been much the poorer without it. All the more am I personally indebted to them as a colleague much their junior; to them collectively this last contribution of mine to the series is dedicated as an *antidoron*.

G.H.R. HORSLEY

1

THE FICTION OF 'JEWISH GREEK'

... Intense study of vocabulary and syntax seem to me to establish that there was a distinguishable dialect of spoken and written Jewish Greek. That is to say, the biblical language was more than a written product of those whose mother tongue was Semitic and who floundered in Greek because they knew so little of it that they must copy Semitic idioms as they penned it. I am not the first to suggest that the Greek of the OT was a language distinct from the main stream of the Koine, yet fully understood by Jews . . . Biblical Greek is so powerful and fluent, it is difficult to believe that those who used it did not have at hand a language all ready for use. This, I submit, was the normal language of Jesus, at least in Galilee — rather a separate dialect of Greek than a form of the Koine, and distinguishable as something parallel to classical, Hellenistic, Koine and Imperial Greek.

So N. Turner, *Grammatical Insights into the NT* (Edinburgh, 1965) 183. Cf. a similar statement in id., *A Grammar of NT Greek*, IV. *Style* (Edinburgh, 1976) 1-2: '. . . The nature of the Greek of the NT demands close attention, raising the question as to what kind of "dialect" it is, and whether it is even a unity within itself . . . Though there is a comparative style for each author, I believe the styles are not so far apart as to impair the inner homogeneity of Biblical Greek . . .' With this we may contrast the view of A. Thumb, *TRu* 5 (1902) 93: '[The NT is] . . . weder eine "spezifische" Sprachform noch ein barbarisches Judengriechisch, sondern eine natürliche Phase der hellenistischen Sprachentwicklung . . .' Again, at *CR* 8 (1914) 203 Thumb declares: 'The most prominent literary monument of the Graeco-Semitic milieu, the NT, does not at all show the character of Jewish Greek, or Grec hébraisant or any other similar terms by which it has been characterised.'

These two pairs of quotations, written two generations apart, illustrate the polarised nature of the debate about Jewish Greek. One might have thought that the acceptance of the existence of a special dialect of *koine* called 'Jewish Greek' was today a minority view, an aberration within the context of NT philological study. Not so. It is in fact widespread and very influential in certain circles. While N. Turner has been perhaps the most forthright and consistent exponent of this position over the last thirty years, a recent SNTS Monograph provides merely the latest vote of acceptance of Jewish Greek, and does so in a way that assumes it is no longer even a matter needing debate. S. Thompson, *The Apocalypse and Semitic Syntax* (Cambridge, 1985), holds that 'the primary contribution of this study has been an increased understanding of the specific nature of semitic influence on the important areas of verbal syntax and clauses in the Apc. The results may be applied to any Jewish Greek document' (103). Later on, after quoting with approval Turner's judgment (*NTS* 1 [1954/5] 219-23) that the *Testament of Abraham* is a clear example of Jewish Greek, Thompson says: 'The Apc. can accurately be described in identical terms, and with no hesitancy be categorised as "Jewish Greek", to the fullest extent of that term, in spite of recent protest' (108; the last phrase alludes to L. Rydbeck, *NTS* 21 [1975] 424-27). A number of observations is offered here in order to suggest that Jewish Greek is a modern fabrication, anachronistically imposed upon the NT and certain other writings. It will be noted that the latter, such as the *Testament of Abraham*, are little more than mentioned in this essay; most attention will be focused on the assumption of a Jewish Greek dialect for the NT. Furthermore, other matters of importance for understanding the language employed in the NT receive less than central attention here. Such questions include the literary influence which the LXX exercised on the NT writers, and the effect on the Greek as we have it of a written Aramaic precursor to sections of the NT, if such existed.

The issue of Jewish Greek has been brought clearly into focus by the studies which have appeared in the *New Docs* series. The sample of inscriptions and papyri collected in the four previous volumes provides a tangible weight of evidence which has steadily reinforced the impression that to claim any such cleavage between the *koine* and 'Jewish' or 'Christian' Greek is quite inapposite. In the present chapter it is intended to show that the erroneous belief in Jewish Greek is dependent on

(a) the acceptance of over-vague terminology; and

(b) lack of contact with linguistic research, particularly in the area of bilingualism.

It will be suggested further that this view represents a misconceived, latter-day revivification of the Hebraist position in the debates that dominated NT philology from the sixteenth to the nineteenth centuries. Discussion of the theory of bilingualism and related phenomena (interference, diglossia, dialect, register, etc.) will lead us to review the question of language use in first-century Palestine, and to show that the only aspect of Jewish use of Greek which may have been distinctive is that of phonology. And just as a different accent does not constitute a separate dialect, so the mere presence of Semitisms in Greek does not permit us to speak of a distinct Jewish Greek dialect either. Finally, and briefly, the modern proponents of Jewish Greek will be set within the historical context of the Hebraist/Purist debate. This study has been written independently of M. Silva, *Biblica* 61 (1980) 198-219. We approach the question from different angles, but share much common ground.

Bilingualism

In this field U. Weinreich's *Languages in Contact* (1953; repr. The Hague, 1974) is already achieving a status commensurate with that of de Saussure's *Cours de linguistique générale* in Descriptive Linguistics. First published in 1953, its influence has been widespread; although not the earliest such treatment of its subject in modern linguistics research — as one precursor particularly relevant for our study we may note J. Vergote, *Phil. Stud.* 5 (1933/4) 81-105 (especially 82, where he actually uses the phrase 'der talen in onderling kontakt'); 6 (1934/5) 81-107 — Weinreich's book is the regular *point de départ* for those researching some aspect of bilingualism.

Weinreich's particular interest lies in **interference phenomena**, 'those instances of deviation from the norms of either language which occur in the speech of bilinguals as a result of their familiarity with more than one language . . .' (1; for the unfortunate choice of the established term 'interference' note the comments of J.A. Fishman, *Linguistics* 39 [1968] 21-49, at 29). More specifically, his focus is upon the extent to which interference is due to the structure of the languages which the bilingual has, as opposed to non-linguistic (social, cultural, etc.) factors (4). He acknowledges (63) that linguistic interference is not something easy to quantify or measure. On this problem note L.G. Kelly (ed.), *Description and Measurement of Bilingualism. An International Seminar, University of Monckton*, 1967 (Toronto, 1969), and within that volume especially N. Hasselmo et al., 'How can we measure the effects which one language may have on the other in the speech of bilinguals?', 121-89. More recently see H. Baetens Beardsmore, *Bilingualism: Basic Principles* (Clevedon, 1982) 69-98. Interference occurs in phonology, word order, vocabulary — the main area where borrowing occurs (Weinreich, 47-67; for Greek influence on Latin in this regard note R. Coleman, *TPS* [1975] 101-56, at 105-07) — morphology and syntax, although (depending on the languages in question) not all these may give evidence of interference. In *Actes du Xe Congrès international de linguistes* (Bucharest, 1970) 4.677-82, F.T. Gignac suggests that while there are many examples of Greek/Coptic syntactical interference in Roman and Byzantine period papyri, there is scarcely any morphological interference because the inflectional systems of these two languages were not parallel. This view is repeated more briefly in id., *Grammar*, 1.46-48. See briefly p.37 below.

The monograph by E.C. Maloney, *Semitic Interference in Markan Syntax* (*SBLDS* 51; Chico, 1981), is one of the most impressive recent contributions to NT work relating to linguistic interference. His book addresses evenhandedly such matters as word order, parataxis, conditional clauses, the definite article, pronouns, nouns, and numerals. Each of the features dealt with is analysed with some care. From these he concludes (243-52) that whereas certain Markan syntactic features which have been regarded as evidence of Semitic influence are in fact quite possible in *koine*, on the other hand some constructions widely claimed to be Greek should be regarded in the context of primitive Christianity as reflecting Semitic interference due to the high frequency of occurrence in the Gospel of Mark. It is particularly relevant to note here one of Weinreich's general observations (92-93), about the conservative nature of religious language: religious differences have the effect of limiting language contact, and therefore the potential for linguistic interference.

While the term 'bilingual' has become a convenient shorthand to refer to people using two or more languages — note, e.g., W. Mackey's important 1962 article repr. in J.A. Fishman (ed.), *Readings in the Sociology of Language* (The Hague, 1968), 554-85, at 555; Baetens Beardsmore, 3-4 — if for the present purpose we think in terms of two languages only, then it is observable that interference *normally* occurs in one direction only: from the language with *high* relative status to that with *low* relative status. Cf., e.g., W. Downes, *Language and Society* (London, 1984) 67. Yet H.St.J. Thackeray's claim is a considerable overestimation, that 'the Greek language was at all times the giver rather than the receiver': *A Grammar of the OT in Greek according to the Septuagint*, I (Cambridge, 1909) 21. Though she deals with the pre-Hellenistic period we may note here that E. Masson, *Recherches sur les plus anciens emprunts sémitiques en Grec* (Paris, 1967), discusses nearly 100 Greek words which certainly/possibly/doubtfully derive from a Semitic language. For previous discussion of Semitisms in earlier Greek note, e.g., A. Thumb, *Die griechische Sprache im Zeitalter des Hellenismus: Beiträge zur Geschichte und Beurteilung der Koine* (Strassburg, 1901) 107-09 (further references at 108 n.1). On Egyptian words borrowed by Greek see B. Hemmerdinger, *Glotta* 46 (1968) 238-47; and A.G. McGready, ibid., 247-54. However, as Coleman has pointed out, *TPS* (1975) 102-03 and n.7, the terms 'higher/lower' need careful definition as the status of a language may vary from one context to another (e.g., among those of different social backgrounds). The same point is made by M.D. McLeod in his review of J. Kaimio, *The Romans and the Greek Language*, in *CR* 32 (1982) 216-18. For example, at Rome Greek could be simultaneously a low-prestige language, because used by a large immigrant slave population, and also enjoy high prestige among the intelligentsia. Further, it is not true that the lower language is always the borrower and never the lender. For example, if a speaker's mother tongue is a low-status language but his second, higher language is not well learned, in such a case interference may well occur in both directions, or perhaps from low to high language alone. Indeed, Baetens Beardsmore points out (48) that occasionally the lower-status language will give to the higher one words with a pejorative connotation.

Bilingualism is often viewed as an individual, not a group, phenomenon: cf. Mackey, 554, 583; J.A. Fishman, *Journal of Social Issues* 23 (1967) 29-38 (repr. with some changes in his *The Sociology of Language* [Rowley (Mass.), 1972] 91-106), at 34. What about 'bilingual societies'? This brings us to the subject of **diglossia**. This term refers to a community which uses two languages — or more: R.T. Bell, *Sociolinguistics. Goals, Approaches and Problems* (London, 1976) 165, speaks of 'polyglossic' societies — for intra-society communication. On this subject note Fishman's article mentioned just above. For examples of diglossic communities today see P. Trudgill, *Sociolinguistics: an Introduction* (Harmondsworth, rev. edn. 1983) 113-21. One set of values and attitudes will be expressed in one language, another in the other. One language will have higher prestige than the other. A most useful article on diglossia is that by C.A. Ferguson, *Word* 15 (1959) 325-40 (repr. in D. Hymes [ed.], *Language in Culture and Society* [New York, 1964] 429-39), in which he lists nine distinguishing features of a diglossic situation. Among these nine we may note here particularly:

(a) specialisation of function (i.e., only in some situations will the High language be appropriate);

(b) the relative prestige of the H(igh)/L(ow) languages;

(c) possible variation in literary heritage;

(d) method of acquisition (e.g., L may be the mother tongue, H the language of education);

(e) stability of relationship: do both have a sufficiently clear, differentiated function that they can coexist peacefully within the society?

All these points are of relevance to the question of language use in Palestine in I AD as, of course, elsewhere. In his excellent contribution on Jews and Syrians in the western part of the Empire, *ANRW* II.29.2 (1983) 587-789 (plus index, 1229-49), H. Solin pays particular attention to the question of language preference. In the case of Rome, inscriptions provide conclusive direct testimony that Greek was the dominant language for the Jewish community. Latin was widely known, however (706); and Solin allows that the Jews may be thought of there as a partly bilingual group (707). The evidence takes us only as far as the fourth century; what position Greek held *vis-à-vis* Latin among the Jews of the city in V AD and later is not so clear (780). In Norman England (to give a rather different example) the relationship between high-status French and low-status English began to alter over the period from the XIII-XVth centuries. As the latter began to be used more in writing it had to compete with both French and the similarly high-status Latin. It was not so much that the status of French and Latin were waning, as that a renewed nationalism about what constituted English saw the status of the latter rise. On this generally see, e.g. A.C. Baugh/T. Cable, *A History of the English Language* (London, 1978³) 126-57, especially 133-38, 152-56.

Returning to interference, a difficulty of which linguists researching bilingualism are conscious (e.g., Baetens Beardsmore, 37-68, especially 41-43; Bell, 116-44, especially 117-18) is the question, when does interference become a switch in language? That is, how much interference from another language is needed to trigger the speakers to shift across into that one entirely in the middle of their conversation? This issue of **code-switching** appears to have little practical application to the study of dead languages, however, since it can really only be tested and observed in oral communication. Languages that are dying are another matter, of course: see N.C. Dorian's discussion of code-switching in N. Scotland between the moribund East Sutherland Gaelic and English, in *Language Death: The Life Cycle of a Scottish Gaelic Dialect* (Philadelphia, 1981) 98-102. A particularly illuminating discussion of code-switching between two dialects of the same language occurs in the study by J.J. Gumperz/J.-P. Blom in Gumperz' collection of essays, *Language in Social Groups* (Stanford, 1971) 274-310. Their point is of great significance, that a bilingual speaker's choice, whether to use the regional or the standard dialect, is conditioned by social factors (281; cf. 294, 307). Some ancient writers certainly provide evidence of the phenomenon of interference in their surviving work, but wholesale code-switching does not occur in the written medium. For a possible example of something akin to code-switching see *CIJ* I.523, discussed below at p.15.

Cicero's use of Greek in his letters illustrates the point. He was clearly a 'productive' bilingual (for this term see p.24 below), whose Latin translation of Aratos' *Phainomena* is extant. Although Greek is frequently employed in the letters, there is never any wholesale shift into Greek from Latin for extensive passages. A phrase or sentence in Greek is the norm. On Cicero's use of Greek see the useful remarks of P. Boyancé, *REL* 34 (1956) 122-24. Of particular interest is *ad Att.* I.19.10, in which he tells Atticus that he is sending him *commentarium consulatus mei Graece compositum* (at *ad Att.* II.1.2 the same work is called a ὑπόμνημα). That this was no mere translation of a Latin original becomes clear shortly afterwards, when Cicero mentions that he is considering writing a Latin version. Atticus is requested to draw attention to any 'un-Greek' features (*minus Graecum*), for he does not wish to include barbarisms merely in order to make plain that the work emanates from the pen of a Roman. From *ad Att.* II.1.2 it is clear that Cicero has a high estimate of his own ability at Greek.

Code-switching is not the only area where students of morbid languages can get into methodological difficulties. R. Coleman has pointed out in an important paper, *TPS* (1963) 58-126 (the methodological questions are raised at 58-69), that '(ancient) Greek dialect studies are often conducted as if they were dealing with a living language'. Since the corpus of any ancient Greek dialect is (to all intents and purposes) closed, as well as being fragmentary, geographically uneven, and diachronically scattered, it has to be approached with full recognition of the limitations thereby imposed upon the possibility that comprehensive understanding can be achieved. Nevertheless, certain overlapping dialectal elements can be taken into account in the study of an ancient writer. Two of these are **social dialect** (the way you speak determined by your social class), and **geographical dialect** (the way you speak determined by where you come from). Amalgamated into any individual they emerge as that speaker/writer's **idiolect**, his uniquely idiosyncratic variety of the language of his language community. Recently the study of the interconnections between dialect and geography has been urged strongly by J.K. Chambers/ P. Trudgill, *Dialectology* (Cambridge, 1980), for which they suggest the term 'geolinguistics' (205-07). As a general introduction to the subject of dialect this book overlaps considerably with D.M. Petyt, *The Study of Dialect* (London, 1980). Note also W.N. Francis, *Dialectology. An Introduction* (London, 1983). Trudgill has (re)published/revised several essays in *On Dialect* (Oxford, 1983), amongst which pp.1-6 (on the problem of the term 'sociolinguistics' meaning different things to different people) and 31-51 (on sociolinguistics and dialectology) are particularly deserving of attention. More recently still, his *Dialects in Contact* (*Language in Society* 10; Oxford, 1986) — the title takes its cue from Weinreich's book — provides expanded sociolinguistic treatment of the interaction of dialects of the same language. Cf. the comments of R. Hasan in B. Bernstein (ed.), *Class, Codes and Control*, II (London, 1973), 253-92, at 256. Little has been attempted by way of the dialect geography of classical languages. A notable exception is J. Whatmough, *The Dialects of Ancient Gaul* (Cambridge [Mass.], 1970), which seeks to illustrate the point that Latin was not uniform across the Empire by means of a very detailed analysis of dialectal features of Latin in the different parts of Gaul and N. Italy.

Dialect is to be distinguished from **accent**. The latter refers only to pronunciation and is merely one element in dialect along with grammar and lexicon. On this point note the brief but perceptive article by D. Abercrombie, repr. in his *Studies in Phonetics and Linguistics* (London, 1965) 10-15. Cf. Petyt, 16-24; Trudgill, *Sociolinguistics*, 56. This differentiation is of some significance for us, for by the range of provenances covered the *New Docs* volumes demonstrate clearly the truth of J.H. Moulton's claim (*The Expositor* ser. vi, 9 [1904] 224) that, allowing for varieties in pronunciation, the great value of inscriptions for *koine* philology is that they show that 'there was little dialectal difference between the Greek of Egypt and Asia Minor, Italy and Syria'. The qualification about pronunciation is important. It may be that we should allow that

Jews who spoke Greek as a second language had a 'marked' pronunciation. Even so, we should expect such differences in accent to be due to geographical, not ethnic considerations: the pronunciation of Greek by Jews in Rome may have differed from that of Jews in Alexandria and in Jerusalem. (For analogous evidence of locally distinctive pronunciation of Greek in Cappadocia and Cilicia see the references in F. Millar, *JRS* 58 [1968] 126-34, at 127.) In any case, pronunciation is not sufficient alone to constitute Jewish use of Greek as a separate dialect. (G. Mussies points out to me [*per litt.* 9.8.85], however, that apart from the fact that there may have existed a specific Jewish accent 'one should also bear in mind that Hebraising translation-Greek may have been imitated, especially in the Apocrypha. In that case it would have led a literary life of its own which can only be evaluated as a genre-dialect'.)

As an analogy, attention may be drawn to a recent study of the Greek dialect used in Pamphylia before the Hellenistic period: C. Brixhe, *Le dialecte grec de Pamphylie* (Paris, 1976). The Greek of this region exhibited certain idiosyncratic features in alphabet, phonology, lexicon, morphology and syntax — the small number of surviving documents, mostly brief inscriptions and coin legends, makes it impossible to extrapolate a complete morphology and syntax, however — the coherence of which justifies the term 'dialect'. The isolation of the region was a major reason for the persistence of these features (ibid., 9). But with Alexander's arrival in Asia Pamphylia was opened up to the outside world. Whereas a genuinely diglossic situation had existed, the *koine* now gradually relegated the dialect 'au rang de "patois" inculte', which the autochthonous inhabitants used solely for communication *inter se* and for documents such as family epitaphs (ibid., 148-50). The latter were on public display, but usually reflected a private, because domestic, context. A significant difference between this example of the use of Greek in Pamphylia and Greek used by Jews is that the former was largely geographically determined. We should expect a Jew brought up in Pamphylia to have used Greek affected by localised interference phenomena. To suggest that the Jews in Italy, in Egypt and in Palestine — to name only the three geo-graphical areas about whose Jews we know most — spoke an identical and identifiably distinct 'dialect' of Greek *because of their ethnicity* ignores those factors such as geography, education and social class, to which allusion has already been made. More recently, Brixhe has contributed further to the question of Greek in Asia Minor: *Essai sur le grec anatolien au début de notre ère* (Nancy, 1987[2]). This excellent, brief analysis focuses upon the inscriptions of Anatolia in II-III AD. In *Hethitica* 8 (1987) 45-80, the same writer provides a detailed essay on interference between Greek and Phrygian as evidenced by the confession and manumission inscriptions from the sanctuary of Apollo Lermenos in SW Phrygia, 35 km. NNE from Hierapolis.

Again, in a recent brief survey, T. Hägg has considered the use of Greek in Nubia (in J.H. Plumley [ed.], *Nubian Studies. Proceedings of the Symposium for Nubian Studies, Cambridge, 1978* [Warminster, 1982], 103-07). The corpus of Greek inscribed texts from Nubia so far published is small, *c.*300 items; but they extend chronologically between V-XII AD, and are geographically distributed over the two northern Nubian kingdoms. Comparative analysis of dated texts does not allow the claim to stand that over time there was a gradual debasement of Nubian Greek. Hägg points out a significant methodological flaw in the study of this Greek, which has application beyond Nubian studies. Scholars have too often compared its syntax, etc., with classical or *koine* Greek usage and concluded that the use of Greek in Nubia was barbaric. Chronologically, a more appropriate comparison would be with Byzantine Greek; geographically, with Greek used in Egypt. The presence of several languages in Nubia of which Greek was a, or possibly the, *lingua franca* (serving, perhaps, as a pidgin language) ensures the likelihood of linguistic interference. Interference from Coptic should be recognisable because of parallels with Greek in Egypt, while interference from Old Nubian may be expected to be unique to the Greek of Nubia.

There are other factors to be taken into account in language choice as well as high/low prestige distinctions. One of these is the matter of **register**. Whereas dialect is 'what a person speaks determined by who he is', register is 'what a person is speaking, determined by what he is doing at the time' (M.A.K. Halliday, *Language as Social Semiotic* [London, 1978] 110-11; cf. 31-35). Among many other discussions of register, a term which entered the linguistics 'lexicon' only in the mid-1950's, we may note the article by Hasan, mentioned above; J. Ure, *IJSL* 35 (1982) 5-23; Downes, *Language and Society*, 27-28. The particular situation in which a speaker finds himself (formal/informal context, relationship with the other speaker, the subject of discussion) will have an effect on the language choices he makes, lexical and syntactic, and sometimes phonological. This is encapsulated in Fishman's dictum, 'Who speaks what language to whom and when'. A revised version of his 1965 article with this title appears in J.B. Pride/ J. Holmes (edd.), *Sociolinguistics. Selected Readings* (Harmondsworth, 1972), 15-32. Cf. Baetens Beardsmore, 6. Register certainly has application to written language as well as to spoken communication, and is therefore a tool for use in studying linguistic phenomena from antiquity. Little has yet been done to tap the potential of 'register' in the study of ancient Greek, to my knowledge; though note J.A.L. Lee, *NovT* 27 (1985) 7-11 (*vis-à-vis* the NT); cf. A.L. Connolly, *Atticism in Non-Literary Papyri of the First Seven Centuries AD* (unpub. B.A. thesis, Univ. of Sydney, 1983) 3-6.

Since Weinreich, two works on bilingualism deserve closer attention for our purposes. One of these is W. Mackey's 1962 article, already noted, which has exercised a wide influence. Of special relevance to the present context is the distinction he draws between interference and borrowing. The latter may be a cultural, not a linguistic phenomenon: foreign elements in a bilingual's speech or writing 'may be the result of an effort to express new phenomena or new experience in a language which does not account for them' (573; cf. Baetens Beardsmore, 40). The relevance of this for our subject is clear in relation to the degree to which lexical Semitisms, such as technical terms of Jewish cultus, can tell us anything about bilingualism. Since borrowings across languages are never haphazard, and loan words occur only in certain domains of language — not among so-called 'empty' words like prepositions, for example — their mere presence cannot constitute an argument for the existence of a bilingual situation.

The second contribution to be taken up here, H. Baetens Beardsmore's *Bilingualism: Basic Principles*, covers in less than 150 pages of text a wide range of questions at impressive depth in a way that makes it quite an exceptional synthesis of the current state of research. Thus, his first chapter (1-36) is devoted to problems of definition and typology in which he demonstrates very clearly how multi-faceted is the phenomenon of bilingualism, and consequently the difficulty of adequate, succinct definition. While he explicitly avoids providing a definition himself (4), the nearest he comes is his statement that the term 'must be able to account for the presence of at least two languages within the same speaker, remembering that ability in these two languages may or may not be equal, and that the way the two or more languages are used plays a highly significant role' (3). Some twenty definitions are quoted and critiqued by M. Beziers/M. van Overbeke, *Le Bilinguisme. Essai de définition et guide bibliographique* (Louvain, 1968) 111-38, who then offer a definition of their own (133).

There is much to be learned from Baetens Beardsmore's short work for research into ancient bilingualism. Studies of bilingualism in the Graeco-Roman period are not common; not surprisingly, most involve Greek as one of the languages. This is due in no small part to our wholesale ignorance about the majority of provincial languages in the Roman world. Among recent studies we may note here R. MacMullen, *AJP* 87 (1966) 1-17 (on Syriac, Coptic, Punic and Celtic in the Roman Empire); F. Millar, *JRS* 58 (1968) 126-34 (mainly on indigenous languages in Roman Africa); id., *JRS* 61 (1971) 1-17, especially 2-8 (on Aramaic, Syriac and

Greek in Roman Syria). P.A. Brunt's article on 'The Romanization of the local ruling classes in the Roman Empire', in D.M. Pippidi (ed.), *Assimilation et résistance à la culture gréco-romaine dans le monde ancien* (Paris, 1976), 161-73, includes an excursus on 'vernacular languages'. (Incidentally, on the difficulties of the term 'vernacular' see briefly Bell, *Sociolinguistics*, 153.) Some attention has been given to bilingualism in Egypt, thanks to papyrus finds. For example, in several studies of bilingualism in Ptolemaic Egypt W. Peremans has shown that more Egyptians knew Greek than there were foreigners who knew Egyptian: *AC* 4 (1935) 403-17; in H. Braunert (ed.), *Studien zur Papyrologie und antiken Wirtschaftsgeschichte* (Festschrift F. Oertel; Bonn, 1964), 49-60; in J. Quaegebeur (ed.), *Studia P. Naster oblata*, II. *Orientalia Antiqua* (Leuven, 1982), 143-54; and in E. van 'T Dack et al. (edd.), *Egypt and the Hellenistic World. Proceedings of the International Colloquium, Leuven, 24-26 May 1982* (Leuven, 1983), 253-80. One of the general points which emerges in A. Momigliano, *Alien Wisdom. The Limits of Hellenization* (Cambridge, 1975), is that, because of the high status of their culture and language, the Greeks could afford to be monolingual, expecting those of other language backgrounds to know Greek (note, e.g., what he says about Greeks and Jews at p.81). Cf. the *obiter dictum* of Baetens Beardsmore: 'A technically and economically more advanced language community tends to export more culture-tied terms than a less advanced community' (49). Yet it was not all one-way traffic: testimony to the opposite trend is provided by a famous letter from a mother to her son(?), congratulating him for 'learning Egyptian', πυνθανομένη μανθά|νειν σε Αἰγύπτια | γράμματα, κτλ., *UPZ* I.4 (1927) 148.1-3 (provenance unknown, II BC. On this text see R. Rémondon, *CE* 39 [1964] 126-46.). F.F. von Schwind wrongly thinks that the give and take of learning each other's language was much more widespread and even: see his essay in *Studi in onore di V. Arangio-Ruiz*, II (Naples, 1953) 440.

Another of Peremans' conclusions in his series of articles is that, although the amount of bilingualism was not great because Greek and Egyptian communities lived largely in isolation from each other, factors encouraging bilingualism included intermarriage — unfortunately, we have no means of estimating the proportion of mixed marriages — and the billeting of civil servants in villagers' homes. Furthermore, the creation of a professional army in the second century BC involved the intermingling of Egyptians and foreigners, who previously had fought in separate corps; this development is of considerable significance for the question of bilingualism in the Ptolemaic period.

A further observation offered by Peremans is that within the government administration it was primarily middle-echelon officials in the *chora* who needed to be bilingual, to serve as the 'interface' between administrative decisions affecting villagers and the latter's petitions, etc., to be relayed to the bureaucracy. Certainly, it was not necessary for all civil servants to be bilingual or monolingual Greek speakers/writers (cf. A.E. Samuel, *From Athens to Alexandria: Hellenism and Social Goals in Ptolemaic Egypt* [*Studia Hellenistica* 26; Louvain, 1983] 115-16). However, H.C. Youtie has drawn attention — *CE* 41 (1966) 127-43 (repr. with addenda in his *Scriptiunculae* [Amsterdam, 1973] II.677-95); *HSCP* 75 (1971) 171-72 (= *Scriptiunculae*, II.621-22) — to two town clerks from later II AD Egypt who are, to all intents and purposes, illiterate. *P.Petaus* (1969) 121 is a sheet of papyrus on which Petaus, *komogrammateus* between 184-87 of an area covering five villages in the S. Fayum, practises over and over writing his name and title. But once he makes a mistake (*l.*5), so completely is he unable to read that he is unaware of the error and preserves the same omission in all the following lines. A plate of this papyrus is provided in the 1966 article at p.135 (= *Scriptiunculae*, II.685). Another papyrus from the same corpus, *P.Petaus* 11 (dated 2 May 184; pl.IV), preserves Petaus' adjudication of a complaint against Ischyrion, *komogrammateus* at Tamais. Among the grounds for which the latter is charged as incompetent is that he is ἀγράμματον (*l.*9). Petaus adjudges that since name he is not illiterate. But of course to say otherwise would expose Petaus himself to the same charge, since all he is able to do is provide a very laboured signature, probably copying out his name letter by letter from an exemplar written for him by one of the scribes in his office.

These instances make it relevant to note here, though only in passing, that the question of literacy in antiquity has numerous points of contact with the subject of bilingualism. To particularise this from Roman Egypt, subscriptions on papyrus documents show what is meant by illiteracy in multilingual Egypt is inability to write Greek, not necessarily lack of facility in other languages in use there. See H.C. Youtie, *ZPE* 19 (1975) 101 (= *Scriptiunculae Posteriores* [Bonn, 1981] I.255); cf. id., *ZPE* 17 (1975) 202 (= *Scriptiunculae Posteriores*, I.180). A text like *SB* 1 (1915) 5117 illustrates this unequivocally. This document in demotic records a sale of a house in 55 AD, to which there is attached a Greek subscription stating that the vendor is illiterate in Greek (γράμματα Ἑλληνικά), though he is able to write Egyptian (Αἰγύπτια). Less explicit is *P.Oxy.* 33 (1968) 2673 (February 304), in which Aurelius Ammonios, the lector (ἀναγνώστης) of a Christian church, is said to be illiterate. This apparent contradiction is resolved when we realise that the reference would be to an inability to read Greek; Ammonios must have been fluent in Coptic. For discussion of these two papyri in relation to the question of literacy see Youtie, *HSCP* 75 (1971) 163 (= *Scriptiunculae*, II.613). The *P.Oxy.* text has provoked a different interpretation from E. Wipszycka, *ZPE* 50 (1983) 117-21, who suggests that given its date during the Diocletianic persecution, Ammonios declared himself illiterate out of religious scruples, not wishing to taint himself by touching physically this document which required him to swear by the *genius* of the emperor. It has been suggested recently, however, that there may have been some lectors unable to read *any* language: G.W. Clarke, *ZPE* 57 (1984) 103-04, responding to part of Wipszycka's argument at 118. Illiteracy among office-holders within the Church was clearly not an isolated phenomenon. A work contract between a deacon and his bishop indicates that the former was illiterate (in Greek, but not in Coptic?): *CPR* V.2 (1976) 11 (early IV?); repr. at *New Docs 1976*, **80**. Deissmann long ago pointed to evidence of intending deacons who did not even know Coptic (*LAE*, 221-24). The converse, that the test of literacy is the ability to write Greek, is implied in *P.Oxy.* 12 (1916) 1467 — repr. at *New Docs 1977*, **3**, p.30 — a petition (probably 263 AD) in which a woman claims the right under the *ius trium liberorum* to act independently of her *kyrios* in business transactions. Aurelia asserts that an added reason in her favour is her ability to 'write with especial ease' (*ll.*13-14). The quality of the Greek in this document bears out her claim: there are particles and other stylistic features indicative of a good education. Nowhere is there confusion over the use of cases.

As with bilingualism, so informed research into literacy in the Graeco-Roman world is still in its infancy. Apart from Youtie's series of useful studies — in addition to the four articles noted above see *GRBS* 12 (1971) 236-61 (= *Scriptiunculae*, II.629-51) — of certain aspects of the question in Roman Egypt as evidenced by the papyri (superseding the older study of R. Calderini, *Aeg.* 30 [1950] 14-41), and some notable contributions by E. Wipszycka on the situation in Byzantine Egypt (especially *REAug.* 30 [1984] 279-96, which challenges the current orthodoxy about diminishing literacy from late IV onwards), the most valuable contribution of late has been provided by W.V. Harris, *ZPE* 52 (1983) 87-111. In focussing upon the question, whether epigraphy can yield us much tangible data concerning the percentage of literates in society, he has most effectively opened up a 'can of worms'. There are few other publications concerned with antiquity which can be mentioned. For two recent studies of women and literacy in antiquity note those by S.G. Cole and S.B. Pomeroy listed in the bibliography below. Comparative evidence from other periods and cultures is only sometimes of real use. The series of sociological essays edited by J.R. Goody, *Literacy in Traditional Societies* (Cambridge, 1968), contains two articles which should be of more than passing interest for research into literacy in Graeco-Roman antiquity: Goody and I. Watt's 'The Consequences of Literacy' (27-68) pays attention to the significance of the development of the Greek alphabet and of literacy there, but overestimates how much there was. R.S. Schofield's essay on 'The Measurement of Literacy in pre-Industrial England' (311-25) is of some interest for comparative purposes, though his claim (319) that the ability to sign one's name is evidence of basic literacy highlights the problem of definition which afflicts this area of research no less than bilingualism, as has been observed above. This same inadequate definition of literacy has been adopted *faute de mieux* by R. Houston in his study of literacy in XVII-XVIIIth century Scotland, *P&P* 96 (1982) 82. More significant than these is L. Stone, *P&P* 42 (1969) 69-139, to which Harris draws attention (90-92) as a particularly useful comparative study for those working on ancient literacy.

Addressing the question of the influence of Latin upon Greek, P.J. Sijpesteijn acknowledges that not much can be expected to have occurred: *Lampas* 15 (1982) 318-30. Cf. J. Kaimio, in *Actes du XVe congrès international de papyrologie, Bruxelles, 1977* (Brussels, 1979) 3.27-33. However, bilingual texts among the papyri occasionally help us perceive whether the writer was a Greek trying to learn Latin, or the reverse. Of the 41 bilingual glossaries known to Sijpesteijn, 33 can be shown to have been devised for Greeks who want knowledge of Latin, their goal being, presumably, access to the civil service. On this point see also A. Bataille, *Rech. Pap.* 4 (1967) 161-69; cf. H.-I. Marrou, *Histoire de l'éducation dans l'antiquité* (Paris, 1948; 1965[6]) 375-76. J. Kramer has recently provided a re-edition of 16 Greek/Latin and Latin/Greek bilingual glossaries covering a wide range of subjects, such as names of fish, months, and gods: *Glossaria bilinguia in papyris et membranis reperta* (Bonn, 1983). His notes and bibliographies provide further references to the secondary literature. In W.C. Weinreich (ed.), *The New Testament Age*: *Essays in Honor of Bo Reicke* (Macon, 1984), 2.327-34, B.M. Metzger has provided a useful, preliminary check-list of NT MSS written in more than two languages. The oldest surviving bilingual NT fragments are 𝔓[6] and 𝔓[62], both from the fourth century. Metzger is rightly cautious about attempts to show that bilingual and multilingual MSS of the NT began to be produced over a century earlier. A late fifth-century Greek/Latin lexicon to some of the Pauline epistles (*CLA* Suppl., no.1683; van Haelst, 511) appears to favour the suggestion that that scribe was more at home with Greek than with Latin: cf. A. Wouters, *Scriptorium* 31 (1977) 240-42, and further, *New Docs 1979*, **105**, p.192. R. Cavenaile discusses evidence for the knowledge of Latin in Christian circles in Egypt in S. Janeras (ed.), *Miscellània Papirològica R. Roca-Puig* (Barcelona, 1987), 103-10.

Spreading well beyond Egypt and Rome, J. Kaimio's stimulating and important study, *The Romans and The Greek Language* (Helsinki, 1979), investigates who used Greek in the Roman world and why. In the next section we shall review the question of language use in Palestine in I AD; suffice it to mention here that of the studies devoted to Greek which take up the question of bilingualism in ancient Palestine those of most help are S. Lieberman, *Greek in Jewish Palestine* (New York, 1965[2]), dealing with the period II-IV; J.N. Sevenster, *Do you Know Greek? How Much Greek could the First Jewish Christians have Known?* (Leiden, 1968); G. Mussies, *The Morphology of Koine Greek as Used in the Apocalypse of St. John. A Study in Bilingualism* (Leiden, 1971).

Discussing minority groups and language use at Rome, I. Kajanto has drawn attention to a small number of Latin epitaphs written with Greek letters, in G. Neumann/J. Untermann (edd.), *Die Sprachen im römischen Reich der Kaiserzeit* (*Bonner Jahrbücher, Beitrag* 40; Köln, 1980), 83-101, at 96-97. As a hypothesis he suggests that those responsible for setting up these monuments wanted to indicate that the deceased was bilingual: the text is Latin to show that he was a citizen, but carved in Greek characters to point to his Greek origin. This is too intellectualised an explanation. We are looking at another facet of interference phenomena, either in those who have commissioned the monument and provided the exemplar for the letter-cutter, or in the latter himself. Either way, these texts do offer evidence of bilingualism, but say nothing about the language attainment of the deceased. If bilingualism were as widespread at Rome as the studies of Kajanto, H. Solin (in ibid., 301-30) and others have shown, and as I believe to be the case, that is not something which warrants advertisement on an epitaph. And if it were really felt necessary to indicate it, writing a Latin text in Greek letters is a most obscure way to make the point. As to the matter of bilingual attainment, it is clearly a rudimentary knowledge of Latin which we are witnessing in these texts; for the person responsible for such an inscription reveals Greek to be his primary language.

As two examples of Jewish epitaphs from Rome written this way we may note *CIJ* I.207, ΑΓΡΙΟ ΕΥΑΝ|ΓΕ(Λ)Ο ΒΕΝΕΜΕ|ΡΕΝΤΙ ΡΗΓΕΙΝΟΥΣ | ΚΟΛΑΗΓΑ; and I.257, ΟΥΛΠΙΑ ΜΑ-|ΡΕΙΝΑ ΚΟΥΑΙ (= *quae*) | ΒΙΞΙΤ ΑΝΝΕΙΣ | ΚΒ ΒΕΝΕΜΕΡ|ΑΙΝΤΙ ΦΗΚΙΤ | C. Other examples may be mentioned: *CIJ* I.460 (Rome), 637 (Ferrare). A non-Jewish example of this phenomenon at Rome is an Imperial-period tombstone for Polymnestos set up by his wife, his daughter Eustorgos, σεμνοτάτη φιλια (= *filia*) Εὔστοργος, and her husband: *IGUR* 3 (1979) 1306 (noted at *New Docs 1979*, **109**). In this case, an additional factor contributing to the interference is the existence of the homophonous Greek adjective φίλιος. A more complex instance linguistically is *CIJ* I.215: ΣΕΜΠΡΩΝΙΟΥΣ ΒΑΣΕΙ|ΛΕΥΣ ΑΥΡΗΛΙΑΙ ΚΑΙΛΕΡΕΙΝΑΙ | ΚΟΖΟΥΓΕΙ ΒΟΝΑΙ ΕΤ | ΔΙΣΚΕΙΠΟΥΛΕΙΝΑΙ ΒΟΝ|ΑΙ | ΚΟΥΝ ΚΟΥΑ ΒΙΞΕΙ ΑΝΝΕΙΣ ΧΖ | ΦΗΚΙΤ | ΚΟΖΟΥΓΕΙ ΒΜ. This equates to the Latin: *Sempronius Basileus Aureliae Caelerinae coniugi bonae et discipulinae bonae cum qua vixi annis KZ fecit coniugi b(ene)m(erenti)*. Here the equation of ΚΟΖΟΥΓΕΙ/ *coniugi* calls for comment. It is not an error, since the letter-cutter has written it twice. J.A.L. Lee has given me the following comment on the words. 'That Greek *zeta* was transliterated as Latin *i* is hardly conceivable, since they are phonetically so far apart. What lies behind ΚΟΖΟΥΓΕΙ is the identification of Greek ζυγόν and Latin *iugum* as equivalent words (at least one example of this equation can be quoted from the Greek-Latin glosses: see A. Debrunner, *Geschichte der griechischen Sprache*, 18). In transferring the Latin *coiugi* (this form without the *-n-* is well established in Latin) into Greek letters, the letter-cutter has not simply transliterated but has introduced ζ from the Greek word because of the equivalence *iugum* : ζυγόν and more particularly *coiunx* : σύζυγος. At the same time he retains the Latin *co-* (> ΚΟ-), the Latin ending *-i* (> -ΕΙ), and the sound of Latin *-u-* (> -ΟΥ). What we end up with is a blend of Latin and Greek. It is possible, moreover, that this blend was not merely the result of this stone-cutter's confused attempt at representing the Latin word in Greek letters but was actually current in the speech of some Latin/Greek bilinguals.' In this inscription the confusion concerning the numeral, due to the loss of aspiration of Greek *chi* may also be observed.

Sometimes a conventional Greek formula is transliterated into Latin letters, as in the case of *CIJ* I.523, where after nine lines of reasonably normal Latin we find *en irenae ai cymysis | autis* (*ll.*10-11), rendering the cliché ἐν εἰρήνῃ ἡ κοίμησις αὐτῆς, 'may she have peaceful repose'. This example provides us with an instance of something akin to code-switching (see above, p.8). Occasionally, too, we find Hebrew written with Greek letters: a number of epitaphs from Beth She'arim contain ΣΑΛΟΜ (*vel sim.*) to render the funerary cliché commonly written in Hebrew even on otherwise Greek inscriptions: M. Schwabe/B. Lifshitz, *Beth She'arim. II, The Greek Inscriptions* (New Brunswick, 1973) nos. 21, 25, 28, 91 (= *CIJ* II.1034, 1036 + 1037; 1038, 1113). Likewise, the first word in a short text (no.148) from the same site reads Χωὴν Βυρίτιος, 'a priest from Beirut', merely transliterating the Hebrew technical term. Of a piece with this is the transliterated reference to Mount Gerizim which has appeared on two recently published inscriptions from Delos and in a papyrus letter. The allusion provides an indication of Samaritan authorship of these texts. For the references see the Addenda section in the present volume, *ad New Docs 1976*, **69** (p.138 below). A related instance of this phenomenon in another context is a list (in unusual order) of 27 books of the OT given both in Hebrew or Aramaic transcribed into Greek letters, and in Greek. This curious item was included in the MS rediscovered last century at Constantinople which contained the *Didache*. While the original date of the OT transcription list cannot be established with certainty, perhaps I *fin.*-II[1] may not be implausible. On this list see J.-P. Audet, *JTS* 1 (1950) 135-54.

Moving further afield both geographically and ethnically, in order to show that the phenomenon is widespread (if not very common), reference may be made to *P.Berl.* 10582, a lengthy fragment on papyrus of a trilingual 'conversation-book', first published by W. Schubart, *Klio* 13 (1913) 27-38 (= *CPL* [1958] 281). Some 140 lines of this papyrus survive, dated V or VI. The manual was intended for those familiar with Greek and Coptic who wanted to learn Latin: Latin words are transliterated into Greek letters, the Greek equivalent is given, and often the Coptic equivalent is added in Coptic (e.g., on the first page, *col.*1, *l.*17 ΔΙΚΙΤΕ : ΕΙΠΑΤΕ : ⲭⲟⲟⲥ ; Coptic omitted two lines later, ΦΙΛΙΚΙΤΕΡ : ΕΥΤΥΧΩϹ). Whereas the Greek is written correctly, the Latin orthography is often quite vulgarised, suggesting that the author is more at home with the former language. R. Cavenaile suggests that this document may have emanated from a Christian, specifically monastic, context: see *Miscellània Papirològica R. Roca-Puig*, 109-10. The writer of the *Psalmus Responsorius* (repr. at *New Docs 1977*, **92**) may also have been more comfortable with Greek than Latin, given the slip *naξarenum* at *l.*9. We may note, further, an altar to Jupiter Optimus Maximus, from Kučar in Pannonia Superior, set up by a slave, Tertullianus, *cum Crhstene co(n)iuge sua . . .*: *AE* (1978) 649. The wife's name, Chrestis, is here written with a Greek *eta*. Analogous to this is another Latin inscription from Andros (I BC *init.*), in which the forms *DIOGENHS . . . [F]HCIT* occur: M. Sašel-Kos, *Inscriptiones Latinae in Graecia repertae. Additamenta ad CIL III* (*Epigrafia e Antichità* 5; Faenza, 1979) 30 (repr. at *New Docs 1979*, **109**, p.200; cf. the form ΦΗΚΙΤ in *CIJ* I.257, quoted above). In these two examples the *eta* apparently represents an attempt (inconsistent though it be for *Crhstene*) to differentiate the Latin homograph *E* as Greek Ε/Η (J.A.L. Lee suggests to me, alternatively, that the writer may have been representing the sound of Latin *ē* as Greek Η = [i].). Since there is a switch only of isolated letters in these last two inscriptions, the shaky bilingualism in evidence is probably to be attributed to the letter-cutter. The mason may also have been responsible for the orthography of the word *arcisina(vac.)γος* in *CIJ* I.681, an Imperial-period funerary monument from Moesia Inferior; here the word ἀρχισυνάγωγος begins in Latin and concludes in Greek, with an intervening syllable omitted (though indicated by the *vacat*). This text is noted at *New Docs 1979*, **113**, p.215 no.20. Not altogether unlike this last item is *CIL* X (1883) 11 (Regium Iulium in Sicily, Imperial), an epitaph which begins in Latin and ends in Greek, with Latin transliteration of the ὁ καί formula at the changeover: *D.M. Fabia Sperata Sallustis Acathocles* (sic) *o cae Rodios* α<ὑ>τοῖς ἐπόησαν. *IMS* 6 (1982) 178 is also noteworthy in this regard (Sredno Konjare, near the Macedonian frontier, SE of Skopje in Moesia Superior, Imperial). Here we have a Latin epitaph written in Greek letters with some letters borrowed from Latin in the middle of the text (the Latin is underlined for clarity): <u>D M</u> | Οὐλπία [Δο]|μιτία ουει (= *quae*) | υιχιτ <u>annic</u> | <u>X X X</u> Αὐρήλιο|υς Διονύσιους | χωειουγι (= *co(n)iugi*) βε|νεμερεντι. The morphological ambivalence in the ending attached to Aurelius Dionysius' name is a tell-tale sign of a bilingual who lacks real control of Greek, which we should probably take to be his second language. Another small example of bilingual interference reflected in morphology is provided by *IMS* 4 (1979) 31 (Naissus in Moesia Superior, Imperial), a Latin epitaph for a soldier who was undertaking his apprenticeship as a marine, *disce(n)s | epibeta* (5-6). The second word equates to ἐπιβήτη (for ἐπιβάτη), mistakenly intended to be the accusative of ἐπιβάτης. Over a longer perspective of several Christian centuries, it is possible to discern in Latin and Old English MSS certain combinations of Greek letters — most notably the *nomen sacrum XP-* — no longer being recognised as Greek: see G.H.R. Horsley/E.R. Waterhouse, *Scriptorium* 38 (1984) 211-30.

To the contributions from classicists on ancient bilingualism should be added mention of a recent discussion by E.G. Lewis, which forms App.3 in J.A. Fishman, *Bilingual Education. An International Sociological Perspective* (Rowley [Mass.], 1976) 150-200. As far as I am aware, this article makes a unique attempt to survey a large chronological period, from antiquity to the Renaissance. Akkadian, Aramaic and Egyptian as lingua francas are dealt with (157-63), in addition to the Graeco-Roman world. Unfortunately, Lewis' work is badly flawed: it is written by a linguist who is clearly out of touch with recent linguistic work on ancient languages. Further, his sense of chronology is badly askew, and unreliable historical statements occur. For example, his implied claim (153) that the Romans had a coherent language policy is very doubtful. Such a view obtrudes into Kaimio's study as well. It is true that there are hints which might be taken to suggest its existence were they not so rare and could they be made to suggest a consistent approach. One such piece of evidence comes from Valerius Maximus, *Mem.* II.2, in which it is said that in time past Roman magistrates would speak only in Latin to Greeks at official meetings, and that even when they knew Greek the magistrates would use interpreters, 'for they think that in every sphere the Greek cloak should be subordinated to the toga', *sed nulla non in re pallium togae subici debere arbitrabantur*. Since Valerius is writing under Tiberius, the implication of *magistratus . . . prisci* at the beginning of this paragraph is that by I AD the action he described was no longer employed. Such behaviour reflects a concern to protect Roman *honos* — Valerius uses this word in the passage of Latin — but is too slender a basis from which to extrapolate the existence of a *coherent* language policy. Recent discussion of this passage is provided by M. Dubuisson, *LEC* 49 (1981) 37-38. Much earlier in Egypt a nice analogy to the Roman magistrates' use of interpreters is provided by the story of Joseph's encounter with his brothers in Egypt when they come to buy grain during a famine: he uses an interpreter even though he naturally understands their language (Gen. 42.23). Reverting to Lewis' essay, it is anachronistic to speak of an 'Hellenic language policy' (167; cf. 170 where he mentions 'the permissive language policy [which] the Greeks pursued . . .'). He is clearly out of touch with research on the *koine* in view of his belief (167) that 'the various Greek dialects levelled themselves in the direction of a uniform Koine'. Lewis is not the only linguist to continue to hold to erroneous views about the evolution of the *koine*: Beziers/van Overbeke relay a similar conclusion (39), relying on a now-outdated publication. On Jewish bilingualism Lewis' view (192) is quite incorrect, that the status of Hebrew as a vernacular was replaced by Aramaic and Greek 'after 200 AD'. And his claim is certainly open to challenge that hellenisation 'was resisted by the [Jewish masses], so that Aramaic was able to coexist as a vernacular with Greek' (ibid.).

Finally, Peremans' observation, noted above, that middle-ranking civil servants in Ptolemaic Egypt generally needed to be bilingual, serves to raise a question of first importance: in what societal context is bilingualism occurring? For example, a social/intellectual/political élite may be bilingual but the populace at large be monolingual, or at best be characterised as 'receptive bilinguals'. On this term see p.24, below. Indeed, it may often be the case that those who control the means of production and its dispersal are bilingual.

In this connection, two stimulating recent studies by M. Dubuisson may be mentioned, both of which show interest in sociolinguistics and bilingualism. In *LEC* 47 (1979) 89-106, an examination of the amount of Latin known by Greek writers of the early Imperial period (such as Plutarch, Dionysios of Halikarnassos, and Diodoros), he demonstrates that of the peoples brought under Roman rule it was only upper-class Greeks who embraced this domination, in contrast to the Jews, Egyptians and others. This conclusion is exemplified by the contrasting attitude shown to two non-Roman writers who had somewhat similar careers: Polybios and

Josephus. Both were (in a sense) 'collaborators' with the Romans: both wrote histories concerning the spread of Roman domination which were sympathetic to the Romans. But whereas Josephus was execrated by his fellow-countrymen, Polybios was accorded honoured status and continued to be held in high regard by later generations (ibid., 100 n.80). Attainment in Latin was sought by Greek authors not because they admired Latin literature, but for reasons of practical politics and because Latin was the language of law (ibid., 103). Thus, these writers' knowledge of Latin was indicative of 'une collaboration massive des classes supérieures du monde hellénique avec le pouvoir romain' (ibid., 101). It was only from this period that upper-class Greeks were finally persuaded of the value to themselves of being bilingual. Apart from isolated individual exceptions, never before had the Greeks bothered to learn the language of any other people. In contrast to this élite, the great majority of Greeks remained monolingual.

Yet brief attention may be given here to one particularly relevant example of bilingualism in a Greek, earlier though it be. Laomedon, a native of Lesbos, was appointed by Alexander the Great as officer in charge of the foreign prisoners-of-war because he was bilingual, ὅτι δίγλωσσος ἦν ἐς τὰ βαρβαρικὰ γράμματα (Arrian, *Anab*. III.6.6). See A.B. Bosworth's note on this passage in his recent *Commentary* (Oxford, 1980), where further references are provided for bilinguals in Alexander's army. This man was presumably conversant in Aramaic, and perhaps Persian as well. E. Badian points to Alexander's ability to travel easily through linguistically-alien territory, by employing such men with bilingual ability, as being one of his most signal achievements: *The Cambridge History of Iran*, II (Cambridge, 1985) 439-40.

As for non-Greeks in the Roman world, when they wanted to make a name for themselves as writers Greek was the inevitable language choice: thus Josephus, Lucian, and Juba, this last an African prince brought up at Rome during the late Republic who wrote various works — including a *History of Rome*: for the fragments see Jacoby, *FGrH* IIIa.275 — in Greek, not in Latin or his native Punic (Dubuisson, 104; cf. G.W. Bowersock, *Augustus and the Greek World* [Oxford, 1965] 60-61, 138-39). Aramaic, the mother-tongue of the Jewish Josephus and of the Syrian Lucian, lacked the status of Greek as a prestige language, a transmitter of culture. On Aramaic and Greek in Roman Syria, see F. Millar, *JRS* 61 (1971) 1-17, especially 7-8. For the broader range of languages in this province see R. Schmitt, in Neumann/Untermann, *Die Sprachen im römischen Reich*, 198-205. For Syriac/Greek bilingualism and translation in both directions between these languages at a later period see the collection of reprinted essays by S. Brock, *Syriac Perspectives on Late Antiquity* (London, 1984), especially nos. II-IV. Josephus' bilingualism is discussed briefly below, p.33. He was by no means the only Jew to write history in Greek: for fragments and testimonia on over a dozen others see Jacoby, *FGrH* IIIC.2 (Leiden, 1969) 722-737, pp.666-713. Similarly, Punic lacked international status. A century before Juba the Carthaginian philosopher Hasdrubal, who taught philosophy there in Punic (τῇ ἰδίᾳ φωνῇ κατὰ τὴν πατρίδα ἐφιλοσόφει), would have remained obscure had he not gone to Athens and become Karneades' most famous student. Karneades helped him learn Greek (γράμματά τ' ἐποίησε μαθεῖν καὶ συνήσκει τὸν ἄνδρα); and under the name of Kleitomachos he wrote over 400 *biblia*, presumably in Greek. In 129 BC he succeeded his mentor as head of the Academy (Diogenes Laertius 4.67). Very few native Greek speakers chose to write in Latin — the best known are Ammianus and Claudian — and to the extent it occurred, this was mostly a phenomenon of the later Empire.

Dubuisson's second article, *LEC* 49 (1981) 27-45, considers the attitude of the Roman élite to the Greek language during the period II BC-I AD. For some there was a cultural 'cringe' leading to the denial of the value of Latin as a flexible medium of expression. Others 'acted ostrich', denying the superiority of Greek. A third reaction perceived by Dubuisson sought to make virtue out of necessity, claiming to see as good qualities in Latin certain features which had previously been considered faults. A fourth response, 'protectionnisme linguistique' (ibid., 44), attempted to disarm the superiority of Greek by emphasising features of Latin in which the latter did not show up to disadvantage.

It was within this very same period that the NT books were written. While it is undoubtedly true that the NT was written in Greek because this was the international language of the ancient Mediterranean world at the time, does this truism provide the whole reason? Certainly, Latin did not yet possess this status, as Cicero acknowledged (*pro Archia*, 23) a century before: *Graeca leguntur in omnibus fere gentibus, Latina suis finibus, exiguis sane, continentur*. But to say that all the NT writers realised consciously the significance for the early Christian mission of the status Greek possessed may be to accord to some of them anachronistically too broad and international a vision. While this reason should not be absolutely excluded, additional and overlapping factors ought to be considered. One of these was the widespread knowledge of Greek in Palestine specifically, rather than whether Greek was the language for a much wider area. Again, a man like Paul, highly-educated not only in terms of Judaism but also by Graeco-Roman standards — see recently C.B. Forbes, *NTS* 32 (1986) 1-30 — may thereby reasonably be presumed to have come from an upper-class family. It is at least conceivable, then, that he may have shared with others of like background a cultural disinclination to employ Latin in his letters, despite his activity and host of contacts with other Roman citizens (see ch.5 below, on *I.Eph.* Ia.20) in numerous Roman cities. And third, as G. Mussies has recently shown (*NTS* 29 [1983] 364-66), Christianity simply responded linguistically like other oriental cults which spread westwards, embracing Greek and later Latin.

This section has sought to show that bilingual theory has much potential for the study of language use in antiquity. The phenomenon of interference is fundamental to any such investigation. A few points to be raised in the following sections have been anticipated here briefly, and some of the theoretical matters raised in this part will be developed later. But this outline at least puts us in a position now to consider the language situation of first-century Palestine.

The languages of Palestine in I AD

What languages were in use in first-century Palestine? This question has attracted a considerable literature this century, and especially since the 1950s, in part because it has far-reaching implications for other areas of NT research. The consensus on this subject, as I perceive it, runs like this: Palestinian Aramaic was the language in most common use among first-century Jews born and domiciled in Palestine, with Biblical Hebrew known by some, and Mishnaic Hebrew used as a spoken medium by others. Knowledge of Latin was fairly limited, whereas Greek was widely understood and used, the amount varying according to locality, social and educational background, and mobility.

Yet the consensus is an uneasy one: rather than that there is general agreement, the state of research seems to have reached something of an impasse. What is provided here is not intended to be a thorough-going review of recent work, since that has been provided by others. The following may be mentioned: H. Ott, *NovT* 9 (1967) 1-25; J. Barr, *BJRL* 53 (1969) 9-29; J.A. Fitzmyer, *CBQ* 32 (1970) 501-31; H. Leclercq, *LEC* 42 (1974) 243-55; M. Schwabe/B. Lifshitz, *Beth She'arim*, II. *The Greek Inscriptions* (New Brunswick, 1974) 217-21; C. Rabin in S. Safrai/M. Stern (edd.), *The Jewish People in the First Century*, II (Assen, 1976), 1007-39; G. Mussies in ibid., 1040-64; A. Díez Macho, *La lengua hablada por Jesucristo* (Madrid, 1976); J.C. Greenfield, in H.H. Paper (ed.), *Jewish Languages: Theme and Variations. Proceedings of the Regional Conferences of the Association for Jewish Studies, 1975* (Cambridge [Mass.], 1978), 143-54, with responses by H.C. Youtie (155-57) and F.E. Peters (159-64); E. Schürer (rev. by

G. Vermes/F. Millar/M. Black), *The History of the Jewish People in the Age of Jesus Christ*, II (Edinburgh, 1979) 20-28, 74-78; H. Rosén, in G. Neumann/J. Untermann (edd.), *Die Sprachen im römischen Reich der Kaiserzeit* (Köln, 1980), 215-39; E.M. Meyers/J.F. Strange, *Archaeology, the Rabbis and Early Christianity* (London, 1981) 62-91; G. Mussies, *NTS* 29 (1983) 356-69. Instead, by focusing upon certain aspects of the problem, and upon some of the contributions, I hope to suggest some ways by which fuller cognisance of bilingualism theory may help to break the deadlock.

The views of G. Dalman have proved a major influence throughout this century. For him, Aramaic was the mother-tongue of Jesus, his everyday language. But since Jesus was educated in the Scriptures he also knew Biblical Hebrew; and in view of the presence of foreigners in Palestine it is likely that he had some acquaintance with Greek. Dalman's stance is laid out clearly in *Jesus-Jeshua. Studies in the Gospels* (1922; ET: London, 1929) 1-37; note also his earlier *The Words of Jesus* (ET: Edinburgh, 1902). In the intervening decades until the 1950s two contributions may be singled out here. S. Lieberman, *Greek in Jewish Palestine* (New York, 1942, 1965[2]), demonstrated persuasively that, although the Rabbinic tradition of the Talmud and the Mishnah survives only in Aramaic and Mishnaic Hebrew, the Rabbis were undoubtedly well-acquainted with Greek. Note also his *Hellenism in Jewish Palestine* (New York, 1950, 1962[2]). Yet Sevenster, *Do You Know Greek?*, 38-61, was right to sound a note of caution, pointing up the difficulty of extrapolating from Lieberman's work conclusions about the use of Greek in the first century, since the material dealt with by the latter belongs to the three subsequent centuries. On rabbinic texts as evidence for Palestinian *koine* see H.B. Rosén, *JSS* 8 (1963) 56-72. The second significant contribution was H. Birkeland's *The Language of Jesus* (Oslo, 1949), in which his claim that the language of Jesus was a certain form of Hebrew served to sharpen that aspect of the matter considerably. Reaction to Birkeland's hypothesis was strongly adverse, but at least the question of the knowledge of Hebrew (and what sort) was reopened and has led to further work in subsequent decades. A similar view is espoused by J.M. Grintz, *JBL* 69 (1960) 32-47. For some useful evaluation of Birkeland's book note Barr, *BJRL* 53 (1969) 13-17. Some of the most productive work on the question recently has been by J.A. Emerton, e.g., *JTS* 24 (1973) 1-23, where he suggests that Mishnaic Hebrew probably continued in everyday use by ordinary people in Judaea at least until the second century, although not to the exclusion of Aramaic. Cf. H.P. Rüger, *ZNW* 59 (1968) 113-22; Meyers/Strange, *Archaeology, the Rabbis and Early Christianity*, 70.

This view has recently been challenged by H. Rosén in *Die Sprachen im römischen Reich*, 223-26, especially 225-26 — see also Mussies' discussion, *NTS* 29 (1983) 362-64 — who argues persuasively that the presence of Hebrew texts among the documents associated with the Bar-Kokhba revolt has misled scholarly thinking concerning the use of Hebrew in Palestine. He suggests that Hebrew was re-introduced at this time as a nationalistic statement of opposition to Rome — 'Keine der Linguae francae konnte den politischen Kontrast zum Römertum so kraß zum Ausdruck bringen wie das Hebräische . . .' (226) — but that it did not survive the failure of the revolt. It follows that Hebrew was not widely spoken or written by Jews in the first century, with the exception of the specific contexts of religious education and cult.

From the 1950s onwards, publications have burgeoned on the subject of the languages in use in Palestine. By no means all of them are worth reading. Some of the weakest discussions have attempted to show that Jesus may have used Greek on a more than occasional basis. While it is reasonable to consider that Jesus had some knowledge of Greek — along with Aramaic as his mother-tongue and some acquaintance with Hebrew: cf., e.g., J. Barr's article in H.H. Paper (ed.), *Language and Texts. The Nature of Linguistic Evidence* (Ann Arbor, 1975), 35-57, at 55-56; M. Black, *NTS* 3 (1957) 305-13, claims that Jesus may have used Hebrew in solemn teaching situations — and that this may have been the medium of communication with foreigners (e.g., with Pilate at the Trial), the debate initiated by A.W. Argyle in the mid-1950s is of low quality because he claimed far too much. At *ExpT* 67 (1955/6) 93 he suggests: 'The importance of establishing that Jesus and his disciples sometimes spoke Greek cannot be overestimated. It means that in some cases we may have direct access to the original utterances of our Lord and not only to a translation of them.' A flurry of debate followed in that journal, not all of it useful: J.K. Russell, ibid., 246; H.M. Draper, ibid., 317; Argyle's reply, ibid., 383; R.M. Wilson *ExpT* 68 (1956/7) 121-22. With the quotation from Argyle given here we may compare R.H. Gundry's claim at *JBL* 83 (1964) 408, that in view of the trilingual language milieu of I AD Palestine it is possible that 'many of the dominical sayings in the present Greek text of the gospels may be closer to the ipsissima verba of Jesus than has been supposed. Many may, in fact, be identical with dominical sayings originally spoken in Greek.' This view is echoed by N. Turner in E.A. Livingstone (ed.), *Studia Evangelica*, VII. *Papers presented to the Fifth International Congress on Biblical Studies held at Oxford, 1973* (Berlin, 1982), 510. B.Z. Wacholder's unguarded claim goes even further, that '. . . in the Gospels Jesus speaks Judaeo-Greek': *Eupolemus. A Study of Judaeo-Greek Literature* (Cincinnati, 1974) 256.

Now, Argyle does not deny that Jesus spoke Aramaic as well; but his arguments in favour of bilingual ability are not sound. For example, he makes much of the word ὑποκριτής at Mt. 6.2, 15, 16, to claim that Jesus taught publicly in Greek: *ExpT* 75 (1963/4) 113-14; id., *NTS* 20 (1973/4) 87-89, at 89. This does not prove his case at all, for he fails to perceive the distinction between loanword borrowings and bilingualism. If an English speaker uses a French word or phrase because it is appropriate and there is no real English equivalent, knowledge of French is not thereby necessarily implied. Cf. Lieberman's point, in A. Altmann (ed.), *Biblical and Other Studies* (Cambridge [Mass.], 1963), 130-31, that rabbinic use of κυνικός has little significance for the question whether the Rabbis knew Greek philosophical terminology. Note also Schürer, *History of the Jewish People* . . . (rev. edn), II.53-78, with the notes. What *does* argue in favour of Jesus possessing some bilingual ability, however, is the more general proposition of the context in which he grew up: on this see especially Mussies, *NTS* 29 (1983) 357-59.

Interest in the language of Jesus is not the only reason to account for the increased attention paid since the 1950s to the subject of the languages in Palestine. The growing amount of archaeological work in Palestine/Israel is a significant factor; for it is noteworthy that the epigraphical yield from archaeological digs has had an impact on the question (cf. Sevenster, *Do You Know Greek?*, 96-175). Even so, it has not led to agreement about the significance of the inscriptions. H. Ott, *NovT* 9 (1967) 6, suggests that they are of little help in determining the language(s) of Jesus. Lieberman claims (*Greek in Jewish Palestine*, 30) that 'the very poverty and vulgarity of the [Greek] language in these inscriptions [in Palestine] shows that it was spoken by the people and not written by learned men only'. This is very much the conclusion of Sevenster (183; note his discussion of the Greek inscriptions and coins, 115-28), although D.M. Lewis, *JTS* 20 (1969) 583-88, especially 588, is critical of the weight Sevenster places on funerary inscriptions to make his case that knowledge of Greek was widespread. In the main, the Greek epitaphs surviving in Palestine from this period reveal only a rudimentary ability in written Greek. Yet the rudimentary facility in *speaking* the language is not thereby proved. The view of which M. Black is representative, that Greek was restricted to educated, hellenised Jews — *An Aramaic Approach to the Gospels and Acts* (Oxford, 1946, 1967³) 15 — founders in the light of M. Hengel's largely persuasive thesis that already from mid-III BC '*all Judaism* must really be designated "*Hellenistic Judaism*" in the strict sense': *Judaism and Hellenism* (2 vols., ET: London, 1974; repr. in one vol.: London, 1981) 104 (his emphasis). S. Freyne, *Galilee from Alexander the Great to Hadrian, 323 BCE to 135 CE* (Wilmington, 1980) 101, concurs with Hengel; at 141 Freyne says that the view that Greek was the language of upper-class, educated Jews, and Aramaic the language of uneducated and rural folk 'is based on a too intellectualist understanding of the whole hellenization process in Palestine'. Contrast W.A. Meeks, *The First Urban Christians* (New Haven, 1983) 15, who says that '. . . in the villages of Galilee, Aramaic was presumably still [i.e., in I-II] the dominant language'. On the other hand, Hengel claims (104) that the first-century Greek inscriptions demonstrate that there must have been 'a quite considerable minority who spoke Greek as their mother tongue'. The 'Hellenists' of Acts 6.1 are most plausibly seen as ethnically Jewish Christians whose primary language was Greek: so, e.g., T. Rajak, *Josephus. The Historian and his Society* (London, 1983) 55 n.26. After examination of the epigraphical and other archaeological evidence Meyers/Strange, *Archaeology, the Rabbis and Early Christianity*, conclude (90-91) that while Greek was first an urban language in Judaea, '. . . it appears that sometime during the first century BCE Aramaic and Greek changed places as Greek spread into the countryside and as knowledge of Aramaic declined among the educated and among urban dwellers . . . Aramaic never died, though it suffered a strong eclipse in favour of Greek.'

The separate contributions of Rabin and Mussies in the Safrai/Stern volume deserve special mention. Both are attuned to linguistic trends, and Rabin's survey of the evidence for the use of Hebrew and Aramaic in I AD takes up very usefully the question of diglossia in particular. Greek and Hebrew were both high-status languages, each possessing a rich cultural component. In contrast, Aramaic had no such status: '. . . it was a means of communication, no more. It commanded no loyalty' (1032). The claim of W. Chomsky, *JQR* 42 (1951/2) 206, that Aramaic was a prestige language among Jews, is baseless. While the high/low relative status of Hebrew/ Aramaic was clear-cut, the relationship between Greek and Aramaic in Palestine was more complex because one was Semitic, the other not: whereas Greek may be known by both Jews and Graeco-Roman Gentiles, Aramaic would be the mother-tongue only of Jews (and of Syrians, of course; see briefly below). The low status of Aramaic *vis-à-vis* Greek was certainly clear by the time of Egeria. In her late fourth-century account of her travels she records (*Peregrinatio Egeriae* 47.3-4) that in Jerusalem at Christian services a presbyter had the task of translating the bishop's words into Aramaic. For even if the latter knew Aramaic, he spoke only Greek during the service. As Millar points out, *JRS* 61 (1971) 7, 'nothing could demonstrate more clearly the values attached to the two languages'. Earlier in the century Hilarion became a hermit near his native Gaza following his conversion to Christianity while at Alexandria. His high-register language was Greek, but in contexts where low register was appropriate (such as his exorcising of a camel!) he used Aramaic: Jerome, *Life of Hilarion* 21 (Migne, *PL* 23.29-54), referred to by Millar, *JJS* 38 (1987) 149.

A further aspect making the status comparison less easy is the apparent fact that Greek was considerably more widely known and used than Hebrew. On Greek as the 'odd man out' in trilingual Palestine see Barr, *BJRL* 53 (1969) 28. For the question, whether the presence of Greek MSS among the Qumran finds means that some members of the sect were more familiar with Greek than with Hebrew, see A.R.C. Leaney's essay in J.K. Elliott (ed.), *Studies in NT Language and Text* (Festschrift G.D. Kilpatrick; Leiden, 1976), 283-300. This question is sharpened for us by the much-discussed sentence in a Greek letter found at Murabba'at, dating from the Bar-Kokhba revolt: ἐγράφη | δ[ὲ] Ἑλληνιστὶ διὰ | τ[ὸ ὁρ]μὰν μὴ εὑρη|θ[ῆ]ναι Ἑβραεστὶ | γ[ρά]ψασθαι (*ll.*11-15), '(the letter) is written in Greek because I couldn't make the effort to write in Hebrew'. First published by B. Lifshitz, *Aeg.* 42 (1962) 240-48, no.1 (pl.), this text has been reprinted in, e.g., *SB* 8.2 (1967) 9843; and in Fitzmyer, *CBQ* 32 (1970) 514, whose comment at 515 deserves notice, that 'at a time when the nationalist fever of the Jews must have been running high [the writer] . . . frankly prefers to write in Greek'. Cf. Meyers/Strange, *Archaeology, the Rabbis and Early Christianity*, 87: '. . . Greek is surely the author's first language'. In the light of Rosén's persuasive argument noted earlier in this section that Hebrew was revived out of nationalism during this revolt, the presence of Aramaic morphological features in some of the Hebrew documents from the Bar-Kokhba letters — see Mussies, *NTS* 29 (1983) 363 — suggests that to write in Hebrew required considerably more effort — hence the plausible presence of the noun ὁρμή here — than to communicate in Greek or Aramaic. In this passage, at least, Ἑβραεστί should therefore probably be taken to mean 'Hebrew', specifically; so, e.g., J.C. Greenfield in H.H. Paper (ed.), *Proc. of the Regional Conference . . .*, 151, with which F.E. Peters concurs in his response to Greenfield's paper, ibid., 162. It should not go unnoticed that the writer of this letter preferred to use Greek over Aramaic, serving to confirm Meyers/Strange's view (90-91; quoted above) that Greek was eclipsing Aramaic, and perhaps reflecting the differences in status between these two languages.

Although Rosén's general point here is compelling, his discussion (*Die Sprachen im römischen Reich*, 224, 225) of this particular letter is flawed; for he fails to note that the wording of this papyrus supports his case in the way indicated above. First, he rejects Lifshitz's reading τ[ὸ ὀρ]μάν (*l*.13) as 'unacceptable' and offers [μη]δ̣[έν](α?) as his own restoration. This entirely ignores the trace visible in Lifshitz's plate of this papyrus. In *l*.13 the lettering begins with most of a *tau*; then the papyrus is blank before a break in the sheet, after which follow traces consistent with MAN before the entirely legible final six letters of the line. (An attractive alternative restoration, τ[ὸ Ἑρ]μᾶν ['because Hermas could not be found to write . . .'], proposed by G. Howard/ J.C. Shelton, *IEJ* 23 [1973] 101-02, also fits the visible traces.) Second, he argues that Ἑβραεστί must mean 'Aramaic', not 'Hebrew', because the addressees are Nabataeans, with whom Jews would naturally correspond in Aramaic. Yet on the basis of his restoration we would have a situation entirely inconceivable for the context, that 'the letter is written in Greek because no one can be found to write in Aramaic'. While usage varies from writer to writer, it may be noted that Josephus employs Συριστί to refer to speaking Aramaic (*Ant.* 10.8). The question, what terms like Ἑβραιστί, etc., mean in Greek texts, remains to be resolved: see the revision of Schürer, *History of the Jewish People . . .*, II.28 n.118. Perhaps it should not be ruled out that when Paul addresses the Jerusalem crowd τῇ Ἑβραΐδι διαλέκτῳ (Acts 21.40; 22.2), he may have spoken in (Mishnaic) Hebrew.

As with Rabin, so Mussies' survey (in the Safrai/Stern volume, II.1040-64; already noted) of Greek used in Jewish and Christian sources down to I AD is also excellent. A particular strength here is his discussion of Jewish papyri and inscriptions in Greek from both Palestine and the Diaspora. The *c*.700 Greek inscriptions of Jews from the Diaspora are concluded to be linguistically indistinguishable from those of Palestinian provenance (1042-47). See further below, pp.35-36. The more recent survey of Jewish inscriptions by L.H. Kant, *ANRW* II.20.2 (1987) 671-713, is both uneven in the quality of its comments on various features, and disappointing in its lack of depth and unawareness of certain major epigraphical publications (e.g., *I.Eph.* is not known at 691 n.121).

What may bilingual theory contribute to this question of language use in Palestine? A number of points may be mentioned from Baetens Beardsmore's recent book.

1. The great majority of bilinguals are **not fluent** in their second language (Baetens Beardsmore, 10). This is of relevance to the use made in the secondary literature of the Greek inscriptions of Palestine, which are sometimes claimed — e.g., by D.M. Lewis, *JTS* 20 (1969) 588 — to be in Greek that is too rudimentary to indicate bilingual ability. Yet, as was noted a little earlier, inability to write well does not allow the presumption of an inability to speak a language.

2. In a bilingual context the dominant or **preferred language may not always coincide with the first language** (Baetens Beardsmore, 30). This may have relevance to the relationship

between Aramaic and Greek in the case of Palestinian-born Jews of permanent residence elsewhere, such as Josephus. See below, p.33. An instance of this phenomenon in another context is provided by that group of bilinguals using a dying language whom N.E. Dorian calls 'semi-speakers': see, e.g., her essay in R. Andersen (ed.), *Pidginization and Creolization as Language Acquisition* (Rowley [Mass.], 1983), 158-59; and further, below, p.26.

3. **Primary bilingualism** should be clearly distinguished from **secondary bilingualism**. The first term refers to a speaker who has picked up a second language by force of circumstances (e.g., from the work environment), without any formal instruction. In contrast, secondary bilingualism refers to the situation of a speaker who has learned a second language via systematic instruction (ibid., 8). The implication of this distinction for our present discussion is that there were people in Palestine who attained to bilingualism by different routes. While it should not be taken as an exact equation there may be some appropriateness in seeing upper-class, urban Jews as those more likely to be secondary bilinguals, primary bilinguals being those with less access to formal education or who lived in rural areas. H.C. Youtie's failure to perceive this distinction between primary and secondary bilingualism has occasioned his erroneous conclusion, that '. . . Greek never became a vital linguistic factor in Palestine comparable to Hebrew and Aramaic. The great mass of Jews made little or no contact with it' (*Scriptiunculae Posteriores* I [Bonn, 1981] 59). A useful example of a primary bilingual is provided by Julianus Euteknios, a businessman from Laodikeia in Syria, who died at Lyon. His Greek verse epitaph (III/IV) — the text is repr. and discussed at *New Docs 1976*, **23** — speaks of his constant travel among diverse peoples, and claims that 'persuasion flowed from his tongue' in his dealings with Kelts (οὐ Κέλτοις λαλέοντος ἀπὸ γλώσσης ῥέε πειθώ, *col.*1, *l.*7). Like Lucian, Julianus' first language was probably Aramaic, but almost certainly he would have been fluent in Greek as well. And this comment in the epigram suggests more than a passable facility in Keltic. In contrast, the Punic philosopher Hasdrubal who, under the name of Kleitomachos, became head of the Academy at Athens in 129 BC (see above, p.18), was clearly a secondary bilingual whose first language ceased to be his preferred one. So, too, with the Lykian Philetos, whose epitaph (*IGUR* 3.1351) is discussed at *New Docs 1979*, **8**. Another secondary bilingual who may be mentioned is the Egyptian Isidoros, who inscribed four hymns to Isis on a temple at Medînet Mâdi in the Egyptian Fayum between *c.*88 and 80 BC. As V.F. Vanderlip points out, *The Four Greek Hymns of Isidorus and the Cult of Isis* (*Am.Stud.Pap.* 12; Toronto, 1972) 97-102, Isidoros' very precise uses of voice, as also his use of the definite article, are indicative of his having had formal schooling in Greek. She characterises him as 'an intelligent man who had learned, but did not easily speak, Greek' (100).

4. Of particular importance is the distinction between **receptive and productive bilingualism**. The former refers to a situation where a second language can be read, and understood aurally, but not written or spoken. The latter term signifies the situation where a second language can be written and spoken as well (Baetens Beardsmore, 13-17). Corresponding to this, Beziers/van Overbeke use the terms 'passive' and 'active' bilingualism (99-105). As K.L. McKay points out to me (*per litt.*, 5.12.88), however, many primary bilinguals do not easily fit into these two classifications, possessing oral/aural ability in a language but unable to read or write it. In my judgement, much of the 'fuzziness' of discussion about bilingualism in Palestine (and elsewhere) in antiquity is due to the failure to differentiate these forms of bilingualism. Consequently, bilingual capacity is often judged solely in terms of its 'productive' aspect. When the chiliarch addresses Paul in surprise, Ἑλληνιστὶ γινώσκεις; (Acts 21.37), he clearly implies recognition that Paul is a productive bilingual. Yet this point is nowhere taken up in the secondary literature, not even in Sevenster's book which takes this

question as its title. From Egypt a useful instance of productive bilingualism may be seen in the person of Dionysios son of Kephalas. He figures frequently over the period 116-104 BC in *P.L.Bat.* 22 (1982), a family archive containing both Demotic and Greek texts (Akoris in Middle Egypt). The editor demonstrates (3) that Dionysios' background is Egyptian, yet he could write Greek as capably as Demotic.

Of some interest for our subject is *P.Col.* 4 (1940; = *P.Col.Zen.* 2) 66 (Fayum, *c.*256 or 255 BC), a Ptolemaic letter of complaint to Zenon from one of his employees, assigned to work in Syria under one of Zenon's agents. The man complains about not being paid or treated properly because he is a non-Greek (βάρβαρος, 19), ὅτι οὐκ ἐπίσταμαι ἑλληνίζειν (21). The editors hold (17) that the letter is probably written by the complainant himself and accordingly deny that the verb can have its usual meaning, to write/speak Greek. They therefore interpret it more generally (17-18) as, 'because I don't know how to act like a Greek'. But this fails to take into account the issue of bilingualism. The man may have been able to write Greek reasonably (so edd.), even if his hand-writing was 'crude' (ibid., 16). He may be a productive bilingual, but not necessarily fluent. And a Greek seeking to 'pull rank' culturally over an Egyptian would find a marked accent one of the most obvious things to which to draw attention. A native Greek speaker may scorn a non-native speaker of Greek as unable to speak it. For recent discussion of this text see C. Orrieux, *Les papyrus de Zénon. L'horizon d'un grec en Egypte au III* siècle avant J.C.* (Paris, 1983) 132-33.

The situation of Ovid in exile is perhaps a special case, but possibly affords evidence of productive bilingualism. While at Tomis he claimed to have learned Getic and Sarmatian (*Trist.* 5.12.57-68). The fact that he attained considerable facility in the former may be inferred from his statement (*Pont.* 4.13.19-20, cf. 65-66) that he composed poems in that language. On Ovid and bilingualism see the article by E. Lozovan in N.I. Herescu (ed.), *Ovidiana. Recherches sur Ovide* (Paris, 1958), 396-403. However, R. Syme, *History in Ovid* (Oxford, 1978), is much more suspicious of this and other passages which suggest that Ovid acquired fluency in such languages, dismissing the idea as 'only a piece of fantasy' (17). Close in time to Ovid was Publilius Syrus, an ex-slave who 'made good' at Rome under Julius Caesar as a writer of Latin mimes (*fabulae riciniatae*). His surviving fragments are collected in the Loeb *Minor Latin Poets* volume. His name betrays his origin (Antioch?), and we may assume that his mother-tongue was Aramaic (or possibly Greek). Several centuries later Honorius' court poet Claudian must be inferred to have been a productive bilingual. A native Greek speaker born at Alexandria *c.*370, he acquired a good education in Latin and was in Italy by *c.*394 where he wrote a number of works in Latin, none of which can be dated after 404.

As for the difficulty of measuring bilingualism, only two studies of my acquaintance consciously attempt this for ancient Palestine. The focus of Lieberman's 1963 essay in A. Altmann (ed.), *Biblical and Other Studies*, 123-41, is very narrow: he limits himself to 'the main stratum which influenced Judaism: namely Rabbinic literature' (123). Even so, his conclusions are very generalised, that we really do not know how much Greek the Rabbis knew. As the subtitle of Sevenster's book indicates, he is particularly interested in how much Greek the first Jewish Christians could have known. The particular strength of his lively and informative volume is its second half, evaluating the archaeological evidence from Palestine which gives some indication of knowledge of Greek. His conclusion is that in first-century Palestine the most common language of communication was Aramaic, although Greek was widely known and Hebrew (written and probably spoken) occupied a more important place than is often allowed (176). In particular, 'the simultaneous occurrence of tidy, correct and clumsy, primitive inscriptions in Greek proves that this language was used in widely divergent layers of the Jewish population in Palestine' (183). A question which deserves to be taken up, though, is: who erected the 'clumsy' inscriptions? Were these texts set up by receptive bilinguals with only a very shaky ability to write Greek? If so, why did they choose to employ Greek rather than their mother tongue? Alternatively, may the choice of Greek for an inscription, even when limited ability is betrayed, allow the inference that the composer's mother-tongue was also Greek, i.e., that considerably greater oral skills were possessed? If not, are we seeing cultural pretension alone at work? Some amount of overlap is to be expected between primary and receptive bilingualism on the one hand, and secondary and productive bilingualism on the other. This matter bears on the wider subject of the pervasive influence of Hellenism beyond educated circles and urban groupings.

In the light of research this century we may say that Thumb was mistaken in his belief (*Die griechische Sprache* . . ., 105-06) that Hellenism and knowledge of Greek was not as widespread in Palestine and among Jews as it was in Syria, Egypt and Asia Minor. At least in the case of Greek Chomsky's assertion is erroneous, *JQR* 42 (1951/2) 206-07, that 'none of the other languages [viz., Persian, Greek, Latin] of the ruling powers in Palestine ever attained such popularity [as Aramaic] . . . These languages failed to encroach upon the position of the vernaculars in Palestine.'

In view of Meyers/Strange's above-quoted conclusion (see above, p.22) on the basis of archaeological data, that by I AD Greek had already eclipsed Aramaic as the major spoken language of Palestine (*pace* Schürer, *History of the Jewish People* . . ., II.74, 79), the question of the relative standing of these two languages needs further reconsideration. Careful attention to developments in linguistics relating to bilingualism may well offer some approaches to help break the impasse concerning the language question of ancient Palestine. Nevertheless, it should be stressed that to expect very specific results may be unrealistic given the implications imposed by working with dead languages. The subject of 'language death' has been receiving increasing attention in linguistic research since the mid-1970s. The contributions of N.C. Dorian may be noted in particular. In *Language* 54 (1978) 590-609 she demonstrates it is the semi-speakers (i.e. receptive, not productive bilinguals) who because of their lack of fluency, are very much the innovators in a language that is dying. These changes (whether morphological, syntactic, or other) are in the direction of simplification, or else will involve expansive paraphrases. Dorian concludes (606) that such linguistic discontinuity is not always caused by social discontinuity but by a gradual narrowing of the context (home, in-group community, religion, work, etc.) in which the language is employed. Some other contributions by her are listed in the bibliography to the present volume. Note most recently ead. (ed.), *Investigating Obsolescence. Studies in Language Contraction and Death* (Cambridge, 1989). One of the syntactic features explored in this volume is the low frequency of relative clauses used by speakers of a language well on the way to disappearing (J.H. Hill, 149-64). Albanian speakers in Greece who speak Arvanitika are the focus of L.D. Tsitsipis' study in this volume (117-37), as elsewhere, e.g., *Zeitschrift für Balkanologie* 20 (1984) 122-31 (on semi-speakers' loss of competence with the subjunctive inflection). L. Campbell/M.C. Muntzel deal with different types of language death and their linguistic characteristics (181-96). The potential of the application of this kind of linguistic research to the study of languages in antiquity warrants consideration.

Semitisms and Jewish Greek

It is not the intention of this section to scrutinise the evidence for Semitisms in the NT (although a few alleged examples of Semitisms will be given brief attention in ch.3 below) for, as with the previous subject of language use in Palestine, that has been done often enough by others. The most recent contribution of substance is M. Wilcox, *ANRW* II.25.2 (1984) 978-1029. Rather, it is intended to show why the presence of Semitisms in the NT does not amount to a case for Jewish Greek.

For Wilcox a Semitism is 'any word or phrase whose use or construction departs from normal idiomatic Greek usage in such a way as to conform to normal idiomatic semitic usage' (*The Semitisms of Acts* [Oxford, 1965] 17). While in general terms this may be unexcêptional, it is in fact somewhat question-begging since it ignores the factor of different levels of idiomatic language. While the word 'Semitism' has become a convenient umbrella term it has rightly been insisted that Aramaisms must be differentiated from Hebraisms: see, e.g., G. Mussies, *NTS* 30 (1984) 416-32. It is a weakness of A. Hilhorst's study, *Sémitismes et latinismes dans le Pasteur d'Hermas* (Nimwegen, 1976), that he does not distinguish sufficiently between Hebraisms and Aramaisms. Failure to observe this distinction is one of J.A. Fitzmyer's main criticisms, in *CBQ* 30 (1968) 417-28, of the third edition of Black's *Aramaic Approach* . . . In his 1975 essay, 'The study of the Aramaic background of the NT', repr. in his *A Wandering Aramean. Collected Aramaic Essays* (Missoula, 1979) 1-27, Fitzmyer raises eight matters needing differentiation in the study of Aramaic and the NT. J. Barr, *BJRL* 53 (1969) 17, 22-23, also offers some methodological criticisms of Black's book. Note also M. Smith, *JBL* 90 (1971) 247-48. M. Silva characterises as Hebraisms those Semitic loans in the NT which are mediated via the LXX, whereas Aramaisms comprise all other examples of Semitic loans found in the NT: *NTS* 22 (1976) 104-10, at 105. After eliminating technical terms he finds only *c*.60 Hebraisms and 20 Aramaisms in the NT (110). On the other hand, the vagueness with which the term 'Semitism' may be invested — cf. Fitzmyer, *A Wandering Aramean*, 5-6 — is illustrated by the introduction to N. Turner, *Grammar of NT Greek*, IV. *Style*, where 'Semitism'/'Semitic' is sometimes used as an equivalent for Jewish Greek, and sometimes not. The need to distinguish Hebrew and Aramaic influences and, for the former, to differentiate OT Hebrew from Mishnaic emerges in S. Thompson's brief survey of the lack of agreement among Semitists in their understanding of the language of Revelation: *The Apocalypse and Semitic Syntax*, 2-7.

At the lexical level it should be clear that technical terms deriving from Judaism and employed in Greek cannot be considered as part of a hypothetical 'Jewish Greek' dialect (so Silva, *NTS* 22 [1976] 109; cf. MM, s.v. πνεῦμα. The quotation from Mackey above [p.11] is apposite in this connection.). Nor does the presence of Jewish names in Greek prove anything about the Semitising of Greek, even where they come across as indeclinable forms (cf. Wilcox, *The Semitisms of Acts*, 87). Nor, again, is it true to say that new coinages in the NT help to establish the claim of the existence of a separate dialect. C. Mohrmann, *VC* 11 (1957) 35, states: 'During the first two centuries, early Christian Greek develops very rapidly, and is distinguished from the general *koine* by numerous semantic innovations, as well as by a number of technical and non-technical neologisms'. I would dissent from this statement if it is to be inferred that 'Christian Greek' is a distinct dialect of the *koine*. Again, in *Humanitas* 13-14 (1961-62) 322-35, Mohrmann suggests (327, 329) that a major influence on the Greek used by Christians was idioms from a Jewish milieu. Such items as new coinings may subsequently have become a part of the technical vocabulary of the Christians, but a dialect cannot be created retrospectively. These new words, and words accorded a new meaning, are to be seen primarily as the result of literary creativity at the time of their coining, and in no way as a self-conscious contribution to the development of a separate dialect. Further, while there are some words which we should not doubt are nonce-words, particularly in the Pauline corpus, e.g., σύσσωμος (cf. MM, s.v. συνσ-), we must always temper any ambition to inflate the number of these with the realisation that new documentary finds are each year bringing to light words previously unattested either in their form or in their meaning. Cf. M. Silva, *ZNW* 69 (1978) 253-57. To the extent that long-attested Greek words are applied to new contexts, that is a normal linguistic phenomenon — cf. R. Merkelbach, *ZPE* 18 (1975) 101-49, with a response by H.C. Youtie, ibid., 150-54 — and nothing special should be inferred from this process merely because it occurs in the Greek Bible and ECL.

Some modern writers have spoken of a 'Christian Greek', above all N. Turner in his most recent book, *Christian Words* (Edinburgh, 1980). Thus, J. de Zwaan held that Acts provides evidence of 'something like a sort of "Christian Greek" ', in F.J. Foakes Jackson/K. Lake (edd.), *The Beginnings of Christianity* I.2 (London, 1922) 63-64. The views of two classicists who mention 'Christian Greek' should not be misconstrued. Writing about Jerome, H.-I. Marrou says that it did not occur to him that '. . . le grec est une langue vivante, qu'il existe un grec chrétien, une langue technique de la théologie, qui évolue et se différencie de jour en jour': *Histoire de l'éducation dans l'antiquité* (Paris, 1948; 1965⁶) 383. It is clear that Marrou is here thinking of the development of a technical theological vocabulary within Christianity, not of a separate language or dialect. More recently, L.R. Palmer gives the heading 'Christian Greek' to one brief section of his recent book, *The Greek Language* (London, 1980) 194-96. But it emerges from these few pages that the caution with which he speaks means that he stands back from any notion of a separate dialect.

It needs to be emphasised that while the literary impact of the LXX on the NT writers is not to be doubted, its actual influence on the *vocabulary* of the NT is small, apart from the obvious matter of theological and other technical terms. 'The vocabulary that the LXX and NT have in common is less than is often supposed. In particular it is to be noted that words common to both often vary considerably in regard to their uses': J.A.L. Lee, *A Lexical Study of the LXX Version of the Pentateuch* (*SCS* 14; Chico, 1983) 9. Cf. Silva, *NTS* 22 (1976) 109-10; *pace* Mohrmann, *VC* 11 (1957) 22. As merely one example to illustrate this, the LXX phrase πρόσωπον λαμβάνω is usually regarded as a Hebraism. It does not appear in the NT, however, although προσωπολημπτέω occurs once (Jas 2.9), along with two related nouns, -λήμπτης (Acts 10.34) and -λημψία (Rom. 2.11; Eph. 6.9; Col. 3.25; Jas 2.1), and the privative adverb at 1 Pet. 1.17. Exactly what the relationship is between the LXX phrase and these NT words has recently been spelled out in detail by P. Ghiron-Bistagne in C. Froidefond (ed.), *Mélanges E. Delebecque* (Aix-en-Provence, 1983), 157-74, where it is shown that the link is more complex than is sometimes claimed. Nearly a century ago H.A.A. Kennedy, *Sources of the NT Greek. The Influence of the LXX on the Vocabulary of the NT* (Edinburgh, 1895), reached the conclusion that while LXX influence on NT vocabulary is indubitable, it must not be exaggerated (164). Kennedy's book, written in reaction to E. Hatch, *Essays in Biblical Greek* (Oxford, 1889), still deserves attention. Its interest lies in the conclusions reached before papyri began to be drawn into the discussion of NT language. A few years before Kennedy, T.K. Abbott had already provided a briefer critique of Hatch, and reached the same conclusion about LXX influence on NT vocabulary: *Essays, Chiefly on the Original Texts of the Old and New Testaments* (London, 1891) 65-109 (especially 66-71 on LXX vocabulary, and 72-86 on Hatch's work).

We shall not concern ourselves here at length with the theory of 'Translation Greek', which claims that behind the Gospels and Acts, and certain other NT books such as Revelation, there may lie an Aramaic original, the translation of which has brought across numerous Aramaisms (or Hebraisms) into the Greek version we have. The LXX provides the most tangible instance of this process, of course. On this see the sensible remarks of E.J. Bickerman in his *Studies in Jewish and Christian History* (Leiden, 1976) 1.167-200. Whatever the merits of this hypothesis for the NT, Barr is surely correct to insist, in his article in H.H. Paper (ed.), *Language and Texts* . . ., 56, that it is the Greek text of the NT which has to be viewed as the 'original' text. Since the Second World War the most famous and influential contribution to this question of a Semitic original behind certain NT books has been M. Black's *An Aramaic Approach to the Gospels and Acts*. Earlier this century there was much speculative activity in this field, partly in reaction to the work of Deissmann, Thumb, Moulton, and others; and the 'Translation Greek' hypothesis itself prompted counter-reactions. One particularly clear exposé of certain weaknesses of the theory was D.W. Riddle, *JBL* 51 (1932) 13-30, in which he reiterated the view that the Greek non-literary *koine* provided the proper basis for comparing the NT writings. Two much weaker discussions appeared in the same journal in successive years: J.M. Rife, *JBL* 52 (1933) 244-52; M. Burrows, *JBL* 53 (1934) 13-30. Riddle's later article in *JBL* 54 (1935) 127-38 is a critique of the work of C.C. Torrey in particular. Unwarranted speculation is still apparent in this sphere, as may be instanced by R.H. Gundry's claim at *JBL* 83 (1964) 408 that in I AD Palestine '. . . the Septuagintal translation of Greek so full of Semitisms must have exerted a powerful influence on the style of Greek spoken by the Jews'. G. Friedrich goes further, *TDNT* 10 (1976) 652, claiming that the Jews' constant exposure to the LXX affected their speech 'so that they could not think in authentically Greek terms'. These are not isolated opinions: as an earlier example reference may be made to two articles by H.F.D. Sparks on Luke as a 'deliberate Septuagintalizer', in which it is suggested that 'his native Greek had become so infected that he not only spoke, but also wrote, quite naturally, in the Semitic-Greek *patois* current among so many of his co-religionists': *JTS* 44 (1943) 131; cf. *JTS* n.s.1 (1950) 26. (Classicists, on the other hand, tend to see in Lk./Acts syntactic and stylistic features which indicate that the author was well versed in the classical authors: see, e.g., the two recent studies by E. Delebecque, *Rev.Bib.* 87 [1980] 590-93; *Bib.* 62 [1981] 229-38.) These writers are suggesting that the LXX influenced Jewish speech patterns. A variation of this is the assertion that the LXX reflected Jewish use of Greek. Thus, H. Pernot, *REG* 42 (1929) 425, states that the LXX '. . . nous a conservé plus ou moins, suivant les parties qu'on envisage, une langue de Juifs, où les hébraïsmes sont indéniables.' Yet well before Pernot's article Thackeray had already rejected the notion that the LXX provides a true picture of the language spoken by Jews among themselves (*Grammar . . .*, 27). It is not to be denied, of course, that Translation Greek can be productively researched, so long as it is recognised that no sharp distinction can be made between Greek translations of Semitic texts and Greek works containing Semitisms. G. Mussies provides a useful list of 15 characteristics of Translation Greek in his contribution in the Safrai/Stern volume, 1048-49. R.A. Martin has employed a statistical approach to see whether some parts of the NT can be shown to be Translation Greek: *Syntactical Evidence of Semitic Sources in Greek Documents* (Cambridge [Mass.], 1974); cf. his two earlier articles in *VT* 10 (1960) 295-310, and *NTS* 11 (1964/5) 38-59. Examination of Translation Technique is one of the most actively researched areas in LXX study today: see, e.g., the illuminating review of this question by E. Tov in C.E. Cox (ed.), *VI Congress of the International Organization for LXX and Cognate Studies, Jerusalem, 1986* (*SCS* 23; Atlanta, 1987), 337-59, which includes a useful classified bibliography (354-59).

Although the LXX is not primarily in view in this study, one further comment is warranted. R. Helbing's important monograph, *Die Kasussyntax der Verba bei den LXX. Ein Beitrag zur Hebraismenfrage und zur Syntax der Koine* (*Göttingen*, 1928), provided a detailed treatment of *c.*350 verbs and the constructions that follow them. While particularly concerned with detecting syntactic Hebraisms, lexical Hebraisms and evidence of a translator's misunderstanding of the original also receive attention. Helbing frequently quotes parallels from non-literary Greek sources, and occasionally refers to the NT and other writers. He finds that there are less than three score syntactical Hebraisms among the verbs examined. The implication of this for the NT is clear: if the number of Hebraisms in the LXX is not large, then the number in the NT should be expected to be even less. This coheres quite reasonably with Silva's tally of *c.*60 Hebraisms for the NT, noted above (p.27), given that the latter is not dealing with syntactical features alone.

In the quotation with which this chapter began Turner claims that 'Biblical Greek' was 'rather a separate dialect of Greek than a form of the Koine, and distinguishable as something parallel to classical, Hellenistic, Koine and Imperial Greek'. Any basis for Turner's differentiation here of Hellenistic and *koine* Greek is non-existent. Further, in one of Deissmann's more polemical moments he prophesied that those who sought to isolate the Bible from contemporary *koine* by calling it 'NT' Greek or a special language 'could only commit one more blunder by speaking of a Biblical or NT *dialect*': The Philology of the Greek Bible (London, 1908) 44-45 (his emphasis). Cf. Thumb, *Die griechische Sprache* . . ., 185. In a review of Turner, *Style*, at *CBQ* 39 (1977) 165-67, F.T. Gignac approves of Turner's position: '[Turner] calls this new community language Jewish Greek, and rightly considers it a distinct dialect or branch of Koine Greek' (167). This view is uncharacteristic of Gignac, and does not accord with the general tenor of the introduction to vol.1 of his *Grammar* (Milan, 1976).

In a useful survey of ancient attempts at dialect study J.B. Hainsworth, *TPS* (1967) 67, has pointed out that despite the canonical number of three *gene* (Doric, Ionic, Aeolic) Attic was accorded the status of a separate dialect by the Hellenistic grammarian Ps.-Dikaiarchos (flor. *c*.250 BC). (On the equation of *genos* and dialect — Athenians speak Attic, etc. — note the question from Ps.-Dikaiarchos given by Hainsworth at 65.) Clement of Alexandria, *Strom.* 1.142.4 Dindorf (= Migne, *PG* 8.800), provides the earliest testimony by a Greek writer for the acceptance of *koine* as a fifth dialect: φασὶ δὲ οἱ Ἕλληνες διαλέκτους εἶναι τὰς παρὰ σφίσι πέντε, Ἀτθίδα, Ἰάδα, Δωρίδα, Αἰολίδα, καὶ πέμπτην τὴν κοινήν . . . Already in the first century, however, Quintilian could speak of the *quinque graeci sermonis differentias* (*Inst.* 11.2.50). As we use the term, 'dialect' does not always correspond exactly to διάλεκτος, and is sometimes used flexibly, without precision. For example, we may speak of both Aeolic and Lesbian as dialects, though the latter is a sub-type of the former. Clement is here referring to Attic, etc., as the recognised *literary* dialects, of course, and when he includes the *koine* we must take him to mean its literary, high register. Thus we see him here as a participant in the Atticist debate. He is ignoring those geographically localised forms of the language that survived for many centuries in isolated areas. Brixhe implicitly endorses Clement's view (*Essai sur le grec anatolien*, 22-23) in his proposal that the only language which may properly be called *koine* is that variety of Greek spoken uniformly across time and geographical regions by the aristocracy of the Hellenistic cities. Other Greek is to be regarded as demotic or popular, evolving from the prestige language. This perspective fails to appreciate the importance of linguistic register. But I take it that the reason why *koine* should not be classed as a dialect entirely commensurate with Doric and others is that to do so not only confuses fundamentally the synchronic/diachronic distinction so important for descriptive linguistics, but in addition it entirely fails to appreciate that *koine* was the internationally used form of Greek which gradually developed from IV BC. It was *the* Greek language of the Hellenistic and early Roman periods. A little more will be said about this in the next chapter. To think of it as a dialect could imply that there existed contemporaneously a 'mainstream' Greek language of which *koine* was one tributary. We may note, further, that although Hainsworth points out (64, 76) that the Greek contribution to dialectology was not without its weaknesses, it seems never to have occurred to later Byzantine scholars that any such dialect as 'Jewish' or 'Biblical' Greek was to be differentiated. On the modern narrowing down of the Greek of the Bible from 'Jewish' Greek to 'Biblical' Greek, since it had to be conceded that Philo's and Josephus' work was different, see Vergote, *Phil.Stud.* 4 (1932/3) 191.

Alexandrian scholars sought to identify Alexandrian Greek as a separate dialect of the *koine*, but the attempt was misconceived, because of the failure to realise that the difference between the colloquial language and the language employed in literary genres is one of register, not dialect. On this see Thumb, *Die griechische Sprache*. . ., 170-72; S.G. Kapsomenos, *Mus.Helv.* 10 (1953) 258-60; and, more recently, P.M. Fraser, *Ptolemaic Alexandria* (Oxford, 1972) 2.147-48, n.197. One particular text should be mentioned in this connection, fragmentary though it is. *P.Giss.Univ.Bibl.* 5 (1939, repr. 1973) 46 provides an extract from the so-called 'Acts of the Pagan

Martyrs', in which an accuser (κ]ατήγο[ρος, *col*.III.6) is denounced while appearing before the emperor Gaius, because he could be shown by his speech not to have been an Alexandrian. The passage runs as follows (*col*.III.8-12):

οὐ [γάρ

ἐστιν ὁ κατήγορος οὗτος] ἔ[τ]υμος Ἕλ[λην.

10 διὸ ὡς ἄδικον κατήγορον ε]ἰσκαλῶ [αὐ-

τὸν εἰς δίκην. ξένον γὰρ αὐ]τὸν δηλο[ῖ τό

τε βαρβαρικὸν σχῆμα καὶ] ἡ γλ[ῶσσα.

'[For this prosecutor is] not a genuine Greek. [Accordingly,] I indict [him as an unauthorised prosecutor. For his non-Greek bearing and his] speech show him [to be a foreigner.]'

The details of this passage cannot be pressed too far because so little is preserved. But for our purposes it may be inferred that a man who had passed himself off as an Alexandrian citizen was apparently unmasked by virtue of his manner of speech (γλῶσσα), viz., his accent. As has been observed already, a marked accent is not sufficient to indicate a separate dialect. The obvious, and striking parallel to this incident in the NT is the identification of Peter as a Galilean because of his speech patterns (Mt. 26.73, καὶ γὰρ ἡ λαλιά σου δῆλόν σε ποιεῖ; cf. Lk. 22.59; Mk 14.70).

There is another factor to be considered here. We know that the Jews adopted the *koine* on a thorough-going basis in the Diaspora; and in Palestine itself Greek was widely known, though in varying degrees. It was a long haul from this to the emergence in mediaeval times of a distinctive Judaeo-Greek, or Yevanic. What distinguishes Yevanic from ancient Jewish use of Greek is that the former is written in Hebrew letters — see R. Dalven, 'Judeo-Greek', *Encyclopaedia Judaica* 10 (1971) 425-27 — although such a feature is not a *sine qua non* of all modern Jewish languages, as C. Rabin points out, *IJSL* 30 (1981) 19-28. Had there been already in antiquity a distinctive version of Greek developed by Jews and used intracommunally — for as observed above (p.29) the view is not infrequently advanced that 'Jewish Greek' was a spoken language, not simply an idiosyncratic literary style: contrast Bauer's introduction in BAGD, xxi — it would be hard to account *both* for its disappearance *and also* for the emergence of a quite differently-based Jewish Greek a millennium and more later, in view of the tenacity of Jewish tradition. This claim is a generalised one, for I am not competent to say much about Jewish use of Greek in the Byzantine period and beyond. But it may be urged that the onus is upon those who hold with a notion of Jewish Greek as a distinct dialect of the *koine* to account for its demise in later centuries coupled with the development of a new Greek distinctive of Jews many centuries later. Cf. J. Juster, *Les Juifs dans l'Empire romain* (Chartres, 1914; repr. New York, n.d.) 1.366 n.3.

Before we leave the question of dialect there is one final matter to be noted where, again, the onus of proof rests firmly with those who adhere to belief in the existence of Jewish Greek. To speak of a dialect as a coherent grammatical subsystem of a language it must be possible to demonstrate that it has a consistent syntax, morphology and phonology, which is definably distinct from and yet related to that language. Despite the promise of the title of K. Beyer's *Semitische Syntax im NT* (Göttingen, 1962, 1968²) this book does not provide that demonstration, even for the temporal and conditional clauses which he investigates in such detail. Indeed, it is clear that his concern is not really with Jewish Greek as such but with Semitic influence on the NT. Further brief comment on this book is provided in ch. 4, p.82, below.

This brings us to our next distinction, arguably the one most fundamental for our discussion: Semitisms do not establish the existence of Jewish Greek. This point is normally widely recognised, at least implicitly: e.g., Bauer's introduction in BAGD, xx-xxi; P.S. Costas, *An*

Outline of the History of the Greek Language, with Particular Emphasis on the Koine and Subsequent Periods (Chicago, 1936; repr. 1979) 55. But there are publications where it is claimed that the cumulative effect of various Semitic features in the NT is such that the latter is to be treated as a distinct form of Greek, composed by Jews. In this way, acknowledgement of the presence of Semitisms is allowed to stray into acceptance of a Jewish Greek. Cf. S.W. Baron, *A Social and Religious History of the Jews* (New York, 1952[2]) 1.186. Although it is true that Deissmann, Moulton and others undervalued the presence of Semitisms in the NT in the first flush of enthusiasm for the Greek documentary parallels they were noting — on this, see J.R. Harris, *ExpT* 25 (1913) 54; and A.T. Robertson, *A Grammar of the Greek NT in the Light of Historical Research* (New York, 1923[4]) 91 — yet it ought not to be forgotten that they never denied them. For example, in *NJA* 11 (1903) 161-77, an article on the importance of the LXX as a landmark in the process of the hellenisation of Jewish monotheism, Deissmann addresses the question, whether the LXX is really a Greek book or a Semitic book in Greek 'covers'. He argues for the former position, though readily acknowledging the presence of foreign features as an indication of its origin. 'Ich denke an die zahlreichen (wenn auch in ihrer Zahl meist stark überschätzten) syntaktischen Semitismen . . .' (171). As for Moulton, it is clear that he modified his views somewhat between the *Prolegomena* and the second volume of his *Grammar*, to acknowledge more fully the presence of Semitic idioms. Cf. Howard's comments in Moulton's *Grammar*, II.413-14. Howard's appendix on 'Semitisms in the NT' (411-84) remains a useful statement of the question. It is his main contribution to the volume which was already mostly written by Moulton before he left England for India in 1915. Of the section on 'Semitic colouring' in the introduction (12-34), pp.12-22 were written by Moulton but left unfinished. Of these pages note particularly p.14 where Moulton acknowledges that his minimising view of Semitisms had been 'too rigorous'. As G. Milligan observed in one of his essays in the collective work, *The History of Christianity in the Light of Modern Knowledge* (London, 1929) 284, why should there be any 'undue anxiety' to deny the existence of genuine Semitisms in the NT? 'The presence of a few "Semitisms" more or less does not prevent our recognizing that the general language of the document in which they occur is Greek.' Lagrange's response to what he perceived to be the refusal by others to see Semitic influence in the NT (quoted by Howard in *Grammar*, II.414 n.1) is an over-reaction simply because no-one, so far as I am aware, has ever totally denied the presence of Semitic features.

> Il n'en est pas moins vrai que lorsqu'un helléniste ouvre le NT, en particulier les évangiles, il se trouve transporté dans les tentes de Sem. L'exagération de quelques hellénistes a été, reconnaissant chaque objet comme déjà vu dans le domaine de Japhet, de prétendre qu'il en venait toujours.

F.M. Abel, *Grammaire du grec biblique suivi d'un choix de papyrus* (Paris, 1927) xxv, over-reacts, too, when he says that one effect of Deissmann's work in demonstrating parallels between documentary texts and the NT, and thereby reducing the number of putative Hebraisms, is the tendency 'à ramener à zéro l'élément sémitique des livres bibliques'.

In the phenomenon of Semitisms in certain parts of the NT and other Judaeo-Christian writings, such as the *Testament of Abraham*, what we are seeing is quite simply examples of bilingual interference. N. Turner, *NTS* 1 (1954/5) 220, claims too much for this latter work calling it 'an excellent example of the "Jewish" Greek language of the early Christian centuries'. R. Sollamo, *VT 25* (1975) 777, unquestioningly includes Ps.-Aristeas, Aristobulus Judaeus, and Ezekiel Tragicus as writers of Jewish Greek. This categorisation does not stand scrutiny. To take the last-named only, the language of Ezekiel's *Exagoge* is in general modelled firmly upon that of the fifth-century dramatists, allowing of course for differences of vocabulary necessitated by its plot. Writing in II BC Alexandria it is clear that Ezekiel knew the LXX, but uncertain whether he knew Hebrew. An excellent recent edition of the play has been provided by H. Jacobson (Cambridge, 1983), which includes a balanced appraisal (40-47) of the language(s) known by Ezekiel.

Some Semitisms have been detected in the *Shepherd* of Hermas, but Hilhorst claims that their presence is due to the author's close knowledge of the LXX: '. . . nous ne trouvons aucune preuve qu' Hermas était familiarisé avec l'hébreu, l'araméen ou le latin. Ses sémitismes sont des emprunts déjà intégrés dans le grec de son temps' (*Sémitismes et latinismes . . .*, 185; cf. 50). This quotation should not be construed as indicating that Hermas knew no languages other than Greek. Hilhorst says (14, 67) we must remain agnostic as to his ethnic origin and the languages he knew. Yet this is over-cautious. Hilhorst is alert to the question of interference phenomena (36-38); and the fact that the number of Semitisms in Hermas is few (together with the virtual non-existence of Latinisms) may rather tell us something about his bilingual ability, viz., that in the case of the former if Aramaic was his mother tongue his grasp of Greek was sufficiently good that the former rarely made its presence felt. Hermas would thus provide us with an instance of someone whose dominant language did not coincide with his first language; cf. Baetens Beardsmore, *Bilingualism*, 30. However, we should allow that his mother tongue may have been Greek, given the dominant language preference of the Jewish community — and accordingly of Jewish Christians, as Paul's letter to the Romans also indicates — in Rome in the first few centuries of the Imperial period; cf. Solin, *ANRW* II.29.2 (1983) 705 and n.263a.

What of Josephus (cf. Sevenster, *Do You Know Greek?*, 61-76)? His *Jewish* War is an expanded reworking of an Aramaic precursor now entirely lost: Ἑλλάδι γλώσσῃ μεταβαλὼν ἃ τοῖς ἄνω βαρβάροις τῇ πατρίῳ συντάξας ἀνέπεμψα πρότερον, κτλ. (*BJ* 1.3; on this passage, and the verb μεταβάλλω, see Rajak, *Josephus*, 176; G. Hata's view, *JQR* 66 [1975/6] 89-108, that a drastic reworking of the original history was involved in the process of recasting *BJ* into Greek, should not be ruled out absolutely, although his case is not argued very persuasively). He tells us himself that he decided to learn Greek more thoroughly so his writings would be available to a wider readership, even though he found it difficult to render his material εἰς ἀλλοδαπὴν ἡμῖν καὶ ξένην διαλέκτου συνήθειαν, 'in the customary usage of a language which is not my native one, and foreign' (*Ant.* 1.7). The decision to immerse himself in Greek may not have been taken before he went to Rome: 'he did not leave Jerusalem equipped to compose the *Jewish War* in Greek' (Rajak, 62); though it need not be excluded that he had already acquired some Greek while at Jerusalem, as J. Bernardi points out at *REG* 100 (1987) 26. To improve the quality of his Greek he enlisted the aid of others proficient in the language, χρησάμενός τισι πρὸς τὴν Ἑλληνίδα φωνὴν συνεργοῖς (*Contra Ap.* 1.50). (H. St. J. Thackeray, *Josephus, The Man and the Historian* [1929; repr. New York, 1967] 106-20, attempted unconvincingly to identify the contribution of two of them, in *Ant.* xv-xvi and xvii-xix. For refutations of this theory see R.J.H. Shutt, *Studies in Josephus* [London, 1961] 29-35, 59-77; and, more recently and bluntly, Rajak, 233-36. A survey of discussion on the assistants is included in L.H. Feldman, *Josephus and Modern Scholarship (1937-1980)* [Berlin, 1984] 827-30.) The result is that in Josephus we have good-quality *koine* which betrays some considerable evidence of Atticism. This point is brought out in the detailed analysis of A. Pelletier, *Flavius Josèphe, adaptateur de la Lettre d'Aristée. Une réaction atticisante contre la Koine* (*Etudes et Commentaires* 45; Paris, 1962). Taking Josephus' paraphrase (*Ant.* 12.11-118) of the *Letter of Aristeas* written some three centuries earlier concerning the translation of the LXX, Pelletier demonstrates how the historian altered the language of this work in ways to make it approximate more closely to classical Attic norms. Although he shows care in this, he is not an absolute purist (Pelletier, 250-59); nevertheless, he may be appropriately associated with the Atticising reaction which began in the first century. The Greek of Lucian of Samosata, whose first language was Aramaic too, is even more faithful to Atticising canons. Indeed, he wishes to pass himself off as completely hellenised, as is shown by *Herc.* 4: Κελτὸς δέ τις παρεστὼς οὐκ ἀπαίδευτος τὰ ἡμέτερα, ὡς ἔδειξεν ἀκριβῶς ῾Ελλάδα φωνὴν ἀφιείς, φιλόσοφος, οἶμαι, τὰ ἐπιχώρια, κτλ, 'A Kelt was standing beside me, not uncultivated by our standards as he showed by his precise use of the Greek language, a philosopher (I suppose) by his own culture's standards . . .'

Even though Josephus' work is literary it is surprising, as Thackeray and others have pointed out (*Grammar* . . ., 28; confirmed again at id., *Josephus*, 102 with n.2; Vergote, *Phil.Stud.* 6 [1934/5] 88-89; endorsed by Abel, *Grammaire* . . ., xxvi; earlier, Thumb, *Die griechische Sprache* . . ., 125-26, with regard to Philo as well as Josephus), that virtually no trace of Semitisms occurs in his material, which might be expected if a distinct Jewish Greek existed. Thackeray detected one Aramaism: *JTS* 30 (1929) 361-70. Yet this construction, pleonastic ἄρχομαι plus infinitive, occurs in Xenophon, as he acknowledges (369-70). On this construction see further, ch. 3, p.55-56 below. More recently, Bernardi has identified (24-26) several Semitisms in *BJ* (though not all his examples seem conclusive), while acknowledging their rarity (27). The fact that Josephus did have some help with his Greek makes it difficult for us to assess his bilingual ability. We may legitimately infer that Aramaic was his first language, though the possibility that he was also at home with Hebrew should not be ruled out (Rajak, *Josephus*, 230-32). As to his attainment of Greek, we must say that he mastered it so thoroughly that no linguistic interference from Aramaic is detectable in what he wrote. Alternatively, we would have to say that the amount of sub-editing by the well-educated helpers he enlisted was very considerable, in that they erased well-nigh all trace of Aramaic interference. Yet as he himself acknowledges, although he came to feel at home in Greek grammar his pronunciation of Greek was marked by Aramaic interference: τὴν γραμματικὴν ἐμπειρίαν ἀναλαβών, τὴν δὲ περὶ τὴν προφορὰν ἀκρίβειαν πάτριος ἐκώλυσεν συνήθεια (*Ant.* 20.263; cf. Rajak, 50). Thus we may conclude that for Josephus, as for Hermas, Greek became his dominant, or preferred language, and it was attained via the secondary route of formal study and instruction. Bernardi makes the intriguing, but insufficiently tested, suggestion (28-29) that the mention of language helpers is a smokescreen by Josephus for the political advisers who helped mould his work of propaganda into its final form; for obviously he could not admit outright that he had such aid.

On a scale measuring the degree of bilingualism the author of Revelation would be positioned rather differently from both Josephus and Hermas. Mussies' very thorough study of the orthography, phonology and morphology of Rev. leads him to the conclusion that Palestinian Aramaic, or possibly Mishnaic Hebrew, was the author's first language, but that his control of Greek was sufficiently weak that numerous Semitic idioms are attempted in Greek dress, resulting in some decidedly odd Greek (*Morphology of Koine Greek*, especially 348-49; cf. 312-21). Note also his more recent essay in J. Lambrecht (ed.), *L'Apocalypse johannique et l'Apocalyptique dans le NT* (Louvain, 1980), 167-77, in which he identifies certain typically Greek constructions that do not at all, or scarcely, occur in Rev., perhaps due to their having no real counterpart in Mishnaic Hebrew or Aramaic.

With this view must be contrasted the monograph of S. Thompson, who rejects Mussies' conclusion and argues that Biblical Hebrew, not Mishnaic, served as the model for the language of Rev. (*Apocalypse and Semitic Syntax*, 1, 34, 53-57, 106-07). It is a frequently recurring element in his book that words and forms in Rev. are 'un-Greek' (ibid., 1, 2, 3, 27, 63, 64, 67, 79, 94, 99, etc.). It is disquieting that he makes no attempt to establish any basis by which this 'un-Greekness' is to be tested. Disquiet grows as awareness increases of methodologically doubtful statements. For example, he claims (59) that if a construction (in this case, the use of a Greek participle with imperatival force) is rare in the papyri 'naturally the case for Semitic influence is enhanced by such findings'. Again, a certain construction (passive use of μνησθῆναι) is said (25) to be 'no doubt a case of Hebrew influence on the voice of the verb, since such usage is neither classical nor is it found in the papyri'. As a third example we may note what Thompson says (36-37) about the use of verbs in the present tense with a past sense: 'It cannot be denied that the Greek Historic present could be used to express similar sense in Koine Greek, although it was never used on a large scale. But in such a text as the Apc., which is noted for its Semitic constructions, this use of the present tense can be described as yet another point of contact with Semitic verbal syntax'.

Thompson's brief chapter on 'Greek verbs with Hebrew meanings' (12-17) builds in particular on the work of G. Ozanne, *TynB* 16 (1965) 3-9 and M. Black, in J.R. McKay/J.F. Miller (edd.), *Biblical Studies: Essays in Honour of W. Barclay* (London, 1976), 135-46. It is critical for his argument that several words in Rev. have un-Greek meanings which are due to Hebrew words in the OT. He holds that the LXX renderings of these Hebrew words illustrate the meaning, and that therefore the occurrences in Rev. may be understood with the same force as they have in the LXX. For example, he suggests that θαυμάζω at 17.6, 7 has the sense 'be appalled', and the meaning 'devastate' at 13.3; again, κληρονομέω at 21.7 means 'take possession' (without any notion of inheritance implied). He suggests (15) that since the verb at Rev. 21.7 does not denote 'inherit', 'it must be understood in its Hebraic sense'. This fails to convince. Thompson needs to demonstrate that these meanings are *intrinsically inappropriate* to the Greek words which possess them in certain passages in Rev. To say that these meanings have carried across from Hebrew does not make them 'un-Greek': we may merely be looking at further lexical instances of bilingual interference.

Additionally, Thompson's approach fails to perceive and address the following difficulty: how did the first Christian readers/hearers of Rev., or Diaspora readers of the LXX, understand these Greek words when they met them *unless* they were already usages current in the *koine*? After all, the LXX was provided for those many Jews who knew no Hebrew, readers who would not be able to 'check back to their Hebrew version' to determine how the Greek was to be understood. Yet, though this may have motivated the undertaking of the translation, the result did not always achieve the aim of easy comprehensibility, as T. Muraoka has observed to me (*per litt.* 22/11/88). Thompson's book provides simply the most recent illustration of the problem of forgetting the situation of the ancient reader. It is true that he does take up this point briefly. Discussing the use of the Greek future indicative to represent the Semitic imperfect (47), he claims it as

> a true Semitism for which non-biblical Greek has no parallel whatever. We are led to the conclusion that here we are dealing with translation Greek, and furthermore, Greek which is intelligible primarily to readers familiar with Semitic languages. An ordinary non-Jew could hardly be expected to understand that the future tense contains a past reference . . .

Embedded in this view is the *a priori* of the existence of a separate Jewish-Greek dialect. But surely it is not only non-Jews who would have difficulty with the tense relationships posited by Thompson. Diaspora Jews whose knowledge of OT Hebrew was slight or non-existent would presumably be in the same position.

If a separate Jewish Greek existed in reality some traces of it should be evident in Jewish non-literary survivals. Yet this is not the case. A feature of Mussies' 1976 contribution in the Safrai/Stern volume is the attention he gives to Jewish inscriptions and papyri. By his count *c*.440 Greek inscriptions by Jews were known from Palestine by the mid-1970s, and nearly 700 from outside Palestine. 'Linguistically, all these inscriptions are hardly different from those found in Palestine' (1043). Of the c.200 inscriptions from Jerusalem printed in *CIJ* II.1210-1414, roughly 100 are in Greek. Since the publication of *CIJ* II in 1952 — it was essentially complete before the Second World War, although it only appeared after Frey's death — several dozen more texts have been published, nearly all of which are in Greek. For details see B. Lifshitz, *ANRW* II.8 (1977) 452-60. Lifshitz's tally of post-*CIJ* II items includes publications from 1937 onwards. For further comment on recent epigraphical finds see Mussies, *NTS* 29 (1983) 359-60. This proportion of Greek inscriptions from Jerusalem and its environs testifies to the use of Greek by a very considerable portion of the city's population (Lifshitz, *ANRW* II.8.459). A recent, specific contribution in this geographical area is L. Roth-Gerson, *The Greek Inscriptions from the Synagogues in Eretz-Israel* (in Hebrew; Jerusalem, 1987). This volume presents approximately three dozen mosaic and other building and dedicatory inscriptions, almost all of which are already known. In nearly all cases their language is quite perfunctory. Two recently-published bilingual Greek/Semitic inscriptions from Palestine are reproduced with brief comment in *New Docs 1976*, **67, 71**. The very great majority of all these items are of Roman date. As for the papyrus texts, of the 450 documents in *CPJ* I-II (vol.III lay outside the chronological scope of Mussies' essay) only 12 are certainly of Jewish authorship, 'or contain portions in the first person representing language actually spoken by Jews' (in Safrai/Stern [edd.], 1046). At n.1 on that page he lists them, though one of these twelve has slipped out: *CPJ* 12, 13, 14, 19, 43, 46, 133, 141, 151, 417, 424 (date range: 241 BC - 87 AD). Of these, no.46 is written on behalf of illiterate Jews, so is not relevant for Mussies' purpose; and no.141 can only be regarded as a possible candidate for inclusion (see ed. n. ad *ll*.9-10). Mussies' list may be supplemented, however, by the following items from *CPJ*: I.128 (a possibility only, depending on whether the female author is in fact to be regarded as a Jew — see the editor's intro. n. ad loc., and n. ad *l*.1), 138 (resolution of a Jewish association), 139 (list of contributions to a club, probably Jewish); II.158a, b (words of Jews quoted), 431 (ditto). For the record we may note the following items from *CPJ* III: 455, 469 (possibly), 474. The language of these documents — letters, petitions, etc. — 'shows the signs of the well-known phonetic and morphological development of the Hellenistic period' (Mussies, ibid.). Mussies has now provided a useful general survey of the Christian inscriptions of Palestine in R. van den Broek et al., *Kerk en kerken in Romeins-Byzantijns Palestina. Archeologie en geschiedenis* (Kampen, 1988), 186-211.

Another very informative analysis from the mid-1970s is H. Solin's survey, in Neumann/ Untermann (edd.), *Die Sprachen im römischen Reich . . .*, 301-30, of language use by Jews and Syrians in the Roman Empire, based primarily upon epigraphical evidence. This article serves as a summary of his extended treatment of the subject in *ANRW* II.29.2 (1983) 587-789 (plus indexes at 1222-49). His geographically-arranged lists (314-26) of Jewish inscriptions from Rome and the provinces serve to update further the situation since *CIJ* appeared. Within this period (I-IV) fall somewhat over 500 inscriptions, a mere fractional glimpse of Roman Jewry (316). The clear preponderance of texts in Greek leads Solin to conclude (316-17) that it was the first language of Jews at Rome, with Latin second-preferred and Aramaic scarcely used. This conclusion is supported by I. Kajanto in the same volume (92). The significance of the presence of Hebrew on some inscriptions has been overrated (Solin, 317). But Greek was not merely the language of the Jewish community in Rome; Solin suggests (317) that for the period of the Empire it was also the primary language of Jews in Palestine. This judgement conforms with the view of Meyers and Strange quoted above at p.22.

Quite independently of these studies the *New Docs* volumes serve only to reinforce Mussies' and Solin's point, that we cannot distinguish *linguistically* the documentary texts written by Jews from those by non-Jews. There may be exceptions to this, as T. Muraoka points out to me (22/11/88), in cases where a host of linguistically-marked features occurs; and the subject-matter may naturally provide a way to discern Jewish authorship. The surveys by Mussies and Solin, together with the material assembled in *New Docs*, thus confirm with specific instances and in detail what Moulton had said 80 years ago, that the value of the inscriptions lies in the demonstration that 'there was but little dialectal difference between the Greek of Egypt and Asia Minor, Italy and Syria' (*The Expositor*, ser. vi, 9 [1904] 224). Cf. S.G. Kapsomenos, *Mus.Helv.* 10 (1953) 263: '. . . In Ägypten, Syrien und Kleinasien, muß in jener Zeit eine ähnliche Form von Griechisch, die eigentliche Koine, gesprochen worden sein . . .' That Thumb had seen the same point is recognised by Vergote, *Phil.Stud.* 4 (1932/3) 214.

One argument adopted by certain Jewish-Greek proponents is that if the documentary texts from Egypt and elsewhere do illustrate the language of the NT, this is because the papyri (in particular) have been subjected to Semitic influence because of the large Jewish population resident in Egypt and elsewhere in the Diaspora. For example, G. Friedrich claims (*TDNT* 10 [1976] 652) that the number of Jews in Egypt 'shaped the Greek character of the *koine* in Egypt, so that the Greek of the papyri is not common Greek, but Jewish Greek, and the Greek of the papyri does not offer clear testimony to the *koine* of the age. The papyri and the NT both came under semitic influence . . .' Likewise, N. Turner, *NovT* 16 (1974) 151 would have us believe that 'many words must have trespassed from the Biblical vocabulary into the secular papyrus texts, passing from the ethos of the Alexandrian LXX into the Greek which the Jews spoke there, for the Egyptian Jews were numerous enough to influence the *koine* spoken by Gentiles'. Another to accept this view is M. Wilcox, *ANRW* II.25.2 (1984) 981. As to the size of the Jewish population in Egypt the latest estimate I have seen is by J. Mélèze-Modrzejewski, in J. Hassoun (ed.), *Juifs du Nil* (Paris, 1981), 15-49, who suggests (20-21) that at the beginning of the Roman period the number of Jews in Egypt may have been *c*.150-200,000 (of whom half resided in Alexandria), or about 3% of the entire population. This percentage appears to be consistent with the situation of first-century Rome, for which H. Solin estimates that the number of Jews may have been somewhere between 15,000-40,000, roughly 2-8% of the half-million total population for the city: *ANRW* II.29.2 (1983) 698-701, at 700. Views like those of Wilcox, Friedrich and Turner are not new, e.g., H.A. Redpath, *AJT* 7 (1903) 11; H.B. Swete, *The Apocalypse of St John* (London, 1907²) cxxiv, n.; J. Vergote, *Phil.Stud.* 6 (1934/5) 90, nor do they require lengthy rebuttal. The decimation of the Jewish population in Egypt during the Revolt of 115-17, together with the 'going to ground' of the survivors who stayed there, is the most obvious point which comes to mind. The suggestion that the Jews had a noticeable impact on the *koine* is an argument without cogency, typifying the general weakness of the theory of Jewish Greek. A direction in which research should be looking, however, is towards Coptic, to investigate the degree of interference it effected in Greek documents from Roman Egypt. This is a question of some importance, raised briefly by Thumb, *Die griechische Sprache* . . ., 124-25, and later by L.-T. Lefort, *Le Muséon* 41 (1928) 152-60, especially 156-60, promoted by Vergote, *Phil.Stud.* 6 (1934/5) 91, 97-107; id., 'Grec biblique', *Dictionnaire de la Bible*, Suppl. vol.3 (1938) 1354-60, and taken into account by Gignac in his recent *Grammar* (cf. id., *YCS* 28 [1985] 155-65). It is beyond the scope of the present discussion to take this up in any detail here, but the point must be broached, at least. It is not inconceivable that for research on subliterary and documentary Greek texts we may need to revise our thinking about what constitutes 'pure' *koine*.

The Hebraist/Purist Debate

To round off this evaluation of Jewish Greek it is useful to set it within an historical perspective. In much of what follows I am dependent upon the excellent survey by J. Ros, *De studie van het Bijbelgrieksch van Hugo Grotius tot Adolf Deissmann* (Nimwegen, 1940). Note also the very useful, slightly earlier survey by J. Vergote, *Phil.Stud.* 4 (1932/3) 28-46, 81-109, 190-215. Much more recent is J.W. Voelz, *ANRW* II.25.2 (1984) 893-977, whose 'History of the investigation of the problem' (894-930) is generally even-handed. The second part of his article (930-70) is a useful but over-brief coverage of features which characterise the Greek of the NT. There are indications here that his reading is out of touch with classicists' publications; Voelz's work may also be contrasted with the present contribution in that he glances only rarely at the papyri, and never at inscriptions. E.C. Maloney's excellent survey (in *Semitic Interference in Marcan Syntax* [*SBLDS* 51; Chico, 1981] 7-34) concentrates almost exclusively on work this century.

The Jewish Greek issue is to be seen as a colophon to the Hebraist/Purist debate begun in the Renaissance, with Theodor Beza earning the reputation of 'Ebraistarum parens' in the eyes of the Purists (Ros, 5-7, though at 57 n.5 he says that Erasmus or Vatablus could more justifiably have been so called), and Stephanus being one of the prominent scholars who sided early with the Purists (ibid., 7; cf. 11). The clash between the two groups over the nature of the Greek in the NT was particularly prominent in the XVIIth and XVIIIth centuries (ibid., 11); one of the most important contributions in the first half of the XVIIIth century was provided by J.J. Wet[t]stein, *Novum Testamentum Graecum . . . nec non commentario pleniore ex scriptoribus veteribus Hebraeis, Graecis et Latinis historiam et vim verborum illustrante* (2 vols: Amsterdam, 1751-52; repr. Graz, 1962); cf. Ros, 26-27. By the end of that century the Hebraists seemed to hold the field (ibid., 18). Among the few classicists to enter the debate in this period was J.A. Ernesti, who defended the Hebraic background of the NT language (ibid., 25). Ros makes the important point that in this period the debate had an almost exclusively theological foundation, and that although the question was not an issue among Roman Catholics it was very live among Protestants (ibid., 17-28). He suggests, further, that whereas the Hebraists were generally moderate in their discussions the Purists often went to extremes in their zeal to find classical Greek parallels for NT language (ibid., 32-33). This led to some transparent absurdities and served to discredit the Purist position.

The Hebraisers' domination continued through much of the XIXth century. G.B. Winer's *A Treatise on the Grammar of NT Greek* (ET: Edinburgh, 1882³) was particularly influential — the German original went through eight editions between 1822-1898; a Latin translation by J.T. Beelen also appeared (Louvain, 1857) — and in it was promoted the notion of Jewish Greek. Perhaps the most systematic espousal of Jewish Greek came at the end of the century in J. Viteau's *Etude sur le grec du NT* (2 vols; Paris, 1893, 1896). Note also D. Schilling, *Commentarius exegetico-philologicus in hebraismos Novi Testamenti, seu de dictione hebraica Novi Testamenti Graeci* (Mechelen, 1886), the first section (1-83) of whose monograph is devoted to illustrating his contention 'linguam Novi Testamenti esse ex omni parte hebraizantem' (29). But the Hebraist position was brought into question at almost exactly the same time by Deissmann's reaction against the isolation of the NT from the *koine*, and his use of non-literary texts to highlight this. He made his mark first with *Bibelstudien* (1895) and *Neue Bibelstudien* (1897), which were collected in English translation in 1901 as *Bible Studies*. Deissmann was not the first to draw upon the non-literary evidence: on his precursors see, e.g., J.R. Harris, *ExpT* 25 (1913) 55; N.A. Bees, *BPW* 40 (1920) 476-78; and see further, ch.4 p.70 below. He was undoubtedly the first, however, to mine this material extensively, and to draw attention to its significance. That his work gained such widespread notice was due in no small part to his undoubted gifts as a populariser, most evident in *LAE*. Deissmann did not deny Semitic influence, but was perceived to stand within the Purist tradition, along with Moulton, A.T. Robertson, L. Radermacher, and others (Ros, 34-44). A. Thumb also belonged to this side of the debate: cf. *Die griechische Sprache . . .*, 182. His comment at 120 is worth quoting: 'Der alte, durch dogmatische Gründe bedingte Streit der "Puristen" und "Hebraisten" musste ergebnislos bleiben, solange die biblische Gräcität als etwas isoliertes, einzigartes betrachtet und nicht in den grossen Zusammenhang der gesamten hellenistischen Sprachentwicklung gestellt wurde.'

In his illuminating survey which takes us down to Deissmann's death (in 1937), Ros undoubtedly regards the resurgence of the Purist position at the start of this century as a deviation from the mainstream, and a temporary one at that. Indeed, he concludes (44) that in the long run Deissmann added surprisingly little to our understanding of the NT. Similarly, Vergote thought that Thumb and Deissmann's views of the papyri have been allowed to exercise too much influence on the study of the *koine* (*Phil.Stud.* 6 [1934/5] 89). In my estimation, and in the light of the next half-century down to the present, Ros has read the actual situation aright. For NT research has indeed come to regard the contribution of Deissmann et al. as a side-road in the Hebraist highway. Cf., e.g., C.K. Barrett, *ExpT* 90 (1978) 71; P. Cotterell/M. Turner, *Linguistics and Biblical Interpretation* (London, 1989) 126 n.6. Yet whether those who study this field have been right to do so is another matter. In discounting so heavily the linguistic contribution of the likes of Deissmann NT philology is in danger of turning in on itself and, in my judgement, closing itself off from the opportunity for continuing stimulus and contact with classicists and linguists. The Hebraist perspective largely holds the field in NT studies today, a significant manifestation of which is the acceptance in certain circles of a separate Jewish Greek.

The weakness of Ros' and others' view of Deissmann's long-term significance is that the latter was too neatly pigeonholed as a Purist. Yet he and Moulton and others emphatically were *not* harking back to Attic models for the parallels they found in the NT. By sifting through the non-literary texts roughly contemporaneous with the NT, their contribution was a distinctive one, which the true Purists of an earlier age would have disowned. Their work was no actual return to the Purist canons, although the conclusions they reached brought them to a position *vis-à-vis* the Hebraists that was not altogether dissimilar. As it turns out then, Milligan's optimistic comment is both right and wrong (in *The History of Christianity in the Light of Modern Knowledge*, 282):

> The discussion of the real character of the Greek of the NT has in recent years entered on an entirely new phase. The old controversy between the 'Purists', who endeavoured to bring all its peculiarities under the strict rules of Attic usage, and the 'Hebraists', who magnified these peculiarities in the interests of a distinctively 'Biblical Greek', or even 'language of the Holy Ghost', is now completely a thing of the past.

Milligan is suggesting here that Deissmann and Moulton's work has been so widely accepted that there is no longer an issue to debate. Yet he did not reckon with the setting aside of the gains made by these men, a reaction which set in during the 1930s. So, to the extent that serious debate on the question is a thing of the past, this reflects the renewed ascendancy of the Hebraist perspective within NT circles.

Yet it should be noted that scarcely anyone outside the NT field who comments on the issue accepts the notion of Jewish Greek. Merely as examples we may note: J. Psichari, *REJ* 55 (1908) 161-210 (repr. in id., *Quelques travaux de linguistique, de philologie et de littérature helléniques, 1884-1928* [Paris, 1930] 1.831-91, at 847-52); Juster, *Les Juifs dans l'Empire romain*, 1.366-67 n.3; Costas, *Outline of the History of the Greek Language* . . ., 55; Baron, *Social and Religious History of the Jews*, 1.186; R. Browning, *Medieval and Modern Greek* (London, 1969) 30; B.G. Mandilaras, *The Verb in the Greek non-Literary Papyri* (Athens, 1973) 50, §22; J. Frösén, *Prolegomena to a Study of the Greek Language in the First Centuries A.D. The Problem of*

Koine and Atticism (Helsinki, 1974) 78-79; Bickerman, *Studies in Jewish and Christian History*, 1.175-77; E. Tov, *Bull. IOSCS* 9 (1976) 22-23; Youtie, *Scriptiunculae Posteriores*, I.57-59; L. Zgusta, in Neumann/Untermann (edd.), *Die Sprachen im römischen Reich der Kaiserzeit*, 125; J. Mélèze-Modrzejewski, in *Juifs du Nil*, 23; M. Harl/G. Dorival/O. Munnich, *La Bible grecque des LXX. Du judaïsme hellénistique au christianisme ancien* (Paris, 1988) 233-35. Among non-NT scholars who accept the notion of Jewish Greek the best known older treatment is that of E. Norden, *Die antike Kunstprosa vom VI. Jahrhundert v. Chr. bis in die Zeit der Renaissance* (Leipzig, 1909[2]; repr. Stuttgart, 1958) 2.484 (note also his supplementary comment at II, Nachträge, pp.2-3). More recent espousals of Jewish Greek have come from, e.g., Wacholder, *Eupolemus*, who sees it as 'a specific kind of *koine*' (256); but he shows little awareness of the debate. In the Neumann/Untermann volume Rosén also accepts (219) in too facile a manner that the Greek of the NT is Jewish Greek, as does R. Sollamo, *VT* 25 (1975) 777.

As far as I am able to ascertain, the great majority of those who nowadays affirm strongly its existence appear to be Protestants. Here some speculation may be offered. If it is a correct perception that the proponents of Jewish Greek are Protestants in the main, perhaps this is to be accounted for partly in theological terms. That is, the notion that the language of the NT is distinct and separate from other contemporary Greek is an unspoken factor employed to undergird the theological tenet, 'Sola Scriptura'. As the Bible is to be interpreted theologically from within, so too linguistically. This is merely a hypothesis, but even if it does not persuasively help to account for the resurgence of belief in Jewish Greek, the foregoing discussion remains unaffected. (It should be appreciated that I am not suggesting that all Protestant scholars adhere to the notion of 'Jewish Greek'.)

Conclusion

The edifice of Jewish Greek lacks foundation in reality, neither does it have any cogent linguistic framework. Accordingly, it is built largely using weak arguments and assertions. While it is not denied that certain Semitic features obtrude into Greek written by Jews and Christians in antiquity, where this occurs it is to be understood as the expected phenomenon of interference which manifests itself in varying degrees in the speech and writing of bilinguals. The door should be left open, however, for the possibility (and even likelihood) that Greek was spoken with a distinct ('marked') accent by those Jews in Palestine whose mother tongue was Aramaic (or perhaps Mishnaic Hebrew). But phonological differences alone are insufficient to establish the existence of a separate dialect. Furthermore, other Aramaic speakers who acquired facility in Greek must have had a similarly marked pronunciation. All that could have distinguished a Jew from a non-Jew in this regard, then, would be the use of certain technical terms distinctive of Jewish culture and religion (cf. F. Büchsel, *ZAW* 60 [1944] 138-39). It was in their social customs that the Jews were distinctive, not in their use of Greek, as K. Treu has emphasised, *Kairos* 15 (1973) 123-44 (at 125).

Problems of definition are one aspect of the question, lack of contact with developments in linguistics another. Possibly a certain theological predisposition has encouraged the continuing acceptance of Jewish Greek in certain quarters. Just as there are ghost words imputed to a language, so it may be urged that Jewish Greek is a ghost language. And like all ghosts it needs to be laid to rest.

2

KOINE OR ATTICISM
— A MISLEADING DICHOTOMY

The previous *New Docs* volumes scarcely addressed themselves to the phenomenon of Atticism, at least explicitly. Yet because the matter is apposite to the present volume which evaluates several aspects of the state of NT linguistic studies, it receives attention here briefly.

Classicists not versed in linguistics and who may not work primarily with post-classical Greek may sometimes hold to a much too confining view of the term '*koine*'. This came home sharply to me at an all-too-rare encounter between a number of classicists and several specialists in the language of the LXX/NT during a conference in America in 1985. One classicist of international reputation indicated that by '*koine*' he meant only the NT. This is to take an exceedingly narrow view of it. In the XIXth century distinctions were made between *koine* and Hellenistic Greek: see J. Vergote, *Phil.Stud.* 4 (1932/3) 29-36. Nowadays, however, '*koine*' is to all intents and purposes interchangeable with 'Hellenistic' Greek, so long as it is recognised that the latter is not tied chronologically to conclude with the end of I BC. Because 'Hellenistic' is a fairly clearly defined term in the study of Ancient History and Greek Literature, it is better to avoid it when talking about periods of development of the Greek language, and to employ the term '*koine*' instead. In this book, therefore, the word is taken quite broadly, to include chronologically all Greek from roughly late IV BC through to the fifth century, during which the first traces of what evolves as Byzantine Greek become detectable. Further, I treat as *koine* writers all authors of the period who wrote in Greek, including those affected by Atticism to a high degree. For Atticism is a linguistic reaction within the period of the *koine*, reflecting merely one part of the spectrum of Greek usage. To say that literary authors of this period are not writers of *koine* is to ignore the question of linguistic register in the language. (The nature of the *koine* is badly misunderstood by P. Cotterell/M. Turner, *Linguistics and Biblical Interpretation* [London, 1989] 107: in discussing Deissmann's contribution they state that ' [the papyri] represented the language of the common people — the *koine* . . .').

The conventionally accepted time for the start of the *koine* is Alexander's conquests. Over-simplification though this be, it underlines the far-reaching changes that political and military conquest can exercise upon a language. We may compare the Norman conquest as merely one analogy, which extinguished the chance of West Saxon becoming the standard speech of England. Of the four dialects of Old English, West Saxon was the one that was on the way to constituting the literary standard; but the arrival of the Normans and the imposition of French as the high-status language 'reduced all [OE] dialects to a common level of unimportance' (A.C. Baugh/T. Cable, *A History of the English Language* [London, 1978[3]] 54). In the case of Greek, the reasons for the association of the start of *koine* with Alexander's reign are severalfold, two of which are particularly appropriate to note here. On the one hand, Phillip II and subsequently Alexander confirmed Athens' political decline permanently; and because the unique literary flowering of Attic literature had occurred in V and IV[1] BC when the *polis*' fortunes had been at their greatest — the resilience of the democracy is nowhere more in evidence than in the city's rapid return to strength after the major defeat in the Peloponnesian War — there has been an almost inevitable tendency to associate the two. Students of Greek at later periods (through to the present) were unable to perceive, or unwilling to acknowledge, that any great works of literature had been written in Greek subsequently, and attributed this to the decline of Athens. The city became the focus for that nostalgia for *res Graecae* which was widely current among the educated in the Roman period. Long after its own pretensions to political and cultural leadership had faded, Athens continued to be a mecca for intellectuals and others who wished to 'finish off' their education. A second reason to be mentioned here for the conventional connection between Alexander and the beginnings of the *koine* is the practical necessity, for the success of his campaigns, that Macedonians and others in his army should be able to communicate easily. It should not be thought that there was any so conscious idea as a 'language policy', simply that the soldiers and others all needed to accommodate themselves to one another's linguistic differences. The compromise led to the emergence of a form of Greek to which the high-status Attic was by far the largest contributor. Although there are signs of *koine* features in earlier writers (perhaps especially in Xenophon, but even Thucydides uses non-Attic forms), we may say that Alexander's spectacularly successful campaigns hastened the process of language change very considerably because so vast an area came under his control in so short a period, and was thereby exposed to Greek cultural and linguistic influence.

Serious study of the *koine* began only last century, and it was at the very beginning of the present one that sharply divergent views of its nature were given their fullest expression. P. Kretschmer, *Die Entstehung der Koine* (*Sitz. der Wiener Ak., ph.-hist. Kl.*, 143.10; Vienna, 1900), won little support for his view that a variety of dialects melded together to form the *koine*. In contrast, A. Thumb's explanation of the koine as being based on Attic exercised great influence: *Die griechische Sprache im Zeitalter des Hellenismus: Beiträge zur Geschichte und Beurteilung der Koine* (Strassburg, 1901). Although he acknowledged that other dialects made some contribution to the *koine*, he did not give enough weight to the presence of Ionic features. Thumb's position on the nature of the *koine* attracted detailed support from E. Mayser's intensive study of Ptolemaic papyri: *Grammatik der griechischen Papyri aus der Ptolemäerzeit* (6 vols; Leipzig/Berlin, 1906-1938). Vergote, *Phil.Stud.* 4 (1932/3) 28-46, 81-109, 190-215, provides a very useful survey of the history of scholarship concerning the nature, spread, and foreign influence upon the *koine*, both before and after Kretschmer and Thumb.

The groundwork for all modern discussion of Atticism was laid by W. Schmid before the end of the last century. In *Der Atticismus in seiner Hauptvertretern* (5 vols; Stuttgart, 1887-97; repr. Hildesheim, 1964) he dealt with a number of authors, from Dionysios of Halikarnassos to Philostratos. Schmid had predecessors, of course; but it was his achievement to build on the often extensive commentaries devoted to particular grammarians by scholars like Lobeck (1820, on Phrynichos) and Pierson (1759, on Moeris), and to provide the first thorough, wide-ranging synthesis. Given the date of his work, it is no wonder that the papyri received scant attention; nor, again, was much notice taken of epigraphic material (that from Pergamon provides a notable exception: 2.19-33). Schmid scarcely addressed himself at all to the NT (2.299; 4.729, both very brief asides); but it might have been expected that under the general stimulus of his work others would take up this question, and investigate in detail the evidence for Atticistic influence upon the NT. Not so. Moulton's *Grammar* is disappointingly lightweight in this regard, e.g., *A Grammar of NT Greek*, I. *Prolegomena* (Edinburgh, 1908[3]) 24-26; ibid., II. *Accidence and Word Formation* (Edinburgh, 1929) 6. Atticism surely demanded some attention in N. Turner, ibid., IV. *Style* (Edinburgh, 1976), yet all that is offered are two passing references (39, 100). The healthy number of references to Atticisms in the index to ibid., III. *Syntax*

(Edinburgh, 1963) gives the false impression that Turner has addressed himself seriously to the matter in that volume, at least. But examination of these passages reveals comments everywhere *en passant*: no discussion of substance occurs anywhere. The same paucity of comment, and all of it brief, is evident in L. Radermacher, *Neutestamentliche Grammatik* (Tübingen, 1925[2]), as well as in BDF and BDR[15]. In 1923 W. Michaelis published an article whose title, 'Der Attizismus und das NT', *ZNW* 22 (1923) 91-121, gives one to hope that he might have offered a thorough study; but it is surprisingly thin in content, its main worth being the publicising more widely to NT studies of Schmid's generation-old work, and raising generally the question how far the text of the NT may have been 'improved' in an Atticising direction by scribes.

Another forty years passed before G.D. Kilpatrick took up the question of Atticism in relation to NT textual criticism, in J. Blinzler et al. (edd.), *Neutestamentliche Aufsätze. Festschrift für J. Schmid* (Regensburg, 1963), 125-37. Kilpatrick had shown an interest in this question well beforehand, but this article is the fullest statement of his views. Kilpatrick takes the argument of this paper further in part of his article in H. Anderson/W. Barclay (edd.), *The NT in Historical and Contemporary Perspective. Essays in Memory of G.H.C. Macgregor* (Oxford, 1965), 189-208. The 1963 essay has been much quoted and critiqued. For example, Kilpatrick's discussion of ζήσω/ζήσομαι (132-33; cf. *Essays Macgregor*, 203) stems from a misperception of how the 'Antiatticist' couches his statements: see J.A.L. Lee, *NovT* 22 (1980) 289-98, to which Kilpatrick's rejoinder, *NovT* 25 (1983) 146-51, is unconvincing. The discussion had already been criticised by C.M. Martini in M. Black/W.A. Smalley (edd.), *On Language, Culture and Religion* (Festschrift E.A. Nida; The Hague, 1974), 149-56. Though his conclusions on specifics are not beyond challenge, yet Kilpatrick's general point (*Festschrift Schmid*, 137) is important: 'But we submit that on the evidence before us there is a case for the view that the NT text has on occasion been revised in the direction of Atticism and that one form of enquiry necessary for any attempt to recover the original form of the Greek Testament is the enquiry in detail into the Atticist element in the transmitted NT text.' Implicit here is the notion that the 'original' Greek text had less-literary features and/or elements reflecting Semitic interference, which were 'tidied up' and made to look more nearly like literary Greek.

Examination of the work of Kilpatrick, and of his pupil J.K. Elliott — in addition to the bibliography in the present volume, a useful list of recent publications may be found in G.D. Fee's article in E.J. Epp/G.D. Fee (edd.), *Studies in NT Language and Textual Criticism* (Festschrift B.M. Metzger; Oxford, 1981), 47-60 — reveals that the question of Atticistic influence upon the text of the NT is one of the two main planks (the other is the basic consistency of an author's style) in their approach to textual criticism. Their conscious weighting in favour of 'internal criteria', in preference to so-called 'external criteria' (such as the date of the MS which attests a particular reading), has occasioned considerable criticism, especially from North American scholars. Attention may be drawn to several articles by E.J. Epp and G.D. Fee listed in the bibliography; cf., too, B.M. Metzger, *The Text of the NT* (Oxford, 1968[2]) 177-79. Kilpatrick, and particularly Elliott at *Rev.Bib.* 84 (1977) 5-25, have sought to defend their position, dubbed 'rigorous eclecticism' by their critics in contrast with the mainstream contemporary position of 'reasoned eclecticism' (see especially Fee, in J.K. Elliott (ed.), *Studies in NT Language and Text* [Festschrift G.D. Kilpatrick; *NovT Suppl.* 44; Leiden, 1976], 174-97). This terminology needs some tightening up. S. Thompson, *The Apocalypse and Semitic Syntax* (Cambridge, 1985), allies himself with the approach of Kilpatrick, styling it 'judicious eclecticism' (10-11; cf. 102).

Features of Greek which may be termed Atticistic can be detected from III BC onwards, but Atticism came into its own as a dominant influence on the Greek language only in II AD. In relation to Atticism it is fundamental for Kilpatrick (*Festschrift Schmid*, 128-131, following

H. Vogels) that most conscious alterations to the NT text had occurred before III AD. Note particularly his comment (131) that '. . . the vast majority of deliberate changes in the NT text were older than AD 200. In other words they came into being in the period AD 50-200.' Because of the great impact of Atticism upon educated writers, he believes that scribes in the second century altered the NT text to conform with these norms. This notion, that virtually all textual corruptions in the NT occurred during II AD, is the basis for his view that the original text of the NT may be represented in any later MS, including those of late Byzantine date and even in Patristic quotations. Fee's counter to this (*Festschrift Kilpatrick*, 179) is telling, and the point is well put that 'Atticism may indeed be a cause of some corruption in the second century, but it is hypothetically equally probable . . . that a Christian scribe in the second century altered a less common form (= the alleged Atticism) to a more common, if less literary, form' (185).

Now, any wholesale discussion of trends in recent NT textual criticism is not simply beyond the scope of the present context; it is rendered unnecessary by several most illuminating recent surveys. E.J. Epp's two articles, *JBL* 93 (1974) 386-414, and *HTR* 69 (1976) 211-57, deserve particular mention. If Epp and others are correct in their assessment, then the discipline is clearly in some disarray. NT textual criticism is subject to two significant complexities which classicists do not have to face:

1. the superabundance of witnesses; and
2. the problem of how the *koine*/Atticism question is to be lined up in relation to the re-emergence in this century of the 'Hebraist/Purist' debate in modified form. Do those who regard the NT as 'pure' Greek — on the whole, i.e., allowing for some Semitic influence, but unwilling to speak of a 'Jewish Greek' — think of it as *koine* or Atticistic?

The second point has been cast in this way deliberately, because attention needs to be drawn to a false dichotomy which NT linguistic research has been content to live with for a very long time. It appears to be accepted as axiomatic that all Greek at the time of the NT and ECL (i.e., I-III AD) is either *koine* (i.e., vernacular Greek) or it is Atticistic and highly artificial. This over-simplistic view may be found in many publications in NT studies, not merely those concerned with textual criticism: e.g., S. Angus, *Princeton Theol.Rev.* 8 (1910) 54-55; Kilpatrick, *Festschrift Schmid*, 132; Elliott, *ZNW* 63 (1972) 133; id., *Festschrift Kilpatrick*, 144, 152; id., *Rev. Bib.* 84 (1977) 20-22; N. Turner, *NTS* 20 (1973/4) 108, 112-14. The same bipartite distinction pervades BDF and Moulton's *Grammar*. J. Frösén's critique of this dualistic breakdown of post-classical Greek into *koine* and Atticism is most useful: *Prolegomena to a Study of the Greek Language in the First Century. The Problem of Koine and Atticism* (Helsinki, 1974) 10-11 (cf. 49-50), and especially his ch.4 (pp.95-133). Pointing out that it leads to the overestimating of the impact of the Atticistic movement upon the language, he observes (99): '"Atticistic language" and "Koine" cannot be regarded as opposed to one another in such a way as to make them mutually exclusive phenomena, rather they are better regarded as representing different levels of linguistic behaviour. The custom of regarding them as different extremes is primarily the result of distinctions popularised by lexicographers.' Cf. Metzger, *The Text of the NT*, 178. This is a point to which we shall return later.

Here is one area where sociolinguistics can be of great use to classical and NT philologists. The literature in this field is considerable. For some items from the 1960s onwards, see bibliography under the following names: Bell, Bright, Currie, Dittmar, Downes, Edwards, Fishman, Hymes, Labov, Lehmann, Romaine, Stubbs, Trudgill. Apart from the obvious differences in style required by different genres — not literary ones only, but also non-literary genres such as wills, private letters, petitions, epitaphs, honorific inscriptions — we have also to deal with a different set of levels of language use which overlap and interact with these, namely the linguistic competence of the writer. That is, style needs to be distinguished from the level of 'literariness'. For example, petitions will conform to the genre of petitions by virtue of the style they adopt and the conventional phrases they employ, but they may be written by people of very different linguistic ability. J.A.L. Lee, *NovT* 27 (1985) 9, draws attention to the range of registers to be found among the papyri: the fact that they are non-literary does not make them homogeneous in register. On linguistic register see ch.1 above, p.11. Such questions are not resolved merely on the basis of criteria like orthographic variation: some types of spelling difference are unimportant, though others (e.g., the use of the iota adscript) provide significant clues to the writer's level of education. Furthermore, some types of non-literary genres exist for which those of little education will seek the skills of professional writers. Petitions are a case in point. In order to be sure that his petition will succeed, a semi-literate will naturally have recourse to someone who knows how to phrase it to greatest effect. *New Docs 1976-79* illustrate this phenomenon by their inclusion of numerous examples of documents belonging to the same genre. In the case of private letters, for example, the *New Docs* entries rarely say much about the level of literariness, but the letters themselves display transparent features. Contrast *New Docs 1978*, **2** or **100**, which clearly emanate from well-educated (and wealthy) people, with the tortuous attempts at Greek of *New Docs 1976*, **84** and **85**. Somewhere in between come letters like *New Docs 1976*, **15**; above this last but below *New Docs 1978*, **2** and **100** is the group reprinted at *New Docs 1977*, **21**. Analysis of vocabulary, morphology, syntax and orthography would help us to arrange these letters on a scale of linguistic competence. Occasionally, the content of the letter may also afford clues. Even if there is room for differing opinions about the precise relative positions of these examples, the general point is clear. Linguistic analysis may be a useful tool to help us evaluate the social status of the writers of such texts. *New Docs 1978*, **4**, pp.18-19, considers briefly the question of the status of fishermen (a feature examined in more detail on the basis of onomastic evidence and other data in the fifth chapter of the present volume), and whether they may have been more skilled at writing than is sometimes assumed (*contra*, for example, the implicit assumption of illiterate tradesmen in L.H. Kant, *ANRW* II.20.2 [1987] 674).

A.D. Nock was surely right to emphasise, at *JBL* 52 (1933) 138-39, the dissimilarity between the papyrus letters and those of Paul: the latter is not writing 'peasant Greek or soldier Greek'. But to imply, as Nock proceeds to do, that the LXX is *the* differentiating factor falls rather short of a satisfactory assessment. The majority of the NT letters (Pauline and other) are addressed to groups; moreover, the members were known personally to the writer in varying degrees, some very well, others not at all. Again, the purpose for which these letters were written was fundamentally different from the reasons for private letters written in Egypt. The latter were primarily addressed to an individual or to immediate family members, very rarely to those with whom the writer was entirely unacquainted, and their brevity was mostly filled with the commonplaces of wishes for health or specific requests about mundane matters ('send me x').

Some genres are ruled out from such an analysis, or at least require much more caution. These are documents which are habitually written by a professional. For example, honorific inscriptions set up by a city to laud a benefactor — on this phenomenon vis-à-vis the NT see F.W. Danker, *Benefactor. Epigraphic Study of a Graeco-Roman and NT Semantic Field* (St. Louis, 1982) — may be composed by the city council's secretary; but the contribution of the mason who actually carves the text may not be inconsiderable (especially at the level of orthography), even if difficult to distinguish. (For one recent attempt to do this see my article in *AS* 37 [1987] 49-80, especially 74-77, concerning a related group of inscribed statue bases from Cremna in Pisidia.) Such texts may yield more information about other linguistic questions, such as shifts in pronunciation of vowels. On this question note the contributions of S.-T. Teodorsson listed in the bibliography, particularly *The Phonology of Ptolemaic Koine* (Göteborg, 1977).

In sum, then, there is a need to be alert to a greater range of language levels than merely two: *koine* and Atticistic, as though the latter were somehow not part of the *koine*. On this point, 'even Deissmann nods'. In opposing the thesis of E. Norden, *Die antike Kunstprosa* . . . (Leipzig, 1898), concerning the style of the Pauline letters, Deissmann sets up too sharp a distinction: 'die Paulusbriefe sind im grossen und ganzen Denkmäler jenes volkstümlichen Weltgriechisch der Kaiserzeit, gegen welches die Atticisten vergeblich ihre Lexika mobil machten' (*TRu* 5 [1902] 68).

It will be hard to detect instances, though they must have occurred, where a writer affects a higher style in some contexts because it is necessary or advantageous. This phenomenon of a shift in stylistic tone may be seen in certain literary genres, such as the Orators. C. Fabricius, *JbAC* 10 (1967) 187-99, suggests that in the fourth century the Church Fathers employed classical Greek, in an attempt to attract the largest number of readers. On Atticism itself he has only brief remarks (190, 191). Cf. more briefly, but with great clarity, R. Browning, *IJSL* 35 (1982) 50. Roman historians writing in Greek afford another example of the phenomenon, as H.J. Mason has observed: *Phoenix* 24 (1970) 150-59. He notes a number of instances of their choice of inappropriate classical Greek technical terms (such as 'harmost') to refer to Roman officials and institutions. Such a writer, reflecting an Atticising preference in lexical choice, selected his terms 'with an eye to literary respectability rather than political aptness', expecting his readership to be sufficiently knowledgeable about Roman institutions to 'perceive the Roman reality under the Attic façade' (159). As for the NT, one recent attempt to apply sociolinguistics has been B.J. Malina, *The Gospel of John in Sociolinguistic Perspective* (*CHS, Colloquy* 48; Berkeley, 1985). Observing the heavy use of personal pronouns in John, as contrasted with the Synoptics, Malina suggests that this was a means by which the writer presented Jesus' encounters with a variety of people using dialogue which then drifts into direct comment by the writer to his readers. To discern such shifts of register in documentary materials, however, is all the harder because of the fragmentary and haphazard survivals. Moreover, there are all too few archives of non-literary texts which can be shown to have been written by the same person. It is extremely rare to have clear evidence of a number of documents embracing several genres, all demonstrably written by the same hand.

In papyrology and, *a fortiori*, in epigraphy the potential of a sociolinguistic approach has scarcely been tapped. This is true of Classical Studies in general, of course, though there are signs of a growing awareness. J. Kaimio, *The Romans and the Greek Language* (Helsinki, 1979), is a recent contribution of particular value; note also Frösén, *Prolegomena*. In *Antichthon* 18 (1984) have recently appeared two useful articles on women's speech: D. Bain, dealing with Menander (24-42), and J.N. Adams, dealing with Latin Comedy (43-77). A brief collection of ancient testimonia concerning women's speech habits is provided by M.E. Gilleland, *AJP* 101 (1980) 180-83, although no evaluation is offered whether all of them can be taken at face value. B.G. Mandilaras, *The Verb in the Greek Non-Literary Papyri* (Athens, 1973), proffers some observations on sociolinguistics (45-46, §§9-12), though they are very brief. More useful, though still only a sketch, are the introductory few pages in a recent thesis by A.L. Connolly, *Atticism in Non-Literary Papyri of the First Seven Centuries AD. A Study in Several Features of Orthography and Syntax* (unpub. B.A. thesis, Univ. of Sydney, 1983) 3-6. It is now usual in NT studies to distinguish stylistic features of Lk./Acts from those of Paul, etc. Yet in my judgement stylistic evaluation of the NT writings is still at a fairly rudimentary level. For example, N. Turner's recent fourth volume in Moulton's *Grammar* (Edinburgh, 1976) is devoted to style, and is most disappointing, *pace* the warm reviews it has received from, e.g., F.T. Gignac, *CBQ* 39 (1977) 165-67, and G.D. Kilpatrick, *TLZ* 104 (1979) 109-11. In part, this is to be attributed to his extreme view of the nature of the Greek of the Bible, a view which pervades the book. But because he is out of touch with recent developments in Linguistics he has not given himself and his readers the benefit of any stimulus which would certainly have been forthcoming from that discipline. Nevertheless, it must be allowed that in short texts like some of the NT epistles, and in lacunose documents as papyri and inscriptions so often are, there is always the danger of trying to press more juice out of the grape than it can yield.

One recent book has attracted considerable attention in NT philological work. L. Rydbeck's *Fachprosa, vermeintliche Volkssprache und NT. Zur Beurteilung der sprachlichen Niveauunterschiede im nachklassischen Griechisch* (Uppsala, 1967) provides a most valuable analysis of ancient (I BC/I AD) technical writings in a number of disciplines, including medicine, mathematics and astronomy. Rydbeck argues that, taken as a whole (and allowing for differences from author to author), the NT should be seen within the context of such technical writing, for its Greek, too, while lacking literary pretension, cannot be called entirely colloquial. His claim is spelled out in detail via his analysis of several diverse syntactical features and two lexicographical studies. The book has received a generally warm reception, especially in NT circles: note, e.g., the reviews of M.E. Thrall, *JTS* 20 (1972) 581-82, G.D. Kilpatrick, *JBL* 88 (1969) 354-56, G.J.M. Bartelink, *VC* 24 (1970) 304-06, E. Pax, *Biblica* 53 (1972) 557-64. It is a particular weakness of Turner's *Style* that he devotes no more than a paragraph (on the very last page of his book) to Rydbeck's monograph, all the more so since he disagrees with him fundamentally. Cf. id., in E.A. Livingstone (ed.), *Studia Evangelica, VII. Papers presented to the Fifth International Congress on Biblical Studies held at Oxford, 1973* (Berlin, 1982), 505. Yet the criticism of Frösén, *Prolegomena*, 25-26, and others, that too few features are examined for Rydbeck to have established his case, must carry some weight. H. Thesleff, *Gnomon* 42 (1970) 551-55, is another who is not altogether persuaded by Rydbeck's case, however useful many of his specific points are. In positing a level of prose between literary and entirely colloquial Greek ('Zwischenschriftsprosa'), Rydbeck should not be inferred to be saying simplistically that there are three levels of register in *koine* rather than two. Rather, his book is a recognition that there is a considerable range of linguistic registers. On this point see also W.F. Bakker, *Pronomen Abundans and Pronomen Coniunctum* (Amsterdam, 1974) 23. Rydbeck's approach is of some moment for NT linguistic research, drawing attention as it does to the much-neglected corpus of technical, sub-literary prose contemporary with the NT. More recently, L. Alexander, *NovT* 28 (1986) 48-74, has reached a similar conclusion by focussing upon the prefaces to Luke/Acts which she sees as unconsciously modelled on the prefaces to scientific treatises.

Schmid's *Atticismus* was devoted to literary authors; and it is usual to see Atticism's most active exemplars in writers who are to be identified with the Second Sophistic, whether men included in Philostratos' and Eunapios' *Vitae* of various sophists and philosophers, or others whose work survives in considerable bulk, such as Lucian. See in general G.W. Bowersock, *Greek Sophists in the Roman Empire* (Oxford, 1969); E.L. Bowie in M.I. Finley (ed.), *Studies in Ancient Society* (London, 1974) 166-209; and C.A. Trypanis, *Ὁ Ἀττικισμὸς καὶ τὸ γλωσσικό μας ζήτημα* (Athens, 1984), a useful brief survey which takes a much broader chronological sweep. But there is another side of the coin: how extensive was the influence of Atticism upon sub- and non-literary texts? If we are to find evidence for such an impact it ought to be most apparent in II and III AD. A satisfactory analysis of Atticism in the NT — for text-critical work as well as other reasons — needs to take into account its prominence (or lack of it) in the documentary sources as well as in literary works.

A promising step in this direction has recently been taken in the thesis just mentioned by A.L. Connolly. His study of a number of features (-σσ-/-ττ-; -ρσ-/-ρρ-; γιν-/γιγν-; the use of ὅπως; and particle usage) in documentary papyri from the *P.Oxy.* series — the data-base comprised *c.*2300 documents — is illuminating at several points. Connolly finds (78) that *c.*10% of the documents examined contain at least one of the five features being investigated. It is not only literary authors but also documentary papyri which attest 'that there actually is an Atticistic style, and not just individuals who prefer ὅπως to ἵνα or -ττ- to -σσ- . . .' (79). Nevertheless, 'the extent of Atticistic influence . . . was limited to a small minority of writers, probably only some of those who were well educated, writing both privately and in official correspondence' (78).

A point of considerable significance flows from this, though Connolly himself does not make the link, and it can only be stated baldly here. If the number of writers influenced by Atticism can be shown to be small on the basis of the number of documents containing Atticistic features, that number of writers can confidently be taken to be even less given that it is particularly in official documents — those of a formal genre — that these features predominate. For these texts were written for the most part by professional scribes for illiterates and others too barely literate to have sufficient confidence to couch their own petitions, wills, etc., in the appropriate manner; cf. Teodorsson, *Phonology of Ptolemaic Koine*, 19, 23. (Words like 'illiterate' and 'semi-literate' are employed here in a generalised sense. For the problems of definition of such terms see M. Stubbs, *Language and Literacy. The Sociolinguistics of Reading and Writing* [London, 1980] 10-14.) The same principle, recognition of the role of the scribe, has been applied by F. Farid, *MPL* 2 (1977) 109-17, to try to determine whether the Christian tone of some of the letters in the Paniskos archive reflect the views of the senders or of those who wrote these particular letters on their behalf. The question receives brief attention in *New Docs 1977*, **22**. T.C. Skeat's illuminating paper on dictation as a feature of book-production in antiquity, *PBA* 42 (1956) 179-208, is also of some relevance.

When consideration is given to this question, it will readily be appreciated that what matters is not so much the number of documents which give evidence of Atticism as the number/ percentage of people, even though that figure or percentage cannot be specified. This approach has the minimising effect, therefore, of restricting the marked influence of Atticism upon the populace to a tiny coterie of highly-educated professionals. It is not denied that Atticism exercised an influence on the whole education system in the second century. The point being made here is that its impact will have been most visible in the work of professional writers. It must be stressed that this hypothesis is a tentative one, which needs to be tested in the context of further work on Atticism in documentary texts, and also when the question of Atticism is addressed thoroughly for the NT. Teodorsson's phonological researches suggest one avenue for the detailed evaluation that is required. Study of the ancient grammarians is another. Renewed attention is being given, especially in Germany in the series *Sammlung griechischer und lateinischer Grammatiker* edited by K. Alpers/ H. Erbse/ A. Kleinlogel, to the men like Phrynichos and Moeris, whose strictures concerning lexical preferences especially are usefully balanced off by the counter-claims of the laconic 'Antiatticist'. These writers had their own particular 'axes to grind', of course, and it is not always appropriate to take their comments completely at face value.

3

THE SYNTAX VOLUME
OF MOULTON'S *GRAMMAR*

Spanning seventy years, the four volumes of J.H. Moulton's *Grammar of NT Greek* (Edinburgh, 1906-1976) have exercised a considerable influence upon NT, particularly British, scholarship. The quality of Moulton's own work, particularly in the *Prolegomena*, resulted in the latter running to three English editions. A German translation (Heidelberg, 1911) was based on the third English edition (1908), and included a preface by A. Thumb. It should be emphasised how rarely a grammar book is translated into another language; that this happened to Moulton's first volume reflects the high regard in which he was held by German contemporaries. Deissmann greeted the first English edition with the comment, 'Viel entschiedener noch als unsere deutschen Grammatiken steht Moultons Buch auf dem Boden der modernen Sprachwissenschaft, . . .' (*TRu* 9 [1906] 220). For a recent appreciation of the *Prolegomena* see C.K. Barrett, *ExpT* 90 (1978) 68-71. It remains an excellent introduction, even allowing for the passage of time and shifts in scholarly consensus. Moulton also wrote the bulk of the second volume, on *Accidence and Word Formation* (1929), though he did not live to see it in print; and W.F. Howard, who assumed responsibility for completing the *Grammar*, himself contributed an important excursus (411-85) on Semitisms in the NT. But in any major grammar work the section most likely to be consulted frequently is that on syntax, and it is vol.3 of Moulton's *Grammar* (Edinburgh, 1963) which takes our attention here. On the comparative lack of syntactical grammars in other fields compared with the interest in syntax shown by NT grammarians see A.T. Robertson, *A Grammar of the Greek NT in the Light of Historical Research* (New York, 1923[4]) 379-83, especially 381.

As a result of the death of those deputed successively to complete the *Grammar* (Howard in 1952, H.G. Meecham in 1955) responsibility for the writing of the syntax volume devolved upon N. Turner, who had been appointed to assist Meecham. He states (preface to *Syntax*) that a bibliography alone had been prepared by the time of the latter's decease. While Turner was the natural person to turn to since he had been Meecham's understudy, it is curious that one whose attitude to the nature of the Greek of the Bible was fundamentally at variance with Moulton's should have been selected for this task. Turner himself implies at *ExpT* 76 (1964) 45 that he held his own views consistently since 1945. It is unsurprising, therefore, that in the preface (vii) to the fourth and final volume of the *Grammar*, on *Style* (1976), Turner acknowledges the lack of unity in the now complete work. No one could have done exactly what Moulton may have, had he lived; but at least the publisher could reasonably have been expected to ensure that the completer of the *Grammar* was approximately sympathetic to Moulton's position without abandoning sufficient detachment to perceive both Moulton's blind spots and the progress of research in the intervening half-century. But as we now have it the Grammar falls into two halves qualitatively, vols. 3 and 4 being markedly inferior.

(As a parenthesis concerning the long delay in completing Moulton's *Grammar*, put back even further by the death first of Howard and then of Meecham, the point may be raised whether it was merely coincidental that the publisher [T. and T. Clark] embarked upon a small host of reprints of older books on NT grammar and vocabulary. Amongst these reprints were Cremer [1954], Burton [1955], Abbott-Smith [1956], and Grimm/Thayer [1956]: for details of these works see the bibliography. In the case of Cremer's *Lexicon*, in particular, it is curious that the reprint was of the translation of the fourth edition of 1895. The eleventh German edition appeared in 1923, a revision by J. Kögel which accorded some importance to the documentary evidence for elucidation of NT vocabulary, while seeking to remain faithful to Cremer's approach. On this see J. Barr, *Semantics of Biblical Language* [Oxford, 1961] 242-44, whom I follow for the information about Kögel, whose revision I have not seen.)

While the focus of the present chapter is upon the *Syntax* volume some comments are included *en passant* about the volume on style. Less needs to be said about it here, however, since its weakness has normally been recognised widely. G.D. Kilpatrick's positive review of *Syntax* and *Style*, in *TLZ* 104 (1979) 109-11, is presumably to be accounted for in terms of his close link with Turner over many years (cf. preface to *Syntax*); yet even he includes some serious criticisms couched in gentle language (e.g., *col*.110, first new para. and last para.). F.T. Gignac's favourable review of *Style*, in *CBQ* 39 (1977) 165-67, is surprising in view of his own notable contribution to Ancient Greek grammar studies. The final sentence of this review may be instanced: 'I think T's interpretation of the multilingual nature of NT Greek is the soundest we have in NT grammatical literature'. (My own comment in *Biblica* 65 [1984] 396 n.14 about the *Syntax* volume being 'excellent in general' I now unequivocally retract.)

Three reasons are advanced here why the *Syntax* volume is seriously deficient.

1. It was already out of date when published

Despite the fact that the book appeared in the 1960s it reflects XIXth-century attitudes in its approach to grammar. There is no awareness of recent developments in General Linguistics in the areas of syntax and semantics, even of those books written specifically within the sphere of Biblical Studies. The most transparent evidence for this is that Barr's *Semantics of Biblical Language* — even allowing that it appeared too late for proper assimilation into *Syntax* — receives no mention at all in *Style*. (Turner is not alone in failing to address himself to Barr's work: see the following chapter on lexicography.) Further, the chronological bibliography in *Syntax*, pp.vii-x, lists 61 items of which only ten are post-1945: fifty titles span the eighty years 1859-1939. Even more surprising is the fact that in a book which draws heavily upon documentary material no papyri or inscriptions are referred to which have been published later than the mid-1930s. The index to papyrological and epigraphical works (381-83) typifies this. Apart from publications for which abbreviations were listed in Moulton/Howard, *Grammar*, II, those items for which full details are given in this index nearly all date from the turn of the century. In two cases alone are works drawn upon which appeared after *Grammar*, II, and both of these date to the 1930s. Thus, though the book was not begun till the mid-1950s, the reader is left with the impression that it is an already outmoded product of the late 1930s which was not published for a further generation. Yet the *Syntax* is not alone in failing comprehensively to take advantage of recent documentary publications: see the discussion below of BDF and BDR[15].

2. It is over-indebted to Mayser

E. Mayser's monumental *Grammatik der griechischen Papyri aus der Ptolemäerzeit* appeared in various editions and reissues over a period of 30 years, from 1906-1938: a revision of i.1 appeared in 1970, thanks to the work of H. Schmoll. For a concise unravelling of the tangled skein of the order in which the six volumes appeared and reappeared see E.G. Turner's review of Mayser/Schmoll i.1 in *CR* 23 (1973) 219. A comparison between Mayser ii.1-3 *Satzlehre* (Berlin, 1926-34; repr. 1970) and Turner's *Syntax* reveals how dependent the latter was on Mayser's work, in two main areas: the overall plan of the enterprise, and his references to documentary evidence for syntactical structures. That Turner draws on the other volumes as well is not in question; it is upon ii.1-3 that the dependence is most perceptible.

a.   The overall scope of *Syntax*

In his introduction to *Syntax* Turner explains (1) the arrangement of his material.

> The plan of this work follows a natural linguistic pattern: the building up of the sentence from its independent elements right to the complicated co-ordinations and subordinations of the period. The student who likes to have all his pronouns or all his prepositions dealt with together in one chapter must console himself by making good use of the index, for he will find that the various parts of speech are treated in the appropriate place as they contribute to the construction of the sentence.

This programmatic statement about how the book is structured implies that Turner has sought to do something original, and that he had good reasons for so doing. Yet as one reviewer observed — M.E. Thrall, *NTS* 10 (1963/4) 305 — the organisation of the volume is not always convenient to the user whose focus is NT. To my knowledge, no one has pointed out what Turner has actually done: the general arrangement of Mayser ii.1-3 has been taken over, almost without change. The following table makes this apparent.

TABLE 1

	Mayser		Turner
ii, 1	§§ 1-8	Substitutes for nouns	Chapter 1 Book One
	9-10	Gender and number of nouns	2 Part I
	11	Comparison of adjectives/adverbs	3
	12	The vocative	4
	13-18	Substantival article and pronoun	5
	19-32	The verb: voice	6
	33-41	The verb: aspect and tense	7
	42-48	The verb: mood, indicative/subjunctive	8
	49	The verb: mood, optative	9
	50	The verb: infinitive	10
	51	The verb: participle	11
	52	Verbal adjective	(cf. pp.89, 91)
ii, 2	(53), 54-56	Individual article with proper nouns	12, §1
	57-63	The article with common nouns	12, §§2-3
	64-65	Attributive relationship: adjectives	13
	66-70	Attributive relationship: pronouns/pronominal adjectives	14
	71-78	Attributive relationship: nouns	15
	79-80	Predicative use of adjectives/adverbs	16
	81-106	Case additions to the verb: without a preposition	17
	107-136	Case additions to the verb: with a preposition	18
	137-142	Negatives	19

Mayser ii.1-3 is not the sole work Turner has used, of course: various observations below show that he has drawn upon other parts of Mayser, and upon other works. But in the overall schema Mayser ii.1-3 has been the model which has been followed very closely for all but the final chapter of the book. Moreover, analysis reveals that this extends to the order in which specific aspects of a construction are treated. As an example of this, comparison might be made between the order of Mayser's treatment of the article and pronoun (§§13-18a) and the handling of the same material in *Syntax*, ch.5; or again, between Mayser on the subjunctive (§§44-48) and *Syntax*, ch.8, §2. Particularising this further, portions of *Syntax* range between close translation and free adaptation of Mayser; and occasionally Turner exposes his flank where he has been careless in the way he has taken over his predecessor's material. As simply one instance of this, in the treatment of μή + subj. expressing a cautious statement, *Syntax*, 98 = Mayser, 234: Turner quotes clauses from Plato though he omits the references which Mayser additionally provided, and he misreads *P.Par.* (1865) 32 (μὴ οὐκ ἀποδῶ σοι, Mayser) as μὴ οὐκ ἀποδώσοι. Given the accentuation, this is not likely to have been a printer's error which slipped through the proof-reading.

b. References to documentary evidence in *Syntax*

Turner's constant distinction between pre- and post-Christian papyri is too sharp (e.g., *Syntax*, 34), and not very useful anyway — as if Greek grammar was altered by the Incarnation! References to 'the pap.' abound, but without specific references there is no way to assess whether Turner's conclusions are correct. Even more seriously, the user of *Syntax* becomes aware of the extent to which papyri of the Ptolemaic period comprise almost exclusively such documentary evidence as is adduced, e.g., *Syntax*, 96, 98, 99, 138, 139 (*ter*), 140 (*ter*), etc. Sometimes Turner calls them 'pre-Christian' papyri, e.g., 206, 217, 220. As will emerge below, it is not coincidental that in several of these latter places the relevant paragraph in Mayser uses the adjective 'vorchristlich': thus, compare Mayser, i^2.2, 69 with *Syntax*, 206; Mayser, ii.2, 143 with *Syntax*, 217, etc. A person researching seriously for documentary parallels to NT syntax might be expected to do some looking in the epigraphical material as well. As merely one example of the potential of this vast bulk of texts see the bibliography to the present work for the series of articles by A.S. Henry which appeared in *CQ* from 1964-1970, which examine various syntactical and other features of Hellenistic Attic prose inscriptions. Although they appeared after the publication of *Syntax*, the *Style* volume shows no awareness of studies like these, which include material of use for a discussion of Hellenistic Greek style (e.g., the 1970 article includes sections on 'co-ordination' and 'word order'). Moreover, to the extent that chronological limits are significant why look only for BC examples? II BC to II AD might seem a more natural, if still somewhat narrow, range for a work focusing strictly on NT parallels. That aside, what Turner means by his constant allusion to Ptolemaic papyri slips out occasionally, e.g., a reference to occurrences of a construction 'in Ptol. pap. in Mayser's list' (140); '. . . in all the Ptol. pap. examined by Mayser' (278). If this implies that there was little or no independent checking for parallels, what follows serves only to reinforce that impression.

At *Syntax*, 101, are listed the dates only (no references to texts are included) of 57 Ptolemaic papyri which use a present subjunctive in a purpose clause. These dates are culled *seriatim* (with a few lacunae) from Mayser ii.1, 241-43, the major difference being that the latter quotes both the references and the relevant clause of Greek. A further example of this procedure occurs at *Syntax*, 130, where seven dates are listed *tout court*. How unprofitable is Turner's dependence on Mayser is shown by the fact that the dates in *Syntax* merely follow the order in which they occur in Mayser: there is no attempt even to re-order them chronologically. At *Syntax*, 116 Turner provides papyrus volume and date for a series of references but neither gives the particular text numbers nor quotes the relevant clause. Here he is apparently drawing upon the work of R.C. Horn, *The use of the subjunctive and optative moods in the non-literary papyri* (Diss. Pennsylvania; Philadelphia, 1926) — *non vidi*. On this work see further below. At p.99 Turner quotes a papyrus text from Mayser (though fails to give the reference which Mayser includes), and then adds the dates for this and other texts quoted by Mayser ii.1, 235-36. With such half-information how is the reader's understanding advanced? This last example is just the sort of place where brief comments on the stylistic genre of each document and its level of 'literariness' could have been of great benefit to a reader investigating the use of the deliberative subjunctive.

Again, in his tables Turner takes over directly from Mayser figures for papyrus attestations of various constructions; but he does so in such a bald way as to be far less helpful than Mayser. The latter often gives a breakdown of instances by century, along with other information; and his tables come at the conclusion of a section after examples have been quoted, to provide a summary of the evidence. Aside from the fact that nearly 40 years' bulk of papyrus publications separate Mayser ii.1 and the appearance of *Syntax* in 1963, Turner has presented his figures in so 'contextless' a fashion that they are meaningless, if not potentially misleading to users who are not on their guard. Some examples of this feature are:

Mayser ii.1, 267 (relative clauses in subjunctive mood with/without ἄν) = *Syntax*, 109
274, table a (temporal clauses in the subjunctive introduced by ἕως (ἄν)/μέχρι (ἄν)) = *Syntax*, 111
274, table b (temporal clauses in the subjunctive introduced by ὅταν, ὡς ἄν, ἐπάν, ἐπειδάν) = *Syntax*, 113
286-88 (conditional clauses) = *Syntax*, 116

In the case of the table at the bottom of *Syntax*, 332, Turner appears to have derived his tallies for papyrus instances of μέν *solitarium* and μέν . . . δέ from Mayser ii.3, 125-131. (On μέν . . . δέ in the NT see now J.A.L. Lee, *NovT* 27 [1985] 1-6.) In this place Mayser quotes examples, though provides (125) a frequency total for μέν . . . δέ only. Turner's figures are to be faulted because he appears to have included in the totals for 'μέν only' Mayser's instances (129-30) of, e.g., μέν . . . πλήν, i.e., where some connective other than δέ follows. Worse still — and this is a general criticism of Turner's statistical charts — the effect of this table, which also lists totals of μέν and μέν . . . δέ for each NT book or group of books, is to convey to the reader the erroneous impression that the papyrus totals are totals for all (Ptolemaic) papyri: they are simply totals of Mayser's list of examples. (The same flaw occurs in R.A. Martin, *VT* 10 [1960] 295-310.) The arrangement of the table in this way may lead the user of *Syntax* erroneously to compare the tally for one homogeneous document like Acts or Hebrews with the tallies Turner gives for the papyri, as if the latter, too, were one homogeneous document. Turner surely cannot have intended his table to be interpreted this way; but the danger is that an incautious user who does not take time to analyse the contents of the chart may come to a false conclusion about relative frequencies.

For another example of uninformative, 'contextless' figures, note the discussion (*Syntax*, 201-05) of the position of πᾶς in relation to its noun and definite article. Turner claims for these tables (202-05) that they 'prove the essential unity of Biblical Greek against that of the Ptolemaic papyri . . .' But in his tabulation papyri of III BC and II/I BC receive one line each, and the figures lack any supporting information for a user to know whether to trust the conclusion that has been advanced.

An instance may be given where Turner has drawn a faulty conclusion on the basis of an error in copying out his statistics from elsewhere. In discussing the relative frequency of ἵνα and ὅπως in final clauses, the table at *Syntax*, 106 appears to be derived for the classical authors represented from W.W. Goodwin, *Syntax of the Moods and Tenses of the Greek Verb* (London, 1897) appendix 3, p.398. But Turner has mistakenly reversed the figures for Homer (Goodwin gives: ἵνα - 145; ὅπως - 9) and for Herodotos (Goodwin: ἵνα - 107; ὅπως - 13 [*sic* — is Turner's '17' a misprint?]). Goodwin's figures for Thucydides are 52 and 114 respectively, and Turner's totals (53, 153) are incomprehensible unless we posit that he wrongly added together the various figures for Thuc. in Goodwin's table. Turner's tally for 'Xen. i-iii' is enigmatic: i-iii = what? — *Hell.*? *Anab.*? 'Xen. i-iii' refers to *Hell.*, in fact. Goodwin's Xen. totals — 213 (ἵνα), 221 (ὅπως) — embrace the entire Xenophontic corpus, I take it. (Incidentally, B.G. Mandilaras, *The Verb in the Greek Non-Literary Papyri* [Athens, 1973] §577, has some of the figures in his table correctly from Goodwin, but in the case of Homer and Hdt. he appears to have carried Turner's reversed figures across into his own chart.) The upshot of this is that the statement (*Syntax*, 106) is false, that '. . . Homer, Thucydides, Xenophon, Herodotus and Attic inscriptions of V-IV BC favoured ὅπως [over ἵνα]'. Only in the case of Thuc. is this claim right, and then it is in the proportion of 2:1, not 3:1. For examination of the use of ὅπως ± ἄν/ἵνα in final clauses in Attic inscriptions from V BC down into the Hellenistic period see A.S. Henry, *CQ* 16 (1966) 291-97, especially 291-93; id., *CQ* 20 (1970) 257. A.L. Connolly, *Atticism in non-Literary Papyri of the First Seven Centuries AD. A Study in Several Features of Orthography and Syntax* (unpub. BA Hons. thesis, Univ. of Sydney, 1983) 51-62, concludes from a search among over 2000 documentary texts in *P.Oxy.* that in imperatival clauses ἵνα and ὅπως are used indiscriminately (60). But ὅπως with various functions occurs more frequently in official documents than in private ones (57). On imperatival ἵνα see further below, p.57.

What are we to make of all this? Turner has in fact done what may loosely be called a free translation of Mayser (omitting portions in the latter which were irrelevant to NT syntax). The detailed evidence of the Ptolemaic papyri marshalled by Mayser is condensed so heavily in *Syntax* that we are presented too often with statistics that are meaningless. It must be emphasised that Turner is not suppressing references to Mayser and passing off the work as his own research. Rather, he has taken over Mayser's evidence and abridged it in such a way that it is no longer of any value. Further, it appears that evidence about grammatical use in literary texts, derived from earlier writers like Goodwin, has sometimes come across into *Syntax* in a confused manner. To this Turner has added NT and LXX references at the appropriate points in illustration of each syntactical feature. Yet even here there are disturbingly inaccurate claims about such straightforward matters as NT frequencies. For example, his claim that γάρ 'is very rare in the Johannine writings' (*Syntax*, 331) is simply not true, as is shown by a quick check of Moulton/Geden. It should not be doubted that Turner has put much labour into the book, e.g., the inclusion of variant readings from many MS witnesses. But an independent contribution to NT syntax it is not. As it stands, the book does not serve specialist users satisfactorily and merely bamboozles students.

3. It exaggerates the impact of Semitic influence

Turner's consistently held position *vis-à-vis* the nature of the Greek of the Bible, not only in *Syntax* but in other publications which predate and postdate it, is idiosyncratic; and with the passage of years his stance has become increasingly extreme. His hypothesis that the Greek of the Bible is 'a unique language with a unity and character of its own' (*Syntax*, 4), i.e., that it is 'Jewish' — or 'Christian' — Greek, has been evaluated already in the first chapter; and we shall have occasion to discuss it further in the following chapter on lexicography. Turner's *Style* is vitiated not simply by the considerable amount of repetition from the *Syntax* volume, but mainly by the assertion of the presence of Semitisms everywhere in the NT. Howard points out (*Grammar*, 2.413-14) that Moulton had already begun to modify his minimising view of alleged Semitisms from what he had said in *Prolegomena*, though that is not to be taken as a surrender of his main thesis; cf. Moulton himself at ibid., 14. It is not to be denied that some Semitic influence and bilingual interference is present; the difficulty lies in establishing which NT features are *indubitably* due to Semitic idiom and not simply coincidental parallel formations. In the course of an informative essay on the καὶ ἐγένετο construction H. Pernot, *Etudes sur la langue des Evangiles* (Paris, 1927) 188-99, states the following general principle which is of wider relevance than to this particular idiom: 'Dans cette question de sémitismes, il importe de ne pas perdre de vue que le grec et l'hébreu coincïdent sur bien des points et que l'existence dans ces deux langues de phénomènes semblables n'implique pas nécessairement une dépendance du grec par rapport à l'hébreu.'

Some syntactical elements which strike me as a 'Semitic amateur' as reasonably persuasive instances are: the influence of the Hebrew construct state upon certain uses of the Greek definite article (*Syntax*, 175, 179-80), and the Hebrew infinitive absolute as an explanation for some pleonastic cognate participles in the NT (ibid., 156-57; *Style*, 15, 47-48; *contra* Moulton, *Prolegomena*, 75-76. For λαβών, however, see p.58 below.). Concerning the latter feature it is to be noted that Turner, acknowledging the existence of a possible papyrus example (157), is yet not fully ready to concede it due weight since it weakens his case that the feature is 'thoroughly Septuagintal' (156). This pair of instances should not be construed as a minimalist list, merely two clear-cut examples of features where linguistic interference by Hebrew upon *koine* appears to have occurred in LXX translation work as taken over by certain NT writers. See further Howard's still very useful section (*Grammar*, 2.477-79) on the classification of Semitisms, and on possible mistranslations (470-77) as evidence for Semitic influence upon the language of the NT. More recently, M. Wilcox has provided a careful survey discussion of the question in *ANRW* II.25.2 (1984) 978-1029. He emphasises the complexity involved in trying to distinguish whether an idiom or syntactical construction owes something to Aramaic, Biblical Hebrew or Mishnaic Hebrew. On the whole he finds evidence of Aramaisms in various features of the Gospels and Acts, whether transliterations, or items of a lexical or syntactic nature. Not all his examples are equally convincing, e.g., εὑρίσκω = 'be able' is claimed as an Aramaism (1011) with no consideration whether it may be idiomatic Greek. Note, for example, the occurrence in the *Sortes Astrampsychi* (*P.Oxy.* 12 [1916] 1477 *col.*2.17) quoted at *New Docs 1977*, **8**, p.42. In a forthcoming article J.A.L. Lee collects a comprehensive range of evidence (literary and non-literary), demonstrating that there is no reason to think that this usage is anything other than normal Greek.

How slippery this question is may be instanced by brief consideration of pleonastic ἄρχομαι in the NT. J.W. Hunkin, *JTS* 25 (1924) 390-402, considered those examples in the Synoptics where it functions as a quasi-auxiliary (three times in Mark, not in Mt. or Lk.), and adduced five parallels for this usage from Xenophon as well as referring to MM, s.v., for non-literary examples. H.St.J. Thackeray, *JTS* 30 (1929) 361-70, acknowledged the significance of Hunkin's discussion but became aware of it too late to incorporate it fully into his own essay five years later. Falling between these chronologically came C.H. Turner's discussion of auxiliary verbs in Mark, *JTS* 28 (1927) 349-62 (ἄρχομαι dealt with at 352-53), which does not go beyond the Synoptics. All three articles appeared within the same decade in the same journal, but *Syntax* refers only to the last mentioned. In discussing ἄρχομαι N. Turner extrapolates a conclusion which goes beyond the view of his namesake, stating that ἄρχομαι is frequent in the Synoptics 'especially in a Semitic pleonastic sense' (*Syntax*, 138). In the light of the examples from Xenophon is it legitimate to think of this usage as an Aramaism in the NT? Thackeray believes so, in view of its frequency: it is an example of the phenomenon of 'the *over-working* of a form of expression, correct but unusual in good Greek, because it happened to correspond to a phrase that was frequent in the Semitic language' (*JTS* 30 [1929] 370; his emphasis). 'Good Greek' is question-begging, of course; but if by that phrase 'Classical Greek' is meant then it is not altogether well-chosen in regard to Xenophon. For it is in the work of this writer that it is possible to discern anticipations of *koine* usage, of which pleonastic ἄρχομαι is one.

The periphrastic tenses (εἶναι/ἔχειν + participle) provide a further illustration of the need for careful scrutiny of the evidence. The diachronic study of W.J. Aerts, *Periphrastica* (Amsterdam, 1974), ranges across three millennia, drawing upon evidence from Homer to Modern Greek. While periphrastic uses are known in the Classical period, they came to be employed more frequently in the *koine*, and new types were developed (e.g., ἦν + aorist participle: Aerts, 84). Aerts discerns (55) the development of what he terms the 'progressive periphrasis' as another *koine* initiative, but it is one which cannot be shown to have existed outside Christian texts, beginning with NT passages such as Lk. 13.10 and 14.1. While it is not a widespread phenomenon, the hypothesis is proposed that this usage may owe its rise to Aramaic (56). Nevertheless, Aerts is at pains not to go too far and, indeed, is firm (75) on the point

> that the language of the LXX and the NT is a good reflexion of the average koine usage of those days. There are few passages, if any, of which it can be said, 'This is not Greek', or, 'No Greek would have said that'. Even those passages of which the translation into Hebrew o[r] Aramaic throws light on the author's actual process of thought or on the source used by him cannot be condemned outright a[s] being 'impossible' Greek. However, this does nothing to alter the fact that, because of the subject dealt with by the OT and the NT . . . the linguistic usage cannot be compared directly with the Ionic linguistic usage of Herodotus or the Attic of Plato. Indeed Luke, who has a good command of Greek but who also, of the four gospel writers, used the most Hebraic expressions, demonstrates that his Greek has become a means of expressing things which are not, in essence, Greek.

Aerts' balanced approach, coupled with well-selected examples, provides a basis for acceptance of his view that the progressive periphrasis may be a Semitism, and specifically an Aramaism.

It is not intended here to challenge Turner's *Syntax* point by point; the matter could be weighed more efficiently when F.T. Gignac's volume on the syntax of the post-Ptolemaic papyri appears. Two volumes have appeared so far of his *Grammar of the Greek Papyri of the Roman and Byzantine Periods* (Milan, 1976, 1981). He has indicated (*per litt.*, 18.1.85) that the Syntax will appear in two parts. Since the weakness of Turner's *Style* in this regard has been more widely recognised it is largely left out of account here. But a few claims from *Syntax* may be noted in summary fashion which can be shown (from recent research known to me) to be wrong.

a.   ὦ — rare in NT, only once certainly 'in pre-Christian papyri' (*Syntax*, 33, following Mayser, ii.1, 55, et al.). 'Semitic and Koine influences once again united in their effect upon the NT, for in the Hell. period ὦ was reserved for emotional or stilted speech' (*Syntax*, ibid.). J.A.L. Lee, *NovT* 27 (1985) 16-18, not only finds some more documentary examples (though it remains exceedingly uncommon), but argues that emotion is not the rationale for its use: it is 'primarily a feature of higher style. Its chief effect in all places [in the NT] is to give a formal and elevated tone' (17).

b.   **Periphrases for the perfect** (*Syntax*, 88-89). Turner's view is overstated and misleading, that where there is no special emphasis the presence of the construction may be attributed to Semitic influence. The case is rebutted by K.L. McKay, *TynB* 23 (1972) 42-43.

c.   **Imperatival ἵνα** (*Syntax*, 94-95). 'In view of this wealth [of LXX and NT examples] and the secular poverty of examples, we may claim the imperatival ἵνα as virtually a Semitism, illustrating the homogeneity of Biblical Greek and its distinction from the Koine' (ibid., 95). Cf. *Style*, 23, where this construction is called 'a Biblical rather than a secular idiom'. Yet Pernot, *Etudes*, 64, had long before alluded to non-NT/LXX attestations. For papyrus examples see Mandilaras, *The Verb in the Greek Non-Literary Papyri*, §§585-589, to which may be added as an example from recent publications *P.Oxy.* 46 (1978) 3314.16 (IV), a private letter: ἵνα οὖν καὶ σοὶ παραβοηθήσῃς μοι, κτλ. (text reprinted and discussed at *New Docs 1978*, **100**). Note also *O.Amst.* (1976) 22.7-8 (region of Egyptian Thebes(?), II), ἵνα μίνῃς αὐτόν, ἐπὶ γὰρ | ὀρτ<ρ>ίζει πρός σε αὔριον (cf. *New Docs 1976*, **43**). In his unpublished thesis (mentioned earlier) Connolly has found 23 examples of this construction in *P.Oxy.* documentary texts dated II-VII (*Atticism in non-Literary Papyri*, 59-60).

d.   **Articular participle acting in place of a relative clause** (*Syntax*, 152-53). Turner believes this may occur in the NT 'because of misunderstanding of an underlying Semitic ptc'. He cites one example from the papyri; for numerous others see Mandilaras, §885.

e.   **Position of unemphatic personal pronoun.** *Syntax* refers (189 n.1) to A. Wifstrand's perceptive article, *Studia Theologica* 3 (1949) 172-84, concerning the word-order of the enclitics μου/σου and με/σε; but its findings are ignored. Wifstrand showed that from the early Hellenistic period there was an increasing tendency in sub- and non-literary Greek to place pronominal enclitics immediately after the word to which they were most closely attached in sense. Literary texts of the period maintained the classical preference for separating these words, with the enclitic frequently placed nearer the beginning of the clause. Wifstrand notes that Semitic influence may be a factor contributing to the high proportion of such immediate post-positions (particularly μου/σου) in the Gospels; but he observes that influence from this direction should not be over-emphasised. On this point see also T. Muraoka, *Studies in Linguistics* 15 (1976) 52. Wifstrand suggests that this feature of word-order reflects the inability of the uncultivated speaker to put together carefully thought-out, complex sentences. If this is so — and the point needs testing in greater detail — there are implications for the question, how closely the Gospels and unpretentious papyrus letters approximate to oral forms. On the whole, W.F. Bakker is right to stress that however colloquial low-register papyri may be, they are nevertheless still written Greek and therefore cannot provide an entirely accurate reflection of the spoken language. See his *Pronomen Abundans and Pronomen Coniunctum* (Amsterdam, 1974) 22. This is a matter of degree, of course; for though written texts may not mirror perfectly oral usage, certain of them may undoubtedly give us a good idea of spoken forms.

f.   **αὐτός standing as a demonstrative for οὗτος/ἐκεῖνος:** Turner is ambivalent whether this occurs in the papyri (*Syntax*, 194). See Gignac, 1.44; 2.166, who sides with Moulton, *Prolegomena*, 91, that it does, against the view of M. Black, *An Aramaic Approach to the Gospels and Acts* (Oxford, 1967³) 96-100, that it does not. At *New Docs 1979*, **23**, p.99 an instance is quoted from a papyrus petition, *P.Oxy.Hels.* (1979) 23 (Oxyrhynchos, 23 April, 212), suggesting that the construction was part of colloquial *koine*: ἐνεποι|ησάμην αὐτῷ τῷ Ἀπίω[νι] (23), 'I pressed my claims with this Apion'.

g.   **Partitive genitive expressed by ἀπό/ἐκ introducing a phrase standing independently of a noun:** 'this is a Bibl. Greek construction, not unknown but rare in class. Greek, really originating in the LXX, and is parallel to similar constructions in Heb., Syriac and Arabic' (*Syntax*, 209). But see Gignac, 1.44 for papyrus examples. See further E.C. Maloney, *Semitic Interference in Markan Syntax* (*SBLDS* 51; Chico, 1981) 134-37, also disagreeing with Turner.

h.   **εἰ in direct questions** 'is a Bibl. Greek usage [NT and LXX references are given], probably a Hebraism . . .' (333; cf. 319 n.1). Yet questions to an oracle commonly use εἰ in this way. See *New Docs 1977*, **8**, p.42 where every one of the questions in the extract given from the *Sortes Astrampsychi* (*P.Oxy.* 12.1477) begins with εἰ. At *New Docs*

1979, **32** (a lead tablet from Dodona, II BC) the question put to the oracle is introduced by ἤ which, by virtue of being phonetically identical with εἰ, was often written for it. The use is not confined to that context, of course. A very clear example comes in a private letter, *P.Mich.* 14 (1980) 679 (provenance unknown, mid-II) in which the writer says, 'On the next day, when there was no longer even a bit to drink, he stood up saying to me, "Do you want a hundred drams of meat bought for you?" ', . . . τῇ ἐφαύριον, ὅτε | [οὐκ]έ`τι´ ἐνῆ πεῖν, ἐστάθη μοι λέ|[γω]ν ὅτι Εἰ θέλις μνᾶν κρέος | [σοι] ἀγορασθῆναι; (*ll*.3-6). J.A.L. Lee refers me also to *P.Oxy.* 9 (1912) 1216 (II or III), another private letter in which the writer asks, ἤ καὶ ἀρσενει|κὸν ἡμῖν ἀφίκατα[ι;], κτλ, 'Have you produced for us a male child?' (*ll*.14-15). Lee suggests that ἤ = εἰ here, and finds a further example of the same way of introducing a direct question at *P.Oxy.* 9.1220.5-9 (III), another private letter.

i.   **Treatment of double-name formulae.** On Σαῦλος ὁ καὶ Παῦλος (Acts 13.9) *Syntax* says (166): 'The NT formula . . . has many parallels in the Koine'. This is not wrong, of course, but falls a good way short of adequacy in that it is so uninformative. Other standard NT Grammars are also wanting in their treatment of the feature. What is said at *Syntax*, 206 on double-name formulae is merely derived (with acknowledgement) from Mayser. The treatment of the phenomenon by BDF §268(1) is similarly derivative, as is also BDR[15] §268.1 n.4. Only BDF troubles to refer to R. Calderini (name misspelled, however), *Aeg.* 21 (1941) 221-60, but fails to note her continuation article in ibid., 22 (1942) 3-45. Given that they deal with the NT, all three of these Grammars might profitably have referred to Deissmann, *Bible Studies*, 313-17. For some further items of bibliography on by-names see R. MacMullen, *AJP* 87 (1966) 1-17, at 9 n.20; cf. *New Docs 1976*, **55**, p.89. I have already pointed out the unsatisfactory treatment of this question by the standard Grammars at *Numen* 34 (1987) 15 n.32. An article to be included in the *Anchor Bible Dictionary* provides representative examples of the diversity of ways by which double names were expressed, and considers reasons for the phenomenon.

In addition to these examples, there are numerous places in *Syntax* where special pleading appears to be used to favour the 'Semitic Greek' hypothesis. This occurs particularly when a syntactical feature is claimed as 'Biblical' Greek even though non-Biblical examples are acknowledged. A sample of instances is listed below with minimal comment.

j.   **The phrase** ἀπὸ μιᾶς at Lk. 14.18 'may be an Aramaism rather than an ellipse . . . but it occurs in secular [papyri] . . . and in MGr.' (18). Yet earlier (6-7) the use of the feminine for neuter in this and similar phrases is said to be 'a peculiarity of Biblical Greek and not of the Koine'. Black, *Aramaic Approach*[3], 113 discusses the phrase; but note A. Pietersma's comment that the presence of the phrase in *P.Chester Beatty* XV, 11.8 militates against it being a Semitism: *The Acts of Phileas Bishop of Thmuis* (*Cahiers d'Orientalisme* 7; Geneva, 1984) 68.

k.   **Reduction of** μᾶλλον ἤ **to simple** ἤ **or** παρά 'is a Semitism but there are classical parallels' (32).

l.   Though **pleonastic participles** are acknowledged to be paralleled in *koine* and the papyri, 'λαβών and some other merely descriptive ptcs. seem to owe their origin in Biblical Greek to a Hebraic pattern' (154). That λαβών is by no means necessarily a Semitism see more recently W.J. Verdenius, *Mnem.* 33 (1980) 196, referring to Hdt. 4.130.

m.   **Use of the cognate participle** to strengthen the verb is 'thoroughly Septuagintal'; yet the counterweight of *P.Tebt.* 2 (1907) 421.12-13, ἐρχόμε|ν[ο]ς δὲ ἔρχου (ε)ἰς Θεογενίδα (which Turner quotes), is not fully conceded (156-57). Cf. Howard in *Grammar*, II.444.

n.   οὐ . . . πᾶς is a 'peculiarly Biblical Greek phenomenon' (196); yet at 196 n.2 one papyrus and two literary parallels are acknowledged.

o.   **The frequent addition of** υἱός to express the relation of parents to children is 'Semitic rather than typically Greek, and even in the papyri this and θυγάτηρ are needed only for clarity (Mayser ii.2, p.9)' (207). From a statement like this it is only a short step to the claim that Semitic influence permeated all the papyri. Turner takes this step a decade later in *NovT* 16 (1974) 149-60 (especially 151), a preliminary study for his *Christian Words* (Edinburgh, 1980). See further, ch.1 above, p.37.

p.   **The genitive of quality** is taken to be a feature of Biblical Greek: 'There may be class. parallels but they are poetic . . . there may be Koine parallels but they are few' (213 n.1). By quoting only one of the several examples given by his source Turner allows the unwary reader to draw the inference that the apparent paucity of classical and *koine* parallels supports his thesis that 'this is a feature of Biblical Greek' (212). Turner indicates (203 n.1) that his source is Moulton, *Einleitung*, 113 n.1. Though he regards this German translation of *Prolegomena*[3] as a fourth edition of Moulton's first volume (p.viii), throughout the book there is no consistent reference to *Einleitung* alone: the *Prolegomena* is also mentioned frequently. In this particular instance, in fact, *Einleitung* 113 n.1 = *Prolegomena*[3], 74 n.1, a cross-reference to *Prolegomena*, 235 where Moulton quotes the *P.Tebt.* text in the form adopted by Turner. Moulton provides three papyrus examples, Turner offers one only, emphasising for his argument the paucity of non-Biblical parallels. Mayser, ii.2, p.139 quotes the passages accurately, and gives their precise date (103 BC). Mayser and Moulton correctly take these phrases to be instances of the genitive after a privative adjective, *not* the genitive of quality which Turner does.

q.   **Pleonastic insertion of the personal pronoun** 'is a Semitism in the sense that the Heb. אֲשֶׁר לוֹ is reflected through LXX usage, helped by a parallel Aramaic idiom [viz., דְּ]; but non-Biblical Greek, and indeed many languages reveal the same pleonasm' (325). This feature is what W.F. Bakker terms the *pronomen abundans*. In his careful presentation of the evidence, *Pronomen Abundans and Pronomen Coniunctum* (Amsterdam, 1974), he suggests (33-42) that it is not really a Semitism for there is a difference in semantic function between it and אֲשֶׁר לוֹ. It is true that the feature is not widespread in *koine* texts outside the LXX (which has many examples) and the NT (with 18); but he suggests that another process was at work which occasions this discrepant frequency: in the case of the NT 'Aramaic supports a tendency which already existed in the Greek language' (35).

r.   Turner's ch.25 on **particles** is weak generally. For example, what are we to make of the following statement at *Syntax*, 329? Speaking of the reduction in the number of particles employed in the NT as against 'more refined Greek', he asserts that 'τοι and μήν (by themselves) and γοῦν are too subtle to be needed in the NT'. Are we to infer that the NT writers consciously decided to dispense with these connectives? He attributes this reduction to 'the double influence of later Greek usage and Jewish background', the last two words being included (I take it) as part of his tendency to argue in favour of a Jewish-Greek hypothesis. A more satisfactory treatment of particles might have been expected in *Style*, in the light of M.E. Thrall, *Greek Particles in the NT: Linguistic and Exegetical Studies* (*NT Tools and Studies* 3; Leiden, 1962), and J. Blomqvist, *Greek Particles in Hellenistic Prose* (Lund, 1969). But the first is referred to only once, the second not at all. It is unfortunate that these monographs have been passed over because their conclusions discount Turner's own hypothesis. Turner knows C.H. Bird's article on γάρ in Mark (*Style*, 30) but ignores Thrall's rebuttal of it (41-50); he knows M. Zerwick's book on Markan style (*Style*, 26), but ignores Thrall's rejection (50-63) of Zerwick's view of how Mark uses δέ — even though he himself discusses the relationship between καί and δέ (*Style*, 17). Worth exploring *vis-à-vis* NT usage is the view of J.J. Fraenkel, *Mnem.* 13 (1947) 183-201, that emphatic particles were made obsolete in the *koine* by the shift from pitch to stress accent. On the function of particles note also A. Hellwig, *Glotta* 52 (1974) 145-71. On adversative καί see J. Blomqvist, *Das sogenannte καί adversativum. Zur Semantik einer griechischen Partikel* (Uppsala, 1979), whose brief monograph includes examination of a number of NT and papyrological texts.

One final matter should be mentioned before leaving this aspect of Turner's work. The last thorough attempt in English at a systematic syntax of the NT prior to Turner is to be found in A.T. Robertson's *Grammar of the NT in the Light of Historical Research*. By 1923, within less than a decade from the time of its first publication, this work reached a fourth edition. (The book was reprinted in 1931 but, *pace* Turner, *Syntax*, ix, this was not a new edition.) In successive editions alterations/additions were not made to the text as such, but were included in a series of appendices. At times this *Grammar* is somewhat overwhelming in its comprehensiveness, even unwieldy. For example, he has 21 pages (1155-75) on negatives; compare Turner, with 6 (281-87) — the latter much smaller pages in format. The syntax section in this tome is over 800 pages in length. Robertson's introduction (1-139) still makes lively reading. His grasp of developments in NT philology is masterly, not to say magisterial; and the judiciousness of his assessment of the contributions of various individuals still rings true half a century later. Thus, although he is an ally of their position, Robertson observes that the enthusiasm with which Deissmann and Moulton embraced the significance of documentary evidence for NT philology led to their underestimating the place of Semitic influence. 'The joy of new discoveries has to some extent blurred the vision of Deissmann and Moulton . . .' (91). His chapter on 'The place of the NT in the Koine' (76-139) remains excellent for its balance and clarity.

This work was the only major English-language Grammar of the NT produced this century available to Turner. The translation of Blass-Debrunner by R.W. Funk appeared only after Turner's *Syntax* volume must have been substantially complete if not already in the press. Yet when a check is made through *Syntax* for references to Robertson's *Grammar* the search is almost in vain: apart from inclusion in the Chronological Bibliography (p.ix) there is one reference only (255), where Robertson's authority is drawn upon because he acknowledges that a particular use of εἰς may reflect Semitic influence. That is, Robertson is invoked at the point where his view coincides with Turner's own general outlook. Yet Robertson's *Grammar* is ignored throughout the rest of Turner's *Syntax*. There is a small number of references to articles by Robertson. It is to be feared that Robertson's *Grammar* is almost totally neglected because Turner's own position on the nature of the Greek of the NT is thoroughly at odds with the judgement of the former. It is sufficient to indicate Robertson's viewpoint by the following statement in his preface (p.xi): 'I have not thought it best to use so much [of the papyrological/ epigraphical evidence] in proportion as Radermacher has done, for the case is now proven [that the NT was written largely in vernacular *koine*] and what Moulton and Radermacher did does not have to be repeated'. Rather than argue his case against Robertson et al., Turner has simply passed over him in silence, in effect a *damnatio memoriae*. The irony is that the influence of Robertson appears indirectly at many points in *Syntax*. For Turner refers to at least eight unpublished dissertations on features of NT grammar completed between the late 1930s to 1951 at the Southern Baptist Theological Seminary in Kentucky, U.S.A. — the very institution where Robertson held his Chair from 1890-1934. These dissertations were written under the supervision of W.H. Davis, Robertson's colleague who succeeded to the latter's chair and held it until his own retirement in 1950. (I owe this information to R.A. Culpepper, *per litt.* 22.9.88.) As for the treatment of Moulton and Radermacher, references to their work are in fact frequent in *Syntax*. Turner draws upon their evidence, but rarely enters into disagreement with them on specifics; he certainly makes plain, however, that he is fundamentally at variance with Moulton on the general issue at stake.

*   *   *

Two further observations are adumbrated much more briefly to underline the fundamentally unsatisfactory quality of Turner, *Syntax*. These comments apply to many other works, of course, and by no means to this book alone. They are included here because *Syntax* happens to typify these weaknesses. First, indications of hazy and misleading chronological statements have been offered in passing above. Here we merely instance the confusing use of the term 'Hellenistic', as applied to a conventionally agreed historical time period, and as applied to language (= *koine* Greek). This problem has already been raised in the previous chapter. Thus, Malalas is spoken of as a Hellenistic author (*Syntax*, 134); *P.Oxy.* 3 (1903) 526 (dated II AD) is also so characterised, as are Hermas and Epiktetos (ibid., 136). With the exception of Malalas who reflects usage of the Byzantine phase of Greek, these authors and texts are all writing Hellenistic (= *koine*) Greek, though employing different registers of language; but none belongs to the Hellenistic *period*. The following statement at *Syntax*, 123-24, may also be quoted: 'In this respect [use of potential optative + ἄν] LXX and NT are much of a unity, and because of the infrequence of this opt. the LXX should be classified with the papyri of i/BC-i/AD rather than with those of iii/BC.' It would be easy for a novice to come away with the erroneous impression that the LXX is being down-dated to I BC.

Second, reverting to the programmatic explanation about the organisation of material in *Syntax* (quoted above at p.51), Turner observes that 'the student . . . must console himself by making good use of the index . . .' In fact, the indexes are defective and far from comprehensive. A couple of examples only are given here to illustrate the point. R.C. Horn's 1926 Dissertation (noted above) on the subjunctive and optative in non-literary papyri is referred to several times (see index, 391), but only at p.383 (in the middle of another index!) are its title and date of publication given. The first of the sparse references to A.T. Robertson in the index (398) is to *Syntax*, 80, where n.1 refers to his work as 'A.T. Robertson, op. cit.' For the detail of this publication the reader needs to go back to p.79 n.2. Small points these, undoubtedly; but if clear and accurate indexes are important for any book, they are fundamentally so for a work of grammatical reference. Good indexes are like Ariadne's thread, helping users find their way through a maze of intricate detail which usually has to be laid out very laconically for reasons of space.

*   *   *

It would be both pedantic and unproductive to pick up every flaw in Turner's *Syntax*. Three conclusions are offered on the basis of the foregoing.

1. The syntax part of any major Grammar is the section hardest to write and likely to be the portion most consulted. Turner's contribution to NT syntax fails to meet the required standard of an authoritative and clear guide to its subject. A completely new NT Syntax is needed for Moulton's *Grammar*, not merely a retouched version of Turner. If this task seems daunting, that is probably as it should be; but it is not a task to be despaired of, given that Gignac's *Syntax* of post-Ptolemaic papyri is expected to appear in the near future. Furthermore, D.A. Carson and P. Miller are near to completing a *Syntactical Concordance to the Greek NT*, a hard-copy version of their GRAMCORD software. Between Mayser and Gignac (and not forgetting Mandilaras) papyrology is exceptionally well served now for grammars — the situation could not be more different for Hellenistic and Roman-period epigraphy. A list of epigraphic grammars is provided in J.J. Hondius, *Saxa Loquuntur* (Leiden, 1938; repr. Chicago, 1976) 147-52, but few deal with Hellenistic and Roman period inscriptions. For a more recent, brief survey see *New Docs 1979*, **138**; some supplementary references are provided in the present volume at p.150 below. But it is not merely the documentary and other contemporary literary evidence which will have to be taken into account: awareness and assimilation of modern linguistic theory is needed, too.
2. The aura of association with Moulton's name may serve to lull users into accepting that the quality of vol.3 of the *Grammar* is as good as vol.1. Moulton's name has been used as an imprimatur of quality for the later volumes in the *Grammar*, conveying the impression that their authority is unimpeachable. By having his name associated with that of Moulton and yet disagreeing with him fundamentally on the importance of the documentary evidence for appreciation of NT language, Turner has helped to foster the impression that Moulton's position on this matter is passé. Moulton's reputation has been diminished, unjustifiably.
3. Ought the book ever to have been permitted to be published? Certainly it should, were the question simply one of differing perspectives about the degree of Semitic influence in the Greek NT. However, since the use of documentary evidence is so misguided and misguiding some responsibility must be sheeted home to the publishing company and its Readers for allowing the book to proceed at all. It does not automatically follow that such close adherence to Mayser's arrangement of his material is inappropriate. What is inadmissible,

however, is the taking over of his statistics in a way that renders them valueless. Anyone who consults *Syntax* cursorily for guidance on this or that grammatical feature may naturally be impressed to see such an accumulation of detailed references and tables arrayed on page after page. The danger lies, however, in the (often unconscious) equating of the industriousness involved in collecting such data with the accuracy both of the data themselves and of the conclusions drawn from them.

*   *   *

Far briefer discussion is accorded here to R. Funk's English translation (Chicago, 1961) of the ninth/tenth edition of F. Blass/A. Debrunner, *Grammatik des neutestamentlichen Griechisch*. The English version amounted to a new edition, in fact, as it included material which Debrunner had been assembling for a new German edition (BDF preface, xiii). English-speaking scholarship has regarded itself as generally well served by this Grammar, and certainly its syntax section is far more reliable than Turner, and more manageable than Robertson. But with the appearance of F. Rehkopf's thorough revision of the German Blass/Debrunner to produce the 14th edition in 1976 — the 15th edition (1979) incorporates merely minor corrections — the need for a revision of the English edition deserves consideration.

It is in layout that BDR's great advance over its predecessors is particularly to be discerned. Material has been thoroughly reorganised, although so faithful has Rehkopf remained to his heritage that the same number of sections has been retained. The rearrangement of the information within individual sections undoubtedly achieves greater clarity and ease of use for the reader. When it is compared with BDF in this regard, the latter begins to look rather muddled.

Nevertheless, some omissions are evident in BDR. (Perhaps 'omissions' is not the most appropriate word: I take it that Rehkopf worked from the previous German editions for his revision, whereas BDF is a translation of no German edition as such. Nevertheless, Rehkopf presumably took BDF into account.) This matters less, arguably, when what is lacking consists of bibliographical references to modern discussion. E.g., BDR §4 is very similar in content to BDF §4, but the information in the last paragraph in the English version is virtually obliterated in BDR. (On BAGD's citation of secondary sources see the comment at *New Docs 1977*, **1**, p.8.) More serious, though less common, is the omission of germane observations on syntax and stylistic 'levels'. E.g., J.A.L. Lee, *NovT* 27 (1984) 14 n.46, points to a useful observation in BDF §385(1) which is passed over in silence by BDR. In his review of BDR at *NovT* 20 (1978) 332-34, G.D. Kilpatrick has drawn attention to the jettisoning of the evidence provided by variant readings, as though BDR were a Grammar of a particular edition of N/A. G.B. Caird has observed in his evaluation of the book, *JTS* 28 (1980) 139-41, that discussion of matters like orthography and phonology is dated.

Concerning phonology, among recent works of major importance relevant for NT linguistic research may be noted S.-T. Teodorsson, *The Phonology of Ptolemaic Koine* (Göteborg, 1977); id., *The Phonology of Attic in the Hellenistic Period* (Göteborg, 1978). The latter work concludes his earlier study, *The Phonemic System of the Attic Dialect, 400-340 BC* (Lund, 1974). Teodorsson provides a useful summary of the conclusions of his monographs in *Glotta* 57 (1979) 61-75. For NT work Teodorsson's contribution ought to be taken into account for any new edition of N/A or UBS, for there are orthographical implications which flow from his studies of phonological change. For discussion of evidence for phonological developments in Hellenistic Attic prose inscriptions see A.S. Henry, *CQ* 14 (1964) 241-45; id., *CQ* 17 (1967) 257-95. Note also L. Hjelmslev in *International Congress of Classical Studies, 1954* (Copenhagen, 1958) 1.101-13.

For phonological evidence from the papyri in the Imperial period Gignac's *Grammar*, I is the natural starting point; it catches up the material in his earlier article in *TAPA* 101 (1970) 185-202.

Another feature which needs re-evaluation in NT Grammars is the question of aspect. This is a subject to which K.L. McKay has given concerted attention over the last two decades: see, e.g., *BICS* 12 (1965) 1-21; *TynB* 23 (1972) 39-57; *BICS* 27 (1980) 23-49; *NovT* 23 (1981) 289-329; *NovT* 27 (1985) 201-26; and most recently in A. Rijksbaron *et al.* (edd.), *In the Footsteps of Raphael Kühner* (Amsterdam, 1986), 193-208. W.F. Bakker's tightly focussed monograph, *The Greek Imperative* (Amsterdam, 1966), examines the question of aspect in the use of present and aorist imperatives within prayers. Within the broad time-span of this diachronic study (ranging from Homer to Modern Greek) some attention is given to the LXX and NT, as well as to a few papyrological examples. Bakker suggests that in contrast to the aorist (used in prayers to gods), present imperatives are used particularly in address to mortals and carry an implied emotional pressure for the hearer. He provides (82-84) some interesting instances of this characteristic in the NT and papyri. Nevertheless the aorist imperative increases in relative frequency in Greek from the *koine* onwards (79, 86-87). J. Thorley's article in *NovT* 30 (1988) 193-211 is the most recent contribution to discuss aspect, with a reconsideration of how the present and aorist subjunctives are used in this regard. A useful bibliography is included in an article by O. Szemerényi on the origin of aspect in Indo-European languages, *Glotta* 65 (1977) 1-18. I have not yet seen S.E. Porter, *Verbal Aspect in the Greek of the NT, with Reference to Tense and Mood* (*Studies in Biblical Greek* 1; New York, 1989).

As for BDR's bibliography, references like that at §4, n.1 to A. Hilhorst, *Sémitismes et latinismes dans le Pasteur d'Hermas* (Nimwegen, 1976) give the impression that the new (14th) edition is very up-to-date. It is always inevitable, of course, that some items fail to be gathered into the net. L. Rydbeck's *Fachprosa* (Uppsala, 1967) is known (BDR §3; note also Rydbeck's article in *NTS* 21 [1975] 424-27). Yet there is no awareness of J. Frösén, *Prolegomena to a Study of the Greek Language in the First Centuries AD: the Problem of Koine and Atticism* (Helsinki, 1974), which includes criticisms of Rydbeck's approach; see above, p.47. As for earlier works of importance, Robertson's *Grammar* is among those now lost to sight. LSJ is mentioned but not the *Supplement*.

Two final comments may be made, both of which have wider application to other work on NT Grammar.

1. BDF and BDR both perpetuate the dogma (at §4(3)) that there was a spoken Jewish Greek. This view may be found in a number of modern writers, as we have seen in ch.1: e.g., N. Turner, in the quotation with which ch.1 began (above, p.5); R.H. Gundry, *JBL* 83 (1964) 408 (quoted above in ch.1, p.21). M. Black also shares this opinion, e.g., *ExpT* 77 (1965) 20-23, while Hilhorst, *Sémitismes et latinismes dans le Pasteur d'Hermas*, believes there were milieux where a semitised Greek was spoken (38; cf. his comments on p.9). As for what BDF/BDR actually say the German edition is quoted here as being the most recent: 'Es hat gewiss ein gesprochenes Judengriechisch gegeben, in dem Sinn, dass auch die profane Sprechweise eines Juden sein semitisches Denken verriet.' This passage offers an interesting small example of the way progress in scholarship can be reversed. When Deissmann's *Bibelstudien* appeared in 1895, Blass' review, *TLZ* 20 (1895) 486-88, especially 487, expressed doubt whether the documentary texts were really of great service for understanding the language of the NT. By the time of the publication of the first edition of his *Grammatik* the following year, Blass' views had changed considerably. He now recognised (*Grammatik*[1], p.2) that the NT and the papyri had much in common, with the latter providing some evidence for the language spoken at the time. Hebraisms and Aramaisms were regarded as mainly lexical (ibid., §2.3), though these languages exercised an influence on Greek-writing

Jews (ibid., §4(1)-(3)). The second edition (1902) was no mere reprint, although the same wording was preserved concerning this question. The third edition (1911) was an unaltered reprint of the second. The real change comes with the fourth edition (1913), in which A. Debrunner completely worked over Blass' text. In the case of the issue of Jewish Greek, we now find (*Grammatik*[4], §4) for the first time in Blass' work the specific wording quoted above. This statement has been preserved in all subsequent editions, most of which were little more than corrected reprints, with no substantive changes incorporated, down to BDR[14] and BDF. So then, the inconsistency becomes explicable. There was only one *volte-face* by Blass, not two. He did not return to his pre-1896 view of the documentary texts and the NT. A later editor of Blass' *Grammatik*, with a different perception of the matter, has included a statement at odds with Blass' own position.

The question ought to be pondered, whether the failure of much NT philological research to keep abreast of relevant linguistic developments may be due in part to the continuing acceptance and popularisation of the misconceived hypothesis that 'Jewish Greek' was an actual, spoken dialect of the *koine*, though one unaffected in large measure by the surrounding developments in Greek.

2. 'Abbreviations, IV' in BDF (pp.xxiii-iv) lists papyrus and epigraphical volumes. One-third of the *c*.70 works included are epigraphical, though that proportion is reduced when other items given in 'Abbreviations, V' are included (pp.xxv-xxxiii). To draw upon inscriptional evidence in such quantity is rare in NT Studies. It is not an unfair generalisation to observe that most researchers in this field, particularly in the last generation, proceed as though the papyri were the only documentary evidence which exists, or at least as though they were the only non-literary material worth consulting. This is true of specific monographs such as Thrall's *Greek Particles in the NT* (which contains not a single epigraphical reference), or D. Hill's *Greek Words and Hebrew Meanings* (Cambridge, 1967). The latter includes (24 n.2) one solitary reference to an inscription in his entire discussion of the ἱλάσκομαι word-group (derived from MM anyway, not his own reading?). This inscription is considered at length in *New Docs 1978*, **6**. The same lack of attention to inscriptional sources proportional to their potential is also in evidence in grammars such as Turner's *Syntax*, in whose index of documentary sources the ratio of epigraphical works to papyrus corpora is 1:8, even though the number of inscriptions which have been published vastly outweighs the number of papyri.

BDR's list of abbreviations is heavily truncated compared to what BDF provides. The ratio between papyrus and epigraphical corpora listed is fairly even; but the number of works listed is minimal, and (for papyri at least) unrepresentative. The epigraphical works mentioned are predominantly the large collections (*CIG, CIL, IG, OGIS*, etc.). As for papyrus letters, Rehkopf includes mention of G. Ghedini, *Lettere cristiane dai papiri greci del III e IV secolo* (Milan, 1923), but not of M. Naldini, *Il cristianesimo in Egitto* (Florence, 1968). In this sphere, a future edition of BDR/BDF will need to take into account G. Tibiletti, *Le lettere private nei papiri greci del III e IV secolo d. C. Tra paganesimo e cristianesimo* (Milan, 1979). See further *New Docs 1979*, **16**.

Furthermore, when one examines the documentary volumes listed in BDF and BDR, it is clear that only older works have been included. To find publications in their lists which appeared later than 1950 is a rarity. In this respect, the comments made above about Turner's *Syntax* being out of date are applicable also to other NT grammar work of the last generation. With the increasing separation of Classics and Biblical Studies the proverb, 'Out of sight, out of mind', unfortunately sums up the disregard which much of NT Studies has shown for documentary publications since roughly the 1930s. It is possible that a comment in a letter by Moulton to J.R. Harris may have served as a cue to Turner and others that there was no need to take further account of the papyri. Writing in July 1910, Moulton offered the opinion: 'I do not think that papyrology will take us much farther. New papyrus collections will only add details now' (quoted in W.F. Moulton, *James Hope Moulton* [London, 1919] 69). The reason that Moulton gave for believing that the subsequent yield would not be as great was the building of the Aswan Dam, and the consequent change in the level of the water table. The effect of this would be to hasten deterioration of those papyri still preserved in the sand. Yet the culling of those works acessible to me which appeared in a mere four-year span illustrates strikingly how many are the gains still to be made. There is no reason to suppose that the years 1976-1979 reviewed by the four previous *New Docs* volumes were unusually rich in their potential for NT studies.

4

THE GREEK DOCUMENTARY EVIDENCE AND NT LEXICAL STUDY: SOME SOUNDINGS

Three works which have appeared in the last decade provide an opportunity to assess the state of NT lexicography, and to some extent more generally work in semantics. In the context of the *New Docs* series, the concern here is to focus particularly on the degree of profit derived by these books from non-literary sources. Naturally, the emphasis on the latter in the series should not be taken to imply a down-valuing of literary texts. The various publications, both monographs and articles, by those involved in the *Corpus Hellenisticum Novi Testamenti* project are underlining the illustrative importance of those texts; and cf. more generally F.G. Downing, *NovT* 30 (1988) 212-30.

The publications which have been selected here all profess to be substantive contributions; yet by virtue of the different form each takes and their different provenances, they afford a means of evaluating what is occurring at a range of levels of scholarship in several places. These three works are:

1. C. Brown (ed.), *The New International Dictionary of NT Theology* (3 vols; Exeter, 1975-78); a translation, with extensive revisions and additions, of L. Coenen et al. (edd.), *Theologisches Begriffslexikon zum Neuen Testament* (Wuppertal, 1965-71; *non vidi*). A fourth volume, consisting of indexes to vols. 1-3, has been produced by D. Townsley/R. Bjork (Grand Rapids, 1985).
2. N. Turner, *Christian Words* (Edinburgh, 1980); and
3. C. Spicq, *Notes de lexicographie néo-testamentaire* (2 vols + Suppl., *Orbis Biblicus et Orientalis* 22.1-3; Göttingen, 1978-82). This work has already received mention at *New Docs 1979*, **93**.

In what follows these items will be abbreviated as *NIDNTT*; Turner, *CW*; and Spicq, *NLNT*, respectively. It is because a full-scale treatment would be required that BAGD has not been selected here. However, some comments on it are offered in an excursus at the end of this chapter, together with brief observations on the sixth German edition of Bauer's *Lexikon* (1988).

The *NIDNTT* is a collaborative effort. The English edition has retained a large portion of the (mainly) German original contributions, but they are expanded and new entries are provided by (with very few exceptions) British and British-trained scholars. Its three volumes of entries comprise nearly 350 articles (English head-words) which discuss over 760 Greek words in some 2900 pp. (omitting the voluminous indexes). *NIDNTT* 1.13 notes that many other Greek words are discussed than are listed in the contents pages of each volume. As well as word entries there is a small number of essays on widely ranging topics which serve as excursuses to certain entries, e.g., 'Animals in the NT' (1.114-19); 'Parts of the body' (1.239-42); 'Language and meaning in religion' (3.123-46). Comparison is inevitably invited with the even larger Kittel/Friedrich *Theological Dictionary of the NT* (10 vols; ET: Grand Rapids, 1964-76. Hereafter referred to as *TDNT*), and some comments will be offered below in this regard.

Turner, *CW*, is much more modest in scope. Its *c*.500 pages treat *c*.450 Greek terms under *c*.250 English head-words. The author views this contribution to NT vocabulary studies as a rounding-off of his earlier work on NT syntax and style, namely vols. 3 and 4 in Moulton's *Grammar* (see ch.3 above); and, further, claims that the words he discusses are merely 'a sample of the speciality of Biblical and Christian language' (*CW*, ix).

Like Turner's new book, Spicq's *NLNT* comes at the end of a long career: his publications extend back over more than half a century. In view of this great productivity the mere collecting together (if that were all it was) of this series of lexicographical studies from his earlier books and articles would be in itself a great service. About 670 Greek words (including a small number of phrases) are dealt with in just over 400 entries (Greek head-words) spanning *c*.1700 pp. Spicq has written several other studies (listed in the bibliography to the present volume) on the *NLNT* model.

Although they emanate from different backgrounds and aim at different readerships, all three works are unequivocally theological in thrust. This is explicit in the title of *NIDNTT* (and cf. Brown's preface to vol.1, p.11), in the preface to Turner, *CW*, and in Spicq's comment, '*notre intention est théologique*' (1.7; his emphasis). The Swiss Dominican Spicq has an academic audience in view, and while theological perspectives are certainly present, they do not obtrude upon his philological judgements. Turner's book is for semi-popular consumption, the product of an English scholarly Anglican clergyman. A homiletical element looms large in it. Numerous references to primary and secondary literature are provided in the footnotes, however. And the reader is assumed to be well-acquainted with a good deal more of early Jewish and Christian writings than the Bible and some of the other main texts. For example, s.v. 'Compassion' (78-80), the reader is expected to know the names Aquila, Symmachus and Theodotion and to be aware of the fact that 'Pr 17^{5}A' refers to the reading of one particular MS. The general reader is offered no guidance about the date of Aquila etc., nor about the date of such texts as the *Test. XII Pat.* The envisaged readership of *NIDNTT* appears to be somewhere in between these two positions; the great bulk of its contributors appear to share a theologically conservative, Protestant background.

When we ask whether these three contributions are up-to-date in various respects, their paths begin to diverge. Spicq seems thoroughly aware of recent secondary literature relevant to the words he is studying, and he has undoubtedly kept in touch with recent papyrological and epigraphical publications. Neither of these comments would be true of Turner. On the latter score his work was already out of date by the time it was published, as we shall see below. As for the modern secondary literature one example must suffice here to point up the contrast with Spicq. S.v. 'coarse jesting' (72-73), Turner is unaware (forgivably, in view of the small date gap) of P.W. van der Horst's useful study of εὐτραπελία, *Miscellanea Neotestamentica* 2 (1978) 163-90, and begins his entry with the bald and inaccurate statement: 'Christians have given *eutrapelia* a bad sense'. Spicq, who knows van der Horst's article, is much more careful in his discussion of the word (3.322-25). As for *NIDNTT*, while its bibliographies of secondary literature (appended to the end of each entry) are inevitably selective and arranged primarily with a monolingual English reader in mind, they are very up to date on the whole.

Yet none of these books gives much confidence that developments in the field of Linguistics are having a thoroughgoing impact on Biblical studies. This is above all true of Turner, all of whose work is entirely untouched by these winds of change. This is one of the criticisms made by G.D. Kilpatrick, though too briefly and allusively, in his review of Turner's *Syntax* and *Style* at *TLZ* 104 (1979) 110. See further, ch.3 above, especially p.50. In the case of *NIDNTT*, the large number of contributors makes unevenness inevitable. Clearly some of them are abreast of what has been happening, and do perceive the application of certain features of linguistic study to their work. Notable among these is A.C. Thiselton, whose several contributions in this *Dictionary* — 1.573-84 ('Explain'); 1.678-82 ('Flesh' — part of article only); 3.874-902 ('Truth'); 3.1123-43, 1145-46 ('Language and meaning in religion', s.v. 'Word') — illustrate his interest in the contribution which philosophy can make to the relationship between linguistics and hermeneutics. The comparative lack of interest in Greek usage of earlier or later periods — a feature so marked throughout *NIDNTT* as to be indicative of editorial policy — could be taken to reflect an acceptance of the prior importance of synchronic over diachronic studies. More will be said about this below (p.79), for this is not the only way to interpret the lack of inclusion of much extra-biblical evidence about Greek vocabulary. The starting point for the synchronic/ diachronic distinction is usually taken to be F. de Saussure's *Cours de linguistique générale* (1915; repr. Paris, 1968) 141-260, though the Czech linguist V. Mathesius actually raised the matter prior to this, in 1911: see F.W. Danker, *A Century of Greco-Roman Philology, Featuring the American Philological Association and the Society of Biblical Literature* (Atlanta, 1988) 213. It should be noted that some sociolinguists are no longer entirely satisfied with this distinction. The earliest such comment I have found is in U. Weinreich's *Languages in Contact* (1953; repr. The Hague, 1974) 103. Note also, more recently, R.T. Bell, *Sociolinguistics. Goals, Approaches and Problems* (London, 1976) 19-21, cf. 42, 162; and the brief comments of K.M. Petyt in *Linguistic Controversies* (Festschrift F.R. Palmer), ed. D. Crystal (London, 1982), 207-08. Appendix 2 (below) provides some indications of a renewed appreciation among Linguistics researchers of the importance of the diachronic study of languages. Historical Linguistics, out of fashion for two generations after de Saussure, is again on the agenda, especially in lexical work. F.I. Andersen has pointed out to me (*per litt.*, 22/3/89) that a distinction needs to be made between the priority to be accorded to synchronic studies for descriptive syntax, and the quite different situation that obtains when lexicography is in view.

As for Spicq, the impression gained is that he has not taken much account, formally at least, of newer linguistic trends. It should not be inferred from this that his work is thereby vitiated, for what is so admirable about it is the thoroughgoing collection of documentary examples coupled with cautious discussion. But his work lacks that 'larger leap forward' which might have occurred had certain fruitful areas of Linguistics been exploited for his studies. For example, I can detect no appreciation of the potential of sociolinguistics for NT studies. This may be illustrated by contrasting his entry on φιλόστοργος (2.944-48) — which assembles an impressive range of data — with *New Docs 1977*, **80** (especially the point raised in the central paragraph on p.103), and *New Docs 1978*, **11**. Nor does the de Saussurean distinction between synchrony and diachrony appear to be consistently built into his treatment. Again, it is not uncommon for Spicq to discuss etymologies. This does not constitute a fault *per se*, of course: etymologising becomes a problem only when undue weight is given to it in determining meaning. J. Barr, *The Semantics of Biblical Language* (Oxford, 1961) 107-60, is still the benchmark in this field for discussion of the danger of the etymologising interpretation of words. Building upon Barr's work and popularising it (but without the same astringency) is M. Silva, *Biblical Words and their Meaning* (Grand Rapids, 1983) 35-51. Note also P. Cotterell/M. Turner, *Linguistics and Biblical Interpretation* (London, 1989) 106-28, 132-33. What Barr has to say was prefigured briefly in J.H. Moulton's Inaugural Lecture of 1906, 'The Science of Language and the Study of the NT', repr. in his posthumous collection of essays and addresses, *The Christian Religion in the Study and in the Street* (London, 1919) 122-23. J.F.A. Sawyer, *Semantics in Biblical Research. New Methods of Defining Hebrew Words for Salvation* (London, 1972) 89-91, thinks that while Barr was right to be so critical of excessive etymologising, he nevertheless did not give enough weight to diachronic semantics. For there are occasions when a word's etymology *may* be useful for deducing its meaning in a specific passage. So long as the historical (diachronic) information provided by etymological investigation remains secondary to synchronic evaluation of the particular context where a word occurs, it may be of some help. Most recently, Barr has developed his ideas about etymology in relation to Hebrew in *TPS* (1983) 41-65; and this reflects the very prominent place which etymology and comparative philology have had in the study of ancient Semitic languages. Barr explores the possibilities of a 'pan-Semitic lexicography' as a more useful way forward, in preference to the traditional lexicography of individual languages.

All three works share with the vast majority of other treatments of Ancient Greek — by classicists as well as those in Biblical studies — a disregard for the help afforded by Modern Greek (i.e., the *demotike*, rather than the *katharevousa*) for our knowledge of the ancient vocabulary. This is a case of the pot calling the kettle black, I confess; for my knowledge of modern demotic Greek — to say nothing of the dialects — is slight. It is true that a large diachronic leap is involved between the *koine* and Modern Greek; but as was mentioned above the worth of diachronic studies is once again being recognised in Linguistics, and in this case real returns have been forthcoming. Despite a time gap of nearly two millennia *koine* exhibits certain linguistic features which are more closely akin to Modern Greek than to the much less distant in time Classical dialects. The general point needs to be made, that NT philological studies are not availing themselves of the help afforded by this particular resource. Yet, considerable caution and expertise is needed in the application of Modern Greek to our understanding of the language in antiquity if it is not to lead to false results; and this is partly the reason for its not being given much attention. In the case of NT studies the linguistic contributions of A. Thumb do not deserve the neglect which they nowadays appear to receive. His *Die griechische Sprache im Zeitalter des Hellenismus: Beiträge zur Geschichte und Beurteilung der Koine* (Strassburg, 1901) is a work of enduring importance. The first essay (1-27) gives particular emphasis to the usefulness of Modern Greek for the study of the language at a much earlier stage (note also what he has to say on p.123). Among his last publications we may note particularly *CQ* 8 (1914) 181-205, a masterly lecture on the subject delivered at Manchester in 1913. (From the date of its delivery it may be inferred that he was one of those who came to Manchester for the celebration of J.H. Moulton's 50th birthday. Moulton's last surviving child, Mrs. H.H. Hollings, tells me that she was then aged 9 and still has a clear memory of the party on the lawn of Didsbury College. In particular she remembers meeting G.A. Deissmann who came across from Germany for the celebration.) Moulton himself was another who had mentioned the great potential of Modern Greek for NT work in his Manchester Inaugural Lecture (noted above), 134-36; but he had nothing independent to contribute on this score. Indeed, the preface to the first fascicule of MM (1914) gave special acknowledgement to Thumb's help in indicating words in their dictionary which still survived in *demotike*. Modern Greek as evidence for the *koine* was also drawn upon to good effect by J. Psichari, in a discussion of the Greek of the LXX included in his *Quelques travaux de linguistique, de philologie et de littérature helléniques, 1884-1928* (Paris, 1930) 1.831-91 (repr. from *REJ* 55 [1908] 161-210), especially 846, 871, 886. J.R. Harris, *ExpT* 25 (1913) 55, drew attention to the all-too-brief observations on the importance of Modern Greek for the NT made by E. Masson, in his translation of the second English edition of G.B. Winer's *A Treatise on the Grammar of NT Greek* (Edinburgh, 1860; based on the sixth German edition). It was on the basis of his knowledge of Modern Greek that Masson reached his conclusions (i, vii, viii) about the nature of the Greek of the NT, thus prefiguring Deissmann although coming at the question from a different angle. Another precursor who saw the importance of Modern Greek for understanding the *koine* was J.J. Bjornstahl (*ob.* 1779): see N.A. Bees, *BPhW* 40 (1920) 476-78.

Much more recent is G.P. Shipp's final book, *Modern Greek Evidence for the Ancient Greek Vocabulary* (Sydney, 1979), which, although unfortunately somewhat incoherently written, is a treasure-trove of both information and insight. The incoherence reflects the fact that the book was entirely recast from an original chapter arrangement to the present alphabetical word list. Thus, the book contains many discussions of NT usage (some of them short articles in themselves), but they are widely scattered. A comprehensive index to the book is a desideratum if it is not to suffer neglect (see Appendix 1, below). One other reason why the book does not make easy reading is Shipp's very laconic style: he assumes (over-optimistically) that most of the modern scholarly literature (especially work done in Greece) is familiar to his reader. To take two examples only of the potential of such a contribution: *pace* the view of N. Turner, *NovT* 16 (1974) 156 — following an earlier proposal by van Unnik — that the Semitic background is what invests παρρησία with the meaning 'unconcealment' at Jn 7.4, Shipp sees in this Johannine usage 'a specially close anticipation of Mod. Greek' (442), taking the dative there to mean 'publicly'. Shipp provides other observations (e.g., 429, 541) on Johannine language in which he detects the same process at work, lexical uses in the *koine* which have their echo in the modern colloquial language. Second, τί at Mt. 7.14 is shown by modern demotic parallels to mean 'because' (ὅτι); the case which has generally been accepted in NT circles (BAGD, s.v., 3b; Bauer[6] s.v., 3b; BDF §299(4), etc.) that it is a Semitism meaning 'how' (exclamatory) comes undone (Shipp, 533-34). Shipp also draws attention to the text of an undated bronze amulet from antiquity, *SB* 6.1 (1958) 9125, in which τί introducing a series of clauses is to be interpreted in the same way (*pace, ed. pr.*). C. Bonner, who published the text, *Hesperia* 20 (1951) 334-35, notes that there are Byzantine parallels to the incantation on the obverse, whose ten lines run as follows: λιμός σε ἔσπιρε|ν, ἀὴρ ἐθέρισεν, φλ|έψ <σ>ε κατέφαγεν· τί | ὡς λύκος μασᾶσε, τί | ὡς κορκόδυλλος κα|ταπίννις, τί ὡς λέω|ν ορωχις, τί ὡς ταῦρ|ος κερατίζις, τί ὡς δ|ράκων είλίσσι, τί ὡ|ς παρᾶος κυμᾶσε, 'Hunger sowed you, air harvested you, vein devoured you, because you munch like a wolf, because you devour like a crocodile, because you bite like a lion, because you gore like a bull, because you coil like a serpent, because you lie down like a tame creature.'

We must ask next, what extra-biblical — specifically, documentary — evidence does each work adduce and how useful does it prove to be? Although Turner acknowledges (*CW*, xi-xii) that the papyri and inscriptions do shed light occasionally on usage in the NT, his consistent emphasis is on how little they have aided our understanding of NT usage. 'The early Christians had their own form of speech and I account it to be as "sacred" in vocabulary as I found it in syntax and style' (*CW*, xi).

Turner's decision to take little account of non-literary evidence is borne out strikingly by his bibliography. Apart from the fact that editions used of classical authors are too often out of date (e.g., those of Aischylos and Menander), volumes of *BGU* are listed only up to 1933; *P.Oxy.* only to 1927 (vol. 17; in 1980, the year when his book appeared, *P.Oxy.* 47 was published). The only epigraphical corpora included are *CIG, IG, OGIS* and *SIG*[3]. The impression left with the reader is that Turner's reading of documentary texts had ceased before the Second World War. In this *CW* is closely akin to what has been noted in the previous chapter (p.50) about the non-literary sources drawn upon in his *Syntax* volume in Moulton's *Grammar*.

The fundamental flaw which vitiates his book is the claim implied throughout that the Christians invented the word if it is nowhere attested except in the NT. How fallacious this view is may be seen at a glance from his entries on (e.g.) ἀνεμιζόμενοι (119) and ταρταρόω (210). On this basis other theologically quite innocuous words, such as διϊσχυρίζομαι and ὀρθρίζω, could also be 'sanctified' as 'Christian' words but for the fact that there are now documentary attestations for each (*New Docs 1977*, **39**; *New Docs 1976*, **43**, respectively). At *NovT* 16 (1974) 151 n.1 Turner is rather more circumspect in his approach to such words. I do not wish to deny that Paul (and others, but he pre-eminently) made imaginative, figurative use of quite ordinary words. But that it was done on the scale Turner urges, and by so many writers of disparate literary skill *because* they were Christians, involves misconceiving seriously the way a writer writes unless the latter is merely eccentric.

In emphasising the debt of the NT writers for vocabulary and usage to the LXX, Turner suggests that research has moved on since Deissmann and Moulton. This is scarcely fair to the former, in particular; but more than that, Deissmann's *Bible Studies* placed special weight (x; 72) on the light that the documentary texts shed on the language of the LXX. What Turner has in fact done is ignore the debt of the LXX translators to 'Egyptian' Greek. With this we may contrast the warning note of J.A.L. Lee, *A Lexical Study of the Septuagint Version of the Pentateuch* (*SCS* 14; Chico, 1983), that 'the vocabulary that the LXX and NT have in common is less than is often supposed. In particular it is to be noted that words common to both often vary considerably in regard to their uses' (9; cf. 45). In perceiving a debt to the LXX everywhere in NT vocabulary Turner appears on occasion to choose a view which favours his desired conclusion even when the evidence is against it: so *CW*, 82, on ἀναφέρω in 1 Pet. 2.5, where Deissmann, *Bible Studies*, 88-89, is rejected in favour of the LXX as the source of the usage. Another example to illustrate this propensity in his book may be seen in his treatment of λύτρον (105-07), where he rejects Deissmann's view (*LAE*, 327-30, especially 327-28) of λύτρον in the NT being linked with its epigraphical attestations in contexts concerned with the ransoming of slaves. The basis of his response consists of an appeal to D. Hill's study of the λυτρ- word-group: *Greek Words and Hebrew Meanings* (Cambridge, 1967) 49-81. Whatever its value as a theological essay, I do not share Turner's confidence that Hill's discussion leads to reliable philological conclusions. See the comments in the final paragraph of *New Docs 1978*, **46**. At *New Docs 1977*, **58**, MM's entry for λύτρον is shown to be seriously deficient even in terms of its own time. Spicq, *NLNT*, 3.429-35, also discusses the λυτρ- words. Turner's argument thus appears to be verging upon the claim that if a word occurs in both the LXX and 'secular Greek' the former is to be preferred as the source for the NT usage. To take this last word, λύτρον, however: as Turner notes, it occurs in the LXX as a translation for several Hebrew words. But he does not address himself to the question, why the LXX translators chose this word for their version. Surely no minor factor in their consideration will have been its currency in the *koine*, to which the inscriptions bear witness. That little or no link exists between the Greek of the LXX and other *koine*-period works is the inference Turner means us to draw — I presume — from his so-frequent use of the term 'Jewish Greek'. Thus, to take merely two of the first words which he discusses, βδελυκτός/βδέλυγμα are 'most likely coined in Jewish Greek by way of the LXX' (*CW*, 2); παντοκράτωρ 'seems probably to be a coinage of Jewish Greek, for there are comparatively few secular examples apart from the magical papyri, and these show Jewish influence' (*CW*, 5). This comment on Jewish influence in the magical papyri is far too facile. W. Brashear's discussion of *P.Berl.* inv. 21227 at *ZPE* 17 (1975) 25-27 includes mention of several examples where παντοκράτωρ occurs in a non-Christian/non-Jewish context. Another instance is *I.Nikaia* II, 2 (1982) 1512, a dedication to Zeus Pantokrator (II-III); the ed.n. *ad loc.* refers to another pagan example.

A small number of other examples is listed, with comment as sparing as possible, as further illustration of the point that Turner's approach in *CW* is extremely defective. The words selected here are all of more than incidental importance in early Christian writings.

(a)   ἄγγελος (14-17): no mention is made of the *angelos* inscriptions from Thera and the extra dimension they possibly provide for our understanding of NT usage. The question of the milieu of these texts attracts brief comments in Deissmann, *LAE*, 279-280 and n.1; there is more recent treatment by M. Guarducci, in *Mélanges helléniques offerts à Georges Daux* (Paris, 1974) 147-57 — repr. in ead.,

Scritti scelti sulla religione greca e romana e sul cristianesimo (*EPRO* 98; Leiden, 1983) 60-70 — who suggests that these epitaphs indicate the pagan character of the angels carved on them. This view is at best doubtful: it is probably more appropriate to see them emanating from within a Christian milieu. Cf. *BE* (1976) 520; note also the earlier review of Guarducci's work on this material in BE (1941) 106. References to these inscriptions from Thera, together with further bibliography, are provided at *New Docs 1976*, **79**; and *New Docs 1979*, **122**, p.240 no.4. Material like this is admittedly not always straightforward to interpret. For example, A.A.R. Sheppard, *Talanta* 12/13 (1980/81) 77-100, discusses the evidence (entirely epigraphic) for pagan cults of angels in Western Asia Minor. The texts come from Caria, Lydia, Phrygia and N. Galatia. Sheppard suggests that words like *angelos* were borrowed from the local Jewish communities 'without any real understanding of their original monotheistic background' (77). It is not a situation of actual syncretism, but of 'uninformed borrowing of Jewish terms by pagans' (87; cf.93). See further the Addenda below (p.136), ad *New Docs 1976*, **5**. Recently, M. Smith has analysed *P.Berl.* 5025b (to be dated V init.) and *P.Louvre* 2391 (a century earlier), two metrical texts in *PGM*. He observes, *Stud.Clas.* 24 (1986) 175-79, that their features indicate descent from a common ancestor which may go back to mid-II. He sees both texts in general as invocations of Jewish angels by pagan magicians: 'The original text was written by a pagan who invoked these Jewish angels [Iao, Michael, Gabriel, Abrasax, and Adonai] as powerful, albeit subordinate, members of the imaginary supernatural society' (177). Further, there are instances of the term ἄγγελος occurring in a context which appears unlikely to be derivative for Judaism. At *New Docs 1978*, **6**, p.28 no.6 reference was made to *TAM* V, 1 (1981) 159 (Tarsi, east of Saittai in Lydia, 164/5; = *CMRDM* 1.69; text repr. and discussed by A.A.R. Sheppard, *Talanta* 12/13 [1980/81] 92-94 no.10) in which, after the god Men has recovered a stolen cloak, ὁ θεὸς οὖν ἐκέλευ|σε δι' ἀνγέλου πραθῆναι τὸ εἱμά|τιν καὶ στηλλογραφῆσαι τὰς δυ|νάμεις (8-11). Here, it is not to be ruled out that the *angelos* is a human intermediary. Yet *TAM* V, 1.185, referred to in the same *New Docs* section and also coming from the region of Saittai, is a fragmentary dedication in which some members of a *katoikia* give thanks to Angelos Hosios Dikaios. The association with divinity is also implicit in an unpublished inscription from Uşak — G. Petzl, *ZPE* 30 (1978) 257 n.41 — in which an activity has divine imprimatur: . . . κάθως ἡμῖν ἐδηλώθη ὑπὸ τοῦ ἀνγέλου τοῦ θεοῦ Μηνὸς Πετραείτου 'Αξετηνοῦ.

(b) ἀδελφός (56-57): Turner dismisses what he claims is the sole example of ἀ. used in a pagan religious association with the meaning 'brother'. But cf. *New Docs 1977*, **14**, where an example or two from Rhodes are given — merely the observations of that year's culling — and **60**, where the presence of other words such as μήτηρ in the context of an association adds a degree of weight to the expectation (in itself plausible anyway) that familial terminology would be employed in associations of various kinds. *New Docs 1976*, **18** may well afford further confirmation in the letter reprinted there, as does the Latin text quoted in that entry.

(c) ἐκκλησία (68-71): a particularly inferior entry. Note, e.g., the third paragraph on p.68 which reveals a surprisingly poor understanding of the 'Classical' Greek world. Turner's view of the use of this word in Acts (69, para. 1) may be quoted as illustrative of the extremity of his position (my emphasis):

> It was in St. Luke's earlier years as a Christian, while he was writing the diary which is thought
> to have been incorporated in the complete edition of Acts, that he used the word *ekklesia* in the
> secular way to which he was accustomed (Acts 19 [vv.32, 39, 41]). I presume that *his language
> subsequently suffered a change in the direction of a new dialect*, in which Christians had made
> *ekklesia* a special name for the believing brotherhood.

Turner's discussion of ἐ. illustrates clearly, too, that he makes far too little differentiation between the usage of the various NT authors (69, paragraphs 3, 4).

(d) εὐαγγέλιον (190-191): Turner notes the existence of *OGIS* 458 (Priene, 9 BC), in which Augustus' birthday is said to inaugurate *euaggelia* for the world. But 'the first Christians would not be aware of so definitive a use of the word and would be likely to avoid the association even if they were'

(190). Turner's treatment is pervaded with special pleading because he cannot escape the fact that there are 'secular' parallels. Note his first paragraph on p.191, in which the Christians are said to have rejected the option of using κῆρυξ because of its 'undesirable associations', and chosen εὐαγγελίστης which was 'untainted by pagan overtones. Early believers could not have been aware that *euaggelistes* had indeed been used of a pagan priest on a faraway inscription.' On this inscription from Rhodes see *New Docs 1978*, **2**, p.14. Turner's case depends on the transparent fallacy that if only one attestation survives the word was employed only once. For a collection of documentary instances of the εὐαγγελ- word-group see *New Docs 1978*, **2**; Spicq, *NLNT*, 3.296-306.

(e)   κύριος (257-260): here Turner appears to be endeavouring to ward off the possibility that the NT writers availed themselves of words used in contexts other than 'pure', biblical Greek. Thus he seeks to persuade the reader that a LXX background provides a 'sufficient origin' for the use of κύριος as a 'name' (*sic*) of Jesus (259):

> If the Christian title did come from Hellenistic paganism, then pagan influence seeped into the brotherhood at a curiously early stage, for the title was used in the first days of the Church — as witness St. Paul's letters to the Thessalonians. Is it conceivable that, so soon, pagan influences from Egypt were affecting a primitive and largely Jewish community?

The views embedded in this statement (e.g., the implied monolithic purity of Judaism and its imperviousness to the winds of Hellenism) take little account of the reality. To take up Turner's example, was it only Christians of Jewish origin that Paul addressed in Thessalonike? Even if Paul were consciously thinking of the LXX background, could he count on convert readers there from outside Judaism making the same link? In the first instance the sort of association they might more reasonably be expected to make is the use of κύριος (and θεός) as designations of the Caesars in inscriptions, and the occurrence of κύριος as an epithet for gods; see *New Docs 1977*, **4, 6**. It makes of Paul a very naïve 'apostle to the Gentiles', and renders the success of his mission incomprehensible, if we are to suppose that his non-Jewish converts were expected to understand his statements entirely within the framework of LXX terminology. Writing about usage in the Fourth Gospel, G.B. Caird is right, *NTS* 15 (1968/69) 275-77, to stress the role of analogy in semantic development, observing that '. . . we should hesitate before attributing to John any Greek usage, however well attested in the LXX, which he knew to be unintelligible to those whose only language was Greek' (275).

There are, of course, some exceptions to this general thrust in *CW* of playing down the possibility that extra-biblical texts may provide a significant context for the language of the NT writers. Thus, s.v. μυστήριον, Turner acknowledges (284) that 'on occasions the first Christians borrowed a term from the contemporary Mystery religions'. Cf. 404, s.v. παρουσία. Yet such concessions are all too rare in the book. At *NovT* 16 (1974) 160 Turner cautions NT researchers 'against relying overmuch on secular parallels' because of 'the uniqueness of the Biblical Greek vocabulary'. Note further the earlier statement in *ExpT* 71 (1960) 104-07, in which he says (106) that the LXX and the Church gave new meaning 'to so many old Greek words' — and these are 'key words' — 'not mere trifles about accountancy and the adulteration of milk, which is the kind of thing the papyri had illustrated'.

In sum, Turner has consistently sought over many years to revive what had been — before Deissmann — the consensus view of the nature of the Greek of the NT. It was against just such a perspective that Deissmann had argued (*Bible Studies*, 65), whereby 'the notion of the Canon is transferred to the language [of the NT] and so there is fabricated a "sacred Greek" of Primitive Christianity'. M. Silva, *Bib.* 61 (1980) 200, summarises Deissmann's position well: 'While certain peculiarities of NT Greek give it away as having been written by Semites, they are not so many that the language should be "sharply distinguished" from non-biblical Greek or "isolated" from the normal tasks of Greek philology'. This point has been stated well, too, by C.J. Hemer at *TynB* 38 (1987) 88, in a context where he is dealing with the Lydian confession inscriptions (85-89):

> . . . whereas we are accustomed to envisage the specifically theological words [of the NT] as standing in relative isolation, so that we may give free rein to interpreting them as peculiarly Jewish and Christian and as representing a Jewish or a very primitive Christian creativity, the suggestion here is rather that their rise is embedded in a much larger matrix, in which the nature of the relationship is a study in itself.

The situation is altogether different with Spicq, *NLNT.* Not only does he collect documentary evidence in a thoroughgoing manner, but he draws upon recent items no less than those long-known. (Perhaps it should be pointed out that I had not seen Spicq's vol.3 until the writing of *New Docs 1978* was complete and with the typesetter, and had no access to his vols 1 and 2 until *New Docs 1978* had actually been published.) Comparison of his treatment of the εὐαγγελ- word-group with *New Docs 1978*, **2** will illustrate this clearly. The first example of the middle verb which he cites (3.299) from documentary sources is *P.Oxy.* 46 (1978) 3313, which happens to be the papyrus letter reprinted in that *New Docs* entry. The same situation obtains if Spicq's entry on the λύτρον word-group (3.429-35) is compared with the evidence collected at *New Docs 1977*, **58** and *New Docs 1978*, **46**. Yet some caution is needed about the condition of the Greek texts he quotes: see *New Docs 1979*, **93**.

Turning, finally, to *NIDNTT*, the inclusion of extra-biblical, and particularly documentary, evidence is minimal. Because this is so consistently the pattern from entry to entry it is to be inferred that it was an editorial decision to prevent the enterprise becoming too bulky. Some exceptions occur, of course. A notable instance is to be found in the discussion of λόγος (s.v. 'Word', 3.1801-87); clearly more diverse material was included because of the importance of the term for Greek philosophy. In general, however, there is a major difference from *TDNT* in this regard, for not a few of the latter's contributors sought to give some serious attention to extra-biblical *koine* usage.

From its approach to NT vocabulary each of the works being considered can be seen as heir to a particular tradition. Whether or not Spicq, Turner, and Brown (and his team) are conscious of the link, it may be suggested that there exists for each an identifiable antecedent work. For Spicq it is the collective contribution of Deissmann and Moulton/Milligan; for Turner it is Cremer's *Lexicon*; for Brown it is *TDNT.* This case does not need to be argued in detail; for it should be strikingly obvious as soon as the identification is made. Nevertheless, some comments of a briefer kind are offered.

Spicq appears to be quite conscious of the tradition in which he stands: see first paragraph of his Preface, vol. 1.7. The work of Deissmann and of Moulton is too well-known to require detailed elucidation here. For a brief assessment of the former see ch.1 above; more will be said about the lexical contribution of the latter below, in the context of an evaluation of MM. Spicq is more explicitly theological than they; but linguistic observations are not subordinated to his theological concerns such as to affect the former. Among all their writings it is Deissmann's *Bible Studies* which provides the closest analogy to Spicq's *NLNT.* It should not be thought that Deissmann, Moulton, and Milligan were the only three substantive contributors earlier this century to NT lexicography. As merely two further examples, we may note, first, T. Nägeli's *Der Wortschatz des Apostels Paulus* (Göttingen, 1905), which draws considerably upon papyrus and inscriptional evidence in its discussion of Pauline vocabulary (see especially 12-58). His brief contribution, like that of Deissmann and his British friends, is all the more impressive in the light of subsequent work when it is realised that, by the time his work appeared in 1905, the first three volumes of *BGU*, and four of *P.Oxy.*, were all that had appeared from these now-large series. Nor had Dittenberger's *OGIS* been published, to name merely one important epigraphical anthology. Nägeli certainly made excellent use of what was available to him. Rather different in conception is L. Schlageter, *Der Wortschatz der ausserhalb Attikas gefundenen attischen Inschriften. Ein Beitrag zur Entstehung der Koine* (Strassburg, 1912). This dissertation (supervised by A. Thumb) contains useful lists of words found in inscriptions and also attested in literary texts, including the NT.

Cremer's *Lexicon* is nowadays less well-known; the English translation (of the fourth edition, 1895) of Cremer was last reprinted in 1954, so far as I can discover. J. Kögel produced a revised German edition, the eleventh, in 1923. It would be well-nigh forgotten today but for J. Barr's critique of it in his *Semantics of Biblical Language*, especially 238-44, including discussion of Kögel's influence as subsequent editor of Cremer's *Lexicon* upon G. Kittel. J.W. Voelz, *ANRW* II.25.2 (1984) 905-06, offers brief comment on Cremer and his influence; cf. Cotterell/Turner, *Linguistics and Biblical Interpretation*, 106-09. With Turner, *CW*, it is unclear to me how fully he perceived his antecedents, although his desire to 'turn the clock back' to the pre-Deissmann era is unmistakable. Though different in its outward form from a lexicon such as Cremer's, Turner's book reflects a similar commitment to attributing to primitive Christianity a serious and widespread conscious influence upon the Greek language in its creation of a special vocabulary, distinctive syntactical features, etc. In this formulation of their position the critical word is 'conscious'. Turner's grammatical and lexicographical work is pervaded by the belief that from the outset Christians deliberately eschewed certain words, and searched out others which they could employ more comfortably. While every writer is always making choices about which word to use, this is presented by Turner as something distinctive of the early Christians, as if they had an agreed and coherent language policy before any of them began to write. Undoubtedly there are words which were coined by NT writers, and others which developed as technical terms within the NT and ECL: any in-group requires its own jargon. But to see it in Turner's terms is quite inappropriate. In this connection mention may also be made of F.W. Gingrich's article in J.M. Myers, *et al.* (edd.), *Search the Scriptures. NT Studies in Honor of R.T. Stamm* (Leiden, 1969), 173-78. His turns of phrase reflect an approach very similar to Turner's, e.g., '. . . the NT takes a great many words commonly found in classical Greek, and turns them in a direction which is distinctively Christian' (173); *agape* 'was seized upon by the Christians and employed to designate their highest virtue' (174). That Gingrich had not developed in his way of thinking about such questions is clear when this last quotation is compared with his earlier, very similar statement at *JBL* 73 (1954) 190. Even granting that there are new coinages and new uses, that does not constitute these words as 'Christian' words. The writers were simply writers — who happened to be Christians — trying to express their ideas, not consciously inventing a Christian vocabulary. The critical test is whether a NT writer can be shown to have invented/selected a word *because* he was a Christian. I doubt whether this can ever be demonstrated, but in any case it seems Turner has never addressed himself to this question. Cremer devised his work before papyrus discoveries had begun to occur in any numbers, and therefore before Deissmann had shown their value to NT philology; and though Kögel accommodated the *Lexicon* to reflect these new finds, he nevertheless continued to justify Cremer's method. In his unwillingness to appreciate the value of the documentary finds for the context of the language of the NT, Turner shows himself to be at one with the pre-Kögel editions of Cremer. This attempt to revert to the approach taken a century ago, in the face of both the documentary evidence and Barr's critique of Cremer, exemplifies the extremity of Turner's position. (It may be that I have missed some references, but I have noticed mention of Barr's contribution only once in all Turner's work which

I have read: *Grammatical Insights into the NT* [Edinburgh, 1965] 2-3. The paragraph reads almost as though Turner considers that he and Barr are in considerable agreement. Some comment on Barr might have been expected in the introduction to *CW*, but he is passed over in silence.)

Once we move into the Patristic period, there is undoubted evidence for new coinings of words (particularly compounds) as a response to the needs of the theological debates which occurred. Yet as M. Harl has pointed out, *JTS* 14 (1963) 406-20 (especially 408-09), the use of asterisks beside many words in Lampe's *Patristic Greek Lexicon* may give an impression of a greater degree of linguistic innovation by Christian writers than is the reality. The purpose of the asterisk in Lampe is simply to signal words not in LSJ[9]; but many of them may also occur in non-Patristic texts which fall outside Lampe's scope.

The potential danger of a blinkered acceptance of a special Jewish/Christian vocabulary may be illustrated by a different example. J. Amstutz's study of the ἁπλότης word-group has much of interest in it; but its very subtitle — ΑΠΛΟΤΗΣ. *Eine begriffsgeschichtliche Studie zum jüdisch-christlichen Griechisch* (*Theophaneia* 19; Bonn, 1968) indicates the prior assumption that there may have been something distinctive about this Greek. While Amstutz is correct to say that Hellenistic Jewish and early Christian use of these words differs from the classical sense of 'single', etc., there is no discussion of other attestations contemporary with the Jewish and Christian material which might have served as a control for his thesis. Spicq, *NLNT* 1.125-29, includes some documentary instances of ἁπλῶς which, however, lack the moral denotation. Yet MM, s.v. ἁπλοῦς *ad fin.*, long ago drew attention to an instance of the adjective in a sense which does parallel the 'Jewish/Christian' use. That important inscription (*IG* II². 1366 = *CMRDM* 1.13) concerning the cult of Men in Attika (Sounion, II/III) was reprinted at *New Docs 1978*, 6; the adjective occurs at *l.*12, 'may the god be merciful to those who serve him with a pure soul', ἁπλῇ τῇ ψυχῇ. The adverb occurs at *l.*26 in very similar wording. The moral integrity or sincerity of the adherent is the characteristic being looked for. The mere fact that we have this documentary example alone — to my knowledge — does not mean that the attestation can be discounted. Its very existence indicates that such a denotation was current in the *koine* contemporary with the alleged late Jewish and early Christian development of the word. The natural conclusion to draw is that its presence in the *koine* explains how it came to be adopted by the LXX translators and early Christian writers. That they may have used it more frequently with this denotation — at least, so far as our surviving sources indicate — does not constitute an argument that they developed the meaning themselves.

Though Brown does not allude to *TDNT* in his Prefaces, yet it is unimaginable that associations with *TDNT* were not in his mind, or at least in the mind of the German editors, given their choice of the term 'Begriffslexikon' in their title. Inclusion of the relevant *TDNT* articles is a virtual *sine qua non* in the bibliographies appended to each entry in *NIDNTT*. It is patent that the criticisms of *TDNT* by Barr in his *Semantics* have not been taken to heart by those responsible for *NIDNTT*. (Barr was discussing *TWNT*, of course, but for the sake of consistency in this survey I continue to refer to the faithful English translation of the German original.) True, in the preface to *NIDNTT* vol.1 Brown refers to Barr's book with approval, acknowledging the dangers of linguistic 'illegitimate totality transfer' and etymologising. These constitute only two of the points in Barr's armoury, and only the latter occurs in his chapter devoted to *TDNT*. Together with 'the prevailing unsatisfactory system of classifications of meaning', these matters constitute three 'serious misconceptions' affecting lexicographical work in Biblical Studies, according to E.A. Nida, *JBL* 91 (1972) 84-87. In the light of the subsequent 2900 pages of *NIDNTT* these two paragraphs in Brown's preface in fact appear to be no more than a superficial attempt by the Dictionary to guard its flank against potential criticism that the

implications of Barr's critique of *TDNT* have been ignored. *NIDNTT* is not alone in this course
of action: we may compare Hill's *Hebrew Words and Greek Meanings*, noted above. Remove the
'protective encasing' of the first and last chapters and the rest of that book gives no hint that
Barr's work has had any effect on that author's approach to his word studies. This weakness in
Hill's monograph is patent even without digesting the observations in Barr's own review article,
Biblica 49 (1968) 377-87.

In *NIDNTT* we find perpetuated the same confusion between 'word' and 'concept' upon which
Barr had laid considerable stress as a vitiating factor in the linguistic worth of *TDNT*. (Cotterell/
Turner, *Linguistics and Biblical Interpretation*, summarise clearly Barr's critique of *TDNT* [115-
23, and more broadly, 106-28], but refer only briefly to *NIDNTT*.) It should be noted that Barr
was at pains to stress that his criticism applies at the point of philology. This focus emerges again
in the critique of Cullmann, Robinson and others in his *Biblical Words for Time* (London,
1969[2]). At *Biblica* 49 (1968) 386 he allows that the later volumes of *TDNT* do give evidence of
some changes for the better in linguistic method. In *NIDNTT* the word/concept confusion is
most obviously revealed when the bibliographies appended to each entry are scanned:
philological studies of words are included along with studies of (usually theological) ideas. As
merely one specific example of a word entry we may cite 'Gospel' (*NIDNTT* 2.107-15). Its
opening discussion succumbs to the 'etymologising fallacy', *tout court*. For the confusion of
word/concept we may quote from p.108:

> It is not difficult to trace the connection between this religious use of the word *evangelion* in
> the Hel. world, especially in the imperial cult, and its use in the NT. The latter takes up a term
> widely used in the Hel. world and loaded with religious concepts, when it speaks of its own
> *evangelion* or *gospel*. At the same time the OT roots of the NT concept of *evangelion* must
> not be ignored.

Or again, p.109:

> When the LXX was translated, this concept of the messenger of glad tidings and his powerful,
> effective word was no longer understood, and the meaning was weakened . . . Neither Philo
> nor Josephus takes up the concept of the messenger of glad tidings as found in Isa. in their
> use of *evangelion* and *evangelizomai*. They use the words in the normal Hel. sense . . . They
> do not therefore contribute anything further to our understanding of the NT use of these
> terms.

And again, p.110 (after remarking on the fact that the Johannine books do not use this verb or
noun):

> It would be a mistake, however, to assume that because certain NT writings do not use the
> vb or noun, the thought expressed by them is therefore completely lacking. In the Johannine
> writings, for instance, the concept is expressed by terms like *martyreō* . . . and *martyria*.

As a final instance from this entry we may compare the first sentence of the final paragraph on
p.110 with the first sentence of the first paragraph on p.111:

> There is good reason to believe that it was Paul who established the term *evangelion* in the
> vocabulary of the NT . . . In Paul *evangelion* has become a central concept of his theology.

This approach is not found in every article, by any means, nor indeed often in quite so blatant
a form as in the example instanced here.

An example may be given of a different kind of weakness which the *NIDNTT* shares with *TDNT*. In the latter a number of articles were co-authored. This occurs on a much more extensive scale in *NIDNTT* because the latter is not only a translation of the German original (like *TDNT*), but has also been considerably revised and expanded (unlike *TDNT*). When two or more writers contribute a part each to an entry there is always the potential for some information to be treated by neither, each assuming it will be handled by the other. One minor philological example from *NIDNTT* must suffice here. The entry 'cry' (1.408-12) has discussions of κράζω by D.A. Carson and of βοάω by C. Brown. Neither attempts to discuss the extent of semantic overlap of these words in the *koine*. Further, the etymologising derivation of κράζω — onomatopoeic, 'reflecting the cry of a raven' (408) — is implicitly allowed to have too much weight (in my judgement) for *koine* usage. Naturally, contributors of such entries are not to be held responsible for the use or misuse that readers may make of their material. But to discuss s.v. κράζω not only ἐπιφωνέω but also κέλευσμα has at least the potential to engender some misapprehending of the meanings of these words. Carson does seek to differentiate the three words in question, but the problem is symptomatic of a larger flaw in the whole undertaking: the decision to use English head-words to discuss Greek terms, and thence Christian theological ideas. This point applies as well to the entirety of Turner, *CW*. Undoubtedly, *NIDNTT* is designed for use primarily by those with no ancient language skills; but there are far too few warning signals provided for such users to help them be alert to quite basic questions, such as the fact that an English word may represent several different Greek words in different contexts, and vice versa. For example, will many users who lack Greek simply expect to find s.v. 'cry' a discussion of 'weep'? In fact, this does not occur s.v. 'weep' for which there is no entry, but s.v. 'lament' (2.416-24), a decidedly high-level — if not obsolescent — word in English, selected, presumably, because it has a 'biblical ring' to it. The potential to mislead will always remain in dictionaries of this sort; and though the very fine indexes at the end of vol.3 and in vol.4 will in practice help users find their way about in *NIDNTT*, it is those very Greekless readers, in need of the index constantly, who will be most at the mercy of the entries. Thus, though the *NIDNTT*'s comparative neglect of classical and non-biblical/non-Jewish *koine* usages (both literary and documentary) may reflect editorial policy, in order to save space, or on the ground of the priority of synchronic linguistic studies over those that are diachronic (see above, p.69), yet the lack of provision of a *balanced* context against which to study NT word use may only confirm readers in the belief that 'Biblical Greek' is a distinct entity with an existence separate from other Greek.

Let it not be concluded that the value of *NIDNTT* is here suggested to be minimal. No comment is offered here on its theological discussions; and — even leaving aside the great merit of attempting conscientiously to popularise recent work in the discipline — there are unquestionably useful insights in many articles. But in its attempt to discuss theological ideas starting out from an analysis of individual words, the *NIDNTT* is firmly espousing the approach of *TDNT* which has been shown a generation ago to be philologically wanting. Thus in M.J. Harris' appendix, 'Prepositions and Theology in the Greek NT' (3.1171-1215), 'attention is focused on some uses of the major prepositions which are judged to be theologically significant'. Earlier, B.F.C. Atkinson's *The Theology of Prepositions* (London, 1944) was even more extreme in its treatment. It is highly dubious, in my opinion, to suggest that such function-words as prepositions (or conjunctions) could ever bear a semantic weight which qualifies them as 'theologically significant'. Their main role is 'to mark the relationships between content words, phrases and clauses' (J.P. Louw/E.A. Nida, *Greek-English Lexicon of the NT based on Semantic Domains* [New York, 1988] I.vi). While on the subject of prepositions, a useful recent contribution on 'improper' prepositions in the LXX and contemporary *koine* is R. Sollamo,

Renderings of Hebrew Semiprepositions in the LXX (Helsinki, 1979); cf. her earlier article, *VT* 25 (1975) 773-82. Note also J.J. Hessinger, *CP* 73 (1978) 211-23, whose study of prepositions in Greek argues that their use as true prepositions is primary: they were not originally adverbs or preverbs in function. The investigation of prepositions, and whether certain adverbs gradually acquired a new grammatical status as prepositions, has the potential to be enriched by recent linguistic work on grammaticalisation. For example, in S. Axmaker *et al.* (edd.), *Proceedings of the Fourteenth Annual Meeting of the Berkeley Linguistics Society, February 13-15 1988* (Berkeley, 1988), E.C. Traugott offers (406-16) a number of examples where a word has gained a new grammatical function apparently to strengthen the informativeness of what the speaker wishes to say. This pragmatic shift for the sake of clarity may occur particularly (though not solely) where a non-native speaker, for lack of awareness of the correct usage he needs, employs a known word in a way different from the current norm, the effect being to give it a new grammatical function. Traugott's examples include the shift from 'hwilum' ('at times') to temporal 'while' to concessive 'while' ('although'); temporal 'since' acquiring a causal function; and the development of the spatial markers 'before' and 'after' into markers of time. Investigation of the grammaticalisation of a multi-function word like ὡς could provide an illuminating study of this process. Research such as Traugott's reflects the renewed emphasis being given to diachronic studies in Linguistics.

Just after the German predecessor to *NIDNTT*, the *Begriffslexikon zum NT*, was brought to completion in 1971, G. Friedrich published a long, theoretical paper outlining the need for such a work, in which he laid out various possible concept domains for the NT: *NTS* 19 (1973) 127-52. He is right that alphabetically-arranged dictionaries do not provide all the answers that a researcher may need; and he properly emphasises the danger of etymologically-based interpretations in a work like *TWNT* (to which he had made no minor contribution) because of its arrangement on the basis of word stems. It may be said that in this respect at least *NIDNTT* is not altogether heir to *TDNT*, since the former groups words of similar meaning which are not always etymologically related.

This provides the opportunity to note the appearance after many years of preparation of what is by far the most innovative Greek lexicon with such an orientation, the two-volume Semantic Domains lexicon of Louw and Nida referred to just above. The theoretical approach for this dictionary was laid out for other linguists in their article in W. Cole (ed.), *Current Issues in Linguistic Theory* (Bloomington, 1977), 139-67. Since this work does not concern itself explicitly at all with any extra-NT evidence such as the documentary texts which are the primary concern of the present book, brief comments only are offered. The lexicon, whose data-base is the entire UBS[3] text (including variants noted in the apparatus), focuses on the related meanings of different words. These meanings are indicated by definitions, not simply by glosses as in traditional dictionaries. The editors accept that although the NT contains words and phrases with specialised meanings, 'it is not a distinct form of Greek, but . . . typical Hellenistic Greek' (I.xvi). This contribution by Louw and Nida will not replace historical dictionaries, nor is it intended to; for its goal is different. In general, they have provided a most useful ancillary tool for NT philological research, which draws upon recent linguistic work in lexicography. Yet it will not answer everyone's questions about the language of the NT. To take simply one example, if we allow the editor's point (I.xv) that there are 'no synonyms' in a language, what is it that differentiates two nouns like ῥαφίς and βελόνη in the Synoptic parallel passages (Mk 10.25 = Mt. 19.24, and Lk. 18.25 respectively)? Louw/Nida do not address this question (I.79, no.6.215), though I take it that the difference is one of linguistic register: βελόνη is higher style (cf. Shipp, *Modern Greek Evidence*, 143-45).

* * *

In the light of the foregoing, two conclusions may be proffered: that the application to NT linguistic research of the contribution of Barr merits renewed attention, and that the increasing interest in the Semitic background of the NT has led to a diminution of interest in the Greek documentary sources.

1. Barr's *Semantics* appeared over a quarter-century ago; yet despite the widespread recognition of its importance it has not had the impact upon NT vocabulary studies which it deserves. (Only passing acknowledgment of the importance of Barr's work appears in J.W. Voelz, *ANRW* II.25.2 (1984) 930 n.221.) Is his contribution to be seen with hindsight as a failure? No, for there have been attempts to rectify linguistic method in Biblical studies, as he himself has pointed out in the postscript to the second edition of *Biblical Words for Time*. Yet whether there has been a real change of atmosphere, or a more superficial attempt to grapple with the problem, is harder to decide. In my judgement Barr's case needs to be restated, in the light of the last generation's work in NT philology. But this restatement needs to be done by someone else, since Barr's polemical approach has been used almost as an excuse for some to ignore the important issues at stake when he particularised his criticisms by focusing on works like *TWNT* or T. Boman's *Das hebräische Denken im Vergleich mit dem griechischen* (Göttingen, 1954²). For example, in an essay which contains a number of otherwise useful insights, O.A. Piper says that the remarks of Barr in *Semantics* were 'so biased and so thoroughly tinged by his positivistic views that no serious refutation was undertaken' (*Festschrift to Honor F.W. Gingrich*, edd. E.H. Barth/R.E. Cocroft [Leiden, 1972], 192). Granted that Barr is somewhat 'one-eyed' in his approach, it was nevertheless a necessary — and to date the only thoroughgoing — critique of Kittel, *TWNT*. Yet to ignore Barr's work because it reacted so strongly is not satisfactory in itself; nor is it sometimes, I suspect, more than an excuse for the discomfort of NT students. For Barr's critique appears to have made many aware of their own 'lack of depth' liguistically. After a generation enough heat has surely gone out of the controversy for a 'serious refutation' of Barr to have emerged if one were to be attempted. Perhaps the best attempt is G. Friedrich's long review of the German edition of Barr's *Semantics*, in *TLZ* 94 (1969) 801-16; *TWNT* and Kittel are defended, while Barr is taken to task for the extremity of his views, which are suggested to be over-influenced by American structuralism. Friedrich provides some interesting observations, but what he writes falls well short of a refutation of Barr's position. While there will undoubtedly be need for modification in details, the latter's general thesis seems irresistible. I would have thought that NT studies cannot afford *not* to build upon the start which Barr has initiated to rescue it from linguistic isolation and the possibility of being stranded in a cul-de-sac. The danger of a similar situation for Classics appears to be becoming slightly more remote in recent years. For although Classical Philology had for nearly half a century since de Saussure largely turned its back upon modern linguistic theory, on the ground that in its move away from historical to descriptive work the latter had little to offer languages which are no longer spoken, some important publications by European and British scholars in the last twenty years testify to the beginnings of a rapprochement. The renewed appreciation by linguists of the contribution of diachronic studies has encouraged this trend. On this question see Appendix 2, below.

2. *NIDNTT*'s down-weighting of extra-biblical/non-Jewish usage has the effect of aligning that dictionary roughly with Turner's work, in which low value is placed upon the usefulness of documentary evidence. Both works reflect the trend which has been occurring in NT studies for well over a generation, to give greater prominence to the Semitic background of

the NT. In part, this is an inevitable 'swing-of-the-pendulum' reaction against the emphasis earlier this century on the Graeco-Roman milieu in which Christianity had its beginnings; and the Qumran finds provided a particular catalyst. Now, this reconsideration of the relative weighting to be given to Graeco-Roman and Semitic elements contributing to the origins of Christianity has resulted in some important gains. One of these is a rethinking of how hellenised the Jews were. Easily the most productive historical contribution here has been M. Hengel's *Judaism and Hellenism* (ET: London, 1974). One consequence has been a strong spill-over effect into NT philology, leading to the renewed investigation of the influence of Semitic languages upon the Greek of the NT. Since the Second War the best-known such study is M. Black's *An Aramaic Approach to the Gospels and Acts* (Oxford, 1967[3]); and many have joined this wave of research. As one among many recent contributions there may be mentioned here only K. Beyer, *Semitische Syntax im NT*, I.1 (Göttingen, 1968[2]). This has been well received, I gather; yet it strikes me — a confessed amateur in Semitics — as an exercise in overkill: a voluminous amount of detail (*c.*200 pages on conditional clauses alone) for a surprisingly slight result. See further ch.1 above, p.31. Nevertheless, Beyer's work has proved a stimulus to others, e.g., E. Pax, *SBF* 13 (1963) 136-62.

One effect of this development has been that the contributions of Deissmann, of Moulton, and of others earlier this century have been seriously down-valued. Examples of this trend include Piper, in *Festschrift . . . Gingrich*, 191-92; and G. Friedrich, *TDNT* 10 (1976) 646-53. The earlier, influential dictionary article by J. Vergote, 'Grec biblique', in *Dictionnaire de la Bible*, Suppl. vol.3 (1938) 1320-69, gives considerable attention to the work of Deissmann and Thumb and the reaction against them. For the views of J. Ros, *De Studie van het Bijbelgriecksch van Hugo Grotius tot Adolf Deissmann* (Nimwegen, 1940) see ch.1 above, p.39. Deissmann and Moulton's separate and various demonstrations from papyrus and inscriptional finds that the Greek of the NT formed an integral part of the *koine* is in danger of being neglected. Bauer's *Lexicon* in concert with the complete MM appear to have satisfied the large majority of those in NT studies that the documentary texts are not likely to throw up much more of use for their work. Cf. the quotation from a letter of Moulton to Rendel Harris, given above, p.65. That this is not the case is amply demonstrated in the four previous volumes of *New Docs*. They reflect the reading of four years' publications: since the entire culling task and most of the writing has been done by one individual some idiosyncrasies in selection are inevitable, as is also the likelihood that some items of interest to NT work have been missed. But whatever their imperfections in this regard — let alone in other ways — they do at the very least indicate that there is a wealth of new primary material of relevance to NT philological studies and early Church History being published year by year. The *New Docs* volumes are set firmly in the tradition of Deissmann and Moulton, and thus have close affinities with Spicq's work. An important difference from the latter, however, is that Spicq's orientation is theological, whereas the lack of any such thrust in *New Docs* has been intentional.

It is not by chance that this pair of names, Deissmann and Moulton, has been frequently conjoined in the present volume. Not only did they see eye-to-eye on the academic question of the nature of the Greek in the NT. They were able to admire each other's contribution without envy, as is evident from Deissmann's proposal of an honorary doctorate to be conferred on Moulton by Berlin University in 1911, and Moulton's securing a like award by Manchester for his German colleague the following year (C.E. Bailey, *HTR* 77 [1984] 198-99). More than this, they had developed a firm friendship which transcended the outbreak of the War (ibid., 215, where it is noted that they met in 1915 at Bern). It may be mentioned in passing that Bailey's interesting study (195-221) of the response of British Protestant theologians to Germany in the First War gives considerable, though not disproportionate, attention to Moulton. The article is somewhat flawed by a too-simple distinction of people's positions as 'conservative' or 'liberal'; Moulton is pigeon-holed as the latter (202). Further, Moulton's pacifist views and his move away from that stance were more complex than Bailey allows. In suggesting that he 'compromised' his position (221), 'overwhelmed by the enormity of Germany's "bad faith"' (211), Bailey fails to take into account the personal sufferings of Moulton. In a short succession of years his elder daughter died, then his wife in 1915, and finally his elder son Ralph was killed on the Somme in 1916. The effect of Ralph's death appears to have exercised a particular influence in his shift from pacifism, as I have gathered from discussions in Sydney with Moulton's sole surviving child, Mrs H.H. Hollings.

*   *   *

This second conclusion leads us to our next question. Turner's work has been criticised above on the ground that he seeks to revert to a nineteenth-century view of the Greek of the Bible. But what of *New Docs*? Is it also 'turning the clock back', in this case to the Deissmann/Moulton approach? If *New Docs* is making a new contribution within this tradition of scholarship, in what does the contribution consist? In seeking to answer this some comments on MM are in order. A useful evaluation of that work was published by C.J. Hemer, *NovT* 24 (1982) 97-123; and it is not intended here to retread that ground. But some additional things need to be said, and observations developed further from that article.

In *An Analysis of the Lexicographical Resources used by American Biblical Scholars Today* (Missoula, 1972), J.E. Gates reports (12-13) that, after BAG, MM was the most frequently-consulted lexicon (taking a very broad definition of that term), ranging from high occasional use to a much lower rate of regular use. The proportion was very similar to the use of LSJ. A new lexicon of *koine* papyri and inscriptions is one of the three specialised lexica for which he identifies a need (130). On Gates' contribution see F.W. Danker, *SBL Seminar Papers* 24 (1985) 235-41. It has been claimed that MM was useful in its time but quickly became 'superannuated by the increasing volume of newly discovered papyri' (Piper, *Festschrift . . . Gingrich*, 177). I have put the point rather differently in *Biblica* 65 (1984) 395, suggesting that in Biblical Studies MM 'is in the unfortunate position of being accorded greater authority than it now deserves . . .' The welter of publications of inscriptions and papyri since MM (and especially since the 1960s) makes this inevitable. C.J. Hemer's posthumously-published article in *TynB* 38 (1987) 65-92 is a wide-ranging essay which considers in general how to nuance the question, What (if anything) is special about the Greek employed by the NT writers? After consideration of various linguistic questions and emphasis on the epigraphical evidence, he concludes (89-92) with a brief resumé of a conference held at Princeton in late 1985 which considered the need for a new MM. More germane in the present context, however, is it to ask a couple of questions of MM itself, in order to take it on its own terms.

1. What is not in MM?

(a) Entries omitted

Of some 6,150 words in very round figures occurring in the NT, I have counted (by checking against BAGD) 1,035 for which MM has no entry at all (see Table 1).

TABLE 1
NT WORDS OMITTED BY MM

I letter	II no. of words omitted	III no. of words in *col*.II which are *v.l.*/*t.r.*	IV no. of words in *col*.II which are proper nouns (incl. adj./adv. forms)	V total of *col.* II less *cols* III + IV
A	226	35/3	62	126
B	48	4/1	27	16
Γ	26	2.5/0.5	14	9
Δ	67	15/1	10	41
E	146	33/2	25	86
Z	13	3/-	7	3
H	11	-/-	8	3
Θ	31	5/-	7	19
I	37	1/-	32	4
K	90	17/5	28	40
Λ	18	2/-	11	5
M	32	4/1	15	12
N	20	-/2	15	3
Ξ	-	-/-	-	-
O	18	3.5/0.5	3	11
Π	71	22.5/4.5	9	35
P	17	4/-	11	2
Σ	88	22/7	25	34
T	26	5/1	8	12
Y	12	2/-	-	10
Φ	16	2/3	5	6
X	12	1/-	5	6
Ψ	9	-/-	-	9
Ω	1	-/-	1	-
TOTAL	1035	183.5/31.5*	328	492

* Half-score means one word attested as both *v.l.* and *t.r.* only

The tally in *col*.II of this table includes words for which there is no separate entry, even if those words are discussed under another word-entry, e.g., ἀδιαλείπτως, s.v. -τος; ἀσφαλῶς, s.v. -λής; θεῖον, s.v. θεῖος. I count only 32 such instances, and in some of these no documentary attestations are adduced anyway (e.g., ἁγιωσύνη and ἁγνισμός, both s.v. ἁγιάζω). It may be mentioned that of these 32 words 14 occur under the letter A, 7 are spread across B-Δ (these were the first two fascicules, produced in Moulton's lifetime), with only 11 for the remaining portion of the alphabet. This is consistent with the inference drawn below (p.85) about Milligan's concern to have a separate entry for every word. The only letter for which there are no omissions is Ξ. Of the 1,035 words for which MM is lacking an entry, 215 occur in the NT only as *v.l.* or *t.r.* (see *col*.III). The total for *v.l.* is 183.5, and for *t.r.* 31.5, the half-scores being due to the occurrence of one word as both a *v.l.* and in *t.r.* only. Letters for which there are no omissions in this regard are H, Ξ, Ψ, Ω. As *col*.IV shows, a further 328 are proper nouns (including adjectival and adverbial forms). Letters for which there are no proper noun omissions are Ξ, Y, and Ψ. Even if these two groups were disregarded — MM is very haphazard, including some examples, not others — this leaves a tally of 492 NT words for which an entry is entirely lacking (*col*.V), say, 8% of the NT vocabulary.

(b) Words for which MM provide no documentary parallel
This, after all, was the rationale for their Dictionary, to offer documentary parallels to the NT under the stimulus of the papyrus finds. Here I have counted a total of 800 words in whose entry

no documentary attestation is given (see Table 2). The tally includes entries where the only quotation is from *literary* papyri (e.g., Bacchylides, Menander, Herondas). Milligan refers to the decision to include such evidence in the Prefatory Note to the complete, one-volume edition (p.v).

TABLE 2
NT WORDS IN MM FOR WHICH NO DOCUMENTARY PARALLEL IS PROVIDED

I letter	II no. of words lacking doc. reference	III no. of words in *col.*II which are *v.l./t.r.*	IV no. of words in *col.*II which are proper nouns (incl. adj./adv. forms)	V total of *col.*II less *cols* III + IV
A	96	-/-	2	94
B	20	-/-	2	18
Γ	9	-/-	-	9
Δ	36	3/1	4	28
E	84	2/-	2	80
Z	4	-/-	-	4
H	3	-/-	-	3
Θ	10	-/-	-	10
I	23	-/1	13	9
K	64	3/1	10	50
Λ	15	-/-	6	9
M	47*	1/2	6	38
N	18	1/-	6	11
Ξ	2	-/-	-	2
O	38*	1/1	1	35
Π	130*	2/1	7	120
P	18*	-/1	3	14
Σ	82	1/2	14	65
T	26*	1/-	2	23
Y	27*	1/-	1	25
Φ	24*	-/-	6	18
X	15*	-/-	4	11
Ψ	6	-/-	-	6
Ω	3*	-/-	-	3
TOTAL	800	16/10	89	685

* This total is larger than that for the corresponding letter in Table 1, *col.*II.

Included in this tally are all instances where for a verb (for example) MM can only provide a documentary citation with a related noun or a compound form of the verb. Items where the reading is in considerable doubt are also included (e.g., ἀντιπέρα, ἀπατάω, ἀποτολμάω — but see BAGD on all these). The total would be lowered only slightly if entries were excluded from the count where MM say, e.g., 'We are unable to quote the word from papyri before vi/A.D.' (s.v. διακονία), or where they acknowledge the existence of documentary attestation but quote no examples (e.g., s.vv. Ἀσιάρχης, δεκαοκτώ, θυγάτηρ). Of these 800 words, 26 are *v.l.* (16) or *t.r.* (10) only: see *col.*III. *Col.*IV indicates that another 89 are proper nouns (including adjectival and adverbial forms). Even if these two groups are subtracted, a total of 685 remains, say 11% of the total NT vocabulary.

As is shown by the presence of an asterisk in *col.*II, for the following letters the total number of words for which no documentary reference was provided (category (b)) is greater than those lacking an entry altogether (category (a)): M, O, Π, P, T, Y, Φ, X, Ω. Moulton had died well before the Dictionary was half-way complete — in fact, only the first two fascicules (A-Δ) can be fully said to have been jointly authored; fasc.iii appeared in late 1919 — and my impression is that Milligan chose increasingly to provide a parallel from documentary texts which contained *related* lexical forms rather than the actual word, and attestations from *koine* literature (especially

Jewish), rather than have no entry at all. This observation receives confirmation from the point mentioned above, that there is a clear trend in the last six fascicules (E-Ω) of the Dictionary to avoid dealing with related words under one entry.

Even if we work with the minimised totals in (a) and (b) above — i.e., 492 and 685, respectively — it is obvious that

(i) MM's inclusion of nearly 700 entries for which it contributes nothing germane to its subject (namely, illustrating specific NT vocabulary from documentary sources) has the misleading effect of conveying the impression of a greater comprehensiveness than is the reality; and

(ii) its exclusion of entries for *c.*500 words leaves a constant query in the user's mind: was the omission due to inability to find a documentary parallel, or to mere oversight (as in the case, presumably, of πεντάκις: cf. *New Docs 1977,* **106**, p.191)?

2. Are there irrelevant inclusions in MM?

(a) Non-NT words

MM supply a small number of entries for non-NT words. I count 38 of which 10 are *t.r.* only (see Table 3).

TABLE 3

NON-NT WORDS FOR WHICH MM SUPPLY ENTRY

NT *t.r.* (only)	10*
LXX	13
Other Greek OT versions	2
ECL	5
no explicit reason/other	8
	38

* Where an entry mentions both *t.r.* and LXX, this is included in the tally for *t.r.*

Of these 38, 13 are included solely because they are found in the LXX. How these words came to be included is easy to see. In the preliminary studies which were done for the Dictionary, Moulton — later in collaboraton with Milligan — collected a large number of documentary parallels to NT lexical usage: *The Expositor,* ser. vi, 5 (1901) 271-82; 7 (1903) 104-21, 423-39. Though these articles set out to make known to a theological readership his grammatical gleanings published in *CR* in 1901 and 1904 (see below), they are largely lexical gatherings. These three pieces are of especial interest because in them Moulton's research focus can be seen to be drifting towards lexicography. Note his comment at 7 (1903) 423, for example: 'To examine the vocabulary of the papyri was not my object when I began reading them, and I have never made any systematic effort to do so.' The 'systematic effort' began after a gap of some years, when the sequence of these three articles was revived by Moulton beginning his collaboration with Milligan. 'Notes from the papyri, I-III' were continued as 'Lexical notes from the papyri, IV-XXV', beginning in The *Expositor* ser. vii, 5 (1908) 51-60. In pp.51-53 Moulton explains that the amount of new material persuaded him of the need of a co-worker. It is with this article that the systematic alphabetical listing of lexical items starts. In fact, there were more than 25 articles in the series, for two pieces were numbered XVIII — ser. vii, 10 (1910) 89-96, and 282-88 — and another two numbered XXI — ser. viii, 1 (1911) 284-88, and 380-84. The series remained incomplete, judging by the final article, ser. viii, 4 (1912) 561-68, whose last entry deals with ὑποστέλλω. The more than 250 pages in this extensive series help us to appreciate how fascicules i and ii of MM could appear in such quick succession (May 1914, and Oct. 1915). But for the War the entire undertaking may well have been brought to completion by the end of that decade.

Impressive, too, are Moulton's grammatical studies in *CR* 15 (1901) 31-38, 434-42; 18 (1904) 106-12, 151-55, which cover all sorts of features: accidence, syntax, morphology, orthography. In conjunction with his more discursive series of ten articles in *The Expositor* ser. vi, vols.9-10 (1904), entitled 'Characteristics of NT Greek', these tightly-packed articles serve as preliminary studies for his *Grammar*, disclosing his mastery of detail together with a recognition of the need to treat all facets of *koine* grammar. The combination of this very solid groundwork along with his very readable style in the *Grammar* helps us appreciate more clearly why the *Prolegomena* volume was, and is, so good.

Looked at as a whole the series of lexical articles is impressive indeed; it is also revealing of how Moulton and Milligan cast their net for the data which eventually found their way into the Dictionary; on this point cf. Hemer, *NovT* 24 (1982) 115. Among their preliminary gleanings most of the 38 non-NT words (noted in Table 3) are to be found. There is no gain in listing them all; merely three instances are given: ἀναχρονίζω, *Expositor* ser. vii, 5 (1908) 270; δεκανός (out of alphabetical order in MM), ibid., ser. vi, 7 (1903) 110; ὑπερευχαριστέω, ibid., 121. It is clear from the preface to fasc. i of MM (not preserved in the complete Dictionary) that such inclusions were consciously decided upon, not mere inadvertent slips.

No doubt, the idea to produce a dictionary was Moulton's own, but at what point was the notion conceived? Examination of Moulton's correspondence (deposited in the John Rylands University Library, Manchester, I understand) may resolve this little curiosity one day. It would be intriguing to discover how much Deissmann influenced him to gather the piecemeal notes into a coherent volume; for he regarded Moulton as the most productive contributor to NT philology in the early years of the century, stating that it was now time for him to embark upon 'ein *opus vitae*' (*TRu* 9 [1906] 220).

(b) Inclusion of documentary examples which do not illustrate NT usage

I have no detailed figures to offer here: they could not be provided accurately without every quotation in MM actually being checked. Furthermore, we are brought rapidly towards the difficult question of language levels, which received brief attention in chapter 2 above. For a few scattered examples of citations which MM themselves acknowledge do not illustrate NT usage we may note ἐθνικός, ἐκδοχή, ἐντροπή, ἐπίθεσις, παραβολή.

*   *   *

What do *New Docs 1976-1979* contribute in these spheres? Listed below are 60 words for which these volumes provide documentary attestation (or comment on its absence) but which either lack a separate entry in MM (a), or for which MM's entry adduces no documentary parallel (b).

ἄγρα (a): *New Docs 1978*, **4**.

ἀδιαλείπτως (a), see MM, s.v. -τος: *New Docs 1977*, **95**, p.153, notes a papyrus whose reading is heavily restored. About a dozen examples in Spicq, *NLNT*, 1.41-43.

αἰών (b): *New Docs 1979*, **16**, p.58.

ἄκακος (b): *New Docs 1979*, **102**, item (c).

ἄλαλος (a): *New Docs 1979*, **54**.

ἀμέμπτως (a): *New Docs 1979*, **39**.

ἄμωμος (a): *New Docs 1978*, **11**, p.41.

ἀνασῴζω (a): *New Docs 1979*, **41**.

ἀντίτυπον (b): *New Docs 1979*, **12**, p.42.

ἀντίτυπος (a): *New Docs 1979*, **12**, pp.41-42.

ἀρρωστέω (a), *v.l.* only in NT: *New Docs 1977*, **82**.

ἀσιάρχης (b): *New Docs 1979*, **14**; cf. *New Docs 1976*, **32**.

ἀσφαλῶς (a): see MM s.v. -λής: *New Docs 1978*, **1**. Several examples in Spicq, *NLNT*, 3.74-78.

ἀφθονία (a), *v.l.* only in NT: *New Docs 1976*, **27**.

γενεαλογέω (a): *New Docs 1976*, **5**, p.29.

γέν(ν)ημα (b): cf. *New Docs 1977*, **34**.

γνόφος (b): *New Docs 1979*, **43**.

διανύω (b): *New Docs 1976*, **26**, p.77.

διάστημα (a): *New Docs 1979*, **20**.

διϊσχυρίζομαι (a): *New Docs 1977*, **39**; cf. *New Docs 1978*, **36**.

ἐκσῴζω (a): *New Docs 1979*, **58**, p.153.

ἐξολοθρεύω (b): *New Docs 1978*, **64**.

ἑπτάκις (b): *New Docs 1979*, **54**.

εὐλογέω (b): *New Docs 1979*, **56**.

εὐνοῦχος (b): *New Docs 1978*, **11**. (One late [VI] Christian papyrus is quoted in MM; even apart from its date it may not provide independent testimony to NT usage.)

εὐωχία (a): *New Docs 1979*, **1**.

θεῖον (a), see MM, s.v. θεῖος: *New Docs 1978*, **39**.

θυσιαστήριον (a): *New Docs 1977*, **110**, p.197, largely restored in a Christian text. Cf. Turner, *CW*, 8-10.

ἱλασμός (b): *New Docs 1978*, **6**, p.25. (MM provide three late [VI¹] Christian attestations; cf. Turner, *CW*, 26-27. The comment on εὐνοῦχος above applies here too.)

κανών (b): *New Docs 1976*, **9**.

κατασκηνόω (b): *New Docs 1978*, **89**, p.106 (Christian text).

κηδεύω (a): *New Docs 1979*, **6**, p.28.

Κίλιξ (a): *New Docs 1979*, **87**.

μακαρίζω (b): *New Docs 1979*, **11**.

μεγαλοπρεπής (b): *New Docs 1977*, **85**, p.109. Spicq, *NLNT*, 2.543-47 has numerous examples at 544 and nn.2, 3.

μελετάω (b): *New Docs 1977*, **82**.

μισθαποδοσία (a): *New Docs 1978*, **49** mentions that no documentary attestation is yet known (cf. Turner, *CW*, 368).

νηστεία (a): *New Docs 1976*, **84**, p.133, where it is noted that the particular attestation does not illustrate NT usage.

ὀρθρίζω (b): *New Docs 1976*, **43**. The two documentary citations provided rebut the suggestion of H.S. Gehman, *VT* 3 (1953) 147, about this word; cf. Winer, *Grammar of NT Greek* (1882³), who mentions ὀρθρίζω as his first example of words in the *koine* which were 'coined by the Greek-speaking Jews or the NT writers themselves . . .' (27). See the useful comment in J.A.L. Lee, *A Lexical Study of the Septuagint Version of the Pentateuch* (*SCS* 14; Chico, 1983) 46.

παραλυτικός (b): *New Docs 1978*, **55**.

παράλυτος (a), *v.l.* only in NT: *New Docs 1978*, **55** mentions that no documentary attestation is yet known.

παραπλησίως (b): *New Docs 1977*, **57**. Cf. Spicq, *NLNT*, 2.664, who says cautiously that it 'ne semble pas jamais attesté dans les papyrus'.

παροράω (a): *New Docs 1976*, **19**.

πλησμονή (b): *New Docs 1979*, **6**.

πορισμός (b): *New Docs 1979*, **79**.

πρεσβῦτις (b): *New Docs 1976*, **79**.

προευαγγελίζομαι (b): *New Docs 1978*, **2**, p.14, mentions that no documentary attestations are known.

προκυρόω (a): *New Docs 1979*, **82**.

προστάτις (b): *New Docs 1979*, **122**, p.243.

πρωτοστάτης (b): *New Docs 1979*, **122**, p.244, whose instances are nevertheless not true parallels to the more generalised sense found in the NT.

Σαμαρίτης (b): *New Docs 1976*, **69**, p.110.

σητόβρωτος (b): *New Docs 1976*, **26**, p.77.

σκήνωμα (b): *New Docs 1979*, **85**.

σκώληξ (a): *New Docs 1978*, **65**. Cf. Turner, *CW*, 368.

συμμερίζω (b): *New Docs 1979*, **86**.

Ταρσεύς (b): *New Docs 1979*, **87**.

τεκνόω (a): *New Docs 1979*, **65**.

τετραπλόος (-οῦς) (b): *New Docs 1977*, **23**. Spicq notes documentary examples at *NLNT*, 2.866 nn.2, 4.

τύχη (a): cf. *New Docs 1976*, **16**.

φιλόθεος (b): *New Docs 1977*, **79**; cf. *New Docs 1978*, **6**, p.28.

This list does not include the numerous items which improve on MM's entries by citing more examples to add to the one or two which many MM entries have. For example, MM s.v. ἀρχισυνάγωγος quotes or refers to four epigraphic attestations, one of which is uncertain because of the amount of restoration. At *New Docs 1979*, **113** some 40 certain or probable instances are listed, together with another 14 which are considerably less definite attestations. In the Addenda to volumes 1-4 included later in the present work a further example is noted, s.v. *New Docs 1979*, **113**, p.214. The total number of MM entries which receive comment and supplementary documentation in the first four volumes of *New Docs* is *c*.280 (there is also a considerably smaller number of comments concerned solely with the entries in BAGD or LSJ[9]). Furthermore, the list above does not include items which merely improve on MM by citing texts closer in time to I AD. These instances by no means constitute all such items contained in the texts quoted in *New Docs*. It should not be doubted that another eye and mind would have noticed other examples worth recording. Allowing for words that are treated more than once within the four volumes, *c*.1200 Greek words receive some comment. Spicq treats *c*.175 of these, Turner, *CW*, *c*.100. Yet the point to be made here is not how many words are receiving this illustration, but that the flow of new publications — no mere trickle — continues to offer much of benefit to NT lexicography. By my count Spicq provides documentary parallels for the following words which have either (a) no entry in MM or (b) an entry but no documentary attestation cited:

(a) ἀδιαλείπτως, ἀδόκιμος, αἰσχροκερδῶς, ἀμέμπτως, ἀναστρέφω, ἀνάψυξις, ἄντλημα, ἀσφαλῶς, ἀτάκτως, δυσκόλως, ἐπιποθέω, εὔσπλαγχνος, καύχημα, μωραίνω, μωρία, ὑστέρημα — a total of 16;

(b) ἀλαζονεία, ἐξαγοράζω, ἐπιούσιος (the example he adduces is tenuous, as he acknowledges; on this word see now C.J. Hemer, *JSNT* 22 [1984] 81-94, rebutting Turner, *CW*, 98-100), ἐριθεία, εὐδοκία, ἱεροπρεπής, μεγαλοπρεπής, ὀθόνη, πειράζω, περικάθαρμα (a possible example only), ταπεινόω, τάραχος, τετραπλοῦς, τυφόω, ὑπόκρισις, ὑπομονή — a total of 16.

It may be observed that *New Docs* has turned up 60 such instances in the culling of four years' publications (though where texts published earlier have been brought into the discussion they have yielded some of these items), as against Spicq's 32 instances gleaned from all previous publications. This suggests that there remain many items of interest for NT lexicography as yet unnoticed in past publications; for there is no reason to think that the years 1976-79 have thrown up an atypically rich sample of finds.

Now, *New Docs* is not tied so strictly to MM, nor even to the NT, that comment on LXX, ECL and other material is excluded. One instance of this is the registering of hitherto unattested words as they turn up in newly published papyri and inscriptions. In the four volumes well over two dozen of these are noted in the index of Greek words. The noting of these 'new' words is merely a *parergon* in *New Docs*; no item has been picked up which had not already been perceived to be new by the first editor of the relevant text, or by a later commentator. For more comprehensive addenda to LSJ[9] and its *Suppl.* see J.A.L. Lee, *Glotta* 47 (1969) 234-42 (on LXX material); T. Drew-Bear, *Glotta* 50 (1972) 61-96, 182-218 (epigraphical annotations); S.S. Tigner, *Glotta* 52 (1974) 192-206 (pre-Platonic cosmological vocabulary); S.B. Aleshire/J.B. Bodoh, *Glotta* 53 (1975) 66-75 (verb-forms needing correction in LSJ); R.J. Durling, *Glotta* 57 (1979) 218-24, 58 (1980) 260-65, 59 (1981) 108-16, 60 (1982) 236-44 (all on Galen); and R. Renehan, *Greek Lexicographical Notes. A Critical Supplement to the Greek-English Lexicon of Liddell-Scott-Jones* (2 vols; Göttingen, 1975, 1982). While Renehan concentrates upon literary authors, some documentary items are included. A revision of LSJ is planned. The first two fascicules (α-ἀλλά, ἄλλα-ἀποκοινώνητος have appeared of the new *Diccionario Griego-Español* (Madrid, 1980,1986), which aims to include non-literary evidence on a greater scale than LSJ has been able to do. Its editors have published a group of useful essays, covering historical questions and dealing with practical problems: F. Rodríguez Adrados, et al., *Introducción a la lexicografía griega* (Madrid, 1977).

A useful contribution of a different kind is A. Cameron, *AJP* 52 (1931) 232-62, in which he draws attention to the general neglect accorded by lexicographers to Latin words taken across into Greek. Drawing his evidence from inscriptions of the Eastern Empire, he addresses the question, how to determine whether a Latin word has been really borrowed by Greek as opposed to being a 'temporary intruder' (232). A long list of words (including several found in the NT) and attestations comprises most of the article (237-62). Relevant to this subject is H.J. Mason, *Greek Terms for Roman Institutions. A Lexicon and Analysis* (*American Studies in Papyrology* 13; Toronto, 1974), which does not altogether supersede D. Magie's *De Romanorum iuris publici sacrique vocabulis sollemnibus in Graecum sermonem conversis* (Leipzig, 1905), as certain very critical reviews have pointed out.

In one important respect *New Docs* redresses an imbalance visible throughout MM and, through its influence, in Biblical lexicography and philology more generally ever since. It was the papyrus finds which sparked off Deissmann's work, and then Moulton's. But whereas the former continued to pay much attention to epigraphical resources — the even balance between papyrological and epigraphical evidence is very noticeable in *Bible Studies* and *LAE* — inscriptions are drawn upon relatively slightly in MM. The preface to fasc. i (not included in the preface to the final one-volume work, and so largely lost to sight) makes clear that they look to others to supplement their epigraphical gleanings.

> Students will see at once that we have dealt very differently with the various sources of vernacular Common Greek. The record of New Testament words in the non-literary papyri is intended to be given with fullness, though in the case of very common words we have not sought to be exhaustive where practical purposes are not served. The inscriptions are quite another matter. To deal with their material on anything like an adequate scale appeared to us hopeless. But we have used some easily accessible collections as carefully as possible; and we have cast our net fairly wide for illustration. Specialists in later Greek epigraphy will certainly be able to supplement our articles with riches we have been unable to quarry. And if our book prompts work of the same kind in this still wider field, no one will rejoice more than we.

MM did of course draw upon publications which drew explicit links between inscriptions and the language of the NT. And, as Moulton himself observes in his 1906 Manchester Inaugural Lecture (noted above), since inscriptions come from all over the Greek world they 'give us invaluable help in showing the essential homogeneousness of the world-language as spoken in widely distant countries' (134). Three items may be mentioned here, each of which made the epigraphical remains of Asia Minor its focus in order to pursue the question, what bearing this material has on the NT. G. Thieme, *Die Inschriften von Magnesia am Mäander und das NT* (Tübingen, 1905), is a Heidelberg dissertation written under Deissmann's supervision. While it includes some discussion of orthography and morphology, over half this short work (pp.14-38) addresses itself to vocabulary and syntax questions. It is a useful model of the fruitfulness of such work, concentrated as it is upon the epigraphy of one city, and illustrating the value of covering a range of grammatical features. Little needed to be said about syntax in this case because E. Nachmanson's *Laute und Formen der magnetischen Inschriften* had only just appeared (Uppsala, 1903). A few years after this J. Rouffiac published *Recherches sur les caractères du grec dans le NT d'après les inscriptions de Priène* (Paris, 1911). Clearly Thieme's monograph served as a model for Rouffiac, who similarly dealt with the evidence which Priene's inscriptions provided about *koine* orthography, morphology, vocabulary and idiomatic uses. But he also shows interest in onomastics (87-92) *à propos* the NT (specifically Rom. 16), a subject accorded discussion in the following chapter of the present work. In between Thieme and Rouffiac came W.H.P. Hatch's short article in *JBL* 27 (1908) 134-46, which drew upon some of the finds made in Asia Minor by J.R.S. Sterrett in the 1880s. All three works are now superseded, at least in the sense that their material has been incorporated into MM and BAGD. Why has there been virtually nothing relating to the NT since? These three works really reflect the tail-end of the 'saeculum inscriptionum' (Thieme's phrase, p.1), which overlapped with the start of the 'saeculum papyrorum'. J. Vergote's article on Biblical Greek in *Dictionnaire de la Bible*, Suppl. vol. 3 (Paris, 1938) mentions (1329-30) two other much earlier works (by Walch in 1779, and Sturz in 1808) which used inscriptions in relation to the Greek Bible. Note now, however, F.W. Danker, *Benefactor: Epigraphic Study of a Graeco-Roman and NT Semantic Field* (St. Louis, 1982), a volume with much learning spread through the notes which nevertheless makes a not altogether satisfying attempt to establish the semantic field of terms concerning benefaction in Graeco-Roman antiquity and the implications of this for NT study.

Thieme's distinction noted above may have seemed a neat one, but must not be pressed. It constitutes a positive response to the burgeoning number of papyrus publications; in no way could it have been intended to imply that the flow of new inscriptions was drying up. Of the *c*.30,000 documentary texts read for *New Docs 1976-79*, the proportion of inscriptions to papyri (taken to include ostraka and parchment fragments) which receive comment (whether detailed or in passing) is more than 3:1. The actual count is *c*.1500 inscriptions, and *c*.475 papyri. The word 'documentary' is used here loosely to mean texts written on stone, papyrus, wood, lead, pottery, etc. Literary survivals on these materials are part of the count (e.g., papyrus and parchment fragments of the NT and LXX). This was not so much a conscious policy to rectify MM's imbalance as a simple reflection of the proportionate amount of material being published. Deissmann's observation, made in the course of a running review of new books relevant to the language of the Greek Bible at the point where he deals with epigraphical grammar and Thieme's contribution, is worth quoting (*TRu* 9 [1906] 221):

Wahre Schätze direkter und indirekter Erkenntnis liegen überhaupt in den kleinasiatischen Inschriften für den Neutestamentler verborgen; man sollte das über der Fülle der Belehrung durch die ägyptischen Papyri nicht vergessen: dem Neuen Testament steht Kleinasien immer noch näher, als Aegypten, wenn auch die landschaftliche Differenzierung der Koine in den Randgebieten des Mittelmeerbeckens nicht eben sehr bedeutend war.

It is not often realised that, in terms of its authors' original conception, MM as we have it remains incomplete. In the preface to the first fascicule Moulton and Milligan state (5) their intention to complete the dictionary in six parts (in fact, eight were required): 'A concluding part will, we hope, present not only the addenda which new publications and continued reading will make necessary, but also *some systematic survey of results*' (my emphasis). While the addenda provided by Milligan in the completed one-volume edition are quite perfunctory, what is really missed is some attempt to tie together the massive harvest of lexical detail which they garnered. The extended discussions of certain words in the *New Docs* volumes were not included with this lack consciously in mind. But taken together, a number of these entries — such as the discussion of φιλοστοργ- words at *New Docs 1977*, **80**, or of προστάτις at *New Docs 1979*, **122** — reflect an awareness that something more needs to be provided than a catalogue of attestations.

This chapter may be rounded off with the claim that the *New Docs* series, independently of Spicq, calls attention to the neglect of Greek documentary sources for illustration of the language, and especially the vocabulary, of the NT. It is not merely that the great work of Deissmann and Moulton deserves to be re-appreciated, but that their work should be carried forward in NT philological studies.

*   *   *

EXCURSUS

Three observations on documentary evidence referred to in BAGD

Any full analysis of the second English edition of Bauer's Lexicon (BAGD), which appeared in 1979, is quite beyond the scope of the present discussion. This new English edition is based on the fifth German edition (1958), together with additions incorporated by the American editors. *New Docs 1976-79* provides comment on a number of BAGD entries, mostly the addition of documentary references. Occasionally, the definition in BAGD is queried, e.g., *New Docs 1976*, **82**, pp.129-30, on σχολή. (On the possibility that the word may mean 'synagogue' at Acts 19.9 see P. Wexler, *REJ* 140 [1981] 123-24, 133.) Further, comment is offered at *New Docs 1977*, **1**, p.8, about the inclusion of bibliographical references to the secondary literature. Since, however, *New Docs* is concerned with non-literary material, three specific observations are offered here which bear on BAGD's use of such evidence. All three are stated baldly; the first two are adumbrated in *New Docs*.

1. The unhelpfulness of the general rubric in so many entries, 'inscr., pap., LXX . . .', is transparent; cf. *New Docs 1977*, **1**, p.8. Here again the question of stylistic genre and level of 'literariness' in documentary texts confronts us (see chapter 2, above). Given the date when they began to be produced, it is not surprising that the standard dictionaries like LSJ, MM and Bauer were insufficiently alert to this linguistic question. But future revisions and editions of these works cannot but address this matter seriously.
2. The problem for any large dictionary of achieving consistent forms of reference to the same ancient text, and consistent dating of it, is noted at *New Docs 1978*, **6**, p.26, and at *New Docs 1979*, **113**, p.220. This point applies to MM and LSJ no less than to BAGD.
3. The use of 'MM' at the end of BAGD entries is misleading. Its function appears to be to indicate to the reader that BAGD has culled MM's entry *and* that MM provides documentary references for the word in question, whether or not BAGD provides specific

citation of these. That this is not consistently the case can be seen if the two dictionaries are compared for the following sample of entries: ἀκροβυστία, ἀκρογωνιαῖος, ἀλαζονεία, ἀλοάω (MM provides documentary parallels only for the related noun), ἀμαθής (ditto), ἀνατάσσομαι, ἀνεκδιήγητος, ἀνεμίζω, ἀνεξεραύνητος, ἀνεπαίσχυντος, ἀνθρωποκτόνος, ἀντιμετρέω, ἀντιμισθία, ἀντιπαρέρχομαι, ἀποδιορίζω (MM provides documentary reference for simple verb only), ἀποκάλυψις, ἀποκαραδοκία. BAGD does not add 'MM' merely because MM has an entry for the word, if the latter provides a general comment only. Thus 'MM' does not occur at the end of BAGD's entries for, e.g., ἀνεξιχνίαστος, ἀπαρτί. In both of these MM entries a documentary parallel is lacking. Conversely, BAGD occasionally omits to include 'MM' where it would be appropriate to have done so (i.e., when MM does have a documentary parallel), e.g., ἀκμήν, δικαίως (see MM, δίκαιος, *fin.*), δυσκόλως (see MM, δύσκολος, *fin.*), ἐκκακῶ (see MM, ἐνκ-), Εὐοδία.

Behind each of these observations is a question of methodology of some importance. The third point, for example, exemplifies the problem of one lexicon being dependent for part of its word-gathering on the authority of another dictionary, even though the latter is rather dated. BAGD does, of course, include many references to particular inscriptions and papyri which appeared after MM was completed. When a new edition of this Lexicon appears the present edition needs to be combed very thoroughly to pick up such minutiae and to resolve inconsistencies in order to avoid misleading and confusing the user. Bauer's single-handed achievement was so great that the rectification of such matters is owed to his memory as much as to future users.

A sixth German edition of Bauer's *Wörterbuch* has now appeared (Berlin, 1988), edited by K. Aland/B.Aland. Unfortunately, I have seen a copy too late for more than minimal comment. The slight change in the subtitle — 'und der übrigen urchristlichen Literatur' has become 'und der frühchristlichen Literatur' — signals the major new contribution of this edition. By greatly increasing the coverage for the Apostolic Fathers and by covering the Apologists too (some 70 new authors are culled), the new editors have rendered a signal service. Furthermore, there is increased citation of apposite passages; this has been made possible by new typesetting which makes each entry extremely compact while nevertheless ensuring considerable variety for the eye. In content, though not in length, the dictionary has been expanded by one-third. However, given the availability of *EBB*, *NTA* and other bibliographical series for NT studies, and since it is not possible to include in dictionary entries all the relevant modern literature (let alone keep these data up to date), it might have been hoped that for a new edition of Bauer all the secondary references would be deleted to make room for the citation of more ancient parallels (not merely references to them). Although the Foreword (p.viii) to the new *Wörterbuch* addresses this question, perusal of the entries themselves reveals how much secondary literature is still featured. If we sample the letter Γ, for which Bauer[6] has 129 entries, 31 items include some reference to modern literature. The most recent I have noted was published in 1979, but far more commonly references are to publications which appeared much earlier in the century. Naturally, there is value in providing this information; but the question comes down to the best use of available space in a lexicon. Concerning the NT itself, the *Wörterbuch* is now based on the text of N/A[26] and UBS[3]; and more detail is given about variants. As for documentary texts, reference is made to Spicq, *NLNT* at the end of the relevant entries. But the list of epigraphical and papyrological corpora (pp.xviii-xx) includes nothing which appeared later than the 1960s, with much older publications predominating.

5

A FISHING CARTEL
IN FIRST-CENTURY EPHESOS

In the very year that MM first appeared in the complete, one-volume edition, J. Keil, *JÖAI* 26 (1930) Beiblatt *cols.*48-57 (fig.24), published an inscription from Ephesos which has been undeservedly neglected. This well-preserved *stele* (1.91H x .81B x .31D m.), found *in situ* in the SE corner of the harbour area at Ephesos, has much of interest to illustrate the context of first-century Christianity, for it concerns an association of fishermen. Even more, it is of very considerable significance for its onomastic content. The following discussion includes a consideration of the onomastic 'mix' among the members of the group, and of the significance of this as an analogy to the names of those associated in some way with Paul in the NT. At the risk of clumsiness, the translation below latinises Roman names, while Greek names retain Greek orthography. Of Neronian date (54-59), this long text contains over 60 lexical items (some of which occur several times) which would be included in a new MM. Keil published the main face (side A), and simply listed in a note those names on side B which he could read. The entire text has now been published by H. Wankel in *I.Eph.* Ia (1979) 20 (pl.20, showing side A only); and that version is reproduced here. (Note, however, that most abbreviations have been resolved.) I understand that the projected *I.Eph.* Ib, intended to provide a commentary on the texts in Ia, will not appear. Although this inscription has been picked up in a number of places in LSJ[9], we may note that ἐξευρίσκω (side A.67) occurs here in a sense not offered there; and that lexicon lacks altogether an entry for προσκαταφέρω (A.10-11).

side A

]εφισι[
[Ν]έρ[ω]νι Κλαυδίωι Καίσαρι Σε[βα]στῶι
Γερμανικῶι τῷ αὐτοκράτορι κ[αὶ Ἰουλίᾳ]
Ἀγριππείνη Σεβαστῆι τῇ μητρὶ αὐτ[οῦ]

    5   καὶ Ὀκταουίᾳ τῇ γυναικὶ τοῦ αὐτοκράτορος
καὶ τῶι δήμωι τῶι Ῥωμαίων καὶ τῶι δήμω[ι]
Ἐφεσίων οἱ ἁλιεῖς καὶ ὀψαριοπῶλαι τὸν
τόπον λαβόντες ψηφίσματι ἀπὸ τῆς πόλεως
τὸ τελωνῖον τῆς ἰχθυϊκῆς κατασκευάσαν-
  10 τες ἐκ τῶν ἰδίων ἀνέθηκαν. οἵδε προσκατή-
νενκαν εἰς τὸ ἔργον κατὰ τειμήν·

Πόπλιος Ὀρδεώνιος	Ἕσπερος Δημητρί- δη(νάρια) κε´
Λολλιανὸς σὺν γυναικὶ	ου μετὰ τῶν υἱῶν·
καὶ τοῖς τέκνοις κίον(ας) δ´·	Κό(ϊντος) Λαβέριος Νίγερ δη(νάρια) κε´
15 Πόπλιος Κορνήλιος	μετὰ τοῦ υἱοῦ·
Ἀλέξανδρος τοῦ ὑπαί-	Εἰσᾶς Ἑρμοχάρεως δη(νάρια) κε´
θρου στρῶσαι λίθωι	μετὰ τῶν υἱῶν·
Φωκαϊκῶι πήχεις ρ´·	Γάϊ(ος) Φούριος μετὰ δη(νάρια) κε´
Τιβ(έριος) Κλαύδιος Μητρόδω-	τοῦ υἱοῦ·

20 ρος σὺν γυναικὶ καὶ τοῖς
τέκνοις κείονας γ´
καὶ στρῶσαι τὸ τετράσ-
τυλον τὸ παρὰ τὴν στή-
λην λίθωι Φωκαϊκῶι·
25 Πό(πλιος) Γερελλανὸς Μελλεῖ-
τος κείονας β´·
Εὔπορος Ἀρτεμιδώρου
κείονα α´ καὶ δην(άρια) ιβ´·
Φιλοκράτης Ἀπελλᾶ
30 σὺν τοῖς τέκνοις
κείονα α´ καὶ δην(άρια) ιβ´·
Λεύ(κιος) Ὀκτάουιος Μάκερ
μετὰ τῶν ἀδελφῶν
κείονα   α´·
35 Πό(πλιος) Ἀνθέστιος Ποπλίου
υἱ[ὸς] κείονα   α´·
Ὀνήσιμος Ἀπολλωνίου
καὶ Διονύσιος Χαρει-
σίου κείονα ποικίλον·
40 Πό(πλιος) Κορνήλιος Φῆλιξ
σὺν Κορνηλίᾳ Εἰσίωι
κείονα   α´·
Σεπτούμιος Τρόφιμος
μετὰ τῶν τέκνων κίονα·
45 Ἡρακλείδης Ἡρακλίδου
τοῦ Ἡρακλείδου δην(άρια)·
Ἐπαφρᾶς Τρυφωνᾶ με-
τὰ τοῦ υἱοῦ κεραμίδας τ´·
Πό(πλιος) Νάιουιος Νίγερ μετὰ
50 τῶν τέκνων δην(άρια) ν´·
Πό(πλιος) Οὐήδιος Οὐῆρος
μετὰ τοῦ υἱοῦ δην(άρια) ν´·
Λεύ(κιος) Φαβρίκιος Τοσίδης
μετὰ τοῦ υἱοῦ δην(άρια) ν´·
55 Πό(πλιος) Κορνήλιος Φιλισ-
τίων μετὰ τοῦ υἱοῦ δην(άρια) ν´·
Λε(ύκιος) Ὀκτ[ά]ουιος Ῥοῦφος
μετὰ τῶν υἱῶν δην(άρια) ν´·
Τρύφων Ἀρτεμιδώρου
60 δηνάρια   λζ´·
Εἰσᾶς Ἀρτεμιδώρου δη(νάρια) λζ´·
Ἄτταλος Χαριξένου
Ἀμαξᾶς μετὰ τοῦ υἱοῦ δην(άρια) λ´·
Ἐπικράτης Ἀντιόχου   δη(νάρια) λ´
65 Κρουκρᾶς μετὰ τῶν υἱῶν·
Ἰσᾶς Ἰσιδώρου δη(νάρια) λ´·

Μᾶρ(κος) Οὐαλέριος Φρόν-   δη(νάρια) κε´
των μετὰ θυγατρός·
Ἀρτεμίσιος Λεσβίου δη(νάρια) κε´·
Πό(πλιος) Σαβίδιος Ἀμέθυσ-   δη(νάρια) κε´
τος μετὰ τῶν υἱῶν·
Ἱέραξ Ἑρμοκράτου   δη(νάρια) κε´
σὺν γυναικί·
Δίδυμος Θευδᾶ δη(νάρια) κε´·
Δημήτριος Δημη-   δη(νάρια) κε´
τρίου Κηναρτᾶς·
Ξάνθος Πυθίωνος β
πλίνθους·
Φόρβος παραφύλαξ α
πλίνθους·
Σεκοῦνδος παραφύλαξ α
πλίνθους·
Μᾶρ(κος) Ἀντώνιος Βάσσος
μετὰ τῆς θυγατρὸς τῶν
στοῶν τὰς ὀλένας πάσας·
Συνέρως Κλεάνα-   δη(νάρια) κ´
κτος μετὰ τοῦ υἱοῦ·
Οὐετλῆνος Πρῖ-   δη(νάρια) κ´
μος μετὰ τοῦ υἱοῦ·
Γν(αῖος) Κορνήλιος Εὔ-   δη(νάρια) ιε´
νους μετὰ παιδίου·
Ἄτταλος Ἀττάλου   δη(νάρια) ιε´
τοῦ Κασιάδου·
Διογένης Διογέ-   δη(νάρια) ιε´
νου μετὰ τοῦ υἱοῦ·
Οὐεττίδιος Νεί-   δη(νάρια) ιε´
κανδρος σὺν υἱοῖς·
Γάϊος Ῥωσκίλιος   δη(νάρια) ιε´·
Ζώσιμος Γαΐου Φουρίου   δη(νάρια) ιε´·
Βάκχιος Εὐφροσύ-   δη(νάρια) ιε´
νου μετὰ τῆς μητρός·
Λού(κιος) Οὐιτέλλιος   δη(νάρια) ιε´
μετὰ τοῦ υἱοῦ·
Λού(κιος) Κώνσιος Ἐπα-   δη(νάρια) ιε´
φρόδειτος·
Ἀριστέας Ἀριστο-   δη(νάρια) ιε´
βούλου μετὰ τοῦ υἱοῦ·
Ῥουφίκιος Φαῦστος   δη(νάρια) ιε´·
Πό(πλιος) Λείουιος   δη(νάρια) ιε´·
Ἀντίοχος Ψυχᾶς   δη(νάρια) ιε´
μετὰ τοῦ υἱοῦ·
Χάρης Χάρητος   δη(νάρια) ιε´
μετὰ τῶν υἱῶν·

ἐργεπιστατήσαντος καὶ ἐξευρόντος τὴν κατασκευὴν
τοῦ ἔργου Λευκίου Φαβρικίου Οὐιταλίου τοῦ καὶ ἀνα-
θέντος ἐκ τῶν ἰδίων μετὰ τῆς ἰδίας γυναικὸς
70 καὶ τῶν ἰδίων θρεπτῶν κείονας β΄ τοὺς παρὰ τὸ Σα-
μοθρᾴκιν σὺν τοῖς ὑποκειμένοις βωμοῖς.

side B

[ ]τραθ[
[. . .]ανε[
[. . . .]οσ[
[   ]λιος Ε[
5 [   ] δη. [
[   ]υμενος Ἑρμη[σία-]
[να]κτο[ς] μετὰ μητρὸς [δη.]
[Ἀ]ντιμήδης Μητροδ[ώρου]
μετὰ υἱοῦ   δη. [ ]
10 [Φ]ιλωνᾶς Εἰδᾶ   δη. [ ]
[Ὀ]ρδιώνιος Λαῖνος με[τὰ]
[υ]ἱοῦ   δη. [ ]
[.]αλιος Μουντᾶνος [δη.]
[Π]ολύβιος Τρύφω[νος   δη.]
15 [.]ου[δη.]
[.]αιλιος Λέσβιο[ς   δη.]
[   ]
[.]δ . ρανοπ[
[.]ατιο[ς
20 [Δ]ιονύσ[ιος
[. . . .]σιφ[
[. . . .]τερ[ος Φι]λοφίλου [δη.]
[. . . .] Λόλλιος Ἀρούντιος [δη.]
[. . . .] Λικίννιος Ναύκληρ[ος δη.]

25 [. . .]ις Ἐπαφρᾶς   [δη.]
[. . . .] Ποπίλλιος Ἑρμᾶς   [δη.]
[. . . .]κιος Κωλιοθήρας   [δη.]
[Τύρα]ννος Τρύφωνος   δ[η.]
[. . . .]ερως Σηκρῆτος   δη. [ ]
30 [. .]ας Θιάσου   δη. ε΄·
[. .]μος Φιλωνᾶ   δη. ε΄·
[. . . .] Ἀπολλωνίου   δη. ε΄·
[. . . .]λαος Διοφάντου δη. [ ]
[Λ]εύ(κιος) Στάκιος Γραφικὸς [δη.]
35 [Πο]μπώνιος Στατηρι[
[Ὀνή]σιμος Ἑρμησιάνακ[τος δη.]
[Οὐ]αλέριος Ἄνεκτος δ[η.]
[Μ]ᾶρκος Ὀνέρις [δη.]
[Ἑρ]έννιος Καλλίνικ[ος δη.]
40 [Κ]λώδιος Τύρανν[ος   δη.]
[Ἀ]ντώνιος Ῥουφ[
[. .]λ . ουριος καὶ[
Φ[ίλω]ν Φιλωνίδ[ου δη.]
[Ὀ]νήσιμος [
45 [Π]αυλῖνος [
[Π]ονπώνιος Ἐπαφρό[δειτος δη.]
[Ε]ὔτυχος Φυγέλου [δη.]
[Κ]ορνήλιος Πεῖος [δη.]

side A

To Nero Claudius Caesar Augustus Germanicus the Imperator, and to Julia Agrippina
5 Augusta his mother, | and to Octavia the wife of the Imperator, and the *demos* of the
Romans and the *demos* of the Ephesians, the fishermen and fishmongers, having received
10 the place by a decree from the city (and) | having built the customs house for fishery (toll)
at their own expense, dedicated it. The following provided subventions to the work
according to the amount (indicated):

col. 1
Publius Hordeonius Lollianus with
    his wife and children, 4 columns.
15 | Publius Cornelius Alexandros,
    for paving of the open area
    with Phokaian stone, 100
    cubits.

col. 2
Hesperos, son of Demetrios,
    with his sons, 25 den.
Q. Laberius Niger, | with his son, 25 den.
Isas, son of Hermochares, with his sons, 25
den.
C. Furius, with his son, 25 den.

20 Tib. Claudius Metrodoros | with
 his wife and children, 3 columns;
 and for paving the colonnade that
 is beside the stele with Phokaian
 stone.
25 | P. Gerellanus Melleitos,
 2 columns.
 Euporos, son of Artemidoros,
 1 column and 12 den.
 Philokrates, son of Apellas,
30 | with his children, 1 column and
 12 den.
 L. Octavius Macer with his brothers,
 1 column.
35 | P. Anthestius, son of Publius,
 1 column.
 Onesimos, son of Apollonios, and
 Dionysios, son of Charisios, a
 painted column.
40 | P. Cornelius Felix, with Cornelia
 Ision, 1 column.
 Septimius Trophimos, with his
 children, (1) column.
45 | Herakleides, son of Herakleides,
 grandson of Herakleides, (   ) den.
 Epaphras, son of Tryphonas, with his
 son, 300 tiles.
50 P. Naevius Niger, with | his children,
 50 den.
 P. Vedius Verus, with his son, 50 den.
 L. Fabricius Tosides, with his
 son, 50 den.
55 | P. Cornelius Philistion, with his
 son, 50 den.
 L. Octavius Rufus, with his sons,
 50 den.
60 Tryphon, son of Artemidoros, | 37 den.
 Isas, son of Artemidoros, 37 den.
 Attalos, son of Charixenos, (also
 called) Hamaxas, with his son,
 30 den.
65 Epikrates, son of Antiochos, | (also
 called) Kroukras, with his
 sons, 30 den.
 Isas, son of Isidoros, 30 den.

| M. Valerius Fronto with his daughter,
 25 den.
Artemisios, son of Lesbios, 25 den.
P. Savidius Amethystos, with his
 sons, 25 den.
| Hierax, son of Hermokrates, with his wife,
 25 den.
Didymos, son of Theudas, 25 den.
Demetrios, son of Demetrios, (also called)
 Kenartas, 25 den.
| Xanthos, son of Pythion, 2000 bricks.
Phorbos, watchman, 1000
 bricks.
Secundus, watchman, 1000
 | bricks.
M. Antonius Bassus, with his daughter,
 (donated) all the rush mats(?) of the
 stoa.
Syneros, son of Kleanax,
 | with his son, 20 den.
Vet(u)lenus Primus, with his son, 20 den.
Cn. Cornelius Eunous, with his
 child, 15 den.
| Attalos, son of Attalos, grandson
 of Kassiades, 15 den.
Diogenes, son of Diogenes, with
 his son, 15 den.
Vettidius | Nikandros, with his sons, 15 den.
Gaius Roscilius, 15 den.
Zosimos, son of Gaius Furius, 15 den.
Bacchios, son of Euphrosynos, with his
 mother, 15 den.
| L. Vitellius, with his son,
 15 den.
L. Consius Epaphroditos, 15 den.
Aristeas, son of Aristoboulos,
 | with his son, 15 den.
Ruficius Faustus, 15 den.
P. Livius, 15 den.
Antiochos, (also called) Psychas, with his
 son, 15 den.
| Chares, son of Chares, with
 his sons, 15 den.

67 L. Fabricius Vitalis was works superintendent and deviser of the construction of the work.
70 He also dedicated at his own expense, with his wife | and their *threptoi*, 2 columns, the
 ones beside the temple of the Samothracian gods, with the adjacent altars.

side B

5 - - - | - - - -ymenos, son of Hermesianax, with his mother, [( ) den.]. Antimedes, son of
10 Metrodoros, with his son, ( ) den. | Philonas, son of Idas, ( ) den. Hordeonius Lainos,
with his son, ( ) den. -alius Montanus, [( ) den.]. Polybios, son of Tryphon, [( ) den.].
15,20 | - - - -aelius Lesbios, [( ) den.]. - - - | Dionysios - - - -teros, son of Philophilos, [( ) den.].
25 - - - Lollius Arruntius, [( ) den.]. - - - Licinnius Naukleros, [( ) den.]. | - - - Epaphras,
[( ) den.]. - - - Popilius Hermas, [( ) den.]. - - - -cius Koliotheras, [( ) den.]. Tyrannos,
30 son of Tryphon, ( ) den. - - - -eros, son of Sekres, ( ) den. | *N.*, son of Thiasos, 5 den.
N., son of Philonas, 5 den. *N.*, son of Apollonios, 5 den. -laos, son of Diophantes, ( ) den.
35 L. Staccius Graphikos, [( ) den.]. | Pomponius Stateri[- -, ( ) den.]. Onesimos, son of
Hermesianax, [( ) den.]. Valerius Anektos, ( ) den. Marcus Honerius, [( ) den.].
40 Herennius Kallinikos, [( ) den.]. | Clodius Tyrannos, [( ) den.]. Antonius Ruf(us?) - - -
45 Philo, son of Philonides, [( ) den.]. Onesimos - - - | Paulinus - - - Pomponius
Epaphro(ditos?), [( ) den.]. Eutychos, son of Phygelos, [( ) den.]. Cornelius Pius, [( )
den.].

This monument records the erection of a customs building near the harbour at Ephesos at almost exactly the time when Paul was living in the city. The guild is composed of fishermen and fishmongers, and the importance of this industry should not be lost on us. We are not dealing here with an indigent group of men: corporately, they have the means to erect a public building (which will serve their own interests in part; see below), and mark the event with a very large, pretentious *stele*.

The fundamental importance of fish for the ancient diet

Fish was a staple element in the diet of people in the ancient world, virtually regardless of geography. Accordingly, it was a significant factor in the ancient economy. It was one industry which became highly organised, both economically and technologically: see, in general, M.I. Rostovtzeff, *A Social and Economic History of the Hellenistic World* (Oxford, 1941; repr.) 2.1177-79. In the Hellenistic and Roman Imperial periods, handbooks on fishing techniques were written, of which the sole survivor today is Oppian's *Halieutika* (late II or early III); quotations also survive of a *Halieutika* wrongly attributed to Ovid. For the presence of the industry in different geographical areas during the Imperial period, see the various contributions in T. Frank (ed.), *An Economic Survey of Ancient Rome* (6 vols; Baltimore, 1933-40; repr. Paterson, 1959): 2.374-78 (Egypt); 3.181-83 (Spain); 3.283-85, 352 (Sicily); 4.24 (N. Africa); 4.154 (Syria); 4.626-27 (Asia Minor). In Italy, Ostia was well placed to provide Rome with fresh sea-fish as well as fish from the Tiber. While only one inscription survives which refers to the guild there — *CIL* XIV (1887) 409.17 (= *ILS* II, 1.6146), an Imperial-period text, which names Cn. Sentio Felix as patron of the guild of *piscatores* <*et*> *propolae* — the prominence of this economic sphere is indicated on paintings and mosaics, according to R. Meiggs, *Roman Ostia* (Oxford, 1973[2]) 267-68. A large shop near the Macellum appears to have belonged to the fish guild (ibid.). In Rome itself, the fish market (*forum piscatorium*) burned down in 210 BC (Livy 26.27.3), but was rebuilt north of the Forum in the Macellum area in 179 BC (Livy 40.51.5). The industry did not founder in this thirty-year interval, of course. Plautus, *Rudens* 290-305 (first staged *c*.200-190 BC), suggests that fishermen formed a readily identifiable part of the large urban 'rump' that was poor though not actually destitute. The *ludi piscatorii* were celebrated by the Tiber fishermen at

Rome on 7 June (Ovid, *Fasti* 6.237); and the association provided fish for sacrifice gratis at the annual festival to honour Vulcan on 23 August (see G. Lafaye, in C. Daremberg/E. Saglio [edd.], *Dictionnaire des antiquités grecques et romaines* IV.1 [Paris, 1907; repr. Graz, 1969] 492). There are numerous epigraphical attestations (either dedications to *patroni*, or epitaphs; largely II-III) at Rome to the fishing corporation (*corpus piscatorum et urinatorum*): *CIL* VI.1 (1876) 1080, 1872; VI.2 (1882) 9799-801 (this last an epitaph for a *piscatrix* who is a freedwoman) ; VI, 4.1 (1894) 29700-02; XIV (1887) 409; cf. Athenaeus, *Deipn.* 6.224c (ἰχθυοπῶλαι). 140km. north of Rome on Italy's west coast lies Cosa, the subject of a recent major archaeological study: A.M. McCann et al., *The Roman Port and Fishery of Cosa. A Center of Ancient Trade* (Princeton, 1987). No epigraphical or other evidence survives which actually proves the existence of an association of fishermen there; but the well-organised nature of the industry there makes the inference very plausible (see below).

No doubt partly because it was a staple element in the ancient diet, the fishing industry was subjected to numerous governmental controls. This is in evidence, at least in Egypt, from Ptolemaic times as *P.Tebt.* 3.1 (1933) 701 shows. In this long but fragmentary register of official business (Tebtynis, 235 BC), the fishing trade has considerable prominence. The text provides a basis for J. Dumont's discussion of the fishing industry in the Fayum during the Hellenistic period: *CE* 52 (1977) 125-42. For an earlier treatment which also draws heavily upon this papyrus see C. Préaux, *L'Economie royale des Lagides* (Brussels, 1939) 202-06. This register indicates that the business was a state monopoly, with only a small margin of profit finding its way to the fishermen themselves (cf. Rostovtzeff, *SEHHW*, 1.297, with n.101 at 3.1387). S. Freyne, *Galilee from Alexander the Great to Hadrian, 323BCE to 135CE* (Wilmington, 1980), who follows Rostovtzeff in this (174), speculates that the situation may have been similar in Palestine. On commercial fishing in I AD Palestine, see generally W.H. Wuellner, *The Meaning of 'Fishers of Men'* (Philadelphia, 1967) 26-63, especially 43-45, 61-62. Note, too, M. Nun, *Ancient Jewish Fishery* (in Hebrew; Merhavia, 1964) — *non vidi* (cf. summary of contents in *IEJ* 14 [1964] 195). By comparison with Hellenistic-period epigraphical evidence from Delos and elsewhere, Dumont draws on the work of T. Homolle, *BCH* 14 (1890) 391-444, to show (137-41) that governmental tax on the sale of fish products was mostly considerably heavier in Ptolemaic Egypt. At Delos the 5% tax in the 270s BC had risen to 10% by 250 BC. While a tax of this size was very widespread in the Greek world — though higher imposts are attested — in Egypt the Ptolemies exacted up to 25%, and occasionally even more (up to 40%) if an advance was provided for the purchase of materials (nets, etc.) by the fisherman (id., *REA* 78/79 [1976/77] 114). As in Egypt and some other places, the fishing industry was organised as a state monopoly at Byzantion even before the Hellenistic period (ibid.).

The question of the cost of fish could sometimes be a problematic one at the political level, precisely because it was a basic constituent of the diet. Fishermen and fishmongers receive 'bad press' generally in the literary sources from Greek comedy onwards, being characterised by greed, cheating and over-pricing. Athenaeus, *Deipn.* 6.224b-228c, makes the high price of fish at Rome the starting point for his quotation of numerous passages from earlier authors in which the stupidity and the deceptions practised by those in this trade are illustrated. So, too, in Apuleius, *Met.* 1.24-25, where the overcharging of a fishmonger in a Thessalian town forms the context for the author's humorous depiction of an officious magistrate. Comic exaggeration needs to be allowed for in these passages; but there must have been some basis for so constant a refrain in the sources, perhaps reflecting the dependence of so many in society on the availability of cheap fresh fish since meat was beyond the means of most on a regular basis.

Official concern at the cost of fish is reflected in *IG* II^2 (1913; repr. 1974) 1103, a fragmentary rescript of Hadrian (Athens, 124/5 or slightly later), in which it is noted that those not directly involved in the industry have been purchasing the commodity for resale at a price which could not be afforded by the poor. The action taken over this matter is of a piece with state attitudes to those who hoarded grain and other longer-lasting staple foods.

πιπρασκέ[τω]σαν δὲ πάντα ἢ αὐτοὶ οἱ
10 κομίζοντες ἢ οἱ πρῶτοι παρ' αὐτῶν ὠνού[με]νοι· τὸ δὲ καὶ τρίτους ὠ-
νητὰς γεινομένους τῶν αὐτῶν ὠνίων με[τα]πιπράσκειν ἐπιτείνει
τὰς τειμάς.

10 **Either those who catch the fish are to sell them all themselves, | or the first people who purchase the catch from them. The resale of the same purchases by those who are third buyers adds to the prices.**

Because of the difficulty of keeping meat and fish fresh, a major aspect of the fishing industry was the subsidiary development of pickling and the production of fish sauces, of which *garum* is the best known (for this last, see the references in the index to Frank, *Economic Survey*, 6.31; and on the survival into Modern Greek of the word see G.P. Shipp, *Modern Greek Evidence for the Ancient Greek Vocabulary* [Sydney, 1979] 189). On the technique of preserving fish in antiquity (mainly by salting) see M. Ponsich/M. Tarradell, *Garum et industries antiques de salaison dans la Méditerranée occidentale* (Paris, 1965). Some areas specialised in these secondary industries, and the products attracted different rates of tax at toll-houses. The renaming of Magdala, on the west coast of the Sea of Galilee, as Tarichaia is testimony to the importance of the dried fish industry in that area for purposes of export: see Freyne, 173-74. At the northern end of the sea lay Bethsaida, the home of Peter and Andrew's fishing family (Jn 1.44); its name, too, indicates the focal role of fishing for the city's economy (cf. Wuellner, 28-31, 62). Sometimes individuals specialised in the sale of salted fish, as we may glean from a Byzantine loan document, *P.Coll.Youtie* 2 (1976) 92 (Antinoopolis, 569): the Christian Martha is able to earn sufficient income from the sale of salted fish to redeem her sister from slavery. See further brief comment on this text at *New Docs 1977*, **3**, p.31.

The Ephesos fishing organisation as a typical association

Associations for this trade are attested in many places — for some examples, see the references in Dumont, *REA* 78/79 (1976/77) 115 — and the Ephesos inscription is entirely typical in indicating (A.7) that members comprised both those who caught and those who sold the commodity. That such a guild could flex its political 'muscle' is suggested by *CIL* IV (1871) 826 (Pompeii, before 79 AD), a short, painted inscription in which the *piscicapi* urge the election of a particular aedile. As with the incident concerning the silversmiths at Ephesos (Acts 19.23-41; cf. *New Docs 1979*, **1**), it may be assumed that the large, high-profile guild which represented the local fishing industry could also exercise political power when its members' interests were at stake. Strabo, writing in late I BC/early I AD, was aware (14.1.24, 641c) of the problem of the silting up of the harbour caused by deposits from the Kaystros River and exacerbated by faulty engineering under the Attalids. So bad must the situation have become by the time of the erection of the fish guild's *stele* that in 61 AD the proconsul, Barea Soranus, had the harbour dredged (Tac., *Ann.* 16.23). The association which erected our stele must have been an influential lobby group in ensuring it was done.

In general, we may expect that fishing guilds normally existed wherever this industry had become established on a basis involving more than a few families. For example, *PSI* 8 (1927) 901

(Tebtynis, 46 AD) records the oath (written in duplicate) taken by Herakleides γραμματεὺς ἁλιέων (*ll*.7, 17) and οἱ δεκατρῖς πρεσβύτεροι ἁλιέων (*l*.10; cf. 19-20), that members had not caught any fish sacred to the gods (for sacred fish see *New Docs 1979*, **25**). At Nova Carthago in Spain, the *piscatores* | *et propolae* (4-5) dedicate *lares Augustales* (3): *CIL* II Suppl. (1892) 5929 (= *ILS* II, 1.3624; time of Augustus or a little later). In Asia Minor, the Black Sea coast was a particularly bountiful fishing area, as were the Bosphorus and Propontis. From the last of these regions, a fishing guild is attested at Kyzikos: E. Schwertheim, *Die Inschriften von Kyzikos und Umgebung*, 1 (*IK* 18.1; Bonn, 1980) 260 (Imperial period), though the text is fragmentary. A major plank in Hellenistic Byzantion's economy was the harvesting in the Bosphorus of great numbers of tuna. Teams of professional fishermen using specialised equipment were needed for this work; and it is no wonder that we hear of the *thiasitai* (of fishermen) making a dedication to Dionysos Parabolos: L. Robert, *BCH* 102 (1978) 532-35 (Byzantion, time of Hadrian; = *SEG* 28 [1978] 562). In the same article Robert publishes (522-28) a related dedication (= *SEG* 28.561), which suggests that this fishing association called itself the Dionysoboleitai. Useful discussion of the tuna-fishing enterprise at Byzantion is provided by Dumont, *REA* 78/79 (1976/77) 96-119. Odessos, on the Thracian (west) coast of the Black Sea, also had an association of the θυνεῖται Ἑρμᾶντος in Imperial times: *AE* (1928) 146. It is unclear whether this organisation of tuna fishermen was named after its founder, Hermas — for the phenomenon, cf. *New Docs 1976*, **2 bis** — or whether the word indicates a geographical location. M.I. Rostovtzeff, *A Social and Economic History of the Roman Empire* (Oxford, 1957²) 2.689 n.100, believes that *IGRR* 1.817 (Kallipolis in Thrace, Imperial) may also refer to an association of fishermen, although the ed. n. to the *IGRR* text doubts this. At Cosa in Italy there was a tuna lookout post (θυννοσκοπεῖον, Strabo, 5.2.8, 225c) on the promontory above the port. The presence of a well-organised fishing industry, both catching and processing these fish for export, may be inferred (cf. McCann et al., *The Roman Port . . . of Cosa*, 17-18). Harvesting the tuna schools was seasonal work (roughly May-October), however, and it is no surprise to find evidence of various kinds of ponds and barrages for raising fry (ibid., 141-55). The lagoons at Cosa yielded a rich supply of fish: under the control of the municipal government, a monopoly franchise over it was leased out during the late Republic to one family, the Sestii (ibid., 41).

Yet we should not assume that wherever there were fishermen there were always guilds. In some places, the fishing industry may not have been large enough to lead to the formation of one; alternatively, religious scruple may have forced others to abstain (see below, on *I.Eph.* V.1503). Jewish fishermen come particularly to mind here. At *New Docs 1976*, **40**, it was suggested that *CIJ* II.945 (Joppa, II) offers evidence for a fishing co-operative that may fall somewhat short of a formalised association. The NT evidence leads us in the same direction: the families of Zebedee and Jonah help each other as need arises, and to that extent may be considered μέτοχοι (Lk. 5.7; cf. κοινωνοί in vs.10. For Jonah as the father of Peter see Mt. 17.17.). The speculation of S.W. Baron, *A Social and Religious History of the Jews*, I (New York, 1952²) 254-55, that Galilean fishermen formed a professional association, is dubious, though perhaps not altogether to be ruled out. In any case, the evidence from which he derives his inference, *j. Pesaḥim* IV.1.30d — translated by M. Schwab, *Le Talmud de Jérusalem*, V (Paris, 1882; the repr. of 1960 combines vols. IV and V into a composite third vol.) 49 — does refer to fish-ponds on Lake Tiberias. At least by the late third century fish products were being imported to Palestine from the Nile delta and Apamea in Syria — D. Sperber, *ZDMG* 118 (1968) 265-269 — which may betoken not only cheaper labour costs in those places, but also that there was insufficient local fish available to satisfy demand. The latter point in turn suggests an economically depressed situation for Palestinian fishermen, hardly conducive to belief in the existence of an active trade association. Concerning trade associations in general in I AD Jerusalem, J. Jeremias, *Jerusalem in the Time* *of Jesus* (ET: London, 1974) 21, acknowledges that the evidence is very sparse. Even if he is right to infer their existence at Jerusalem from this data, that proves nothing about the existence of organised trade associations in rural Palestine.

The usual mechanism by which taxes on fish products were collected was the standard Roman one of farming out the task to *publicani* (τελῶναι). E. Badian's *Publicans and Sinners. Private Enterprise in the Service of the Roman Republic* (Oxford, 1972) provides the best general coverage of the *publicani*, tracing the growth of their power from *c.*170 BC and discussing such questions as the sources of their profits. Simultaneously with the publication of Badian's lectures there appeared J.R. Donohoe's study, *CBQ* 33 (1971) 39-61, which focussed particularly on Rabbinic evidence for the attitudes to *telonai* in the Gospels. Succinct analysis, why Jewish attitudes to the *publicani* differed from the way the latter were usually regarded in other parts of the Empire, is offered most recently by M.D. Goodman, *The Ruling Class of Judaea. The Origins of the Jewish Revolt against Rome AD 66-70* (Cambridge 1987) 131-32. Donohoe is right to differentiate the collection of direct taxes from those of an indirect nature (imports on goods being brought in and out of a region, etc.), but fails to appreciate the semantic range of τελώνης. This term is more common than δημοσιώνης, and although the latter is the etymological 'twin' of *publicanus*, τελώνης is applied widely to anyone involved in tax-farming, whether the actual individuals who obtain the contract or their sub-lessees and hirelings; and the term is used of those collecting both direct and indirect taxes. That there was clearly no shortage of tenderers for the work of collecting imposts on imported fish produce reflects the lucrative nature of the fishing industry as a whole, even if the primary producers themselves often saw merely a fraction of the profits. Accordingly, the question must be asked of our Ephesian inscription, why an association of those involved in the catching and marketing of fish should build a customs house at their own expense. Its position at the harbour indicates that altruism was not the primary motive in such self-promotion: provision of this building, whose purpose was to levy a tax, must have been intended to ensure that those who were not members of the group at Ephesos were barred from bringing their catch ashore there and marketing it in the city. We may infer from its general, undifferentiating self-description (A.7) that there was only one such group in the city. Corporate public-spiritedness is not to be ignored as a motive in this action of the fishing association; but neither is self-interest. In effect, we see in this inscription evidence of a cartel in operation at the city. A fragmentary papyrus, *PSI* 7 (1925) 798 (provenance unknown, II-III), which mentions fishermen (a8) and fish-sellers (ἰχθυοπ(ώλης), b10), apparently refers to the illegal sale of fish in an Egyptian town-market.

The city harbour was the obvious location of a customs house whose particular role was to collect tax concerned with the fishing industry, as well as other items which were imported to and exported from a city by ship. Parallels are known to the harbourside siting of the Ephesos building. At Aquileia there were actually two buildings for this purpose in the harbour area by the time of Caracalla (Rostovtzeff, *SEHRE*², 2.609 n.24). Meiggs, *Roman Ostia*, pl.26a, is a marble relief (Portus, III), which may well illustrate a customs house on the dock with the imported cargo of wine amphorae being recorded. L. Casson, *Ships and Seamanship in the Ancient World* (Princeton, 1971) pl.174 and comment on p.xxvi, interprets this relief a little differently, as involving a shipping clerk. On the development of *portoria* in II BC under the Romans see Badian, *Publicans and Sinners*, 63-64. The brief note on Mt. 9.9 in W.F. Albright/ C.S. Mann's *Anchor Bible Commentary* (Garden City, 1971), that the customs house would have been on the outskirts of Capernaum, does not register the reality of this town's location on the NW edge of the sea of Tiberias. Matthew/Levi's role there as a τελώνης (Mt. 10.3; Lk. 5.27) may well have brought him into contact with Peter and James and their respective brothers before his invitation to join Jesus. At Palmyra in Syria, there was discovered in the *portus* area a particularly important but fragmentary bilingual inscription (Greek and Palmyrene Aramaic), dated 18 April 137. This tax law, *CIS* II.3, 1 (1926) 3913, publishes revised regulations concerning the local economy, specifying the tariff to be applied by the *publicani* on goods being brought in and out. In addition to items such as slaves, oil, perfumes and spices, salted (i.e., dried) fish is one of the commodities subject to impost. The Greek section of the inscription is lost at this point, and the Palmyrene version (*ll.*34-38) is lacunose. From this section the editor infers (p.61) that the tariff was heavier for imported items. He concludes that 10 denarii were exacted per imported camel-load of salted fish, 6 den. per exported load; while for donkey-loads of the same material, the import fee was 5 and the export fee 3 den. A recent, thorough discussion of this inscription, with bibliography and an English translation, is provided by J.F. Matthews, *JRS* 74 (1984) 157-80. That tariffs could vary from place to place is shown by comparison of this text from Syria with *P.Wisconsin* 2 (1977) 80 (Bacchias in the Fayum, 1 Oct. 114; see the informative commentary on part of this papyrus by N.Y. Clauson, *Aeg.* 9 [1928] 240-80; = *SB* 4 [1931] 7365), in which the impost on a donkey-load of fresh fish (νεαρὰ ἰχθύς, *col.*5.151, 152) is 2 dr., and that on a *chlibion* — a unit of measurement for estimating duty — of salted fish (τάριχος, *col.*5.169) is 7 dr.

Concerning the design of the Ephesian toll-house, mention of τῶν | στοῶν (A2.37-38) provides one clue, as I. McPhee has pointed out to me. The plural suggests there may have been more than one colonnaded portico; and it would not be unusual for shops to have opened on to them. Since the building is specifically concerned with the fishing industry, the obvious proprietors of these shops would be the fishmongers, themselves members of the association, selling the freshly-landed fish. This inference, that the customs building may also have housed a (the?) fish market for the city, confirms the point made earlier, that the association acted in its own interest in having it erected. A harbourside site for the sale of fish products is less essential, however, when dried and pickled goods are in view. Thus, E. Pemberton has drawn to my attention the so-called Punic Amphora building in the forum at Corinth, the excavation of which has shown that an enterpreneur in late V BC imported large quantities of dried or pickled sea bream and tuna in Punic amphoras from the Western Mediterranean. He may have been forced out of business by the outbreak of the Peloponnesian War. For details of this building and the fish remains see C.K. Williams, *Hesperia* 47 (1978) 4, 15-20; 48 (1979) 107-24, especially 117-18; 49 (1980) 108-10.

In Asia Minor and elsewhere, fishing rights in lakes and rivers were commonly owned by cities and temples as part of their estates from which regular income was derived for the upkeep of buildings, etc. Strabo informs us (12.8.14, 577c) that under Augustus the cult of Men at Pisidian Antioch lost a considerable portion of its domains when they were allocated to Roman *coloni* (cf., briefly, *New Docs 1978*, 6, p.30). As these areas came under Roman control, the right to tax a fisherman's haul (for example) could become a matter of dispute between the traditional possessors of the lakes and rivers and the *publicani*, with the Roman government often backing the former (Rostovtzeff, *SEHRE*[2], 2.689 n.100, a long note full of interesting references and observations). A particularly long-standing dispute is recorded in *SEG* 1 (1923) 329 (Istros, Nov. 100 AD), a bilingual inscription which contains five letters (some in Greek, others in Latin) of legates in Moesia, ranging in date from 43-49 to 100 AD. The Roman officials had successively attempted to resolve the dispute, which concerned the fishing areas and rights of the fishermen of this Black Sea coast city (cf. Rostovtzeff, ibid., 2.609 n.24, 689 n.100).

Strabo provides unequivocal evidence (14.1.26, 642c) of the attempt by the *publicani* to control the revenues for fishing the lakes near Ephesos. Two lakes near the city formed part of the temple estate of Artemis. The Attalids had deprived the goddess of the revenues from them, but the Romans had returned this right to the temple. Subsequently, 'the publicani by coercion transferred the taxes to themselves', οἱ δημοσιῶναι βιασάμενοι περιέστησαν εἰς ἑαυτοὺς τὰ τέλη (the participle here may indicate that litigation was involved). An Ephesian embassy sent to Rome saw the return of the lakes to the goddess' domain. This evidence from Strabo underlines something else which is occasionally insufficiently appreciated: the vast bulk of fishing in antiquity was carried on in lakes and rivers (Rostovtzeff, *SEHHW*, 2.1177). For example, the Euphrates was a famous source of fish, which were often depicted in mosaics. Excavation of skeletal remains at sites in Syria shows fish and crustaceans to have formed part of the diet of those living near the river: see A.T. Clason/H. Buitenhuis, *Jnl of Archaeological Science* 5 (1978) 81-83, a reference I owe to G.W. Clarke. In fact, sea-fishing was a comparatively small part of the total picture, owing to the small size of boats and the risk of sudden weather changes. Such working of the open sea as there was — e.g., off Sidon, whose name is suggestive of a fishing industry based there; see Wuellner, 33 — must almost always have kept the littoral in sight. Passing remarks on fishing boats may be found in Casson, *Ships and Seamanship*, 162, 330. See also his pl.192 for an illustration, and pl.194 in particular, a photograph of the remains of a fishing boat found in the mud of the harbour of Claudius at Portus (also reproduced in McCann, *The Roman Port . . . of Cosa*, fig. VIII.11. Each of the other fishing boats illustrated there — figs. VIII.7-10 — are from North African mosaics, in every case showing two men in each boat.). The boat recently discovered in the Sea of Galilee — see S. Wachsmann, *BAR* 14.5 (1988) 18-33 — may or may not have been a fishing boat. Dated I BC-late I AD, it was big enough (*c*.8.1m. long x *c*.2.3m. wide) for four rowers plus passengers, a size consonant with the boats mentioned in certain Gospel passages (e.g., Mk. 4.35-38).

In many areas artificial ponds were built to harvest fish and eels commercially, or simply as holding areas so fish could be eaten fresh. For a sample of evidence from the Iberian peninsula see A. Moreno Páramo/L. Abad Casal, *Habis* 2 (1971) 209-21; for Roman Crete, C. Davaras, *ABSA* 69 (1974) 87-93; and see the comment already given above for Cosa in Italy. When we consider the fish traders at Ephesos in mid-I AD, therefore, we are looking at a group which must have leased from the goddess exclusive rights to fish the lakes and stretches of the Kaystros River. A useful map in *I.Eph.* VII, 2 (1981) p.296 delineates the Artemision's estates in the Kaystros valley, to the extent that they may be deduced from the find spots of a number of early Imperial boundary-markers (*I.Eph.* VII, 2.3501-12; cf. *New Docs 1979*, **28**, pp.128-29). According to this map, two sections of the river passed through these estates; the tariffs collected at the fishing toll-house built by the guild at the city harbour will have been directed to the Artemision. We may presume that, in addition to fish, the Ephesian association had the rights to harvest other produce of the waterways. Athenaeus, *Deipn.* 3.90d, 92d, rates highly mussels and cockles from the Ephesos area. So important was it to ensure that no one poached in leased areas, that overseers were appointed to police them. Evidence for this comes from Pisidia, where near Lake Eğridir has been found an epitaph for a man who was ἐπεὶ (= ἐπὶ) λίμνης ἐπιστάτης (*l*.3) for twenty years: *SEG* 2 (1925) 747 (Imperial?). In addition to the prevention of poaching such officials were also responsible to ensure that sacred fish were not being caught: see H. Henne, *Aeg.* 31 (1951) 184-91, discussing *PSI* 901 (noted above) in this regard.

Further information about the Ephesian fish-traders' association is provided by the sole other epigraphical reference to this same building, *I.Eph.* V.1503. This dedication from the time of Antoninus Pius was also found in the harbour area.

> ['Αρτέμιδι 'Εφεσίᾳ]
> καὶ Αὐτ[οκράτορι Τ. Αἰλί]ῳ
> 'Αδριανῷ 'Αντωνείνῳ
> Καίσαρι Σεβαστῷ Εὐσεβεῖ

5   καὶ τῇ πρώτῃ καὶ μεγίστῃ
    μητροπόλει τῆς Ἀσίας
    καὶ δὶς νεωκόρου τῶν Σεβαστῶν
    Ἐφεσίων πόλει καὶ τοῖς ἐπὶ
    τὸ τελωνῖον τῆς ἰχθυϊκῆς
10   πραγματευομένοις
    Κομινία Ἰουνία
    σὺν τῷ βωμῷ τὴν Εἶσιν
    ἐκ τῶν ἰδίων ἀνέθηκεν·
    πρυτανεύοντο[ς Τιβ. Κλ. Δ]ημ[οσ]τ̣[ρ]άτ[ου].

[To Artemis Ephesia] and Imperator T. Aelius Hadrianus Antoninus Caesar Augustus
5 Pius | and to the city of the Ephesians, the first and greatest metropolis of Asia and twice
10 *neokoros* of the Augusti, and to those who | conduct business at the customs house for
fishery (toll), Cominia Junia dedicated the statue of Isis with the altar at her own expense.
In the prytany of Tiberius Claudius Demostratos.

This woman, who is known also from *I.Eph.* IV.1266, may have had some link with the fishing
association a century after our Neronian text. If it is asked why she, rather than a member of the
fishing association, is the donor, the answer could be that she has exercised some patronal
relationship to the group (cf. R. MacMullen, *Historia* 29 [1980] 208-18, who suggests [211] that
*c.*10% of the patrons of associations is the donor, were women); but since this would be likely to
be advertised in a dedication, it may be more simply concluded that Junia had a familial link
with one of the members. In an Imperial-period Latin text from Holland, *ILS* 1 (1892; repr.
1962) 1462, the contractors of fishing (*conductores piscatus*) make a dedication to the indigenous
goddess Hlundana. The assimilation of Isis/Artemis is attested elsewhere and was achieved well
before the beginning of the Christian era: see R.E. Witt, *Isis in the Graeco-Roman World*
(Ithaca, 1971) 65, 68, 69, 127, and especially 141-51 (note also his pl. 36); G. Hölbl, *Zeugnisse
ägyptischer Religionsvorstellungen für Ephesos* (*EPRO* 73; Leiden, 1978) 64, 84-85 (he reprints
this text at 52, no.6). For coins of Ephesos from I BC which depict Isis see Witt, 305 n.28. The
assimilation of the two goddesses is visible, too, in the *Ephesiaka* of Xenophon (mid-III AD?):
see R. Merkelbach, *Roman und Mysterium in der Antike* (Berlin, 1962) 92. But it is not actually
a conflation of the two deities that we are witnessing in this inscription. Isis had a special connection with fishermen: cf. Apuleius, *Met.* 11.8, where a fisherman takes part in the procession
at Kenchreai to honour the goddess. Dittenberger's succinct n.1 *ad OGIS* 496 (which reprints the
Junia dedication) indicates the correctness of the restoration of Artemis' name in *l*.1. If accepted,
this wording allows us to draw the inference that the goddess was still in possession of her temple
estates — at least insofar as the lakes and river stretches were concerned — beyond the time of
the latest (Trajanic) boundary-markers so far located. The participial phrase in *ll*.8-10 is common
enough; but in the present context the absence of any reference to the τελῶναι confirms that a
century after *I.Eph.* Ia.20 the dues collected were continuing to be directed to the temple
revenues, not to the state via the *publicani*. The phrase ἐπὶ | τὸ τελωνῖον (*ll*.8-9) provides an
excellent illustration of the wording in the Gospel passages where Matthew/Levi is called from
his occupation (Mk. 2.14 and parallels). The dedication of this statue of Isis typifies the difficulty
faced by pious Jews and new Christian converts in addressing themselves to earning their living
in a cosmopolitan city. In order to ply the fisherman's trade in Ephesos and to sell their wares
there, it was essential to gain membership of this corporation which paid dues to the city's patron

deity. That is not to say that all Jews and Christians thereby excluded themselves from such involvements: eclecticism in religious outlook leading to (from our distance in time) behavioural inconsistency was not unusual: cf. M.H. Williams, *JTS* 39 (1988) 97-111, at 104-105, 110.

The order of names in *I.Eph.* Ia.20

To return to *I.Eph.* Ia.20 and focus more closely upon the inscription itself, we may observe, first, that the text is sufficiently complete to indicate that $c.100$ members made a contribution. Of this total number, the names of some 89 donors survive well enough to attract analysis. These donors are recorded in descending order of the size of their contribution to the construction of the toll-house. Fragmentary though side B is, it may be inferred from the surviving numerals there (B.30-32) that this part of the text is not a later addition consisting of people who gave money subsequently. Rather, all donors have been listed at the one time, but the bottom of side A breaks that sequence in order to draw special attention on the most visible face of the stele to the multi-faceted help provided by Vitalis (*ll*.67-71). Given this, we may infer that the omission of numerals in a couple of places is due to mere oversight by the stone-cutter: at A1.44, read κίονα $<α'>$; in *l*.46 a numeral ought to have been included which lies between the cost of a column and 300 tiles, but which is at least more than 50 den. K.L. McKay suggests to me, however, that the lettering may be better resolved as δη(νάρια) ν', as in the case of A1.56, with the mason having overlooked until too late the entry for Epaphras, which was then added out of sequence (A1.47-48) after Herakleides' contribution. Haplography could explain both omissions.

Since we lack details of the size of the building, these subventions do not allow us to ascertain the cost of pillars, tiles, bricks and mats(?) in other than relative terms. The total surviving monetary value indicated is just short of 1000 den.; and, in view of the loss of numerals being confined largely to side B where the smallest contributions are listed, the full sum cannot have been much more. (The publication of side B by Wankel in *I.Eph.* Ia.20 allows us to modify T.R.S. Broughton's comments in Frank, *Economic Survey*, 4.719: the smallest sum donated was 5 den., not 15; and he states without basis that the largest was 200.) What is important, however, is that each gift is specified, and it is on that basis that the members of this group are ranked. So paramount is the mason's concern to include the amount of money contributed on the first line of each entry on side A *col*.2 that several words are actually split in two (A2.12-13, 20-21, 23-24, 28-29, 39-40, 41-42, 43-44, 47-48, 49-50, 53-54, 57-58, 59-60). In most other instances in this column the amount intrudes into the grammatical sequence, a feature which occurs only once in *col*.1 (*ll*.64-65), and apparently not at all on side B.

A contrast with this Ephesian list readily comes to mind: in the major new Jewish inscription from Aphrodisias — J. Reynolds/R. Tannenbaum, *Jews and Godfearers at Aphrodisias* (*Camb. Phil. Soc. Suppl.* vol. 12; Cambridge, 1987) — the donors who subscribed funds to have the soup-kitchen (?; πάτελλα, face a, *col*.i.1) built are listed at least partly in order of status within the Jewish, not the city, community (see Reynolds/Tannenbaum's commentary, especially 128; cf. 122, 127). The size of the contributions of the Aphrodisias group is nowhere given. That probably III AD text includes only a tiny number of people related to one another (ibid., 23); contrast the Ephesos text, where a large majority of the donors (all of whom are male) expressly includes mention of wife/child(ren)/brother/mother, although almost none of these is named (yet note A1.41). We are looking, therefore, at familial donations to this building project, and in almost every case the man so named is to be interpreted as the *pater familias*. The implication of the inscription is that while husbands/fathers are the only ones named, family members are considered to be linked with the association in some less formal sense than actual membership.

It is improbable that the list testifies to family members who have joint right of disposal over their funds: such pairings as father and daughter (A2.20-21, 36-38) rule out consideration of such a situation. This notion of household members being affiliated to an association provides a suggestive analogy for early Christian congregations into which family members were incorporated by virtue of the adherence of the head of the household (cf. Acts 16.14-15, 31-34). Apart from points of difference between these inscriptions from Aphrodisias and Ephesos, we may point to several features which both share. The two *stelai* are of considerable size: at 2.8m. high, the Aphrodisias text is even larger than the one from Ephesos. In both cases, the rank range extends from Roman citizens (of some local eminence in certain cases at Aphrodisias) to slaves (A2.32, 34 in the text above; for Aphrodisias, cf. Reynolds/ Tannenbaum, 135). Yet, since we are witness to two groups of donors, we are seeing people none of whom is really indigent (cf. ibid., 124). In both cases, too, we have evidence of a trade being pursued by people of varying status, whether slave or free (cf. ibid., 122).

The onomastic importance of *I.Eph.* Ia.20 for the NT

Turning to the question of the onomastic significance of the Ephesos *stele*, and leaving aside the names of the Imperial family mentioned in the dedication (A.2-5), at least 25 — and possibly as many as 28 — of the surviving names of the members and their fathers/grandfathers (papponymics at A1.46, A2.46, 52) are also attested in the NT. Up to 18 of these names are also held by people who have some connection with Paul. The significance of this overlap lies in the point that the total number of male names associated in some way with him is less than 80. It is useful here to distinguish Latin names from Greek/indigenous ones; those italicised below are attested as having some connection with Paul (greetings lists, travelling companions, etc.; the Pastorals are included for present purposes); an asterisk indicates that the name occurs in the NT in some connection with Ephesos (if bracketed, the asterisk indicates some uncertainty).

Latin (10 + 1 uncertain): Claudius, *Cornelius*, *Felix*, *Gaius, *Lucius* (Λεύ(κιος) mostly in text, though note Λού(κιος) at A2.55, 57; Λούκιος, NT), *Marcus*, *Niger*, Publius, *Rufus*, *Secundus*, Tiberius;

Greek (15 + 2 uncertain): *Alexandros, Apellas (? — NT has Apelles), *Apollonios* (variant for Apollos at Acts 18.24D), Aristoboulos, *Demetrios, Didymos, *Dionysios*, *Epaphras* (cf. *New Docs 1979*, **5**, pp.22-23), *Epaphroditos* (cf. ibid., pp.21-23), *Eutychos*, *Hermas*, Lainos (? — NT has Linos), *Onesimos* (cf. ibid., **96**, p.179), (*)*Phygelos*, Theudas (cf. ibid., **101**, p.183), *Trophimos*, *Tyrannos.

G.A. Deissmann (*apud* Keil, *col*.56) had already noted the significant number of names in common between the list and the Pauline 'connection'. But the group of men in this inscription may be analysed in other ways as well. The stone appears to have listed 99 or 100 members (i.e., excluding patronymics and the Imperial family to whom the building is dedicated), of which perhaps 89 are identifiable in the following categories (a little fluidity must be allowed in the tallies in view of the very lacunose state of side B):

A. **Roman citizens** (43-44; i.e., *c*.50% of identifiable members; the one named woman [A1.41] is not included in this tally)
    i. of Roman/Italian descent: 18-19
       B.42 is less than certain: possibly a member of the *familia Caesaris*, or the name should perhaps even be treated as irrecoverable.
    ii. with Greek *cognomina*: 9
       Such names suggest an honorific grant. Note A1.19, a freedman from the *familia Caesaris*.

iii. with Greek or Latin *cognomina* attested as of servile currency: 16

Such names imply manumission (or army service in the case of Latin names).

The large number (at least 20, possibly up to 24) of *duo nomina* may be observed, the majority of which appears on side B where the stone is much narrower; and we may infer that the shortening of the name from the standard *tria nomina* was done in view of the more limited space available. There are up to 15 on side B if Pomponius Stateri[os] and Antonius Ruf[us] are read at B.35 and 41, and noting that nominatives are no less likely than genitives at B.8 and 14. Those listed at B.23, 24 and 26 are not *duo nomina*, since a *praenomen* must have preceded the surviving lettering, given the lacuna in each case.

B. **Others of non-servile status**, i.e., Greeks, citizens of Ephesos (at least 36, possibly as many as 41, i.e., up to 46%)

This group is somewhat fluid: names like Onesimos, Xanthos, etc., which are attested in Rome in I AD of high servile frequency, do not mean that every instance of the name elsewhere must be servile. E.g., Epaphras (A1.47) is unlikely to be a slave since his son is mentioned.

C. **Slaves** (2, possibly as many as 10; 3% +)

The only fairly certain ones are A2.32, 34 (occupations given in lieu of patronymic); a further possible candidate is Paulinus (B.45), for only here does a *cognomen* begin the line. Its position in the line is what allows this possibility to the entertained. But for that, this *cognomen* of distinguished families is unlikely to be a slave-name. L. Vidman, *Index Cognominum ad CIL VI* (Berlin, 1980), has no servile instance; but E.A. Judge has drawn to my notice *CIL* VI.15190, which records a Claudian freedman who used Paulinus as the *cognomen* of his son. The following names have a high frequency of attestation among slaves at Rome in I AD: Onesimos (A1.37, B.36, 44), Dionysios (A1.38, B.20), Xanthos (A2.30), Zosimos (A2.52): see, respectively, Solin, *GPR* 1.913-19, 302-06; 2.693-94, 819-22. The following genitive *could* be taken in each instance as the owner's name rather than a patronymic, although the model of A2.32, 34 militates against this. B.42 may also belong here, if he is not a Roman citizen or to be classed as an irrecoverable name.

D. **Irrecoverable** (9-11)

Nothing useful can be extrapolated from B.1-5, 15, 17-19, 21. Perhaps B.42 should be added here. If Wankel's position of the lettering in B.4-5 reflects the layout on the stone there may have been only one name here, rather than two.

Several points of interest emerge from this analysis. First, the range in civic status, from Roman citizens of Italic descent to slaves, of those involved in this trade at Ephesos provides an intriguing analogy for the similar spread in rank that is attested of the Pauline churches. Second, as reported in *New Docs 1978*, **4**, p.19, E.A. Judge has drawn attention to the large proportion of citizens in this inscription at a date when Roman citizenship was by no means widely held in the East. Those thereby attaining to high rank in a formal sense will mostly have gained it via manumission or military service. Of the 44 Roman citizens in our inscription 17 have Latin *cognomina*, 21 Greek *cognomina*, and the remainder have none recorded (i.e., *duo nomina* only are given). A similarly high percentage of people with Latin names may be observed in NT church groups, and especially among those with some kind of connection with Paul. W.A. Meeks, *The First Urban Christians* (New Haven, 1983) 47-48, observes this phenomenon for Corinth in the course of a useful survey (55-73) of the names attested in the NT of those linked in some way with the Pauline churches. Drawing here upon an unpublished paper by E.A. Judge ('The Latin names in the Pauline Connection', given at a conference on the Roman Family in July 1981 at the Australian National University, Canberra; cf. *New Docs 1977*, **84**) it may be noted that of 78 male names (treating by-names as separate items here) in the Pauline 'onomasticon' — females are excluded from the present discussion, since the fisheries association at Ephesos directly concerns males only — 23 have a Latin name and 45 a Greek name, while

Semitic names account for the remainder. Excluding this last group as not being relevant for a comparison with the inscription, we find a ratio of 1:2 for Latin:Greek names. The Ephesian fishing association yields an almost identical proportion of Latin:Greek names, 24:55, ≃ 3:7. (This calculation takes the *cognomen* or the 'next best thing' as the determiner. Eight names are excluded as not Latin or Greek in origin. By-names are treated as separate names, though most of these are excluded anyway, as being of indigenous origin. The proportion is much higher, 17:21, ≃ 4:5, if *cognomina* of the 44 Roman citizens alone are compared; but this provides a less relevant point of comparison with the Pauline names.) Accordingly — and herein lies the main importance of the inscription for NT research — this group of fishermen and traders from Ephesos provides the first really comparable evidence known to me from a group contemporary with the NT in which we encounter a social 'mix' closely akin to that represented in the Pauline congregations. There are of course other texts where expatriate Roman citizens feature; but although this could be the case for our inscription, the Greek *cognomina* imply not. It is worth noting, too, that only two of the legible Latin names of members are not held by Roman citizens; and both of them may be slaves (A2.34, B45; see group C above). How is such a high percentage of Latin names to be interpreted? After all, the Christian groups have often been thought to have a large number of members of low status and low rank, which is what may be thought about the occupations spawned by the fishing industry. J. Dumont, *CE* 52 (1977) 141, accepts without question that in the Hellenistic period fishermen in Greece and Egypt were at the bottom of the social ladder. In fact, as our inscription from Ephesos shows, there was a considerable spread in formal civic rank and wealth attested for those involved in this industry. We may allow that not every individual who belonged to this association may have rowed his own boat or cast his own nets, as M.J. Osborne has observed to me. Some of the larger donations may have come from men in whose boats and shops hirelings or slaves actually did the physical work. This serves to underscore the point being made here about the 'mix' in formal rank within this industry: even the wealthy are quite happy to identify themselves as fishermen or fishmongers. On the other hand, the two *paraphylakeis* in A2.32-35 may be considered, with Keil (*cols.*56-57), to be watchmen responsible for keeping safe the customs house and the shops which have been inferred (above) to adjoin it. In view of their job designation in lieu of the lack of patronymic, Phorbos and Secundus are presumably of servile status. Yet each has the means (presumably from his *peculium*) to make a donation of 1000 bricks, the cost of which must have been *c.*20-25 den. Others in the list of donors who are possibly to be regarded as of servile status on the basis of nomenclature are noted in group C above. The same range in rank attested by this inscription, from Roman citizen (rich and poor) to slave, exactly parallels the Pauline onomastic evidence.

Apparent support for this view, that there were Roman citizens among the Christian congregations, is to be found some two generations after our Ephesian inscription. Pliny, *Ep.* 10.96.9 expresses his bewilderment at the phenomenon of so many converting to Christianity even in rural parts of Bithynia-Pontus, and seeks Trajan's advice: *multi enim omnis aetatis, omnis ordinis, utriusque sexus etiam, vocantur in periculum* . . . Taken at face value, and even allowing for some exaggeration, *ordo* ought to imply that there were Roman citizens among the Bithynian Christians. Yet *omnis ordinis* cannot be pressed too far: in early II there were hardly any provincial senators from Bithynia. It is less likely, though not to be ruled out, that Pliny alluding to the Greek civic structure of the eastern cities.

At one level, the NT gives implicit information that Galilean fishermen were of low status, at least from the perspective of urban dwellers in Jerusalem (Lk. 22.59) and foreign visitors to the city (Acts 2.7-8). Yet the families of Peter and Andrew, and of James and John, must have been of at least moderate means, since each owned a boat and other fishing equipment; furthermore, these families were each able to release two sons for a three-year period (Mk. 1.16-20, noting especially μετὰ μισθωτῶν). That there was no rupture with their families is implicit in these disciples' easy access to a fishing boat at various times during Jesus' ministry (e.g., Mk. 3.9; 4.1; 6.45-52), and is also confirmed by their immediate return to their fishing work after the Resurrection (Jn 21.1-13). In a rural context such as Galilee, where the lake was rich in its fish yield (Freyne, 14-15; cf. 129, 133, yet note 173-74; the situation may have altered by late III, as noted above), those occupied with the fishing trade will certainly not have been the poorest in the region. This may encourage us to conclude that at least some people from this occupational background were not illiterate. See the brief comment on this subject at *New Docs 1979*, **4**, p.19, with which it should be recalled that authorship of over one-quarter of the NT books is attributed to some of these 'unlearned' men (Acts 4.13, on which see useful comment in Wuellner, 55-59), as well as leadership roles in the first generation of the church.

The conclusion which Deissmann drew about the social level of the early Christians from his observation of the parallels between the NT and documentary texts has been in considerable doubt for some time now, owing to sociological perspectives being brought to bear upon the NT and the debate they have occasioned over the last quarter-century. Deissmann made his view explicit throughout *LAE*, e.g., 'By its social structure Primitive Christianity points unequivocally to the lower and middle classes' (7); his n.1 on that page says that the whole of *LAE* is 'an illustration' of this sentence. Or again, that the earliest Christians were 'men of the non-literary classes has been so often indicated in these pages from a variety of points of view that I should have no objection if this thesis were described as a main feature of my book' (290). Other comments in *LAE* relevant to this hypothesis may be found at 6 n.1, 8, 9, 55, 62, 144, 159-60, 174, 241, 246-47, 272, 299, 338, 339, 340, 385, 394, 395, 396, 466. A major fallacy in his argument is that he did not take sufficient account of the fact that a considerable proportion of the writers of (e.g.) papyrus private letters were individuals whose status and rank ensured that they are not to be identified with the poor, the 'lower classes', the majority of whom were totally illiterate. The occurrence of orthographic forms considerably at variance with Attic and Atticising norms provides no proof *per se* of a low level of literacy. It is intriguing that in all of N. Turner's work, he approaches most nearly to agreement with Deissmann's view of the nature of the Greek of the NT at the very moment when he advances the flawed proposition, in *ExpT* 71 (1960) 105, that since ostraka were pottery sherds they were the writing material 'used by the poorer classes'; and that even they are of value 'coming as they do from the lowest grades of society and helping to illustrate that NT language is in some ways the language of the working classes'. Meeks, *The First Urban Christians*, 51-53, surveys differing views this century about the social level of the early Christians, taking Deissmann as his starting-point.

Finally, very brief annotations are provided for selected names in the inscription, including a few of the patronymics. Where appropriate, reference is made to W. Schulze, *Zur Geschichte lateinischen Eigennamen* (Göttingen, 1904; repr. Berlin, 1966); and to F. Dornseiff/B. Hansen, *Rückläufiges Wörterbuch der griechischen Eigennamen* (Berlin, 1957; repr. Chicago, 1978). The 1978 reprint of the latter includes as an appendix L. Zgusta's reverse index of indigenous names from Asia Minor, taken from his *Kleinasiatische Personennamen* (Prague, 1964). References to Zgusta are to the page numbers in the Dornseiff/Hansen volume. The abbreviation *LGPN* refers to P.M. Fraser/E. Matthews (edd.), *A Lexicon of Greek Personal Names*, of which vol. I, covering the Aegean islands, Cyprus and Cyrenaica has recently appeared (Oxford, 1987). Where a merely general comment is included about the attestation of a name at Rome, the starting-point for the observation is L. Vidman's *Index Cognominum* (Berlin, 1980) and M. Bang's *Index Nominum* (Berlin, 1926) to *CIL* VI.

[..]ailios Lesbio[s (B16) — could this be *N*. Aelius Lesbios, a freedman?

Anektos (B37) — this *cognomen* is attested nine times from Delos (*LGPN*, I.41, III-II BC) and in papyri, but rarely enough to indicate that it was probably not a servile name.

Anthestius (A1.35) — = Antestius = Antistius (Schulze, 124 n.1). *CIL* VI, 4.2 (1902) 32776 (Rome, Imperial), an epitaph for the soldier C. Anthestius Niger, reflects the same orthography as found in our text here. In *I.Eph.* III.973.5, 6, two members of a religious association possess this *nomen*; while at V.1601, frag. δ.15, Γ. Ἀνθίστιος is named in a list of Dionysiac initiates.

Arruntius (B23) — a *nomen* of Etruscan origin (Schulze, 175; cf. 263), here acting as a *cognomen*. Attested of eminent people.

Bassus (A2.36) — quite frequently attested in *I.Eph.*, including people who have achieved eminence.

Tib. Claudius Metrodoros (A1.19-20) — a freedman of the *familia Caesaris*. Another Metrodoros at *I.Eph.* 3.666a.22.

P. Cornelii (A1.15, 40-41, 55) — It is possible that Alexandros and Felix were freedmen of Philistion (this name — only *CIL* VI.24101 at Rome, and two other instances at Ephesos, one a Roman citizen — is too rarely attested to be servile in origin). Cornelia Ision may likewise have been a *liberta* of Philistion. Against this is the latter's smaller contribution. It is very likely that Felix and Ision are *contubernales* both manumitted by the same owner; on *contubernales* see B. Rawson, *TAPA* 104 (1974) 279-305, especially 293-99.

Dionysios (B20) — very common; some people of high standing have this name at Ephesos. The 15th most common Greek name at Rome (Solin, *GPR* 3.1439), with frequency peaking in I AD (ibid., 1.302-06), often servile.

Epaphras (A1.47, B25) — two other instances at Ephesos. Although a common servile name (see *New Docs 1979*, 5), the man at A1.47 is unlikely to be a slave even though he has only one name, since mention of his son is included.

Epaphroditos (A2.57-58, B46) — a dozen instances in *I.Eph.* for this frequently servile name: cf. *New Docs 1979*, 5.

Fronto (A2.20-21) — an eminent *cognomen*, rarely servile; three others attested in *I.Eph.*

Gerellanus (A1.25) for its occurrence as a *nomen* cf. *CIL* VI, 4.2 (1902) 35377 (Rome, Imperial). Schulze (592 n.357) mentions an instance from Ravenna with the Latinised spelling Gerulanius. The -anus spelling is common in *I.Eph.* (eight examples, a couple possessing some status), and rather more so in the form Gerillanus.

Hamaxas (A1.63) — As with Kroukras (A1.65) and Kenartas (A2.29) this non-Latin, non-Greek name is inferred to be of indigenous origin. Each man has taken a Greek name, indicative of the social circles in which he wishes to mix.

Honerius (B38) — a rare Etruscan name (Schulze, 292). Schulze's epigraphical references (292, 358) are somewhat confused. *CIL* VI.3 (1886) 19510 has a *libertus* M. Honerius Gargallus; M. Honerius is visible in the fragmentary *CIL* XIV (1887) 2544, from the Tusculan region. In *CIL* VI.3.19510 Foneria Tyche sets up an epitaph, and the ed. n. ad loc. suggests Honeria should be read. Finally a daughter called Honeratia is memorialised in *CIL* VI.2 (1882) 9800.

Hordeonius (A1.12) and Hordionius (B11) — This *nomen* is of Etruscan origin (Schulze, 306). The spelling -deon- is less common but more eminent: e.g., Hordeonius Flaccus the consular legate in Germania Superior under the Flavians in 69 AD (Tac., *Hist.* 1.9, etc.). Schulze (ad loc.) notes a couple of inscriptions (Rome and Athens) with the -deon- orthography. That the name belongs to a high social echelon is confirmed by *I.Eph.*, where three of the four other males who possess this name and both the women (Hordeonia) are of some status.

Kallinikos (B39) — half-a-dozen others in *I.Eph.*; rarely servile at Rome.

Kassiades (A2.46) — a hybrid name, apparently, consisting of a Greek termination affixed to a Latin stem (cf. Cassius).

Kroukras (A1.65) — see on Hamaxas, above. The name is attested in Zgusta, 327.

Laberius (A2.14) — Two of the other three in *I.Eph.* are of high status (the third text is lacunose). See further Schulze, 162.

Lainos (B11) — This appears to be unattested as a *cognomen*, so cannot be regarded as a servile name.

Licinnius (B24) — geminated -nn- not attested in *CIL* VI; cf. Schulze, 107-08.

Livius (A2.62) — Schulze, 178. Three others in *I.Eph.*, at least one of whom is of high status.

Lollius (B23) — eminent *nomen* (eight attested in *I.Eph.*), also occasionally appearing as a *cognomen*: *CIL* X.1403 (Schulze, 519).

Macer (A1.32) — only here in *I.Eph.* This man and Rufus (A1.57) may be patron and freedman respectively (Macer as a servile name is rare), or two freedmen of the same master.

Melleitos (A1.25-26) — The origin of this *cognomen* is unclear: Greek, probably, but Latin (= Melitus) not to be ruled out.

Montanus (B13) — rarely servile.

Naevius (A1.49) — Schulze, 263 and n.2; only one other example in *I.Eph*.

Naukleros (B24) — unattested at Rome, so unlikely to be in use as a servile name. This is the only attestation in *I.Eph*. The name Naukles is attested six times in *LGPN*, I.323-24 (IV-I BC).

Niger (A1.49, 2.14) — only here in *I.Eph*.

Onesimos (A1.37, B36, 44) — very commonly servile, cf. *New Docs 1979*, **96**; over a dozen other instances in *I.Eph*.

Philistion (A1.55-56) — See on P. Cornelii, above.

Phorbos (A2.32) — only here in *I.Eph*. See Dornseiff/Hansen, 218.

Phygelos (B47) — To illustrate this uncommon name for the NT onomasticon *I.Eph*. yields both this example and III.909a, a fragmentary list of names where the ed. n. treats the occurrence as a *cognomen* or an ethnic.

Pius (B48) — quite common at Ephesos (about 10 others); the name is almost never servile.

Popillius (B26) — non-geminated -ll- is the more respectable orthography, preferred by the senatorial class. Cf. Licinnius above.

Roscilius (A2.51) — once elsewhere in *I.Eph*.; not in *CIL* VI.

Rufus (A1.57, B41) — See above, on Macer. Rufus is common in *I.Eph*. Cf. Ruficius at A2.61, for which Keil had read Fuficius.

Stateri[(B35) — this *cognomen* unattested at Rome, so unlikely to be servile in origin.

Tosides (A1.53) — unparalleled(?), or even if attested only very rarely too infrequent to be servile in origin.

Trophimos (A1.43) — cf. *New Docs 1978*, **80**.

Tyrannos (B40) — a useful contemporary illustration from the same city for the Tyrannos mentioned in Acts 19.9.

Vedius (A1.51) — a notable *gens* at Ephesos; many attestations in *I.Eph*. of members of this family who attained social eminence.

Verus (A1.51) — three others in *I.Eph*. The name appears to be servile in origin only rarely.

Vetulenus (A2.41) — a name of Etruscan origin (Schulze, 256-57). The form found most commonly among the senatorial class is Vett-. Schulze provides (from *CIL*) over a dozen examples of Vetulenus, Vetulenius (this last attested three times in *I.Eph*.), and variants.

Xanthos (A2.30) — servile here (the following genitive indicating the owner rather than acting as a patronymic)? At Rome the name is surprisingly uncommon: Solin, *GPR*, 2.693-94 can provide only 18 attestations (the bulk from I AD). None of these is of higher status than *libertus*, at most. From Ephesos this is the sole attestation.

Zosimos (A2.52) — very common at Ephesos. The 17th most common Greek name at Rome (Solin, *GPR*, 3.1439), prevalent in I AD above all. Of 269 attestations in Solin (ibid., 2.819-22) only one is certainly of the senatorial class, another three freeborn.

]l ourios Cae[(B42) — Perhaps, e.g., Ai]lourios or O]lourios, both attested in the papyri. This presupposes no letter gap between the first two surviving letters. Cae[is more likely to be Latin than Greek and implies a preceding *nomen*; alternatively, have we an imperial freedman (reading Καί[σαρος])?

Conclusion

The lengthy dedication which has been dealt with here has much to offer NT work in four ways. First, given its date, it yields a rich harvest for the lexicographer. Next, the information which may be extrapolated from it (in conjunction with other evidence) about the fishing industry in first-century Ephesos — and elsewhere, by cautious analogy — is of significance for the social historian of the NT world in view of the work background of a number of the first disciples. Third, *I.Eph*. Ia.20 is our first really illustrative indication that the composition of the Pauline churches reflects closely the same spread in civic rank found in a contemporary association at the metropolis of Asia. Finally, if the analogy holds good, this leads to the most far-reaching conclusion, namely the possibility that the Pauline congregations had a large number of Roman citizens among their membership. This hypothesis — adumbrated briefly in several places by E.A. Judge: *Rank and Status in the World of the Caesars and St Paul* (*Broadhead Lecture* 4; Christchurch, 1982) 13; *New Docs 1977*, **84**; *New Docs 1978*, **4**, pp.18-19; *TynB* 35 (1984) 16 — requires careful evaluation, for it has implications for our view of the Pauline Mission. Did Paul focus attention particularly upon those who possessed citizenship in order that, when he moved elsewhere, adherents would be left in those cities who in many cases possessed the means to host gatherings at their own homes? Further, in the light of his own and Silas' experience at Philippi (Acts 16.19-40, especially *vss*.37-39) did he come to appreciate the 'protective' value of having Roman citizens among the membership, whose very identification with the group may have helped to shield it from some of the more open expressions of hostility?

The neglect of this inscription with so much of interest for the NT appears to be symptomatic of a more widespread failure of NT studies to keep abreast of the progress of archaeological work at Ephesos, if the blunt comments of R.E. Oster are justified in his *Bibliography of Ancient Ephesus* (*ATLA Bibliog. Series*, 19; Metuchen, 1987) xix-xxiv. Numismatic evidence is even more rarely used than inscriptions by NT research on cities like Ephesos. For a recent attempt to relate special silver coin issues of Claudius at the city with the Acts 19 riot see L.J. Kreitzer, *JSNT* 30 (1987) 59-70, though the case is overstated. This marvellous site, which is being so methodically excavated, is continuing to yield finds of real significance for the world of early Christianity. It is time for more NT scholars to cast their net into this area and ensure that they catch some of these prize fish; they will surely enrich the dinner table of NT research.

APPENDIX 1

G.P. SHIPP'S DISCUSSIONS OF NT USAGE
IN THE LIGHT OF MODERN GREEK

(see above p.71)

Listed below in summary form are those words treated (in certain of their uses) by Shipp in *Modern Greek Evidence* . . ., where he includes discussion (whether brief or extended) of NT passages. This does not amount to an index, but will give those not familiar with his book some idea of the range of treatment. While the book is arranged alphabetically, related or contrasting words are often dealt with in a composite entry. The number in brackets refers to pages in the book. Attention may also be drawn in passing to Shipp's article, not widely-known, it seems, 'Some observations on the distribution of words in the NT', in E.C.B. MacLaurin (ed.), *Essays in Honour of G.W. Thatcher* (Sydney, 1967), 127-38.

ἀγαλλιάω (24)
ἀγρεύω group (28-29)
ἄγχω (31-32)
ἄγω, προάγω, συνάγω, ὑπάγω, αἴρω, φέρω, βαστάζω (32-38)
αἰδώς, αἰσχύνομαι, αἰσχύνη, ἐντρέπομαι, ἐντροπή (45-47)
αἴρω — s.v. ἄγω
αἰσχύνη — s.v. αἰδώς
αἰσχύνομαι — s.v. αἰδώς
ἅλας (53-54)
ἀλγέω — s.v. πονέω
ἀλεκτρύων — s.v. ἀλέκτωρ
ἀλέκτωρ, ἀλεκτρύων, φωνέω, πετεινά, ὄρνεον (55-56)
ἄλλος, ἕτερος (58-61, 251-53)
ἅλων (62)
ἀμάω, θερίζω (63)
ἀμφότεροι, ἑκάτεροι (67)
ἀναστατόω (70)
ἀνθήμερον (73-74)
ἀνθρώπινος (74-75)
ἀνίστημι, ἐγείρω, ἐξυπνίζω (75-80)
ἀποκρίνομαι (88-89)
ἄρτι (101-02)
ἀχρεῖος (120-22)
βαδίζω (122-24; not NT, but instructive negative evidence)
βαίνω and compounds (125-26)

βάλλω, ἐκβάλλω (129-31)
βαστάζω (132-37; q.v. sub ἄγω)
βαττολογέω (141-42)
βελόνη, ῥάφις (143-45)
βία (147-48)
βλέπω, θεάομαι, θεωρέω, ὁράω (151-57)
βοάω, κράζω (157-58)
βορέας, βορρᾶς (161-63)
βορρᾶς — s.v. βορέας
βότρυς (163-64)
βούλομαι, θέλω (166-67)
βουνός (167-70); cf. C.J. Hemer, *NovT* 24 (1982) 121-23
βρέφος (175)
βρέχω (176)
βρίθω (176-77; negative evidence)
βρύω — s.v. πηγή
δέρω (212-13)
δίδωμι (216)
διψάω (219)
δύσκολος (223-24)
δῶμα (225)
ἐγείρω — s.v. ἀνίστημι
ἑκάτεροι — s.v. ἀμφότεροι
ἐκβάλλω — s.v. βάλλω
ἐκεῖ, ἐκεῖσε (227-28)
ἐλαύνω and compounds (233)
ἐνιαυτός — s.v. ἔτος
ἐντρέπομαι — s.v. αἰδώς

ἐντροπή — s.v. αἰδώς

ἐξαίφνης — s.v. ἐξάπινα

ἐξάπινα, ἐξαίφνης (240-41)

ἐξυπνίζω — s.v. ἀνίστημι

ἐπιτάσσω — s.v. κελεύω

ἑσπέρα, ὀψέ, ὀψία (246-47)

ἕτερος — s.v. ἄλλος

ἔτος, ἐνιαυτός (253-54)

εὔμορφος (256; negative evidence)

εὑρίσκω (258)

ζυγός (261-62)

θαρρέω, θαρσέω, θάρσος (265-66)

θαρσέω — s.v. θαρρέω

θάρσος — s.v. θαρρέω

θεάομαι — s.v. βλέπω

θέλω — s.v. βούλομαι

θερίζω — s.v. ἀμάω

θεωρέω — s.v. βλέπω

θύω, σφάζω (274)

ἴσχω (285; negative evidence)

ἰχθῦς — s.v. ὀψάριον

καιρός, χρόνος (290-92)

καλός (296)

κάμνω — s.v. ποιέω

κἄν = καί (297-98)

κέλευσμα — s.v. κελεύω

κελεύω, κέλευσμα, λέγω, ἐπίτασσω
        (310-11; more on κελεύω at 418-20)

κεράννυμι (312-13)

κλέος (317)

κλίβανος (318-19)

κολαφίζω (326-27)

κολυμβάω (330)

κράββατος (106-07)

κράζω — s.v. βοάω

κρατέω (339-40)

κωφός (349-51)

λέγω — s.v. κελεύω

λικμάω (363-68)

μακάριος (375-76)

μωρός (398)

ὄνομα (416)

ὅραμα (418)

ὁράω — s.v. βλέπω

ὄρνεον — s.v. ἀλέκτωρ

οὖς, ὠτίον (425)

ὀψάριον, ἰχθῦς (427)

ὀψέ — s.v. ἑσπέρα

ὀψία — s.v. ἑσπέρα

παιδάριον — s.v. παιδίσκη

παιδίον — s.v. παιδίσκη

παιδίσκη, παῖς, παιδίον, παιδάριον (430-35)

παῖς — s.v. παιδίσκη

πάντοτε (438-39; read 'Philemon 4' ad loc.)

παρρησία (441-42; see further above in the present
        volume, p.71)

πενής, πενιχρός (446-47)

πενιχρός — s.v. πενής

πετεινά — s.v. ἀλέκτωρ

πηγή, βρύω (449-53)

ποῖ, ποῦ (461)

ποιέω, πράσσω, κάμνω (461-68)

πονέω, ἀλγέω (470-71)

ποταπός (471)

ποῦ — s.v. ποῖ

πράσσω — s.v. ποιέω

προάγω — s.v. ἄγω

προσφάγιον (428-29)

πρότερος, πρῶτος (475)

πρῶτος — s.v. πρότερος

ῥάφις — s.v. βελόνη

σάμβατον = σάββατον (490-91)

σκύλλω (505-06)

συνάγω — s.v. ἄγω

σφάζω — s.v. θύω

τέκνον (530)

τελώνης (530-31)

τί = ὅτι 'because' (533-34; see further above in the
        present volume, p.71)

τρώγω (540-41)

ὑπάγω — s.v. ἄγω

ὗς — s.v. χοῖρος

φαιλόνης (550)

φέγγος (495)

φέρω (553-54; q.v. *sub* ἄγω)

φωνέω — s.v. ἀλέκτωρ

χαλάω (564-65)

χοῖρος, ὗς (210)

χρόνος — s.v. καιρός

ψωμίον (582-84)

ὠτίον — s.v. οὖς

APPENDIX 2

LINGUISTICS AND ANCIENT GREEK
(cf. pp.69, 81 above)

A useful survey of the application of Linguistics to research in Ancient Greek may be found in F.W. Householder/G. Nagy, *Greek. A Survey of Recent Work* (*Janua Linguarum* 211; The Hague, 1972). I have largely confined my attention here to the period after that, and included mention of some titles in Biblical Studies. What is offered here aims to be a representative sampling, and does not at all claim comprehensiveness. A number of other relevant publications have been referred to in various places in the present volume: see index 3.

On the estrangement between Classics and Linguistics for much of this century see J. Frösén, *Prolegomena to a Study of the Greek Language in the First Centuries AD. The Problem of Koine and Atticism* (Helsinki, 1974) 9-15; cf. A. Bartoněk, 'On the application of modern linguistic methods to the study of Classical Languages, especially Greek', *Eirene* 4 (1965) 123-32. W.P. Lehmann suggests in *IJSL* 31 (1981) 11-27 that A. Meillet's expressed concern to link Linguistics with the Social Sciences was not built upon by successors in Historical Linguistics, partly because of the influence of de Saussure and later on partly because of the intervention of World War II. Undoubtedly, one of the finest recent contributions to Historical Linguistics is P. Chantraine's *Dictionnaire étymologique de la langue grecque* (4 vols., the last largely written by several of his students; Paris, 1968-80). Its subject naturally makes it a diachronic lexicon, but entries show awareness of evidence of developments in modern Linguistics. For corrections to Chantraine's first vol., particularly in the area of Semitic borrowings, note B. Hemmerdinger, 'De la méconnaissance de quelques étymologies grecques', *Glotta* 48 (1970) 40-66. In the same sphere of research H. Frisk's *Griechisches etymologisches Wörterbuch* finally reached completion in the early 1970s (22 parts, plus suppl. vol.; Heidelberg, 1954-72). In *New Horizons in Linguistics*, ed. J. Lyons (Harmondsworth, 1970), P. Kiparsky suggests (302-15) that Historical Linguistics is once more being recognised to have a contribution to make to the question of how a language has changed, which may help the synchronic description of that language to be seen in perspective. Indeed, there is now a clear indication that the pendulum has swung back to a better balance. Diachronic studies are firmly back on the agenda with the recognition that synchronic investigation of a language cannot explain how it has developed to its present form. An interesting small example of how both synchrony and diachrony may be drawn upon to illuminate a syntactical question is provided by V.A. Friedman, 'Dialectal synchrony and diachronic syntax: the Macedonian perfect', in S.B. Steever et al. (edd.), *Papers from the Parasession on Diachronic Syntax, April 22, 1976* (Chicago, 1976), 96-104.

In Germany the journals *Glotta* and *Gymnasium* have included a number of articles discussing the relationship between Linguistics and Classical Philology. Among them the following may be mentioned as a sample: H. Weinreich, 'Die lateinische Sprache zwischen Logik und Linguistik', *Gymnasium* 73 (1966) 147-63; K. Strunk, 'Historische und deskriptive Linguistik bei der Textinterpretation', *Glotta* 49 (1971) 191-216; K. Beyer/D. Cherubim, 'Linguistik und alte Sprachen. Eine Polemik?', *Gymnasium* 80 (1973) 251-79; J. Latacz, 'Klassische Philologie und moderne Linguistik', *Gymnasium* 81 (1974) 67-89. The last two provide useful bibliographies, and Latacz includes a brief critique of Beyer/Cherubim (83-84). J. Barr, 'The ancient Semitic languages — the conflict between Philology and Linguistics', *TPS* (1968) 37-55, may also be mentioned here, for he includes discussion which has application more generally than to Semitics alone.

In Britain, interest in Classical Greek phonology which draws upon advances in linguistic research has been revived largely under the stimulus of W.S. Allen, whose *Vox Graeca. The Pronunciation of Classical Greek* (Cambridge, 1987[3]) makes all-too-modest claims for itself. Allen was responsible in part for the supervision of A.H. Sommerstein's Cambridge thesis, subsequently published as *The Sound Pattern of Ancient Greek* (*Publications of the Philological Society* 23; Oxford, 1973). Note also J. Aitchison's phonological study, 'The distinctive features of Ancient Greek', *Glotta* 54 (1976) 173-201. Allen's other major contribution for this general area is his *Accent and Rhythm* (*Cambridge Studies in Linguistics* 13; Cambridge, 1973); and his programmatic Inaugural Lecture, *On the Linguistic Study of Languages* (Cambridge, 1957) is also worth noting (repr. in P. Strevens [ed.], *Five Inaugural Lectures* [London, 1966], 1-26). On the other hand, W.B. Stanford's Sather Lectures, *The Sound of Greek* (Berkeley, 1967), consciously eschews modern linguistic theory (although he is not oblivious to it), pursuing instead an 'aesthetic' approach (v).

J. Lyons' work in semantics should be mentioned. His *Structural Semantics. An Analysis of part of the Vocabulary of Plato* (*Publications of The Philological Society* 20; Oxford, 1963; repr. 1972) is most useful even apart from the analysis itself (which constitutes only some 90pp. of the monograph), for it includes discussion of the theory of Structural Semantics and provides a very clear exposition of his analysis. Like Sommerstein, Lyons is conscious of a major debt to Chomsky's work, although he has developed certain approaches of his own; indeed, the bulk of his subsequent research has not been oriented to Classics *per se*.

A Structuralist approach has been taken to Homer by H.B. Rosén, *Struktural-grammatische Beiträge zum Verständnis Homers* (Amsterdam, 1967) — *non vidi*; cf. C.J. Ruijgh, 'A propos d'une nouvelle application de méthodes structuralistes à la langue homérique', *Mnem.* 21 (1968) 113-31. Note also R.G. Tanner's study, 'Aristotle as a Structural Linguist', *TPS* (1969) 99-164.

Structuralism is not the only method being attempted. For example, D. Lightfoot's analysis of the different contexts in which the subjunctive and optative are used adopts a Generative Semantics method: *Natural Logic and the Greek Moods* (*Janua Linguarum, series practica* 230; The Hague, 1975). A clear survey of structuralist and transformational-generative models of language development (as well as of the neo-grammarian approach) is provided by T. Bynon, *Historical Linguistics* (Cambridge, 1977).

Important contributions have been emanating from Scandinavia, too. Honourable mention should be made, for example, of a number of Finnish researchers — some (all?) of them pupils and/or colleagues of H. Zilliacus — who have been applying sociolinguistics to classical studies. Of these one particularly stimulating recent contribution has been J. Kaimio, *The Romans and the Greek Language* (Helsinki, 1979), a wide-ranging sociolinguistic study which attempts to analyse who used Greek in the Roman world, and why. Also of interest, though not altogether satisfying (because so theoretical), is Frösén's *Prolegomena*. From Sweden the contributions of S.-T. Teodorsson to our understanding of Greek phonology, and of J. Blomqvist to our appreciation of Hellenistic use of particles, warrant particular mention here; see bibliography for several of the publications of each. The contributions of these four researchers are noted elsewhere in this volume. From the Netherlands mention should be included of A. Rijksbaron, *The Syntax and Semantics of the Verb in Classical Greek* (Amsterdam, 1984). This linguistically-sensitive volume concentrates on Greek of the fifth and fourth centuries BC, and is impressive for its concise yet comprehensive scope, and excellent choice of illustrative passages. Rijksbaron is also the editor of a colloquium on Greek grammar: *In the Footsteps of Raphael Kühner* (Amsterdam, 1986), which contains essays ranging from sentence structure to purpose and conditional constructions, and from the use of the modal particle to the role of the accusative.

Turning now to NT Studies, in Germany a structuralist semantic approach has been used by E. Güttgemanns in his attempt to integrate Biblical exegesis and Linguistics. His *Studia Linguistica Neotestamentica. Gesammelte Aufsätze zur linguistischen Grundlage einer neutestamentlichen Theologie* (*Beiträge zur evangelischen Theologie* 60; Munich 1973) reprints six essays from the late 1960s/early 1970s, some in revised form. I have not seen any complete numbers of the journal of which he is the founding editor, *Linguistica Biblica. Interdisziplinäre Zeitschrift für Theologie and Linguistik* (1970—); nor have I seen the book on which he collaborated with U. Gerber, *'Linguistische' Theologie. Biblische Texte, christliche Verkündigung und theologische Sprachtheorie* (Bonn, 1975[2]). Güttgemanns' earlier book, *Offene Fragen zur Formgeschichte des Evangeliums* (*Beiträge zur evangelischen Theologie* 54; Munich, 1971[2]) was translated with the title, *Candid Questions concerning Gospel Form Criticism* (Pittsburgh, 1979); neither version makes for easy reading. W.G. Doty, who translated this book, also reviewed the German original in 'Fundamental questions about literary-critical methodology. A review article', *JAAR* 40 (1972) 521-27; subsequently he provided a broader evaluation of the work of Güttgemanns and his collaborators, 'Linguistics and Biblical criticism', *JAAR* 41 (1973) 114-21. The very dense language in which these works are couched is likely to impede their receiving widespread attention. Even portions of Doty's critiques are obscure. However, the work of Güttgemanns is accorded a chapter in the clearest recent book which introduces Structuralism to those working in Biblical Studies. D. Greenwood's *Structuralism and the Biblical Text* (*Religion and Reason* 32; Berlin, 1985) provides a critical synthesis of the contribution of this linguistic and literary field as expressed through Lévi-Strauss, Barthes, Greimas and others. A useful bibliography in Greenwood's book has appended to it a list of those journals which have devoted a particular number to questions concerning Structuralism. In the Biblical field *Semeia* is one of these. Thus, an article by Güttgemanns which originally appeared in *Ling. Bib.* 13-14 (1972) 2-18 has been translated in *Semeia* 6 (1976) 181-213 under the title, 'Linguistic-literary critical foundation of a NT Theology.' Whatever estimate is to be made of Güttgemanns' contribution, his insistence that Biblical studies as a discipline has given too little attention to Linguistics does ring true. This view is endorsed by P. Cotterell/ M. Turner, *Linguistics and Biblical Interpretation* (London, 1989) 26; indeed, this is the whole rationale for thier book, which offers a useful, introductory guide to the importance of Linguistics for the study of the Bible.

While on the subject of Linguistics and NT studies in Germany, we may note here R. Wonneberger, *Syntax und Exegese. Eine generative Theorie der griechischen Syntax und ihr Beitrag zur Auslegung des NT, dargestellt an 2. Kor. 5.2f. und Röm. 3.21-26* (*Beiträge zur biblischen Exegese und Theologie* 13; Frankfurt am Main, 1979). He applies Chomsky's notion of Generative Syntax to develop a syntactic theory of ancient Greek, which he then tests out by analysis of two NT passages. The work of Wonneberger and Güttgemanns has yet to make a major impact on mainstream NT philological work. On the application of de Saussure's work to theology see Y. Simoens, 'Linguistique saussurienne et théologie', *Rech. Sc. Rel.* 61 (1973) 7-22.

The mid-1970s has witnessed a considerable growth of interest in 'Biblical Semantics' in English-speaking countries. Mention should be made here of A.C. Thiselton's article, 'Semantics and NT Interpretation', in I.H. Marshall (ed.), *NT Interpretation. Essays on Principles and Methods* (Grand Rapids, 1977), 75-104; id., *The Two Horizons* (Exeter, 1980); A. Gibson, *Biblical Semantic Logic. A Preliminary Analysis* (Oxford, 1981); J.P. Louw, *Semantics of NT Greek* (Philadelphia, 1982); and M. Silva, *Biblical Words and Their Meaning. An Introduction to Lexical Semantics* (Grand Rapids, 1983). Also to be noted is E.A. Nida et al., *Style and Discourse, with Special Reference to the Greek NT* (Cape Town, 1983), which includes some discussion of semantics and syntactical structures.

Turning to lexicography, R.L. Collison's recent *History of Foreign Language Dictionaries* (London, 1982) gives attention to a number of works in the field of Ancient Greek, though it is surprising to see all NT lexica ignored, even Bauer. Reference is made to the computerised *Thesaurus Linguae Graecae*, based at the University of California, Irvine. Developments occur so rapidly in the computer field that Collison's information on that project is well out of date already. By early 1989 nearly all Greek literature to 600 AD had been entered, though a fair percentage of this awaits verification (unverified texts are nevertheless over 98% accurate). The development of laser-read compact disks means that all Greek literature is now potentially available on the desk of any individual with a micro-computer which can read the disk. The *TLG* is not a lexicographical undertaking in itself, but is certain to alter the face of this sphere of research into Greek.

As an indication of the increasing sophistication of work in lexicography, one book from each of the last three decades may be mentioned. F.W. Householder/S. Saporta (edd.), *Problems in Lexicography. Report of the Conference on Lexicography held at Indiana University, Nov. 1960* (The Hague, 1962 [= *IJAL* 28.2 (1962)]), was a landmark in its time, and is still of interest. It includes a number of papers on bilingual dictionaries, as well as essays addressing the relation of lexicon to grammar, and lexicographic definition. That parts of this volume seem now rather *passé* is a comment on the pace of developments in this area. A decade later appeared the international collaborative work under the editorship of L. Zgusta, *Manual* of Lexicography (Janua Linguarum, series maior 39; Prague, 1971). This book provides a very full coverage of many of the questions, by no means theoretical ones only. Here, too, attention is given to bilingual dictionaries, and to the question of lexical meaning. D.J. Georgacas offers a lengthy critique of the work in 'The present state of lexicography and Zgusta's Manual of Lexicography', Orbis 25 (1976) 359-400. From the present decade a representative work is R.R.K. Hartman, (ed.), Lexicography: Principles and Practice (London, 1983). Once more, both theory and practice are given their due. As well as a useful contribution on bilingual dictionaries (41-51), there are now essays on more sophisticated problems, such as one on dictionaries for special registers (53-64).

It should not be assumed from this that English-language material is all that is worth reading in this area. Indeed, it rather pales beside some much weightier Continental scholarship, particularly from Spain and France. Deserving particular mention are: J. Casares, Introducción a la lexicografía moderna (Revista de Filologia Española, Anejo 52; Madrid, 1950, repr. 1969); A. Rey/J. Rey-Debove, La lexicographie (Paris, 1970); J. and C. Dubois, Introduction à la lexicographie: le dictionnaire (Paris, 1971), offering many valuable theoretical insights; F. Rodríguez Adrados et al., Introducción a la lexicografía griega (Manuales y Anejos de Emerita 33; Madrid, 1977); G. Haensch/L. Wolf/S. Ettinger/R. Werner, La lexicografía: de la lingüística teórica a la lexicografía práctica (Madrid, 1982). Two contributions from Germany include H. Moser (ed.), Probleme der Lexikologie und Lexikographie (Sprache der Gegenwart 39; Düsseldorf, 1976), and B. Schaeder, Lexikographie als Praxis und Theorie (Reihe germanistische Linguistik 34; Tübingen, 1981). I am grateful to M. Silva for alerting me to a number of these items. Not everything in each of these books is relevant to an historical linguistics interest concerned with the forms no longer spoken of a language. Accordingly, the volume by Rodríguez Adrados and others deserves special mention, for the contributors are indicating in this book the linguistic foundation for the Diccionario Griego-Español, the first two fascicules of which have appeared so far (Madrid, 1980, 1986). The second fascicule includes a supplement to material in the first; for addenda to the second see J. Rodríguez Somolinos, 'Notas lexicográficas. Materiales para un futuro Suplemento al DGE', Emerita 56 (1988) 233-44. A similar undergirding volume for another dictionary project is J.P. Louw (ed.), Lexicography and Translation, with Special Reference to Bible Translation (Cape Town, 1985). Here 'semantic domains' is the approach adopted to lexicography, and this is the explicit orientation of the lexicon which appeared three years later: J.P. Louw/E.A. Nida (edd.), Greek-English Lexicon of the NT based on Semantic Domains (2 vols.; New York, 1988). Brief comment on this last item is given above, p.80. Mention should also be made here of a new journal from Spain devoted specifically to the language of the NT: vol.1 of Filología Neotestamentaria appeared in 1988 under the editorship of J. Peláez. One particularly useful feature is its inclusion of a bibliographical bulletin of research in the area, by A. Piñero Sáenz. Items are arranged by subgroupings (structuralism, morphology, semantics, etc.), with some cross-referencing supplied.

Writing about lexicography continues to be active throughout the 1980s. In L. Zgusta (ed.), Theory and Method in Lexicography: Western and Non-Western Perspectives (Columbia, 1980), particular attention is paid to dictionaries and 'the description of the norm', as well as to the questions of definitions and of the contribution of computers to lexicographical work. These last two issues also receive considerable attention in S.I. Landau, Dictionaries. The Art and Craft of Lexicography (New York, 1984). The volume edited by R. Ilson, Lexicography. An emerging International Profession (Manchester, 1986), looks backwards with a chapter on the history of lexicography, and forward with one on the character of dictionaries of the next century. An essay is included by E. Gates who had earlier provided an assessment of lexicographical tools available for OT/NT work: An Analysis of the Lexicographic Resources used by American Biblical Scholars Today (SBLDS 8; Missoula, 1972); and a summation is provided by L. Zgusta.

SELECT BIBLIOGRAPHY

This bibliography includes nearly all secondary literature referred to in the first four chapters of this volume, apart from standard works of reference (BAGD, LSJ, MM, Migne, etc.), abbreviations for which are given in the Introduction. Works noted only in Appendix 2, on 'Linguistics and Ancient Greek', are not normally included here. Certain items specific only to tangential comments are not listed (e.g., commentaries on certain classical or NT texts). Nor do all book reviews to which reference has been made receive mention here. A small number of other works used but not referred to have been included. Wherever possible, the words 'New Testament', 'Old Testament' and 'Septuagint' have been abbreviated as 'NT', 'OT', and 'LXX' respectively. An asterisk indicates that an item concerns linguistic questions without reference to ancient languages, but nevertheless contributed to the theoretical base for some of the book's essays.

*　　　　　*　　　　　*

Abbott, T.K., *Essays, Chiefly on the Original Texts of the Old and New Testaments* (London, 1891)

Abbott-Smith, G., *A Manual Greek Lexicon of the NT* (Edinburgh, 1937³; repr. 1956)

Abel, F.M., *Grammaire du grec biblique suivie d'un choix de papyrus* (Paris, 1927)

* Abercrombie, D., 'R.P. and local dialect', repr. in his *Studies in Phonetics and Linguistics* (London, 1965) 10-15

Aerts, W.J., *Periphrastica. An Investigation into the Use of εἶναι and ἔχειν as Auxiliaries or Pseudo-auxiliaries in Greek from Homer up to the Present Day* (Amsterdam, 1965)

Aitchison, J., 'The distinctive features of Ancient Greek', *Glotta* 54 (1976) 173-201

Aleshire, S.B./Bodoh, J.B., 'Some corrections to LSJ', *Glotta* 53 (1975) 66-75

Alexander, L., 'Luke's Preface in the context of Greek Preface-Writing', *NovT* 28 (1986) 48-74

Amstutz, J., *ΑΠΛΟΤΗΣ. Eine begriffsgeschichtliche Studie zum jüdisch-christlichen Griechisch* (*Theophaneia* 19; Bonn, 1968)

Angus, S., 'Modern methods in NT philology', *HTR* 2 (1909) 446-64

—————, 'The *koine*, the language of the NT', *Princeton Theol. Rev.* 8 (1910) 44-92

Argyle, A.W., 'Did Jesus speak Greek?', *ExpT* 67 (1955/6) 92-93, 383

—————, '"Hypocrites" and the Aramaic Theory', *ExpT* 75 (1963/4) 113-14

—————, 'Greek among the Jews of Palestine in NT Times', *NTS* 20 (1973/4) 87-89

Atkinson, B.F.C., *The Theology of Prepositions* (London, 1944)

Audet, J.-P., 'A Hebrew-Aramaic list of books of the OT in Greek transcription', *JTS* n.s.1 (1950) 135-54

* Baetens Beardsmore, H., *Bilingualism: Basic Principles* (Clevedon, 1982)

Bailey, C.E., 'The British Protestant theologians in the First World War: Germanophobia unleashed', *HTR* 77 (1984) 195-221

Bakker, W.F., *The Greek Imperative. An Investigation into the Aspectual Differences between the Present and Aorist Imperatives in Greek Prayer from Homer up to the Present Day* (Amsterdam, 1966)

—————, *Pronomen Abundans and Pronomen Coniunctum. A Contribution to the History of the Resumptive Pronoun within the Relative Clause in Greek* (*Verhandlingen der Koninklijke Nederlandse Ak. van Weten., Afd. Lett.*, 82; Amsterdam, 1974)

Bank, J.S., 'The Greek of the LXX', *ExpT* 8 (1898) 500-03

Barclay, W., 'The NT and the Papyri', in H. Anderson/W. Barclay (edd.), *The NT in Historical and Contemporary Perspective. Essays in Memory of G.H.C. Macgregor* (Oxford, 1965), 57-81

Baron, S.W., *A Social and Religious History of the Jews*, I-II (New York, 1952²)

Barr, J., *The Semantics of Biblical Language* (Oxford, 1961)

—————, 'The ancient Semitic languages — the conflict between philology and linguistics', *TPS* (1968) 37-55

—————, 'Common sense and Biblical language', *Biblica* 49 (1968) 377-87

—————, *Biblical Words for Time* (*Studies in Biblical Theology*, First Series 33; London, 1969²)

—————, 'Which language did Jesus speak? — Some remarks of a Semitist', *BJRL* 53 (1970) 9-29

—————, 'The nature of linguistic evidence in the text of the Bible', in H.H. Paper (ed.), *Language and Texts. The Nature of Linguistic Evidence* (Ann Arbor, 1975), 35-57

—————, 'Limitations of etymology as a lexicographical instrument in Biblical Hebrew', *TPS* (1983) 41-65

Barrett, C.K., 'Biblical Classics IV. J.H. Moulton: *A Grammar of NT Greek: Prolegomena*', *ExpT* 90 (1978) 68-71

Bataille, A., 'Les glossaires gréco-latins sur papyrus', *Rech. Pap.* 4 (1967) 161-69

* Baugh, A.C./Cable, T., *A History of the English Language* (London, 1978³)

Bees, N.A., 'Bibelgriechisch und Neugriechisch', *BPhW* 40 (1920) 476-78

* Bell, R.T., *Sociolinguistics. Goals, Approaches, Problems* (London, 1976)

Bernardi, J., 'De quelques sémitismes de Flavius Josèphe', *REG* 100 (1987) 18-29

* Bernstein, B., 'Social Class, Language and Socialization', in P.P. Giglioli (ed.), *Language and Social Context* (Harmondsworth, 1972), 157-78

Beyer, K., *Semitische Syntax im NT. Band* I, *Satzlehre. Teil* 1 (Göttingen, 1968²)

* Beziers, M./Overbeke, M. van, *Le Bilinguisme. Essai de définition et guide bibliographique* (*Cahiers de l'Institut des Langues Vivantes* 13; Louvain, 1968)

Bickerman, E.J., 'The LXX as a translation', *PAAJR* 28 (1958) 1-39 (repr. in his *Studies in Jewish and Christian History* [3 vols: *Arbeiten zur Geschichte des antiken Judentums and des Urchristentums* 9; Leiden, 1976] 1.167-200)

Birkeland, H., *The Language of Jesus* (Oslo, 1949)

Black, M., 'The recovery of the language of Jesus', *NTS* 3 (1956/7) 305-13

—————, 'The Semitic element in the NT', *ExpT* 77 (1965/6) 20-23

—————, *An Aramaic Approach to the Gospels and Acts* (Oxford, 1967³)

—————, 'Some Greek words with "Hebrew" meanings in the Epistles and Apocalypse', in J.R. McKay/J.F. Miller (edd.), *Biblical Studies: Essays in Honour of William Barclay* (London, 1976), 135-46

Blass, F., 'Review of Deissmann, *Bibelstudien*', *TLZ* 20 (1895) 486-88

Blomqvist, J., *Greek Particles in Hellenistic Prose* (Lund, 1969)

—————, 'Juxtaposed τε καί in post-classical prose', *Hermes* 102 (1974) 170-78

—————, *Das sogenannte καί Adversativum. Zur Semantik einer griechischen Partikel* (*Studia Graeca Upsal.* 13; Stockholm, 1979)

Bowersock, G.W., *Augustus and the Greek World* (Oxford, 1965)

—————, *Greeks Sophists in the Roman Empire* (Oxford, 1969)

Bowie, E.L., 'Greeks and their past in the Second Sophistic', repr. in M.I. Finley (ed.), *Studies in Ancient Society* (London, 1974), 166-209 [orig. in *P&P* 46 (1970)]

Boyancé, P., 'La connaissance du grec à Rome', *REL* 34 (1956) 111-31

* Bright, W. (ed.), *Sociolinguistics. Proceedings of the U.C.L.A. Sociolinguistic Conference, 1964* (*Janua Linguarum*, series maior 20; The Hague, 1966)

Brixhe, C., *Le dialecte grec de Pamphylie* (*Bibliothèque de l'institut français d'études anatoliennes d'Istanbul* 26; Paris, 1976)

—————, *Essai sur le grec anatolien au début de notre ère* (*Travaux et mémoires de l'Université de Nancy II. Séries Etudes anciennes* 1; Nancy, 1987²)

—————, 'La langue comme critère d'acculturation: l'exemple du grec d'un district phrygien', *Hethitica* 8 (1987) 45-80

Brock, S., *Syriac Perspectives on Late Antiquity* (London, 1984)

Brown, C. (ed.), *The New International Dictionary of NT Theology* (4 vols: Exeter, 1975-85)

Browning, R., *Medieval and Modern Greek* (London, 1969)

—————, 'Greek diglossia yesterday and today', *IJSL* 35 (1982) 49-68

Brunt, P.A., 'The Romanization of the local ruling classes in the Roman Empire', in D.M. Pippidi (ed.), *Assimilation et résistance à la culture gréco-romaine dans le monde ancien. Travaux du VI° Congrès international d'Etudes Classiques, Madrid, 1974* (Paris, 1976), 161-73

Büchsel, F., 'Die griechische Sprache der Juden in der Zeit der LXX und des NT', *ZAW* 60 (1944) 132-49

Burrows, M., 'Principles for testing the Translation Hypothesis in the Gospels', *JBL* 53 (1934) 13-30

Burton, E. de W., *Syntax of the Moods and Tenses in NT Greek* (Edinburgh, 1898³; repr. 1955)

* Bynon, T., *Historical Linguistics* (Cambridge, 1977)

Cadell, H., 'Papyrologie et information lexicologique', in *Scritti in onore di O. Montevecchi*, edd. E. Bresciani et al. (Bologna, 1981), 73-83

Caird, G.B., 'The Glory of God in the Fourth Gospel: an exercise in Biblical Semantics', *NTS* 15 (1968/69) 265-77

Calderini, R., 'Gli ἀγράμματοι nell' Egitto greco-romano', *Aeg.* 30 (1950) 14-41

Cameron, A., 'Latin words in the Greek inscriptions of Asia Minor', *AJP* 52 (1931) 232-62

Cavenaile, R., 'Le latin dans les milieux chrétiens d'Egypte', in S. Janeras (ed.), *Miscellània Papirològica R. Roca-Puig* (Barcelona, 1987), 103-10

* Chambers, J.K./Trudgill, P., *Dialectology* (Cambridge, 1980)

Chomsky, W., 'What was the Jewish vernacular during the Second Commonwealth?', *JQR* 42 (1951/2) 193-212

Clarke, G.W., 'An illiterate lector?', *ZPE* 57 (1984) 103-04

Cohn, L., 'Griechische Lexicographie', Appendix in K. Brugmann/A. Thumb, *Griechische Grammatik* (*Handbuch der kl. Altertumswissenschaft* II.1; Munich, 1913⁴) 681-730

Cole, S.G., 'Could Greek women read and write?', in H.P. Foley (ed.), *Reflections of Women in Antiquity* (New York, 1981), 219-45

Coleman, R., 'The Dialect Geography of Ancient Greece', *TPS* (1963) 58-126

_____, 'Greek influence on Latin syntax', *TPS* (1975) 101-56

Compernass, J., *De sermone graeco volgari Pisidiae Phrygiaeque Meridionalis* (Bonn, 1895)

Connolly, A.L., *Atticism in Non-Literary Papyri of the First Seven Centuries A.D. A Study in Several Features of Orthography and Syntax* (unpub. B.A. [Hons.] thesis, Univ. of Sydney, 1983)

Costas, P.S., *An Outline of the History of the Greek Language, with Particular Emphasis on the Koine and Subsequent Periods* (Chicago, 1936; repr. 1979)

Cotterell, P./Turner, M., *Linguistics and Biblical Interpretation* (London, 1989)

Cremer, H., *Biblico-Theological Lexicon of NT Greek* (E.T.: Edinburgh, 1895⁴; repr. 1954)

* Currie, H.C., 'A projection of Sociolinguistics: the relationship of speech to social status', repr. in J.V. Williamson/V.M. Burke (edd.), *A Various Language. Perspectives on American Dialects* (New York, 1971), 39-47

Dalman, G., *The Words of Jesus* (ET: Edinburgh, 1902)

_____, *Jesus-Jeshua. Studies in the Gospels* (1922; E.T.: London, 1929; repr. New York, 1971)

Dalven, R., 'Judeo-Greek', *Encyclopaedia Judaica* 10 (1971) 425-27

Danker, F.W., *Benefactor: Epigraphic Study of a Graeco-Roman and NT Semantic Field* (St. Louis, 1982)

_____, 'Lexicographic hazards, pitfalls and challenges, with special reference to the contributions of J.E. Gates', *SBL Seminar Papers* 24 (1985) 235-41

_____, *A Century of Greco-Roman Philology, featuring the American Philological Association and the Society of Biblical Literature* (Atlanta, 1988)

Deissmann, G.A., *Die sprachliche Erforschung der griechischen Bibel, ihr gegenwärtiger Stand und ihre Aufgaben* (Giessen, 1898)

_____, 'Die Sprache der griechischen Bibel', *TRu* 1 (1898) 463-72; 5 (1902) 58-69; 9 (1906) 210-29; 15 (1912) 339-64

_____, 'Hellenistisches Griechisch', *Realencyklopädie für protestantische Theologie und Kirche* 7 (Leipzig, 1899³) 627-39

_____, 'Die Hellenisierung des semitischen Monotheismus', *NJA* 11 (1903) 161-77

_____, *The Philology of the Greek Bible* (London, 1908)

_____, *The NT in the Light of Modern Research* (*The Haskell Lectures, 1929*; London, 1929)

Delebecque, E., 'Sur un hellénisme de saint Luc', *Rev.Bib.* 87 (1980) 590-93

_____, 'L'hellénisme de la "relative complexe" dans le NT et principalement chez saint Luc', *Biblica* 62 (1981) 229-38

Denniston, J.D., *Greek Prose Style* (Oxford, 1952)

Díez Macho, A., *La lengua hablada por Jesucristo* (Madrid, 1976)

* Dittmar, N., *Sociolinguistics. A Critical Survey of Theory and Application* (E.T.: London, 1976)

* Dorian, N.C., 'The problem of the semi-speaker in Language Death', *IJSL* 12 (1977) 23-32

* _____, 'The fate of morphological complexity in Language Death. Evidence from East Sutherland Gaelic', *Language* 54 (1978) 590-609

* _____, *Language Death. The Life Cycle of a Scottish Gaelic Dialect* (Philadelphia, 1981)

* _____, 'Natural second language acquisition from the Perspective of the study of Language Death', in R. Andersen (ed.), *Pidginization and Creolization as Language Acquisition* (Rowley [Mass.], 1983), 158-67

* _____ (ed.), *Investigating Obsolescence: Studies in Language Contraction and Death* (Cambridge, 1989)

Dover, K.J., *Greek Word Order* (Cambridge, 1960)

* Downes, W., *Language and Society* (London, 1984)

Downing, F.G., 'A bas les aristos. The relevance of higher literature for the understanding of the earliest Christian writings', *NovT* 30 (1988) 212-30

Draper, H.M., 'Did Jesus speak Greek?', *ExpT* 67 (1955/6) 317

Drew-Bear, T., 'Some Greek Words, I, II', *Glotta* 50 (1972) 61-96, 182-218

* Dubois, J. and C., *Introduction à la lexicographie. Le dictionnaire* (Paris, 1971)

Dubuisson, M., 'Le latin des historiens grecs', *LEC* 47 (1979) 89-106

_____, 'Problèmes du bilinguisme romain', *LEC* 49 (1981) 27-45

Dunn, J.D.G., *Testing the Foundations. Current Trends in NT Study* (Inaugural Lecture: Durham, 1984)

Durling, R.J., 'Lexicographical notes on Galen's pharmacological writings', *Glotta* 57 (1979) 218-24; 58 (1980) 260-65; 59 (1981) 108-16; 60 (1982) 236-44

* Edwards, A.D., *Language in Culture and Class* (London, 1976)

Elliott, J.K., 'Nouns with diminutive endings in the NT', *NovT* 12 (1970) 391-98

_____, 'Phrynichus' influence on the textual tradition of the NT', *ZNW* 63 (1972) 133-38

_____, 'Moeris and the textual tradition of the Greek NT', in id. (ed.), *Studies in NT Language and Text* (Festschrift G.D. Kilpatrick; *NovT Suppl.* 44; Leiden, 1976), 144-52

_____, 'Plaidoyer pour un éclectisme integral appliqué à la critique textuelle du NT', *Rev. Bib.* 84 (1977) 5-25

_____, 'An eclectic textual commentary on the Greek text of Mark's Gospel', in E.J. Epp/G.D. Fee (edd.), *NT Textual Criticism. Its Significance for Exegesis* (Festschrift B.M. Metzger; Oxford, 1981), 47-60

Emerton, J.A., 'Review of Wilcox, *The Semitisms of Acts*', *JSS* 13 (1968) 282-97

_____, 'The problem of vernacular Hebrew in the first century AD and the language of Jesus', *JTS* 24 (1973) 1-23

Epp, E.J., 'Some important textual studies', *JBL* 84 (1965) 172-75

_____, 'The twentieth-century interlude in NT Textual Criticism', *JBL* 93 (1974) 386-414

_____, 'The eclectic method in NT Textual Criticism: solution or symptom?', *HTR* 69 (1976) 211-57

_____, 'Towards the clarification of the term "Textual Variant"', in J.K. Elliott (ed.), *Studies in NT Language and Text* (Festschrift G.D. Kilpatrick; *NovT Suppl.* 44; Leiden, 1976), 153-73

Fabricius, C., 'Der sprachliche Klassizismus der griechischen Kirchenväter: ein philologisches und geistesgeschichtliches Problem', *JbAC* 10 (1967) 187-99

Fee, G.D., 'Rigorous or reasoned eclecticism — which?', in J.K. Elliott (ed.), *Studies in NT Language and Text* (Festschrift G.D. Kilpatrick; *NovT Suppl.* 44; Leiden, 1976), 174-97

* Felix, S.W. (ed.), *Second Language Development. Trends and Issues* (*Tübinger Beiträge zur Linguistik* 125; Tübingen, 1980)

Ferguson, C.A., 'Diglossia', *Word* 15 (1959) 325-40 [repr. in D. Hymes (ed.), *Language in Culture and Society* (New York, 1964), 429-39]

* Fishman, J.A., 'Bilingualism with and without Diglossia; Diglossia with and without Bilingualism', *Jnl of Social Issues* 23 (1967) 29-38 [repr. in his *The Sociology of Language*, 91-106]

* _____, 'Sociolinguistic perspective on the study of Bilingualism', *Linguistics* 39 (1968) 21-49

* _____, 'The relationship between micro- and macro-sociolinguistics in the study of who speaks what language to whom and when', in J.B. Pride/J. Holmes (edd.), *Sociolinguistics* (Harmondsworth, 1972), 15-32

* _____, *Language and Sociocultural Change* (Stanford, 1972)

* _____, *The Sociology of Language* (Rowley [Mass.], 1972)

Fitzmyer, J.A., 'Review of Black, *An Aramaic Approach to the Gospels and Acts*[3]', *CBQ* 30 (1968) 417-28

——————, 'The languages of Palestine in the first century AD', *CBQ* 32 (1970) 501-31 [repr. in his *A Wandering Aramean. Collected Aramaic Essays* (*SBL Monograph* 25; Missoula, 1979) 29-56]

——————, 'The study of the Aramaic background of the NT', repr. in his *A Wandering Aramean. Collected Aramaic Essays* (*SBL Monograph* 25; Missoula, 1979) 1-27

Forbes, C.B., 'Comparison, self-praise and irony: Paul's boasting and the conventions of Hellenistic rhetoric', *NTS* 32 (1986) 1-30

Foss, C., *Ephesus after Antiquity* (Cambridge, 1979)

Fraenkel, J.J., 'A question in connection with Greek particles', *Mnem.* 13 (1947) 183-201

* Francis, W.N., *Dialectology. An Introduction* (London, 1983)

Fraser, P.M., *Ptolemaic Alexandria* (3 vols: Oxford, 1972)

Freyne, S., *Galilee from Alexander the Great to Hadrian, 323 BCE to 135 CE* (Wilmington, 1980)

Friedrich, G., 'Semasiologie und Lexikologie', *TLZ* 94 (1969) 801-16

——————, 'Das bisher noch fehlende Begriffslexikon zum NT', *NTS* 19 (1973) 127-52

Frösén, J., *Prolegomena to a Study of the Greek Language in the First Centuries A.D. The Problem of Koine and Atticism* (Helsinki, 1974)

Funk, R.W., *A Beginning-Intermediate Grammar of Hellenistic Greek* (3 vols: Cambridge [Mass.] 1973[2])

Garbrah, K.A., *A Grammar of the Ionic Inscriptions from Erythrae: Phonology and Morphology* (*Beiträge zur klassischen Philologie* 60; Meisenheim am Glan, 1978)

Gates, J.E., *An Analysis of the Lexicographic Resources used by American Biblical Scholars Today* (*SBLDS* 8; Missoula, 1972)

Gawthrop, R./Strauss, G., 'Protestantism and Literacy in early modern Germany', *P&P* 104 (1984) 31-55

Gehman, H.S., 'The Hebraic character of LXX Greek', *VT* 1 (1951) 81-90

——————, 'Hebraisms in the Old Greek version of Genesis', *VT* 3 (1953) 141-48

——————, '"Ἅγιος in the LXX, and its relation to the Hebrew original', *VT* 4 (1954) 337-48

Ghiron-Bistagne, P., 'L'emploi du terme grec "prosopon" dans l'AT et le NT', in C. Froidefond (ed.), *Mélanges E. Delebecque* (Aix-en-Provence, 1983), 157-74

Gignac, F.T., 'Bilingualism in Greco-Roman Egypt', *Actes du Xe Congrès international de linguistes* (Bucharest, 1970) IV.677-82

——————, 'The language of the non-literary Greek papyri', Proceedings of the XIIth International Congress of Papyrology (*American Studies in Papyrology* 7; Toronto, 1970) 139-52

——————, 'The pronunciation of Greek Stops in the Papyri', *TAPA* 101 (1970) 185-202

——————, 'Review of Turner, *A Grammar of NT Greek*, IV', *CBQ* 39 (1977) 165-67

——————, 'Some interesting morphological phenomena in the language of the papyri', in R.S. Bagnall (ed.), *Proceedings of the XVIth International Congress of Papyrology, New York, 1980* (Chico, 1981), 199-207

——————, 'The papyri and the Greek language', *YCS* 28 (1985) 155-66

——————, 'The Transformation of the second aorist in *koine* Greek', *BASP* 22 (1985) 49-54

——————, 'Analogical levelling in -μι verbs', in S. Janeras (ed.), *Miscel·lània Papirològica R. Roca-Puig* (Barcelona, 1987), 133-40

Gilleland, M.E., 'Female speech in Greek and Latin', *AJP* 101 (1980) 180-83

Gingrich, F.W., 'The Greek NT as a landmark in the course of semantic change', *JBL* 73 (1954) 189-96

——————, 'The contributions of Professor W. Bauer to NT Lexicography', *NTS* 9 (1962) 3-10

——————, 'Prolegomena to a study of the Christian element in the vocabulary of the NT and the Apostolic Fathers', in J.M. Myers et al. (edd.), *Search the Scriptures. NT Studies in Honor of R.T. Stamm* (*Gettysburg Theological Studies* 3; Leiden, 1969), 172-78

Goodman, M.D., *State and Society in Roman Galilee, AD 132-212* (Oxford, 1982)

——————, *The Ruling Class of Judaea. The Origins of the Jewish Revolt against Rome AD 66-70* (Cambridge, 1987)

Goodwin, W.W., *Syntax of the Moods and Tenses of the Greek Verb* (London, 1897)

* Goody, J.R. (ed.), *Literacy in Traditional Societies* (Cambridge, 1968)

Greenfield, J.C., 'The Languages of Palestine, 200 BCE-200 CE. Jewish Languages', in H.H. Paper (ed.), *Jewish Languages, Theme and Variations. Proceedings of the Regional Conferences of the Association for Jewish Studies, 1975* (Cambridge [Mass.], 1978), 143-54 (with responses by H.C. Youtie [155-57] and F.E. Peters [159-64])

Grimm, C.L.W./Thayer, J.H., *A Greek-English Lexicon of the NT* (Edinburgh, 1901[4]; repr. 1956)

Grintz, J.M., 'Hebrew as the spoken and written language in the last days of the Second Temple', *JBL* 69 (1960) 32-47

* Gumperz, J.J./Blom, J.-P., 'Social meaning in linguistic structures: Code-switching in Norway', repr. in Gumperz's *Language in Social Groups* (Stanford, 1971) 274-310

Gundry, R.H., 'The language milieu of first-century Palestine. Its bearing on the authenticity of the Gospel Tradition', *JBL* 83 (1964) 404-08

Hägg, T., 'Some remarks on the use of Greek in Nubia', in J.M. Plumley (ed.), *Nubian Studies. Proceedings of the Symposium for Nubian Studies, Cambridge, 1978* (Warminster, 1982), 103-07

Hainsworth, J.B., 'Greek views of Greek Dialectology', *TPS* (1967) 62-76

* Halliday, M.A.K., *Language as Social Semiotic* (London, 1978)

Harl, M., 'Remarques sur la langue des chrétiens, à propos du *Patristic Greek Lexicon*', *JTS* 14 (1963) 406-20

Harl, M./Dorival, G./Munnich, O., *La Bible grecque des LXX. Du judaïsme hellénistique au christianisme ancien* (Paris, 1988)

Harris, J.R., 'The so-called Biblical Greek', *ExpT* 25 (1913) 54-55

Harris, M.J., 'Prepositions and Theology in the Greek NT'; Appendix to vol.3 of C. Brown (ed.), *The New International Dictionary of NT Theology* (Exeter, 1978), 1171-1215

Harris, W.V., 'Literacy and Epigraphy, I', *ZPE* 52 (1983) 87-111

* Hasan, R., 'Code, register and social dialect', in B. Bernstein (ed.), *Class, Codes and Control*, II (London, 1973), 253-92

Hata, G., 'Is the Greek version of Josephus' *Jewish War* a translation or a rewriting of the first version?', *JQR* 66 (1975/6) 89-108

Hatch, W.H.P., 'Some illustrations of NT usage from Greek inscriptions of Asia Minor', *JBL* 27 (1908) 134-46

Helbing, R., *Die Kasussyntax der Verba bei den LXX. Ein Beitrag zur Hebraismenfrage und zur Syntax der Koine* (Göttingen, 1928)

Hellwig, A., 'Zur Funktion und Bedeutung der griechischen Partikeln', *Glotta* 52 (1974) 145-71

Hemer, C.J., 'Towards a new Moulton and Milligan', *NovT* 24 (1982) 97-123

_____, 'Reflections on the nature of NT Greek vocabulary', *TynB* 38 (1987) 65-92

Hemmerdinger, B., 'Noms communs grecs d'origine égyptienne', *Glotta* 46 (1968) 238-47

Hengel, M., *Judaism and Hellenism* (2 vols; ET: London, 1974; repr. in one vol. 1981)

_____, *Jews, Greeks and Barbarians* (ET: London, 1980)

Henry, A.S., 'Epigraphica', *CQ* 14 (1964) 240-48

_____, 'Some observations on final clauses in Hellenistic Attic prose inscriptions', *CQ* 16 (1966) 291-97

_____, 'Notes on the language of the prose inscriptions of Hellenistic Athens', *CQ* 17 (1967) 257-95

_____, 'Further notes on the language of the prose inscriptions of Hellenistic Athens', *CQ* 19 (1969) 289-305

_____, 'Some notes on the syntax of the prose inscriptions of Hellenistic Athens', *CQ* 20 (1970) 242-57

Hessinger, J.J., 'The syntactic and semantic status of prepositions in Greek', *CP* 73 (1978) 211-23

Hilhorst, A., *Sémitismes et latinismes dans le Pasteur d'Hermas* (*Graecitas Christianorum Primaeva* 5; Nimwegen, 1976)

Hill, D., *Greek Words and Hebrew Meanings* (*SNTSMS* 5; Cambridge, 1967)

Hjelmslev, L., 'Introduction à la discussion générale des problèmes relatifs à la phonologie des langues mortes, en l'espèce du grec et du latin', *Acta Congressus Madvigiani Hafniae 1954* (Copenhagen, 1958) vol.1, General Part, 101-13

Homeyer, H., 'Some observations on bilingualism and language shift in Italy from the sixth to the third century BC', *Word* 13 (1957) 415-40

Horsley, G.H.R., 'Divergent views on the nature of the Greek of the Bible', *Biblica* 65 (1984) 393-403

_____, 'The inscriptions from the so-called "Library" at Cremna', *AS* 37 (1987) 49-80

_____, 'Name change as an indication of religious conversion in Antiquity', *Numen* 34 (1987) 1-17

Horsley, G.H.R./Waterhouse, E.R., 'The Greek *nomen sacrum* XP- in some Latin and Old English MSS', *Scriptorium* 38 (1984) 211-30

Houston, R., 'The literacy myth?: Illiteracy in Scotland 1630-1760', *P&P* 96 (1982) 81-102

Howard, G./Shelton, J.C., 'The Bar-Kokhba Letters and Palestinian Greek', *IEJ* 23 (1973) 101-02.

Hunkin, J.W., 'Pleonastic ἄρχομαι in the NT', JTS 25 (1924) 390-402

Hymes, D., 'Sociolinguistics: stability and consolidation', *IJSL* 45 (1984) 39-45

Jacobson, H., *The 'Exagoge' of Ezekiel* (Cambridge, 1983)

James, J.C., *The Language of Palestine and Adjacent Regions* (Edinburgh, 1920)

Jannaris, A.N., *An Historical Greek Grammar chiefly of the Attic Dialect as written and spoken from Classical Antiquity down to the present time, founded upon the ancient texts, inscriptions, papyri and present popular Greek* (London, 1897; repr. Hildesheim, 1968)

_____, 'The true meaning of the *koine*', *CR* 17 (1903) 93-96

* Jeffers, R.J./Lehiste, I., *Principles and Methods for Historical Linguistics* (Cambridge [Mass.], 1979)

Judge, E.A., *The Social Pattern of Christian Groups in the First Century* (London, 1960)

_____, 'The early Christians as a scholastic community', *JRH* 1 (1961) 4-15, 125-37

_____, 'St Paul and Classical Society', *JbAC* 15 (1972) 19-36

_____, '"Antike und Christentum": towards a definition of the field. A bibliographical survey', *ANRW* II.23.1 (1979) 3-58

_____, 'The social identity of the first Christians: a question of method in religious history', *JRH* 11 (1980) 201-17

_____, 'Cultural conformity and innovation in Paul: some clues from contemporary documents', *TynB* 35 (1984) 3-24

Judge, E.A./Pickering, S.R., 'Papyrus documentation of Church and Community in Egypt to the mid-fourth century', *JbAC* 20 (1977) 47-71

_____, 'Biblical papyri prior to Constantine: some cultural implications of their physical form', *Prudentia* 10 (1978) 1-13

Juster, J., *Les Juifs dans l'Empire romain* (2 vols: Chartres, 1914; repr. New York, n.d.)

Kaimio, J., *The Romans and The Greek Language* (*Commentationes Humanarum Litterarum* 64; Helsinki, 1979)

_____, 'Latin in Roman Egypt', *Actes du XV⁰ congrès international de papyrologie, Bruxelles, 1977* (*Pap. Brux.* 18; Brussels 1979), III.27-33

Kajanto, I., 'Minderheiten und ihre Sprachen in der Hauptstadt Rom', in G. Neumann/J. Untermann (edd.), *Die Sprachen im römischen Reich der Kaiserzeit. Kolloquium ... April 1974* (*Bonner Jahrbücher Beiheft* 40; Köln, 1980), 83-101

Kant, L.H., 'Jewish inscriptions in Latin and Greek', *ANRW* II.20.2 (1987) 671-713

Kapsomenakis (= Kapsomenos), S.G., *Voruntersuchungen zu einer Grammatik der Papyri der nachchristlichen Zeit* (*Münchener Beiträge zur Papyrusforschung und antiken Rechtsgeschichte* 38; Munich, 1938; repr. Chicago, 1979)

_____, 'Das Griechische in Ägypten', *Mus. Helv.* 10 (1953) 248-63

* Kelly, L.G. (ed.), *Description and Measurement of Bilingualism. An International Seminar, Univ. of Monckton, 1967* (Toronto, 1969 [1971])

Kennedy, H.A.A., *Sources of NT Greek. The Influence of the LXX on the Vocabulary of the NT* (Edinburgh, 1895)

Kilpatrick, G.D., 'Atticism and the Text of the Greek NT', in J. Blinzler et al. (edd.), *Neutestamentliche Aufsätze, Festschrift für Prof. J. Schmid* (Regensburg, 1963), 125-37

_____, 'The Greek NT Text of today and the Textus Receptus', in H. Anderson/W. Barclay (edd.), *The NT in Historical and Contemporary Perspective. Essays in Memory of G.H.C. Macgregor* (Oxford, 1965), 189-208

_____, 'Review of Rydbeck, *Fachprosa*', *JBL* 88 (1969) 354-56

_____, 'Language and Text in the Gospels and Acts', *VC* 24 (1970) 161-71

_____, 'Review of Turner, *A Grammar of NT Greek, III and IV*', *TLZ* 104 (1979) 109-11

Kittel, G./Friedrich, G. (edd.), *Theological Dictionary of the NT* (1932-73; ET: Grand Rapids, 1964-76)

Knox, W.L., *Some Hellenistic Elements in Primitive Christianity* (*Schweich Lectures 1942*; London, 1944)

Kretschmer, P., *Die Entstehung der Koine* (*Sitz. der Wiener Ak., ph.-hist. Kl.*, 143.10; Vienna, 1900)

* Labov, W., 'Hypercorrection by the Lower Middle Class as a factor in linguistic change', in W. Bright (ed.), *Sociolinguistics. Proc. of the UCLA Sociolinguistic Conference 1964* (*Janua Linguarum, series maior* 20; The Hague, 1966), 84-113

* _____, 'The effect of social mobility on linguistic behaviour', repr. in J.V. Williamson/V.M. Burke (edd.), *A Various Language. Perspectives on American Dialects* (New York, 1971), 640-59

* _____, 'The study of a language in its social context', repr. in J.A. Fishman (ed.), *Advances in the Sociology of Language*, I (The Hague, 1971), 152-216

* —————, *Sociolinguistic Patterns* (Oxford, 1978)

Ladouceur, D.J., 'The Language of Josephus', *JSJ* 27 (1982) 18-38

Lapide, P., 'Insights from Qumran into the languages of Jesus', *RQ* 8 (1972-1975) 483-501

Leaney, A.R.C., 'Greek MSS from the Judaean Desert', in J.K. Elliott (ed.), *Studies in NT Language and Text* (Festschrift G.D. Kilpatrick; *NovT Suppl.* 44; Leiden, 1976), 283-300

Leclercq, H., 'Note sur le grec néo-testamentaire et la position du grec en Palestine au premier siècle', *LEC* 42 (1974) 243-55

Lee, J.A.L., 'A note on LXX material in the Supplement to Liddell and Scott', *Glotta* 47 (1969) 234-42

—————, 'The future of ZHN in Late Greek', *NovT* 22 (1980) 289-98

—————, 'Equivocal and stereotyped renderings in the LXX', *Rev. Bib.* 87 (1980) 104-17

—————, *A Lexical Study of the LXX Version of the Pentateuch* (*SCS* 14; Chico, 1983)

—————, 'Some features of the speech of Jesus in Mark's Gospel', *NovT* 27 (1985) 1-26

Lefort, L.-Th., 'Pour une grammaire des LXX', *Muséon* 41 (1928) 152-60

Lehmann, W.P., 'Historical linguistics and sociolinguistics', *IJSL* 31 (1981) 11-27

Leroy, M., 'Théories linguistiques dans l'antiquité', *LEC* 41 (1973) 385-401

Lewis, D.M., 'Review of Sevenster, *Do You Know Greek?*', *JTS* 20 (1969) 583-88

Lewis, E.G., 'Bilingualism and bilingual education: the Ancient World to the Renaissance', Appendix 3 in J.A. Fishman, *Bilingual Education. An International Sociological Perspective* (Rowley [Mass.], 1976) 150-200

Lieberman, S., *Greek in Jewish Palestine* (New York, 1942; 1965²)

—————, *Hellenism in Jewish Palestine* (New York, 1950; 1962²)

—————, 'How much Greek in Jewish Palestine?', in A. Altmann (ed.), *Biblical and Other Studies* (Cambridge, [Mass.], 1963), 123-41

Lifshitz, B., 'Du nouveau sur l'hellénisation des Juifs en Palestine', *Euphrosyne* 4 (1970) 113-33

—————, 'Jerusalem sous la domination romaine', *ANRW* II.8 (1977) 444-89

Louw, J.P./Nida, E.A., *Greek-English Lexicon of the NT, based on Semantic Domains* (2 vols; New York, 1988)

Lozovan, E., 'Ovide et le bilinguisme', in N.I. Herescu (ed.), *Ovidiana. Recherches sur Ovide* (Paris, 1958), 396-403

* Lyons, J. (ed.), *New Horizons in Linguistics* (Harmondsworth, 1970)

McGready, A.G., 'Egyptian words in the Greek vocabulary', *Glotta* 46 (1968) 247-54

McKay, K.L., 'The use of the ancient Greek Perfect down to the second century AD', *BICS* 12 (1965) 1-21

—————, 'Syntax in Exegesis', *TynB* 23 (1972) 39-57

—————, 'On the Perfect and other Aspects in the Greek non-literary papyri', *BICS* 27 (1980) 23-49

—————, 'On the Perfect and other Aspects in NT Greek', *NovT* 23 (1981) 289-329

—————, 'Repeated action, and potential reality in Greek', *Antichthon* 15 (1981) 36-46

—————, 'Aspect in imperatival constructions in NT Greek', *NovT* 27 (1985) 201-26

—————, 'Aspectual usage in timeless contexts in Ancient Greek', in A. Rijksbaron et al. (edd.), *In the Footsteps of Raphael Kühner* (Amsterdam, 1986), 193-208

* Mackey, W., 'The description of bilingualism', repr. in J.A. Fishman (ed.), *Readings in the Sociology of Language* (The Hague, 1968), 554-84

McLeod, M.D., 'Review of Kaimio, *The Romans and the Greek Language*', *CR* 32 (1982) 216-18

MacMullen, R., 'Provincial languages in the Roman Empire', *AJP* 87 (1966) 1-17

—————, *Paganism in the Roman Empire* (New Haven, 1981)

—————, *Christianizing the Roman Empire (AD 100-400)* (New Haven, 1984)

Maldfeld, G., 'Die Papyrologie und die neutestamentliche Textkritik', *Annales Universitatis Saraviensis* 8 (1959) 53-63

Malherbe, A.J., *Social Aspects of Early Christianity* (Philadelphia, 1983²)

Malina, B.J., *The Gospel of John in Sociolinguistic Perspective* (*Centre for Hermeneutical Study, Colloquy* 48; Berkeley, 1985)

Maloney, E.C., *Semitic Interference in Markan Syntax* (*SBLDS* 51; Chico, 1981)

Mandilaras, B.G., *The Verb in the Greek Non-Literary Papyri* (Athens, 1973)

Marrou, H.-I., *Histoire de l'éducation dans l'antiquité* (Paris, 1948; 1965⁶)

Martin, R.A., 'Some syntactical criteria of Translation Greek', *VT* 10 (1960) 295-310

—————, 'Syntactical evidence of Aramaic sources in *Acts I-XV*', *NTS* 10 (1964/5) 38-59

—————, *Syntactical Evidence of Semitic Sources in Greek Documents* (*SCS* 3; Cambridge [Mass.], 1974)

Martini, C.M., 'Eclecticism and Atticism in the Textual Criticism of the NT', in M. Black/W.A. Smalley (edd.), *On Language, Culture and Religion. In Honor of E.A. Nida* (The Hague, 1974), 149-56

Mason, H.J., 'The Roman government in Greek sources. The effect of literary theory on the translation of official titles', *Phoenix* 24 (1970) 150-59

Masson, E., *Recherches sur les plus anciens emprunts sémitiques en grec* (*Etudes et Commentaires* 67; Paris, 1967)

Mayser, E., *Grammatik der griechischen Papyri aus der Ptolemäerzeit* (6 vols; Leipzig/Berlin, 1906-1938; new edn. of vol.i.1 by H. Schmoll, 1970)

Meeks, W.A., *The First Urban Christians* (New Haven, 1983)

Mélèze-Modrzejewski, J., 'Splendeurs grecques et misères romaines: les Juifs d'Egypte dans l'antiquité', in J. Hassoun (ed.), *Juifs du Nil* (Paris, 1981), 15-49

Merkelbach, R./Youtie, H.C., 'Der griechische Wortschatz und die Christen', *ZPE* 18 (1975) 101-54 [A much abbreviated English version of Merkelbach's article appears in H.H. Paper (ed.), *Language and Texts. The Nature of Linguistic Evidence* (Ann Arbor, 1975), 109-20; Youtie's 'Commentary' (149-54) on Merkelbach's essay is repr. in his *Scriptiunculae Posteriores*, 1 (Bonn, 1981) 217-22.]

Metzger, B.M., *The Text of the NT* (Oxford, 1968²)

_____, 'Bilingualism and polylingualism in antiquity', in W.C. Weinreich (ed.), *The NT Age: Essays in Honor of B. Reicke* (2 vols; Macon, 1984), 2.327-34

Meyers, E.M./Strange, J.F., *Archaeology, the Rabbis and Early Christianity* (London, 1981)

Michaelis, W., 'Der Attizismus und das NT', *ZNW* 22 (1923) 91-121

Millar, F., 'Local cultures in the Roman Empire: Libyan, Punic and Latin in Roman Africa', *JRS* 58 (1968) 126-34

_____, 'Paul of Samosata, Zenobia and Aurelian: the Church, local culture and political allegiance in third-century Syria', *JRS* 61 (1971) 1-17

_____, 'Empire, Community and Culture in the Roman Near East: Greeks, Syrians, Jews and Arabs', *JJS* 38 (1987) 143-64

_____, 'The Problem of Hellenistic Syria', in A. Kuhrt/S. Sherwin-White (edd.), *Hellenism in the East* (London, 1987), 110-33

Milligan, G., 'The grammar of the Greek NT', *ExpT* 32 (1920) 420-24

_____, *Here and There Among the Papyri* (London, 1922)

_____, 'The rise, language and form of the NT writings', in *The History of Christianity in the Light of Modern Knowledge. A Collective Work* (London, 1929) 271-99

Mohrmann, C., 'Linguistic problems in the early Christian Church', *VC* 11 (1957) 11-36

_____, 'Les innovations sémantiques dans le grec et le latin des chrétiens', *Humanitas* 13-14 (1961-62) 322-35

Momigliano, A., *Alien Wisdom. The Limits of Hellenization* (Cambridge, 1975)

Montevecchi, O., 'Dal paganesimo al cristianesimo. Aspetti dell' evoluzione della lingua greca nei papiri dell' Egitto', *Aeg.* 37 (1957) 41-59

_____, *La Papirologia* (Turin, 1973)

Morgenthaler, R., *Statistik des neutestamentlichen Wortschatzes* (Zurich, 1973²)

Moule, C.F.D., *An Idiom Book of NT Greek* (Cambridge, 1959²)

Moulton, J.H., 'Grammatical notes from Papyri', *CR* 15 (1901) 31-38, 434-42; 18 (1904) 106-12, 151-55

_____, 'Notes from the Papyri', *The Expositor* ser. vi, 3 (1901) 271-82; 7 (1903) 104-21; 8 (1903) 423-39

_____, 'Characteristics of NT Greek', *The Expositor* ser. vi, 9 (1904) 67-75, 215-25, 310-20, 359-68, 461-72; 10 (1904) 124-34, 168-74, 276-83, 353-64, 440-50

_____, *A Grammar of NT Greek*, 1. *Prolegomena* (Edinburgh, 1906; 1908³) [This third edition served as the basis for the German translation, *Einleitung in die Sprache des NT* (Heidelberg, 1911).]

_____, 'The Science of language and the study of the NT' (Inaugural Lecture: Manchester, 1906), repr. in his *The Christian Religion in the Study and in the Street* (London, 1919) 117-44

_____, 'NT Greek in the light of modern discovery', in H.B. Swete (ed.), *Essays on some Biblical Questions of the Day by Members of the University of Cambridge* (London, 1909), 461-505

_____, *From Egyptian Rubbish-Heaps* (London, 1916)

Moulton, J.H./Howard, W.F., *A Grammar of NT Greek*, II. *Accidence and Word Formation* (Edinburgh, 1929)

Moulton, J.H./Milligan, G., 'Lexical Notes from the Papyri', 24 articles in *The Expositor* ser. vii-viii (1908-1912)

Moulton, W.F./Geden, A.S./Moulton, H.K., *A Concordance to the Greek Testament* (Edinburgh, 1897; 1978⁵)

Muraoka, T., 'Syntax of some types of pronouns in the Greek Genesis', *Studies in Linguistics* 15 (1976) 45-59

Mussies, G., *The Morphology of Koine Greek as used in the Apocalypse of St. John. A Study in Bilingualism* (*NovT Suppl.* 27; Leiden, 1971)

——————, 'Greek in Palestine and the Diaspora', in S. Safrai/M. Stern (edd.), *The Jewish People in the First Century*, II (Assen, 1976), 1040-64

——————, 'The Greek of the book of Revelation', in J. Lambrecht (ed.), *L'Apocalypse johannique et l'Apocalyptique dans le NT* (*Bibliotheca Ephemeridum Theologicarum Lovaniensium* 53; Louvain, 1980), 167-77

——————, 'Greek as the vehicle of Early Christianity', *NTS* 29 (1983) 356-69

——————, 'The use of Hebrew and Aramaic in the Greek NT', *NTS* 30 (1984) 416-32

——————, 'Christelijke inscripties in Palestina', in R. van den Broek et al., *Kerk en kerken in Romeins-Byzantijns Palestina. Archeologie en geschiedenis* (*Palaestina Antiqua* 6; Kampen, 1988), 186-211

Nägeli, T., *Der Wortschatz des Apostels Paulus. Beitrag zur sprachgeschichtlichen Erforschung des NT* (Göttingen, 1905)

Nida, E.A., 'The implications of contemporary Linguistics for Biblical scholarship', *JBL* 91 (1972) 73-89

* Nida, E.A./Louw, J.P./Smith, R.B., 'Semantic Domains and Componential Analysis of Meaning', in R.W. Cole (ed.), *Current Issues in Linguistic Theory* (Bloomington, 1977), 139-67

Nock, A.D., *Conversion* (Oxford 1933; repr. 1972)

——————, 'The vocabulary of the NT', *JBL* 52 (1933) 131-39 [repr. in id., *Essays on Religion and the Ancient World*, ed. Z. Stewart (Oxford, 1972), 1.341-47]

Norden, E., *Die antike Kunstprosa vom VI. Jahrhundert v. Chr. bis in die Zeit der Renaissance* (2 vols: Leipzig, 1898; 1909²; repr. Stuttgart, 1958)

Ott, H., 'Um die Muttersprache Jesu; Forschungen seit Gustaf Dalman', *NovT* 9 (1967) 1-25

Ozanne, C.G., 'The language of the Apocalypse', *TynB* 16 (1965) 3-9

Palmer, L.R., 'Prolegomena to a Grammar of the post-Ptolemaic papyri', *JTS* 35 (1934) 170-75

——————, *A Grammar of the Post-Ptolemaic Papyri*, I. *Accidence and Word-Formation*, I. *The Suffixes* (*Publications of the Philological Society*, 13; London, 1945)

——————, *The Greek Language* (London, 1980)

Pax, E., 'Die syntaktischen Semitismen in NT', *SBF* 13 (1963) 136-62

——————, 'Probleme des neutestamentlichen Griechisch', *Biblica* 53 (1972) 557-64

Payne, D.F., 'Semitisms in the Book of Acts', in W. Gasque/R.P. Martin (edd.), *Apostolic History and the Gospel* (Festschrift F.F. Bruce; Exeter, 1970), 134-50

Pelletier, A., *Flavius Josèphe, adaptateur de la Lettre d'Aristée. Une réaction atticisante contre la Koine* (*Etudes et Commentaires* 45; Paris, 1962)

Peremans, W., 'Over Tweetaligheid in Ptolemaeisch Egypte (3ᵉ e.v.C.)', *AC* 4 (1935) 403-17

——————, 'Über die Zweisprachigkeit im ptolemäischen Ägypten', in H. Braunert (ed.), *Studien zur Papyrologie und antiken Wirtschaftsgeschichte F. Oertel zum achtzigsten Geburtstag gewidmet* (Bonn, 1964), 49-60

——————, 'De la valeur des papyrus comme source d'histoire', in G. Wirth (ed.), *Romanitas-Christianitas. Untersuchungen zur Geschichte und Literatur der römischen Kaiserzeit* (Festschrift J. Straub; Berlin, 1982), 82-97

——————, 'Sur le bilinguisme dans l'Egypte des Lagides', in J. Quaegebeur (ed.), *Studia P. Naster oblata*, II. *Orientalia Antiqua* (*Orientalia Lovaniensia Analecta* 13; Leuven 1982), 143-54

——————, 'Le bilinguisme dans les relations gréco-égyptiennes sous les Lagides', in E. van 'T. Dack et al. (edd.), *Egypt and the Hellenistic World. Proceedings of the International Colloquium, Leuven, 24-26 May 1982* (*Studia Hellenistica* 27; Leuven, 1983), 253-80

Pernot, H., *Etudes sur la langue des Evangiles* (Paris, 1927)

——————, 'Observations sur la langue de la LXX', *REG* 42 (1929) 411-25

Peters, F.E., 'Response [to J.C. Greenfield's paper on the languages of Palestine, 200 BC-200 AD]', in H.H. Paper (ed.), *Jewish Languages: Theme and Variations. Proceedings of the Regional Conferences of the Association for Jewish Studies, 1975* (Cambridge [Mass.], 1978), 159-64

* Petyt, K.M., *The Study of Dialect* (London, 1980)

* ——————, 'Who is really doing dialectology?', in D. Crystal (ed.), *Linguistic Controversies* (Festschrift F.R. Palmer; London, 1982), 192-208

Piper, O.A., 'NT Lexicography: an unfinished task', in E.H. Barth/R.E. Cocroft (edd.), *Festschrift to Honor F.W. Gingrich* (Leiden, 1972), 177-204

Pomeroy, S.B., 'Women in Roman Egypt', in H.P. Foley (ed.), *Reflections of Women in Antiquity* (New York, 1981), 303-22

Price, S.R.F., *Rituals and Power. The Roman Imperial Cult in Asia Minor* (Cambridge, 1984)

Psichari, J., 'Essai sur le grec de la LXX', *REJ* 55 (1908) 161-210 [repr. in id., *Quelques travaux de linguistique, de philologie et de littérature helléniques, 1884-1928* (Paris, 1930) 1.831-91]

Rabin, C., 'Hebrew and Aramaic in the First Century', in S. Safrai/M. Stern, (edd.), *The Jewish People in the First Century*, II (Assen, 1976), 1007-39

_____, 'What constitutes a Jewish language?', *IJSL* 30 (1981) 19-28

Radermacher, L., 'Besonderheiten der Koine-Syntax', *WS* 31 (1909) 1-12

_____, *Neutestamentliche Grammatik. Das Griechisch des NT im Zusammenhang mit der Volkssprache* (Tübingen, 1925²)

_____, *Koine* (*Sitz. der Ak. der Wiss. in Wien, ph.-hist. Kl.* 224, 5; Vienna, 1947)

Rajak, T., *Josephus. The Historian and his Society* (London, 1983)

Redpath, H.A., 'The present position of the Study of the LXX', *AJT* 7 (1903) 1-19

Rémondon, R., 'Problèmes du bilinguisme dans l'Egypte Lagide (*UPZ* 1.148)', *CE* 39 (1964) 126-46

Renehan, R., *Greek Lexicographical Notes. A Critical Supplement to the Greek-English Lexicon of Liddell-Scott-Jones* (2 vols, *Hypomnemata* 45, 74; Göttingen, 1975, 1982)

Riddle, D.W., 'The logic of the theory of Translation Greek', *JBL* 51 (1932) 13-30

_____, 'The Aramaic Gospels and the Synoptic Problem', *JBL* 54 (1935) 127-38

Rife, J.M., 'The mechanics of Translation Greek', *JBL* 52 (1933) 244-52

Robert, L., 'Epigraphie', in C. Samaran (ed.), *L'Histoire et ses méthodes* (Paris, 1961), 453-97

Robertson, A.T., *A Grammar of the Greek NT in the Light of Historical Research* (New York, 1923⁴)

Rodríguez Adrados, F., et al., *Introducción a la lexicografía griega* (*Manuales y anejos de Emerita* 33; Madrid, 1977)

* Romaine, S. (ed.), *Sociolinguistic Variation in Speech Communities* (London, 1982)

Ros, J., *De studie van het Bijbelgrieksch van Hugo Grotius tot Adolf Deissmann* (Nimwegen, 1940)

Rosén, H.B., 'Palestinian *koine* in Rabbinic illustration', *JSS* 8 (1963) 56-72

_____, 'Die Sprachsituation im römischen Palästina', in G. Neumann/J. Untermann (edd.), *Die Sprachen im römischen Reich der Kaiserzeit. Kolloquium . . . April 1974* (*Bonner Jahrbücher Beiheft* 40; Köln, 1980), 215-39

Roth-Gerson, L., *The Greek Inscriptions from the Synagogues in Eretz-Israel* (in Hebrew; Jerusalem, 1987)

Rouffiac, J., *Recherches sur les caractères du grec dans le NT d'après les inscriptions de Priène* (Paris, 1911)

Rüger, H.P., 'Zum Problem der Sprache Jesu', *ZNW* 59 (1968) 113-22

Russell, J.K., 'Did Jesus speak Greek?', *ExpT* 67 (1955/6) 246

Rydbeck, L., *Fachprosa, Vermeintliche Volkssprache und NT: zur Beurteilung der sprachlichen Niveauunterschiede im nachklassischen Griechisch* (*Acta Universitatis Upsaliensis* 5; Uppsala, 1967)

_____, 'What happened to NT Grammar after A. Debrunner?', *NTS* 21 (1974/5) 424-27

Samuel, A.E., *From Athens to Alexandria: Hellenism and Social Goals in Ptolemaic Egypt* (*Studia Hellenistica* 26; Louvain, 1983)

* Saussure, F. de, *Cours de linguistique générale* (Paris, 1915; repr. 1968)

Sawyer, J.F.A., *Semantics in Biblical Research. New Methods of Defining Hebrew Words for Salvation* (*Studies in Biblical Theology*, Second Series 24; London, 1972)

Schilling, D., *Commentarius exegetico-philologicus in hebraismos Novi Testamenti, seu de dictione hebraica Novi Testamenti Graeci* (Mechelen, 1886)

Schlageter, L., *Der Wortschatz der ausserhalb Attikas gefundenen attischen Inschriften. Ein Beitrag zur Entstehung der Koine* (Strassburg, 1912)

Schmid, W., *Der Atticismus in seinen Hauptvertretern von Dionysius von Halikarnass bis auf den zweiten Philostratus* (5 vols.; Stuttgart, 1887-1897; repr. Hildesheim, 1964)

Schmitt, R., 'Die Ostgrenze von Armenien über Mesopotamien, Syrien bis Arabien', in G. Neumann/J. Untermann (edd.), *Die Sprachen im römischen Reich der Kaiserzeit. Kolloquium . . . April 1974* (*Bonner Jahrbücher Beiheft* 40; Köln, 1980), 188-214

Schubart, W., 'Ein lateinisch-griechisch-koptisches Gesprächbuch', *Klio* 13 (1913) 27-38

Schürer, E., *The History of the Jewish People in the Age of Jesus Christ (175 BC-AD 135)*, English version rev. and edd. by G. Vermes/F. Millar/M. Black (3 vols.; Edinburgh, 1973-1987)

Schwind, F.F. von, 'Zur griechisch-ägyptischen Verschmelzung unter den Ptolemäern', in *Studi in onore di V. Arangio-Ruiz* (Naples, 1953) 2.435-51

Sevenster, J.N., *Do You Know Greek? How much Greek could the Early Christians have Known? (NovT Suppl.* 19; Leiden, 1968)

Sheppard, A.A.R., 'Pagan cults of Angels in Roman Asia Minor', *Talanta* 12/13 (1980/81) 77-100

Sherwin-White, A.N., *Roman Society and Roman Law in the NT (Sarum Lectures, 1960/61*; Oxford, 1963; repr. Grand Rapids, 1978)

Shipp, G.P., *Modern Greek Evidence for the Ancient Greek Vocabulary* (Sydney, 1979)

Shutt, R.J.H., *Studies in Josephus* (London, 1961)

Sijpesteijn, P.J., 'De invloed van het Latijn op het Grieks', *Lampas* 15 (1982) 318-30

Silva, M., 'Semantic borrowing in the NT', *NTS* 22 (1975/6) 104-10

_____, 'New lexical Semitisms?', *ZNW* 69 (1978) 253-57

_____, 'Bilingualism and the character of Palestinian Greek', *Biblica* 61 (1980) 198-219

_____, 'The Pauline style as lexical choice. ΓΙΝΩΣΚΕΙΝ and related verbs', in D.A. Hagner/M.J. Harris (edd.), *Pauline Studies Presented to F.F. Bruce* (Exeter, 1980), 184-207

_____, *Biblical Words and their Meaning. An Introduction to Lexical Semantics* (Grand Rapids, 1983)

Simcox, W.H., *The Language of the NT* (London, 1889)

Skeat, T.C., 'The use of dictation in ancient book-production', *PBA* 42 (1956) 179-208

* Slaughter, M.M., 'Literacy and Society', *IJSL* 56 (1985) 113-39

Smallwood, E.M., *The Jews under Roman Rule from Pompey to Diocletian (Studies in Judaism in Late Antiquity* 20; Leiden, 1976)

Smith, M., 'Pagan dealings with Jewish angels: *P. Berlin* 5025b and *P. Louvre* 2391', *Stud. Clas.* 24 (1986) 175-79

Solin, H., 'Juden und Syrer im römischen Reich', in G. Neumann/J. Untermann (edd.), *Die Sprachen im römischen Reich der Kaiserzeit. Kolloquium . . . April 1974 (Bonner Jahrbücher Beiheft* 40; Köln, 1980), 301-30

_____, 'Juden und Syrer im westlichen Teil der römischen Welt. Eine ethnisch-demographische Studie mit besonderer Berücksichtigung der sprachlichen Zustände', *ANRW* II.29.2 (1983) 587-789 (and index, 1222-49).

Sollamo, R., 'Some "improper" prepositions, such as ἐνώπιον, ἐνάντιον, ἔναντι, etc. in the LXX and early Koine Greek', *VT* 25 (1975) 773-82

_____, *Renderings of Hebrew Semiprepositions in the LXX (Annales Academiae Scientiarum Fennicae, Dissertationes Humanarum Litterarum* 19; Helsinki, 1979)

Sparks, H.F.D., 'The Semitisms of Luke's Gospel', *JTS* 44 (1943) 129-38

_____, 'The Semitisms of the Acts', *JTS* n.s.1 (1950) 16-28

Spicq, C., 'Note de lexicographie. Le sens de καταγω dans le NT', *Anagennesis* 1 (1980) 103-09 [cf. id., *NLNT* 3.369-73]

_____, 'ἔθος, εἰθισμένος. Etude de lexicographie néo-testamentaire', in P. Casetti et al. (edd.), *Mélanges D. Barthélemy. Etudes Bibliques offertes à l'occasion de son 60ᵉ anniversaire (Orbis Biblicus et Orientalis* 38; Fribourg, 1981), 485-95 [cf. id., *NLNT* 3.194-201]

_____, 'L' "imitation": une notion paienne empruntée par le NT', in C. Froidefond (ed.), *Mélanges E. Delebecque* (Aix-en-Provence, 1983), 395-404

_____, 'ΑΠΑΡΧΗ. Note de lexicographie néo-testamentaire', in W.C. Weinreich (ed.), *The NT Age. Essays in Honor of B. Reicke* (2 vols; Macon, 1984), 2.493-502

Ste Croix, G.E.M. de, *The Class Struggle in the Ancient Greek World* (Ithaca, 1981)

Stone, L., 'Literacy and Education in England, 1640-1900', *P&P* 42 (1969) 69-139

* Stubbs, M., *Language and Literacy. The Sociolinguistics of Reading and Writing* (London, 1980)

Syme, R., *History in Ovid* (Oxford, 1978)

Szemerényi, O., 'The origin of Aspect in the Indo-European languages', *Glotta* 65 (1977) 1-18

Teodorsson, S.-T., *The Phonemic System of the Attic Dialect, 400-340 BC (Studia Graeca et Latina Gothoburgensia* 32; Lund, 1974)

_____, *The Phonology of Ptolemaic Koine (Studia Graeca et Latina Gothoburgenisa* 36; Göteborg, 1977)

—————, *The Phonology of Attic in the Hellenistic Period* (*Studia Graeca et Latina Gothoburgensia* 40; Göteborg, 1978)

—————, 'Phonological variation in Classical Athens and the development of Koine', *Glotta* 57 (1979) 61-75

Thackeray, H.St.J., *A Grammar of the OT in Greek according to the LXX.* I, *Introduction. Orthography and Accidence* (Cambridge, 1909)

—————, 'An unrecorded "Aramaism" in Josephus', *JTS* 30 (1929) 361-70

—————, *Josephus, The Man and the Historian* (1929; repr. New York, 1967)

Thieme, G., *Die Inschriften von Magnesia am Mäander und das NT* (Tübingen, 1906)

Thiselton, A.C., 'The supposed power of words in the Biblical writings', *JTS* 25 (1974) 283-99

—————, 'Language and Meaning in Religion', in C. Brown (ed.), The *New International Dictionary of NT Theology* (Exeter, 1978), 3.1123-46

Thompson, S., *The Apocalypse and Semitic Syntax* (*SNTSMS* 52; Cambridge, 1985)

Thorley, J., 'Subjunctive Aktionsart in NT Greek; a reassessment', *NovT* 30 (1988) 193-211

Thrall, M.E., *Greek Particles in the NT. Linguistic and Exegetical Studies* (*NT Tools and Studies* 3; Leiden, 1962)

Threatte, L., *The Grammar of Attic Inscriptions*, I. *Phonology* (Berlin, 1980)

Thumb, A., *Die griechische Sprache im Zeitalter des Hellenismus: Beiträge zur Geschichte und Beurteilung der Koine* (Strassburg, 1901)

—————, 'Die sprachgeschichtliche Stellung des biblischen Griechisch', *TRu* 5 (1902) 85-99

—————, 'Review [of NT Grammars by Robertson, Moulton, and Radermacher, of Zorell's NT Lexicon, and of Rouffiac, *Recherches* . . .]', Byz. Zeit. 22 (1913) 484-91

—————, 'On the value of Modern Greek for the study of Ancient Greek', *CQ* 8 (1914) 181-205

Tigner, S.S., 'Some LSJ Addenda and Corrigenda', *Glotta* 52 (1974) 192-206

Tov, E., 'Some thoughts on a lexicon of the LXX', *Bull. IOSCS* 9 (1976) 14-46

—————, 'Die griechischen Bibelübersetzungen', *ANRW* II.20.1 (1987) 124-89

—————, 'The nature and study of the Translation Technique of the LXX in the past and present', in C.E. Cox (ed.), *VI Congress of the International Organization for LXX and Cognate Studies, Jerusalem, 1986* (*SCS* 23; Atlanta, 1987), 337-59

* Traugott, E.C., 'Pragmatic strengthening and grammaticalization', in S. Axmaker, et al. (edd.), *Proceedings of the Fourteenth Annual Meeting of the Berkeley Linguistics Society, February 13-15, 1988* (Berkeley, 1988), 406-16

Treu, K., 'Christliche papyri, I-XIII', *APF* 19 (1969) — 34 (1988)

—————, 'Die Bedeutung des Griechischen für die Juden im römischen Reich', *Kairos* 15 (1973) 123-44

* Trudgill, P., *Sociolinguistics: an Introduction* (Harmondsworth, 1974; rev. edn, 1983)

* —————, *On Dialect* (Oxford, 1983)

* —————, *Dialects in Contact* (*Language in Society* 10; Oxford, 1986)

Trypanis, C.A., Ὁ Ἀττικισμὸς καὶ τὸ γλωσσικό μας ζήτημα (Athens, 1984)

* Tsitsipis, L.D., 'Function Restriction and Grammatical Reduction in Albanian Language in Greece', *Zeitschrift für Balkanologie* 20 (1984) 122-31

Turner, C.H., 'Marcan Usage, VIII. Auxiliary and quasi-auxiliary verbs', *JTS* 28 (1927) 349-62

Turner, N., 'The *Testament of Abraham*: Problems in Biblical Greek', *NTS* 1 (1954/5) 219-23

—————, 'The unique character of Biblical Greek', *VT* 5 (1955) 208-13

—————, 'An alleged Semitism', *ExpT* 66 (1955) 252-54

—————, 'Philology in NT Studies', *ExpT* 71 (1960) 104-07

—————, *A Grammar of NT Greek*, III. *Syntax* (Edinburgh, 1963)

—————, *Grammatical Insights into the NT* (Edinburgh, 1965)

—————, 'The literary character of NT Greek', *NTS* 20 (1973/4) 107-14

—————, 'Jewish and Christian influence on NT vocabulary', *NovT* 16 (1974) 149-60

—————, 'The quality of the Greek of Luke-Acts', in J.K. Elliott (ed.), *Studies in NT Language and Text* (Festschrift G.D. Kilpatrick; *NovT Suppl.* 44; Leiden, 1976), 387-400

—————, *A Grammar of NT Greek*, IV. *Style* (Edinburgh, 1976)

—————, *Christian Words* (Edinburgh, 1980)

_____, 'Biblical Greek, the peculiar language of a peculiar people', in E.A. Livingstone (ed.), *Studia Evangelica* VII. *Papers presented at the 5th International Congress on Biblical Studies held at Oxford, 1973* (Berlin, 1982), 505-12

* Ure, J., 'Approaches to the study of register range', *IJSL* 35 (1982) 5-23

Vergote, J., 'Het probleem van de koine volgens de laatste historisch-philologische Bevindingen', *Philologische Studien* 4 (1932/3) 28-46, 81-109, 190-215

_____, 'Het probleem van de koine in het licht van der moderne linguistiek', *Philologische Studien* 5 (1933/4) 81-105; 6 (1934/5) 81-107

_____, 'Grec biblique', *Dictionnaire de la Bible*, suppl. vol. 3 (Paris, 1938) 1320-69

Vischer, W., 'Savez-vous le grec?', *ETR* 45 (1970) 63-87

Viteau, J., *Etude sur le grec du NT* (2 vols.; Paris, 1893, 1896)

Voelz, J.W., 'The Language of the NT', *ANRW* II.25.2 (1984) 893-977

Wacholder, B.Z., *Eupolemus. A Study of Judaeo-Greek Literature* (*Hebrew Union College Monograph* 3; Cincinnati, 1974)

Weinreich, U., *Languages in Contact* (The Hague, 1953; repr. 1974)

Wet[t]stein, J.[J.], *Novum Testamentum Graecum editionis receptae cum lectionibus variantibus . . . nec non commentariis pleniore ex scriptoribus veteribus Hebraeis, Graecis et Latinis historiam et vim verborum illustrante* (2 vols; Amsterdam, 1751, 1752; repr. Graz, 1962)

Wexler, P., 'Terms for "Synagogue" in Hebrew and Jewish Languages. Explorations in Historical Jewish Interlinguistics', *REJ* 140 (1981) 101-38

Whatmough, J., *The Dialects of Ancient Gaul* (Cambridge [Mass.], 1970)

Wifstrand, A., 'A problem concerning the word order in the NT', *Studia Theologica* 3 (1949) 172-84

Wilcox, M., *The Semitisms of Acts* (Oxford, 1965)

_____, 'Semitisms in the NT', *ANRW* II.25.2 (Berlin, 1984) 978-1029

Wilson, R.M., 'Did Jesus speak Greek?', *ExpT* 69 (1956/7) 121-22

Winer, G.B., *A Treatise on the Grammar of NT Greek* (Edinburgh, 1882³)

Wipszycka, E., 'Un lecteur qui ne sait pas écrire ou un chrétien qui ne veut pas se souiller? (*P.Oxy.* 33.2673)', *ZPE* 50 (1983) 117-21

_____, 'Le degré d'alphabétisation en Egypte byzantine', *REAug* 30 (1984) 279-96

Wouters, A., 'A Greek grammar and a Graeco-Latin lexicon on St. Paul (Rom., 2 Cor., Gal., Eph.): A note on E.A. Lowe, *CLA* Supplement no.1683', *Scriptorium* 31 (1977) 240-42

Youtie, H.C., *The Textual Criticism of Documentary Papyri: Prolegomena* (*BICS Suppl.* 6; London, 1958)

_____, 'Pétaus, fils de Pétaus, ou le scribe qui ne savait pas écrire', *CE* 41 (1966) 127-43 (repr. with addenda in his *Scriptiunculae* 2 [Amsterdam, 1973] 677-95)

_____, 'ΑΓΡΑΜΜΑΤΟΣ: an aspect of Greek society in Egypt', *HSCP* 75 (1971) 161-76 (repr. with addenda in his *Scriptiunculae* 2 [Amsterdam, 1973] 611-27)

_____, 'βραδέως γράφων: Between literacy and illiteracy', *GRBS* 12 (1971) 236-61 (repr. with addenda in his *Scriptiunculae* 2 [Amsterdam, 1973] 629-51)

_____, 'Commentary [on R. Merkelbach, *ZPE* 18 (1975) 101-48]', *ZPE* 18 (1975) 149-54 (repr. in his *Scriptiunculae Posteriores* 1 [Bonn, 1981] 217-22)

_____, 'Response [to J.C. Greenfield's paper on the languages of Palestine, 200 BC-200 AD]', in H.H. Paper (ed.), *Jewish Languages, Theme and Variations. Proc. of Regional Conferences of the Assoc. for Jewish Studies, 1975* (Cambridge [Mass.], 1978), 155-57 (repr. in his *Scriptiunculae Posteriores*, 1 [Bonn, 1981] 57-59)

_____, ' Ὑπογράφευς: The social impact of illiteracy in Graeco-Roman Egypt', *ZPE* 17 (1975) 201-21 (repr. in his *Scriptiunculae Posteriores*, 1 [Bonn, 1981] 179-99)

_____, '"Because they do not know letters"', *ZPE* 19 (1975) 101-08 (repr. in his *Scriptiunculae Posteriores* 1 [Bonn, 1981] 255-62)

Zerwick, M., *Biblical Greek*. English edn by J. Smith (*Scripta Pontificii Instituti Biblici* 114; Rome, 1963; repr. 1977)

Zgusta, L., 'Die Rolle des Griechischen im römischen Kaiserreich', in G. Neumann/J. Untermann (edd.), *Die Sprachen im römischen Reich der Kaiserzeit. Kolloquium . . . April 1974* (*Bonner Jahrbücher Beiheft* 40; Köln, 1980), 121-45

Zwann, J. de, 'The use of the Greek language in Acts', in F.J. Foakes Jackson/K. Lake (edd.), *The Beginnings of Christianity*, I.2 (London, 1922), 30-65

ADDENDA TO *NEW DOCS 1976-1979*

The following notes are intended to provide selective updates on certain of the entries in the previous volumes. In part, they reflect my own further reading, or rethinking of various questions; but a number of colleagues have also kindly offered responses or drawn attention to other perspectives. Abbreviations like *NIP, Anc. Maced.*, etc., refer to works dealt with in earlier volumes of this series; full details of these publications are given in Index 7 in the present volume.

New Docs 1976

1, p.6,   first paragraph: for the text published in *ASNP* 35 (1966) 18-19 no. 7, cf. *SB* 12.2 (1977) 11049. G. Poethke/P.J. Sijpesteijn, *ZPE* 35 (1979) 131 no.1 (provenance unknown, II; = *SB* 16.2 [1985] 12596), publish an invitation to dine at the Hadrianeion; Sarapis is not involved.

2, p.11,   first paragraph below the Greek: for a new inscription from Maroneia which concerns the Egyptian gods note *SEG* 27.341 (Imperial), a very fragmentary dedication to Sarapis, Isis and Anoubis.

    To bibliography on the Maroneia aretalogy (*SEG* 26.821) add *BE* (1977) 287 (pp.364-66); and F.W. Danker, *Benefactor. Epigraphic Study of a Graeco-Roman and NT Semantic Field* (St Louis, 1982) 176-85 no.26. More generally, note V. Longo, *Aretalogie nel mondo greco* I. *Epigrafi e Papiri* (Genoa, 1969), who excludes the hymns which celebrate Isis for the reason that *arete* cannot mean 'accomplishment'. At *HSCP* 82 (1978) 203-11, A. Henrichs surveys the main characteristics of Hellenistic aretalogies, and relates them to Hor., *Od.* 2.19 (cf. *SEG* 28.1634).

    p.12,   first paragraph, b.: the Isis aretalogy from Kyme (*I. Kyme* 41) is repr. and discussed together with other sacred hymns in Guarducci, *EG* IV.137-42. See also Danker, *Benefactor*, 197-201 no.29.

    last paragraph: for hymns to Isis on stone, reference should have been made to V.F. Vanderlip, *The Four Greek Hymns of Isidorus and the Cult of Isis* (*Am. Stud. Pap.* 12; Toronto, 1972). These four inscriptions, carved on a temple at Medînet Mâdi in the Egyptian Fayum, are dated *c*.88-80 BC.

3, p.21,   bibliography: add F. Sokolowski, *ZPE* 34 (1979) 65-69, who suggests that the wording of *ll*.10-11 may reflect a trace of Aramaic syntax; cf. *SEG* 29.1205; *BE* (1979) 431.

4, p.24,   last paragraph: *IGLR* 434 = Barnea, *MPR* 83.

5, p.27,   last paragraph: Drew-Bear, *NIP* (1978) III.8 (Seyitgazi) publishes a fragmentary dedication (clearly non-Jewish) 'to Theos Hypsistos and Hosios and Zeus' (*ll*.7-8). N. Tačeva-Hitova, *VDI* (1978) 133-42 (in Russian; English summary), deals with *Hypsistos* and *Theos Hypsistos* inscriptions from the Bosphorus, concluding that they are pagan not Jewish (*cf. SEG* 28.1648). *SEG* 28.231 (Athens, Imperial), and 890 (Lydia, n.d.), reproduce other dedications for neither of which is there anything to suggest a Jewish milieu. The same may be said of three dedications to *T.H.* (Bithynia, Imperial), in *TAM* 4.1 (1978) 62, 80, 81. The unpublished bronze plaque depicted on the cover of this volume of *New Docs* may be regarded similarly. So, too, with a new inscription found near Lefcopetra, in the territory of ancient Beroia, published by P.M. Petsas in *Ancient Macedonia*, III. *Papers read at the Third International Symposium held in Thessaloniki, Sept. 21-25 1977* (Thessaloniki, 1983) 229-46, at 232. The text on the marble altar reads:

Ἀ[ρ]ιάγνη{ν}, Μητ[ρὸς θεῶν]
ἱερόδουλος, κατ' ἐπιτα-
γὴν Θεοῦ Ὑ[ψί]στου,
μετὰ υἱοῦ Παραμό-
5 νου τὴν ἐπιτ[αγ]ὴν
ἀπέδωκεν τῷ θεῷ.

Ariagne, temple slave of the Mother of the gods, at the command of *Theos*
5 ***Hypsistos* dedicated |what was commanded to the god, with her son Paramonos.**

Petsas suggests no date for this marble altar, though the nearby sanctuary with which this manumission inscription may have been associated testifies to use between late II and early IV.

E. Varinlioğlu, 'Inschriften von Stratonikeia in Karien', *Epig.Anat.* 12 (1988) 84-88 nos.6-11, has published several new inscribed altars with thanksgiving dedications to Διὶ Ὑψί|στῳ καὶ τῷ Θίῳ (6.1-3; nos.10 and 11 are similar), Διὶ Ὑψίστῳ | καὶ Θείῳ Ἀνγέ|λῳ (7.1-3), [Θε]ῷ Ὑψ[ίστ]ῳ καὶ τ[ῷ] | [Θ]είῳ Ἀνγέλῳ (8.1-2), Θείῳ | Βασιλῖ καὶ Ὑ|ψίστῳ (9.1-3). *Theion Angelos* (nos.7 and 8) is taken by the editor to be a clue to a Jewish context for these texts, and thus an indicator of a Jewish presence in the city. This view may perhaps be refined a little. The plurality of address in the dedications may suggest that what we have are texts erected by pagans who are in contact with Jewish ideas. From this a Jewish presence at Stratonikeia may plausibly be inferred. See further above, ch.4 pp.72-73.

6, p.31, main paragraph: another item in the 'letter from heaven' convention is Hermas, *Vis.* 2.1.3-4, with *Vis.* 2.4.2-3. On this see briefly M. Hengel, *Die Evangelienüberschriften* (*Sitz. der Heidelberger Akad. der Wiss.*, ph.-hist. *Kl.* 1984.3; Heidelberg, 1984) 46-47 n.110. Deissmann, *LAE*, 374, regards the seven letters in Rev. 2-3 as part of this tradition. *PSI* 4 (1917) 435 (Philadelphia, 258-257 BC) is a letter of Zoilos to Apollonios which provides a telling parallel to the situation of the inscription from Thessalonike (*IG* X, 2.255) that forms the basis of item **6**. See Deissmann, *LAE*, 152-61, for discussion. Affinities with the inscription may also be seen in an anecdote recorded at Plut. *Mor.* 434 D-F.

7, p.32, last three lines: for a dedication to Hosios and Dikaios see G. Petzl, *ZPE* 30 (1978) 268 no.14 (Lydia, Imperial; = *SEG* 28.889). A dedication to *Theion Hosion* and *Dikaion* is published in *Festschrift Dörner* (Leiden, 1978) 2.756 no. 4 (Sardis(?), Imperial; = *SEG* 28.929).

9, p.38, bibliography on *SEG* 26.1392: add J.F. Strange, *BA* (1983) 167-68.

11, p.46, *BGU* 13.2211, text: more has been lost on the left side than is indicated in *ed. pr.*: see J.D. Thomas, *CR* 48 (1978) 333; J.C. Shelton, *Gnomon* 51 (1979) 609.

15, p.56, *ll*.2-3: for κατ' ὄνομα greetings in a Christian letter note *P.L.Bat.* 19 (1978) 21.16, 20, 24 (Oxyrhynchos, IV).

17, p.59, last paragraph: for some other vets note R.P. Wright, *Britannia* 8 (1977) 279-82, a Greek vet in Britain referred to in the graffito on a funerary urn as μυλοφισι[κός] (*l*.2; i.e. *mulomedicus*, ἱπποιατρός; cf. *BE* [1978] 563); *SEG* 28.1060 (Strobilos in Bithynia, Byzantine), an epitaph for the wife of a vet; and *CPR* VII.4 (1979) 38.3, ἱπποιατρῷ (provenance unknown, IV).

21, p.65, last paragraph: on letters of introduction note the non-Christian example, *P.Tebt.Tait* (1977) 51 (II^2 or III), in which a man asks his brother to receive the letter-bearer 'since he is a *xenos* in these parts.'

22, p.67, first new paragraph: for juxtaposed ΑΩ in non-Christian magical texts see R.W. Daniel, *ZPE* 50 (1983) 153.

23, p.68, bibliography to *SEG* 26.1214: Guarducci, *EG* IV.494-98 (pl.) argues again that this text is Christian; cf. *SEG* 28.826. Her 1976 article is repr. in ead., *Scritti scelti sulla religione greca e romana e sul cristianesimo* (*EPRO* 98; Leiden, 1983) 383-92. In addition to his

AJP article, C.P. Jones has also written on this inscription in *Les martyres de Lyon. Colloque international du CNRS 575, Lyon, 20-23 Sept., 1977* (Paris, 1978) 119-27. On the metre of the text note C. Gallavotti, *Vet.Chr.* 17 (1980) 269-71.

24, p.70, main paragraph: for a scatter of further attestations of the name Abaskantos note *SEG* 27.35, the name attested twice on Roman lamps from Corinth (II/III); ibid., 666 (Cosa, Imperial; = *AE* [1977] 250), Ἡλίου προφήτης |'Αβάσκαντος χαλκεύς; *P.Strasb.* V.3 (1977) 652 (provenance unknown, II); Drew-Bear, *NIP* (1978) IV.10 (Eumeneia in Phrygia, Imperial). For discussion see D. Bonneau, 'L'apotropaique Abaskantos en Egypte', *RHR* 199 (1982) 23-36.

25, p.71, second paragraph: for *virgo/puella sacra* used of those who had taken religious vows see W.H.C. Frend in J.H. Humphreys (ed.), *Excavations at Carthage*, III (Ann Arbor, 1977), 29, referring to *CIL* VIII.25051, 25059, 25251 (all from Carthage).

last paragraph: another recently unearthed *hymnodes* (of Dionysos) occurs in *SEG* 27.399 (Histria, 222-25). Note also Deissmann, *Bible Studies*, 231-32; id., *LAE*, 349 n.1, 346, 360-61.

26, p.74, bibliography on *P. Coll. Youtie* 66: add W.V. Harris, *ZPE* 52 (1983) 100.

28, p.80, last paragraph: add reference to M. Hombert/C. Préaux, *Recherches sur le recensement dans l'Egypte romaine* (*P.L.Bat.* 5; Leiden, 1952).

30 On the Egnatian Way see further, P.A. MacKay, 'The route of the Via Egnatia around Lake Ostrovo', in *Anc.Maced.* II (1977) 201-10.

33 ἀρραβών = 'a first instalment': A.J. Kerr, *JTS* 39 (1988) 92-97.

42 οἶνος ... ὄξος: the words are contrasted thrice in *CPR* VI.3.1 (1978) 12 (300/01), and once in ibid., 24.

55 On double names see W. Clarysse, *Aeg.* 65 (1985) 57-66; R.S. Bagnall in R.S. Bianchi (ed.), *Cleopatra's Egypt: Age of The Ptolemies* (New York, 1988), 21-27. Clarysse (largely followed by Bagnall) suggests that in Ptolemaic Egypt what determined use of an Egyptian or a Greek name was the type of text the person was producing. Private documents (especially those in Demotic) show a preference for the Egyptian name, while in official texts concerned with government administration Greek names preponderate where a double name is known for the individual. The inference is that the phenomenon of double names is largely visible only among those with some public role to play; and, further, 'that at least in the sense of language we are dealing with a context which is Egyptian by choice, Greek only for official purposes' (Bagnall, 23). These propositions have some attractiveness, but do not account for the whole gamut of the phenomenon, whether chronologically or geographically. The motivation for the adoption of an additional name was not so single in all cases. Further discussion of double names: G.H.R. Horsley, *Numen* 34 (1987) 1-17, at 2-5; id., in *Anchor Bible Dictionary* (forthcoming).

p.96, last paragraph: P.M. Fraser/E. Matthews have produced the first volume — six are anticipated — of the *Lexicon of Greek Personal Names* (Oxford, 1987).

56 paragraph two: *IGLR* 61 = Barnea, *MPR* 34 (cf. *New Docs 1977*, **88**, ad fin.).

59 *IGLR* 91 also appears in Barnea, *MPR* 35.

60 *IGLR* 54 also appears in Barnea, *MPR* 42 (cf. his p.240).

61, p.100, last paragraph, *l.*3: this text occurs in *IGCB* (1978) 17.

p.101, last paragraph, fourth last line: on the wording ἀρᾶς δρέπανον see L. Robert, *CRAI* (1978) 276 with the reference in n.33.

66 This item appears as *P.Köln* 1 (1976) 48; cf. van Haelst, 718.

67 The brief, bilingual dedication to 'the god in Dan' is seen by F. Millar to possess a cultural importance in inverse proportion to its size: see his essay on Hellenistic Syria in A. Kuhrt/S. Sherwin-White (edd.), *Hellenism in the East* (London, 1987), 110-33, at 132-33. Its significance is severalfold, which may be summarised as the first 'precise example, from the earlier hellenistic period, of the meeting of two identifiable cultures' (133).

69, p.108,   first paragraph after translation: another example of a *nomen sacrum* in a Jewish inscription occurs in K. Herbert, *Greek and Latin Inscriptions from the Brooklyn Museum* (*Wilbour Monographs* 4; New York, 1972) 32, a bronze incense-burner from Egypt (*c.*300-500) with a menorah and a dedication by a certain Auxanon (= Heb. Joseph), which crudely attempts to render into Greek one of the eighteen Benedictions employed in synagogue services: ὑπὲρ εὐχῆς Αὐξάνοντος | εὔλογα, κ(ύρι)ε χαριτόν οστα (*sic*) | καὶ αν (*sic*). The editor regards Auxanon as 'a semi-hellenized Jew' (62).

last paragraph: for another Samaritan synagogue with three inscriptions on the mosaic floor (two in Greek, one Aramaic in Samaritan script) see *SEG* 27.1021 (Tel Aviv, VI-early VII).

Two new inscriptions published by P. Bruneau, *BCH* 106 (1982) 465-504 attest the presence of a Samaritan community on Delos. The first item (*c.*250-175 BC) is very fragmentary, [οἱ ἐν Δήλῳ] | Ἰσραηλῖται οἱ ἀπαρχόμενοι εἰς ἱερὸν ἅγιον Ἀρ|γαριζείν - - -. The second, dated 150-50 BC, is complete and allows us to make better sense of the first:

> Οἱ ἐν Δήλῳ Ἰσραελεῖται οἱ ἀ-
> παρχόμενοι εἰς ἱερὸν Ἀργα-
> ριζείν στεφανοῦσιν χρυσῷ
> στεφάνῳ Σαραπίωνα Ἰάσο-
> 5 νος Κνώσιον εὐεργεσίας
> ἕνεκεν τῆς εἰς ἑαυτούς.

The Israelites on Delos who provide first fruits for sacred Mt Garizin crown with 5 a gold crown Sarapion son of Jason, | citizen of Knossos, because of his benefaction towards them.

These two monuments were discovered a short distance from a building which is usually thought to have been a synagogue. For a brief account of the importance of these items see A.T. Kraabel, *BA* (1984) 44-46.

Evidence for Samaritans has also emerged recently in *P.Heid.* 4 (1986) 333, a letter (provenance unknown, V) in which the writer swears by Mt Gerizim, μὰ τὸν Ἀργαριζίν (14).

Several major contributions have appeared in the past couple of years on Samaritan studies: note especially A.D. Crown (ed.), *The Samaritans* (Tübingen, 1989); R. Eggers, *Flavius Josephus und die Samaritaner* (Göttingen, 1986); B. Hall, *Samaritan Religion from Hyrcanus to Baba Rabba* (Sydney, 1986); R. Pummer, *The Samaritans* (Leiden, 1987); N. Schur, *History of the Samaritans* (Berlin, 1989).

70   bibliography: add B. Lifshitz, *ANRW* II.8 (1977) 463-64.

73   On *SEG* 26.1178 see H. Solin, *ANRW* II.29.2 (1983) 696-97 n.239.

74, p.116,   main paragraph: on official titles accorded to children note G.W. Clarke, *ZPE* 57 (1984) 103-04, on Christian *lectores infantuli*.

76, p.118,   last paragraph: for *Dis Manibus* in Jewish inscriptions note *AE* (1978) 834 (Segermes in Africa Proconsularis, III *fin.*), *DM s*(*acrum*) | *Iudas I*|*cos*(*itanus*) *m*(*onumentum*) *v*(*ivus fecit*?). Icosium = Algiers. On *DM* cf. L.J. Kant, *ANRW* II.20.2 (1987) 683 n.77. See, too, the discussion of *IGUR* 3 (1979) 1240 at *New Docs 1979*, 5, pp.23-24. For *DM* in Christian texts note as a possible instance *AE* (1977) 104 (Rome, n.d.): on a wall in front of a mausoleum which has the graffito ΙΧΘΥΟ (*sic*) is fixed a marble plaque with *DM* followed by an epitaph for a man who belonged to the *familia Caesaris*. Another candidate is the fragmentary *IMS* 6 (1982) 185 (Scupi in Moesia Superior, n.d.; = *CIL* III.8236), † *DM L*(*ucio*?) | *Alexan*|*drio C*|- - -.

78   On the presence of Jews in Gaul see further Solin, *ANRW* II.29.2 (1983) 753.

80   second last paragraph: for an illiterate lector, and the possibility of lectors really not knowing how to *read* any language, see G.W. Clarke, *ZPE* 57 (1984) 103-04.

82, p.128, first paragraph: on the possibility of apotactic monastics owning property see M. Krause in T. Orlandi/F. Wisse (edd.), *Acts of the Second International Congress of Coptic Study, Rome 22-26 Sept., 1980* (Rome, 1985), 121-33. Relevant to this question is *P.Oxy.* 46 (1978) 3311 (*c*.373/4), mentioned briefly at *New Docs 1978*, **104**. G.M. Parássoglou has published *P.Lond.* 3.1014 (described only in the *P.Lond.* vol.) in S. Janeras (ed.), *Miscellània Papirològica R. Roca-Puig* (Barcelona, 1987), 247-50, a letter to Apa Ioannes from the mother of Philadelphos, the latter being identified twice as an *apotaktikos*. A fourth-century date is suggested.

83 *SB* 12.1.10800, *l*.14: J.C. Shelton suggests (*per litt.*, 19.10.84) that the cancelled words may be understood better if the word were capitalised. Epagathos is a common enough name: 'He would then be a second carrier whom it was decided not to send.'

86, p.137, second paragraph after translation: *SEG* 29.327, gravestone of a Christian butcher (Corinth, VII).

87 The most comprehensive recent study on ancient banking is R. Bogaert, *Banques et banquiers dans les cités grecques* (Leiden, 1968). In *Studia Patristica* 15.1 (Berlin, 1984) 217-20, R.M. Grant discusses some evidence for early Christian involvement in banking. He refers briefly to the Adoptionist Theodotos who was a banker in late II (Eus., *HE* 5.28.9-10). Certain features of the career of Kallistos, a slave set up in the banking trade by his Christian master and subsequently Bishop of Rome, are traced (217-19). Grant also draws attention to evidence for Christians as bankers in two papyri: *PSI* 14 (1957) 1412 (Oxyrhynchos, late II/early III), and *P.Amh.* 1 (1900) 3a (III).

90 *IGLR* 53, 435 and 173 = Barnea, *MPR* 41, 82 and 81, respectively.

New Docs 1977

1, p.8, first paragraph: on nursing contracts see A.C. Johnson, *Roman Egypt* (1936; repr. New Jersey, 1959) 286-90.

2 On the development of the doctor's position in the Imperial period see in general K.D. Fischer, *MHJ* 14 (1979) 165-75; cf. *AE* (1979) 9.

pp.16-17, female doctors: add F. Baratte/B.Boyaval, *CRIPEL* 5 (1979) 237-339 no.1080, a mummy label (II/III). Earlier instances at *CIL* II.497 (Emerita in Baetica, early Imperial period), mentioning a *medica optima*; and *MAMA* 3 (1931) 269 (Korykos, n.d.), an epitaph.

pp.21-23 On the Epidauros testimonials to divine healings (*IG* IV^2.1.121-27) see Guarducci, *EG* IV.147-54; L.R. LiDonnici, *SBL 1988 Seminar Papers* (Atlanta, 1988) 272-76.

3, pp.27-28 On the status of Lydia, C.J. Hemer points out in *The Book of Acts in the Setting of Hellenistic History* (*WUNT* 49; Tübingen, 1989) 114 n.32 that there are women with this name of high civic status attested in I-II, e.g., Julia Lydia Laterane of Ephesos, and Julia Lydia of Sardis.

p.32 On Lydia and Acts 16.15, ἐβαπτίσθη καὶ ὁ οἶκος αὐτῆς, cf. *IGLS* 4 (1955) 1336 (= Lifshitz, *Donateurs*, 55) where Eupithis makes a vow on behalf of her *soteira* and that of her husband, her children καὶ παντὸς τοῦ οἴκου | αὐτῆς (5-6). See too, Ignat., *Smyrn.* 13.2 where he greets τὸν οἶκον Ταουίας; and Ignat., *ad Polyc.* 8.2 where he greets τὴν τοῦ Ἐπιτρόπου σὺν ὅλῳ τῷ οἴκῳ αὐτῆς καὶ τῶν τέκνων.

8, p.39, last two lines: *P.Berl.* 13232 has been repr. as *SB* 14.2 (1983) 11658, and was in fact noted by van Haelst as no.878a (my comment on p.40, paragraph two, was wrong).

14, p.49, *ll*.1-3: for an analogy to Rhodian funerary practice note *SEG* 28.770, providing bibliography on Christian catacombs at Syracuse where slaves and *liberti* were buried with free members of the family.

p.50, item 3, fourth last sentence: Pfuhl/Möbius have many instances of grave reliefs where one person hands a crown to another. Roughly a hundred examples are depicted in their second vol. of plates (240-255). In nearly all these a male is reclining and hands the garland to a seated woman. While not without exception, a good number of these texts are epitaphs for a deceased woman.

p.51,   first new paragraph: on ὁμοίωσις in Christian usage see R. Merkelbach, *ZPE* 18 (1975) 144-46.

text at bottom of page: this inscription is repr. with several different readings at *I.Eph.* VI.2104: cf. *New Docs 1979*, **6**, p.28.

15, p.53,   item 3: cf. the discussion in G.E.M. de Ste Croix, *The Class Struggle in the Ancient Greek World* (London, 1981) 174, where he quotes from *CIL* X, 1 (1883) 4917 (Venafrum in Italy, n.d.) a verse epitaph for a 25 year-old *vilicus* (farm overseer): *debita libertas iuveni mihi lege negata* | *morte immatura reddita perpetua est*, 'the freedom owed to me as a young man but denied by law has been granted on a permanent basis by my early death.'

p.54,   *l.*1: cf. *IGUR* 3 (1979) 1330.5-6 (Rome, n.d.), epigram for a girl aged 6 who was granted manumission from δουλοσύνης . . . στυγερᾶς before she died.

end of same paragraph: for the earth as mother in epitaphs note *IGUR* 3.1164.4, and 1451 (both Rome, n.d.).

item 4: ὁμόδουλος occurs again in Pfuhl/Möbius II.2097 (Smyrna(?), later Imperial). With σύνδουλος we may note the analogous συνεξελεύθερος at *I.Eph.* VI.2276.

16, p.55,   text, *l.*2: G. Mussies points out (*per litt.*, 9/8/85) that Ἔστηκες (for -κας) can be compared to ἀφῆκες at Rev. 2.4 (in ℵ*and C).

bibliography: add *BE* (1978) 332.

18   bibliography for *AE* (1977) 808: add *TAM* V.1 (1981) 687.

19, p.61,   top paragraph: on *patronissa* add *I.Eph.* V.1562 (mid-III), in which Flavius Zotikos erects a statue for Claudia *NN* τὴν ἰδίαν | πατρώνισαν (12-13).

21   bibliography: nos.5 and 6a, b are repr. as *P.Mich.* 15 (1982) 751 and 752, respectively.

p.68,   main paragraph: P.E. Dion, *Semeia* 22 (1981) 59-76, argues that common features of the *proskynema* formula and the initial blessing in Aramaic letters suggest influence from the indigenous Egyptian epistolary tradition.

p.69,   mid-page: on passive of εὑρίσκω + εἰς M. Wilcox, *ANRW* II.25.2 (1984) 1012, sees it as an Aramaism, 'arrive at'.

27, p.75,   last line: ὁμότυπος occurs also at *CPR* VII (1979) 14.17 (Hermopolis, 28 April, 305), with reference to copies of a contract with the same text.

33   For Hades as the βίου βραβεύς see Pfuhl/Möbius I.1021 (Kyzikos, I BC), quoted in part at *New Docs 1979*, **7**, p.31.

51   paragraph one, *l.*7: cf. ὑπόπται εὐσεβεῖς in a late Hellenistic list of initiates from Samothrace, *SEG* 29.799. The same text has the verb ὑποπτεύω. For other instances of ἐπόπτης applied variously, note, e.g., *OGIS* 666 (Abydos(?), time of Nero) which speaks of someone coming to adore Helios, προσκυνήσας τὸν Ἥλιον Ἅρμαχιν ἐπόπτην καὶ σωτῆρα . . . For discussion see *IGA* 3 (1919, repr. 1978) 221 n. In *ILS* 9459, an honorific text for Cn. Pompeius Cn. *f.* Magnus speaks of him as ἐπό|[π]την γῆς τε καὶ θαλάσ|[σ]ης (Miletopolis, 63 or 62 BC); cf. K. Tuchelt, *Frühe Denkmäler Roms in Kleinasien*, I (Tübingen, 1979) 193. R. van den Broek, in *Fest. Vermaseren*, I (1978) 138 refers to the first-century AD *PGM* 12 in which the magician invokes τὸν προπάτορα θεῶν, πάντων ἐπόπτην καὶ κύριον.

67   For Christian use of παρασκευή = Friday in inscriptions note *IG* XIV Suppl. (1890, repr. 1978) 2492 (Vienne in Gaul, 7 Feb., 441), ἐτ[ά]|φη ἡμέρᾳ παρασ|κευ<ῆ> . . . (*ll.*13-15); and *IGCB* (1978) 19, ἡμέρα παρα[σκευή] (Corinth, Byz.(?)).

79   The Greek text taken from Buresch has been improved in *TAM* V, 1 (1981) 457 = Lane, *CMRDM* 1.41 (Ayazviran, Imperial):

[Τα]τιανὸς Γλαῦκος καὶ Ἀμμιανὴ φι-
[λ]όθεοι Μηνὶ Μοτυλείτῃ εὐχαριστ-
[ία]ν ἔθοντο εὐχόμενοι ἀεὶ ὑπὲρ
[θ]ρεπτῆς γένει πρώτης· Σαβείν[η]
5   [δ]ὲ κέκληται, ἥνπερ σώσειες συμ-

80, p.100,　　fourth line from bottom: *SEG* 28.1224 (Telmessos in Lykia, Sept. 279 BC) provides another example. This decree of the city includes a curse on any person who contravenes the decision made: εἴη ἁμαρτωλὸς εἰς τὴν Λητώ, | κτλ (*l*.37).

87, p.112,　　no.2, sixth last line: for ΠΙΠ(Ι) in an inscription note *SEG* 29.1588.2 (Aleppo, n.d.; = *IGLS* 1.224).

91, p.127,　　no.3 (*P.Berl*. 16994): W. Brashear, *APF* 34 (1988) 8 no.4, publishes *P.Berl*. 21290, which adjoins Treu's piece at the top. The whole fragment now yields Lk. 7.20-21, 33-35.

　　　　p.138,　　no.12: newly-published school exercises which use biblical passages include P.J. Sijpesteijn, *ZPE* 55 (1984) 145 (pl. 2k), an ostrakon (*O.Moen* inv. 631; V/VI) which contains parts of Mt. 1.19-20. *MPER* 15 (1985) 88, 89 are two school exercises (both Arsinoite/Herakleopolite nome, VII) which use Ps. 90.1.

92　　　　The '*Psalmus Responsorius*' is no.1210 in van Haelst.

95, p.153,　　first new paragraph: de Ste Croix, *Class Struggle*, 263-64, 265, speaks of the indifference of the peasantry in the Late Empire, both Eastern and Western, to barbarian conquests. Note also his discussion, 474-88, especially 483-84, on the Arab invasion where he argues that Butler's 'Coptic betrayal' thesis is wrong.

98, pp.160-61　To the tabulation of fragments of Hermas the following may be added, all from *P.Oxy*. 50 (1983): 3526 (IV), containing *Mand*. V.3-VI.2, and belonging to the same codex as no.10 in the table (*P.Oxy*. 9 [1912] 1172); 3527 (III init.), containing *Sim*. VIII.4.1-5.2; and 3528 (II fin./III init.), containing *Sim*. IX.20.22. This last item thus vies with *P.Mich*. 130 (no.1 in the table) for the claim to be the earliest surviving fragment of Hermas. Cf. K. Treu, *APF* 31 (1985) 62-63.

101　　　　Note W.H.C. Frend, 'Syrian parallels to the Water Newton Treasure?', *JbAC* 27/28 (1984/5) 146-50.

　　　　p.168,　　*l*.6: note A. Frantz, 'The provenance of the open *rho* in Christian monograms', *AJA* 33 (1929) 16-25.

　　　　p.171,　　second new paragraph: for ⚹ as not everywhere a Christian symbol note the following recent evidence: *P.Strasb*. V.4 (1978) 674 (provenance unknown, IV), a document dealing with land which concludes with *m*.3 writing at *l*.15 ✝ δι' ἐμοῦ Φοιβάμμονος ἐγράφη; *P.Köln* 2 (1978) 102 *verso l*.16 (Oxyrhynchite nome, 30 March 418); F. Baratte/B. Boyaval, *CRIPEL* 5 (1979) 237-339 no.1020, a mummy label dated 29 BC on which the symbol ⚹ is recorded.

　　　　　　Latin text at base of page: this item is repr. in *RIS* 3 (1980) 255. A useful parallel to the presence of the Christogram here is Guarducci, *EG* IV.498, no.3 (Trier, IV²), an epitaph for Ursicinus. At the end of *l*.1 occurs [A] ⚹ ω, though there is nothing else in the text to indicate that it is Christian.

　　　　p.172,　　no.2: another very early example is an epitaph reproduced in Guarducci, *EG* IV.522-23 no.1 (Catania in Sicily, IV¹).

103　　　　*P. Wiscon*. 2.74, *l*.16, and translation: it is better to read ἐλευθέρα σου (not 'Ελ-) and understand the word as 'your wife'; so J.C. Shelton, *per litt*., 19/10/84. Cf. the comment at the base of p.175 and *New Docs 1978*, 12, p.46, Greek text *l*.2, with bibliographical reference.

　　　　p.175　　On the name Martyrios/-ia see Solin, *GPR* 2.1001-02, whose earliest examples are III AD.

　　　　p.176,　　*l*.3: ἀβάσκαντα occurs in a Christian acclamation, *SEG* 28.1404 (Eboda in Palestine, Byz.).

104, p.177,　　*l*.5 below translation: another extremely early instance of the lettering occurs on a brief epitaph from Rome for Ursus, the first line of which reads ΧΜΓ ✝. Guarducci, *EG* IV.549 no.6, dates this text IV init.

　　　　p.178,　　paragraph two, *l*.21: Lefebvre, *Recueil*, (= *IGA* 5) 663 is repr. in Guarducci, *EG* IV.459 no.2, where she dates it V AD and reads Χρίστο<ν> in *l*.21.

p.179,   second new paragraph, *l*.4: J.C. Shelton points out to me (*per litt.*, 19/10/84) that Tjäder's references for *VDN* turn out to be to *verna domini nostri*, i.e., they concern the Emperor's slaves.

G. Robinson, 'ΚΜΓ and ΘΜΓ for ΧΜΓ', *Tyche* 1 (1986) 175-77, has examined texts of the early Arabic period in which these variations of the ΧΜΓ formula occur. He takes them to stand for κύριος/θεὸς/Χριστὸς μαρτὺς γένηται.

106   Two recently published items relating to the turmoil of the Great Persecution and the succeeding years deserve mention briefly because of their importance. *P. Bodmer XXIX*: *Vision de Dorothéos* has been edited by A. Hurst/O. Reverdin/J. Rudhardt (Cologny, 1984), and repr. with many corrections by A.H.M. Kessels/P.W. van der Horst, *VC* 41 (1987) 313-59. This is the oldest surviving piece of Christian hexameters, with nearly 350 lines, many of which are lacunose but not so much so that the context is irrecoverable. Though originally composed in early IV, our copy is to be dated to the end of that century. Dorotheos, whom the 1987 editors identify with the man so named in Eus., *HE* 7.32.2-4; 8.1.4; 8.6.5, and whom they believe may have been the son of Quintus Smyrnaeus, records a mystical experience which reminds him of his weakness in not standing up openly for his faith. The vision encourages him to become a *confessor*. Second, S. Mitchell, *JRS* 78 (1988) 105-24 (pl.16), has published very promptly an important new Latin inscription (Colbasa in Pisidia, 312) which provides an epigraphic example of the rescript of Maximinus which was already known from Eus., *HE* 9.7. Eusebius had taken his version from a stele set up in Tyre (9.7.2); and one other fragmentary epigraphical copy is known, from Arcyanda: *TAM* II, 3 (1944) 785 (cf. *CIL* III.12132). The surviving 16 lines of the new Colbasa inscription equate to that portion of the rescript given by Eusebius at 9.7.10-14. Mitchell argues (121-22) that the enigmatic statement in which Maximinus offers the people of Colbasa 'whatever bounty you want', *qualemcumque* | [*munificentia*]*m volueretis* (9-10), without specifying its nature, may allude to a promise to exempt them from the poll tax imposed by Galerius on the entire Empire in 306. This is in return for their asking him to expel Christians from their city and its territory.

A. Pietersma has now published *The Acts of Phileas Bishop of Thmuis* (*Including fragments of the Greek Psalter*). *P. Chester Beatty XV* (*with a new edition of P. Bodmer XX and Halkin's Latin Acta*) (*Cahiers d'Orientalisme* 7; Geneva, 1984).

115, p.205,   paragraph two: a Syriac text and translation is now available in G. Howard, *The Teachings of Addai* (*SBL Texts and Translations* 16, *ECL Series* 4; Chico, 1981).

116, p.208,   *l*.29: another non-Christian instance of the βοηθός formula occurs in *IGA* 3 (1919, repr. 1978) 221 (Abydos, n.d.), ῞Ηλιε, βοήθησον Δημητρίῳ.

Of general relevance to this entry, but with a much broader scope, note G.G.. Stroumsa, 'Religious contacts in Byzantine Palestine', *Numen* 36 (1989) 16-42.

New Docs 1978

1, p.8,   paragraph two, *l*.3: R.S. Bagnall, in D.S. Whitcomb/J. H. Johnson (edd.), *Quseir al-Qadim in 1978. Preliminary Report* (Cairo, 1979), 243-44, mentions the finding of a sealing plug from a pottery jar with the text Kere onios Σεβ(αστοῦ) ἀπελεύθ(ερος). Given that the evidence for Imperial freedmen in the Greek-speaking part of the Empire is sparse (Weaver, *Familia Caesaris*, 9), this brief text is of some note. According to Bagnall, this is our first clear evidence that an imperial estate in Egypt which produced wine was headed by an Imperial freedman in I-II.

2, p.12,   *sub* εὐαγγελίζω: the *P.Giss.* 27 text should read παι|δαρίῳ . . . |. . . ἐρχομένῳ, κτλ (*ll*.4-7). In addition to the two references to Rev., we may note Acts 16.17D.

sub εὐαγγελίζομαι: *IGRR* 4.1756 comes from Sardis and is dated 5-2 BC. The text is repr. in Ehrenberg/Jones, *Documents*[2], 99.

p.14, The name Euangelos: note further *IMS* 6 (1982) 121 (Scupi in Moesia Superior, Imperial), a Latin epitaph for *Fulcinio Evangelo | marito* . . . (*ll*.1-2), a *libertus* of probably oriental origin (so ed.), with no indication of a Christian connection; *SEG* 29.152, *col*.II.12 (Athens, *c*.140), ephebic list; *SEG* 29.479 (Akarnania, n.d.), dedication to Hermes Euangelos and Pan; Loewy, *IGB* (1885, repr. 1976) 52 (Athens, last decades of V BC), inscription set up by Charidemos son of Euangelos; *CIJ* I.207 (Rome, n.d.), Agrios Euangelos. A literary instance interesting for its testimony to name-change at the instigation of a city is Vitruvius 10.2.15: the shepherd Pixodaros discovered the quarry from which Ephesos took the marble for its temple of Augustus, and the city changed his name to Evangelus, *ita statim honores decreverunt et nomen mutaverunt*. Plut., *Per*. 16.4 mentions a slave of Perikles called Euangelos. For the related formation Agathangelos note, e.g., *IGUR* 3 (1979) 1277.1 (Rome, n.d.); Pfuhl/Möbius I.303 (Byzantion, n.d.); *I.Nikaia* 1.119 (Nikaia, n.d.).

4, p.18, second new paragraph: as a further example of the phrase in a fishing lease note *P.Harr.* 2 (1985) 194 (Oxyrhynchos, 183/4 or 215/6), ἄγραν | ἰχθύ[ων] (*ll*.7-8).

6 *CMRDM* 1.13, *l*.24: the accusative form χοίνικες illustrates the shift from -ας to -ες occurring in the *koine*; so G. Mussies (*per litt*. 9.8.85), who draws attention to accus. τέσσαρες at Rev. 4.4 and 7.1 (both in ms. A). Some other instances of this feature include *New Docs 1977*, 3, p.32 (= *P.Wiscon*. 2.72), *ll*.26-27, πάντες | τοὺς σοὺς . . .; **20**, *ll*.20-21, δραχμὰς . . . | . . . τέσσαρες; ibid., *ll*.23-24, τοὺς παρ' ὑμῶν πάν|τες . . .

p.22, second last paragraph, *l*.8: two other items to be noted are *SEG* 25.173 and 28.233 (cf. 29.138), both dated I AD.

p.27-28 A particularly interesting new confession text concerning Men Axiottenos has been published by G. Petzl/H. Malay, *GRBS* 28 (1987 [1988]) 459-72 (pl.). The inscription, from the region of Kula in Maionia and probably to be dated II[2] or III[1], is a lengthy dedication which details the theft of a precious stone, its retrieval and the god's destruction of the young thief. Divine anger is then directed at the wife of the stone's owner because she had failed to acknowledge publicly the god's role in its restoration. She is punished 'because she acted in men's interests rather than in that of the god' (ὅτι τὸ τῶν ἀνθρώπων μᾶλλον ἐπό|ησεν ἢ τοῦ θεοῦ, *ll*.22-23), and accordingly sets up the inscription. See the editors' notes for references to other recently published items of this genre. Further, in *Epig.Anat*. 12 (1988) 147-52 Malay publishes five new confession texts, for the last of which Petzl provides a detailed commentary, ibid., 155-66. In this inscription (date 235/6) Theodoros confesses his illicit intercourse with three women. These sins are taken away by the sacrifice of various animals. For the use of ἀπαίρω in this context (*ll*.10, 14, 16) Petzl (159) compares 1 Jn 3.5 and Jn 1.29. Especially interesting *vis-à-vis* NT language is Theodoros' comment ἔσχα παράκλητον | τὸν Δεῖαν (*ll*.18-19), for which Petzl (163-64) compares 1 Jn 2.1. The verb ἱλάσκομαι occurs in the dentalised form εἱλαζομένου (*l*.20).

p.28, no.6: text repr. and discussed by A.A.R. Sheppard, *Talanta* 12/13 (1980/81) 92-94.

p.29, second Greek text: on *Menos tekousa* see *SEG* 29.1152.

9, p.38, second last paragraph: another instance where the usage of σύντροφος is less specific or clear is *IGUR* 3 (1979) 1347 (Rome, Imperial), in which σύντροφοι dedicate a statue to Pluto, Lethe and Persephone in memory of the deceased Hygeia.

p.39, *l*.1: some further epigraphical instances of the name Tryphosa from Asia Minor may be mentioned: Pfuhl/Möbius I.1056 (Byzantion, II BC); II.1739 (Odessos, II-III), 2245 (Appa in Phrygia, n.d.), Appendix no.xvi (Kyzikos, n.d.); *I.Eph*. IV.1139; VI.2327a, Tryphosa Elpis (n.d.), 2578 (n.d.); VII, 1.3239a, a priestess of Artemis (n.d.), 3448.7, Flavia Tryphosa (Chondria, NW of Ephesos, n.d.), a Roman citizen ; VII, 2.3481 (Ödemiş, 70 km. NE of Ephesos, n.d.).

10 The Greek text comprises two elegiac couplets. Add to bibliography *I.Nikaia* 1.192; *BE* (1979) 542.

11, p.40,   first paragraph below translation: for demographic studies note (a) on age-rounding in
                  antiquity, R.P. Duncan-Jones, *Chiron* 7 (1977) 333-53, which draws attention to the link
                  with illiteracy; id., *ZPE* 33 (1979) 169-77; (b) on longevity in Egypt, F.A. Hooper, *CE* 62
                  (1956) 332-40.

   p. 41,   first new paragraph: εὐνοῦχος occurs in Pfuhl/Möbius II.2084 (Anazarba in Cilicia, early
                  Imperial), an epitaph on a rock-cut tomb, Ἐρεινύες Τεισιφόνη Ἀλληκτὼ Μέγαιρα ἄγονον
                  εὐνοῦχον φυλάσσομεν· [μ]ὴ ἄνοιγε· οὐ γὰρ θ[έμ]ις.

17, p.56,   second last paragraph: on eye-doctors see V. Nutton, *Epigraphica* 34 (1972) 16-29; and
                  note the epitaph for M. Fulvius Herophilus *medico oc(u)lario* (Patras in Achaia, I): *AE*
                  (1979) 572 = *CIL III Add.* (1979) 60.

39   paragraph two: R.E. Witt, *Isis in the Graeco-Roman World* (London, 1971), observes that
                  'the carvings of footprints such as can be seen at Delos and Beneventum probably
                  symbolise the fact that the pilgrim has trodden in the path of the goddess [Isis]. He could
                  think of himself as "in step" and "foot to foot" with Sarapis' (196; see 313 n.67 for
                  references). At the end of a funerary epigram, Pfuhl/Möbius I.863 (Smyrna, probably I
                  BC fin.; = G. Petzl, *Die Inschriften von Smyrna*, I [IK 23; Bonn, 1982] 521), the text
                  employs ἴχνος in a 'part for the whole' figure: στείχοις ἀβλαβὲς ἴχνος ἔχων (*l*.11).

40   J. Teixidor, *The Pantheon of Palmyra* (Leiden, 1979) 5, reprints a bilingual Greek/
                  Palmyrene inscription (March 51 AD) which mentions that someone gave to the temple
                  a θυμιατῆριν χρυσᾶ.

75, p.88,   first new paragraph: on φίλος as a term used by a *cliens* of his *patronus* see *I.Nikaia* 1.51,
                  52, 58, 60.
                  second paragraph: on *amici principis* see J. Gaudemet in G. Wirth (ed.), *Romanitas-
                  Christianitas. Untersuchungen zur Geschichte und Literatur der römischen Kaiserzeit*
                  (Festschrift J. Straub; Berlin, 1982), 42-60.

76,   paragraph one: note the Roman citizen Ti. Claudius Agapetus in *I.Nikaia* II, 2.1242 (I-II).
79   Two further epigraphical attestations of the name Philemon are *SEG* 29.531 (Larissa,
                  Augustan period), and *I.Nikaia* II, 2.1357 (probably II).

81   Several more epigraphical instances of the name Tryphaina, the first two of which are
                  Roman citizens: *SEG* 29.606 (Kassandreia in Macedonia, n.d.), Cornelia Τρύφενα; Pfuhl/
                  Möbius I.567 (provenance unknown in Western Turkey, probably II BC fin.), Melitine
                  Tryphaina; ibid., 782 (provenance unknown in Western Turkey, 209); II.1977 (Karacebey,
                  III-IV); *I.Nikaia* II, 2.1310 (n.d.; name partly restored); *I.Eph.* VI.2313e (n.d.).

88,   no.9: on *P.Vindob.* L.91 see now *MPER* 15 (1985) 184 (pl.82), where this version of the
                  Lord's prayer is suggested possibly to be from the Hermopolite nome, and dated VI; and
                  K. Treu, *APF* 32 (1986) 94. Van Haelst, 1206.

93, p.118,   last paragraph: note also *I.Nikaia* II, 2.1512, a dedication to Zeus Pantokrator (II-III); see
                  ed. n. ad loc. for discussion and reference to another pagan example.

95, p.123   On the Pontius Pilate inscription see discussion and bibliography in L.H. Feldman,
                  Josephus and Modern Scholarship (Berlin, 1984) 317-20.

96, p.125,   paragraph two: the Aphrodisias inscription has now been published by J. Reynolds/R.
                  Tannenbaum, *Jews and Godfearers at Aphrodisias* (*Cambridge Philological Soc. Suppl.*
                  vol.12; Cambridge, 1987). This edition includes detailed discussion of the question of the
                  'godfearers' (48-66), as well as of the names and trades represented in this text. The
                  inscription has already been the subject of several seminars, and its undoubted importance
                  will ensure it continues to receive active attention. The most recent article known to me
                  which deals with it is P.W. van der Horst, 'Jews and Christians at Aphrodisias in the light
                  of their relations in other cities in Asia Minor', *NTT* 43 (1989) 106-21. He infers from the
                  inscription the strong position of the Jewish community in the city, which may account for
                  the long time it took for Christianity to become well established there. In this he finds an
                  analogy with the situation at Sardis. Support for his proposal, that Christianity was slow
                  in becoming established in Caria because of the well-entrenched Jewish communities

there, is provided by E. Varinlioğlu's publication of a number of new θεὸς ὕψιστος inscriptions from Stratonikeia, *Epig.Anat.* 12 (1988) 84-88 nos.6-11. On these see further above in these addenda, ad *New Docs 1976*, 5. Much new light on Aphrodisias from mid-III onwards in provided by C. Roueché's publication of a large number of inscriptions in *Aphrodisias in Late Antiquity* (*JRS Monograph* 5; London, 1989).

98, p.136,   item 3: a further instance of the formula occurs in S. Mitchell, *The Inscriptions of North Galatia* (*RECAM* 2 = *BAR* S135; Oxford, 1982) 246 (Soğluca, after 212), [ἔ]|ξι πρὸ(ς) τὸν θεὸν | [ὅσ]τις κρείνι δ|[ικαίους καὶ ἀδίκους] (*ll.*7-10). Mitchell thinks the text is either Christian or Jewish.

100, pp.142-44   On θεία πρόνοια note *P.Lond.* 3.1014 (*descr.*), published by G.M. Parássoglou in S. Janeras (ed.), *Miscellània Papirològica R. Roca-Puig* (Barcelona, 1987), 247-50. This fragmentary Christian letter (IV) has the phrase μετὰ τὴν πρόνοιαν (*l.*4), apparently equivalent to θεία π.

New Docs 1979

1, p.8   In addition to the list of attestations from Ephesos, note W. Ameling, *Die Inschriften von Prusias ad Hypium* (*IK* 27; Bonn, 1985) 89 (after 212), an epitaph for the wife of Aur. Sokratianos, son of Pasikrates, ἀργυροκόπου (8).

3   *TAM* V, 1 (1981) 93 (Saittai in Lydia, 225/6) offers another instance of a 'friendly' association, in which a member of the group is honoured in his lifetime: . . . Αὐρ. Πρεῖμον ἐτεί|μησαν Χρυσάνθινοι | οἱ φίλοι τὸν φίλον | ζή(σαντα) ἔτ(η) κε΄ (*ll.*2-5). For the term Chrysanthinoi see the suggestions in the ed. n.

6, p.27   Another variant of the curse formula discussed in the last paragraph on that page is provided by *TAM* V, 1 (1981) 101 (Saittai in Lydia, 108/9). On this epitaph for L. Octavius Glyptos erected by his wife and his siter the warning runs (*ll.*4-8):

> . . . εἰ δέ τις προσαμάρτῃ τῇ στήλ-
> 5 λῃ, μήτε αὐτῷ θάλασσα πλωτὴ μή-
> τε γῆ βατὴ μήτε τέκνων σπορὰ
> μήτε θεῶν καταχθονίων εἴλεος
> τύχυτο.

p.30   On the prothetic vowel, C. Brixhe, *Essai sur le grec anatolien au début de notre ère* (Nancy, 1987[2]) 115-16, points out that its occurrence is rare in Asia Minor except in Phrygia and adjacent border areas.

14, p.49,   first new paragraph: Marcus Julius Aquila, known previously at Ephesos by the title *archiereus Asiae* (*I.Eph.* III.686), appears as an asiarch in a new inscription (Amorium in E. Phrygia, II/III init.): R.M. Harrison, *AS* 38 (1988) 181 no.2 (pl.23). The text is in fact an honorific for the man's mother, Aelia Ammia, who is 'testified to be an *archiereia* of the greatest temples in Ephesos', ἀρχιερατεύου|σ(α)ν τῶν μεγίστων ἐν Ἐφέσῳ | ναῶν ἐμαρτύρησαν (14-16). Further discussion of this inscription may be expected from R.A. Kearsley, who drew my attention to Aquila's link with Ephesos (not noted by Harrison).

p.55,   end of second new paragraph: the article alluded to as forthcoming has now appeared: R.A. Kearsley, 'A leading family of Cibyra and some Asiarchs of the first century', *AS* 38 (1988) 43-51. Note also her further publication, 'M. Ulpius Appuleius Eurykles of Aezani: Panhellene, Asiarch and Archiereus of Asia', *Antichthon* 21 (1987 [1988]) 49-56.

16, p.58,   second paragraph after translation: concerning the mention of cannibalism in *P.Oxy.* 42.3065, reference should have been made to *I.Kyme* 41.23-24, repr. at *New Docs 1976*, 2, p.19. On actual cannibalism in Egypt see Juv. 15.33-92, referring to some event in Upper Egypt after 127 AD; and Dio 72.12.4-5, dealing with an incident in Alexandria in 172/3.

17, p.65,   last paragraph, *l.*4: in addition to the instances of confusion between the oblique cases (most commonly genitive/dative) noted there, attention may be drawn to two papyri exhibiting accusative/genitive ambivalence. *P.Mich.* 14 (1980) 678 (provenance unknown, 17/8/98) is a lease of a house in which the statement is made, 'And after the time I shall hand over the house clean of all dirt', . . . καὶ μετὰ | [τὸ]ν χρόνον παραδώσω τὴν οἰ|[κίαν] καθαρὰν ἀπὸ πᾶσαν ἀκα|θαρσίας . . . (11-14). In the same volume no.679 is a letter (provenance unknown, mid-II), in which the writer complains about another person that 'although he took the two four-obol coins he did not bring the meat or my money, nor have I seen him up to this point', λαβὼν τὰ δύο τετρώ|[βω]λα οὐδὲ τὸ κρέας οὐδὲ τὸν | [χαλ]κόν μου ἤνεγκε οὐδ`ἐ´ ὤφθη | [μο]ι μέκρι τοῦτο (9-12).

18, p.70   On the inscriptions for Ofellius Laetus reference should be made to G. Bowersock, *GRBS* 23 (1982) 275-79 (cf. BE [1984] 45). He notes that in the Athenian text μετάρσιον ὕμνον signifies not a sublime hymn, but a poem concerning the heavens. Plutarch (*Mor.* 911F, 913F) mentions a Laetus who is probably to be identified with the Laetus of the poem, who was thus known to Plutarch at Athens. The name Ofellius may be derived from Ofellius Macedo, procurator in Greece in late I AD. Thus the philosopher praised in these two epigrams belongs to the time and intellectual milieu of Plutarch.

p.71,   first new paragraph: on *I.Eph.* III.789, D. Runia, *ZPE* 72 (1988) 241-43, restores the missing name of the eclectic philosopher as Π[οτάμωνα].

For some other philosophers mentioned in inscriptions, note *IGB* (1885, repr. 1976) 481 (Rome, Imperial(?)), an epitaph which mentions Δίων φιλόσοφος Ἐφέσιος (*l.*1). S. Mitchell, *The Inscriptions of North Galatia* (Oxford, 1982) 519, is an epitaph (Alaca, Imperial) erected by his children for M. Julius Eumelos τὸν φι|λόσοφον καὶ | πάσῃ ἀρετῇ κε|κοσμημένον, | τὸν πιστότατον | καὶ πάντων φί|λον (2-8). Note too ibid., 417 (Büyük Nefes, Imperial), of which the only surviving words are - - - φιλο]σόφου ἀπὸ Μουσείου [- - -.

19, p.80,   second last paragraph: on *I.Eph.* Ia.2, see Danker, *Benefactor*, 289-90 no.46.

20   C.P. Jones points out to me (*per litt.*, 13/10/87) that the best current text of this inscription is W. Ameling, *Herodes Atticus*, III. *Inschriftenkatalog* (*Subsidia Epigraphica* 11; Hildesheim, 1983) 182-205, no.189.

p.85,   last paragraph: on συνευφροσύνη, regarded by C.P. Jones as a ghost-word (*per litt.* 13/10/87), see G. Cortassa, *ZPE* 60 (1985) 177-88.

22   On this text cf. Danker, *Benefactor*, 287-88 no.45.

25, p.112,   The Ostia inscription of Mindius Faustus is repr. by Solin, *ANRW* II.29.2 (1983) 726.

26, p.113,   first paragraph: J. Mateos, *Filologia Neotestamentaria* 1 (1988) 5-25, offers an analysis of the range of meanings of εὐλογία in the NT.

30, p.132,   To the list of items may be added *P.Köln* 4 (1982) 191 (provenance unknown, V/VI), . . . τῆς ἐμῆς χηρίας καταφρονοῦσα, | κτλ (*l.*6).

35   Other recent treatments include M. Marcovich, *ZPE* 50 (1983) 155-71; G. Browne, *ZPE* 52 (1983) 60.

36,   second paragraph: an L. Sergius Paullus was curator of the banks of the Tiber under Claudius (*CIL* VI.31545). Could this be the same man who later became proconsul of Cyprus (Acts 13.7)? If so, can a plausible hypothesis be developed about the usefulness of his social network at Rome for the Christians who went to the capital?

63   Very full discussion of καθηγητής by A. Balland, *Fouilles de Xanthos*, VII. *Inscriptions d'époque impériale du Létôon* (Paris, 1981) 158.

70,   *l.*3: *SIG*³ 1142 = *TAM* V, 1 (1981) 323 (on the findspot, ibid., p.105).

71, p.163,   paragraph two: a further instance of πρωτότοκος at *IMS* 6 (1982) 61 (Scupi in Moesia Superior, Imperial(?)), an epitaph for three people including M. Fabius Julianus πρωτοτόκῳ (*sic*) τέκνῳ ζξ (= ζῇ), *l.*3. On the adjective see further J.B. Frey, *Biblica* 11 (1930) 373-90.

p.164,   last paragraph: with the *MAMA* 7.535 text quoted cf. E. Gibson, '*Christians for Christians' Inscriptions* (1978) no.16.14-18, . . . ὀρφαν|ὰ τέκνα λίποι|το οἶκον †ῆ|ρον βίον ἔρη|μον (Upper Tembris Valley in Phrygia, 304). Note the reversal of the last two adjectives with the nouns, in contrast to the *MAMA* wording. On the cross carved for χ in this clearly non-Christian text see *New Docs 1978*, **98**, p.134.

84	A further example of πρωτεύω to be noted is *IGRR* 3.87 (Amastris in Paphlagonia, II), an honorific text for L. Caecilius Proculus υἱὸν τῆς Λέσβου, πρωτεύοντα τῶν ἐπαρχειῶν. *TAM* V, 1 (1981) 40 (Bagis in Lydia, late Imperial?) is a Christian epitaph for Theodoros ὁ λαμ(πρότατος)	προτεύ(σας) ταύτης	Βαγην(ῶν) λαμ(προτάτης) πόλ(εως) (2-4), where the word occurs again in a civic context.
90,	first paragraph: note also *IGB* (1885, repr. 1976) 154, appendix text b (Pergamon, *c.*190), a dedication by the Achaeans who συναγωνισάμενοι τὴν ἐν Λυδίᾳ	παρὰ τὸν Φρύγιον πόταμον μάχην,	κτλ (*ll.*7-8).
96, p.180,	last paragraph: *AE* (1977) 177 instances an Onesimos who is a *libertus* from Italy.
103, p.187	first sentence after the list: A.B. Shippee (*per litt.* 11/8/88) points out that Wisdom literature is not unexampled in inscriptions. He provides the following references:
	Sir. 5.15: Diehls, *ILCV* 2472 = *CIL* X.1396-1400 (IV/V; Latin)
	38.23: *CIJ* I.97* = *CIL* III *Suppl.* p.1, no.11641 (Greek)
	Wisd. 4.13: *ILCV* 1728 (588(?); Latin)
	Prov. 1.6: *IGLS* 1585 (Greek)
	18.21: *ILCV* 2472 (Latin)
	Eccl. 1.2: *IGLS* 1438 (Greek)
	12.11: *ILCV* 2472 (Latin)
p.189,	*l.*5: Ps. 112.7 is fairly well attested epigraphically in Greek. A.B. Shippee (*ad loc.*) has provided the following references: *IGLS* 1455, 1460, 1461, 2230; *DACL* III.1735, §56 (St. Catherine's, Sinai); *CIG* IV.8912 (Bithynia). The version of the text repr. by Guarducci in *EG* IV is unique; a mason's error, perhaps (Shippee), who notes, however, that *IGLS* 1460 and 1461 read ἐγείρει to fit the context.
	second new paragraph: Shippee points out that Guarducci's transcription of Ps. 79.2-16 is wrong at several points against the copy in H. Grégoire, *Recueil des inscriptions grecques chrétiennes d'Asie Mineure*, I (Paris, 1922; repr. Amsterdam, 1968), and *DACL* III, fig.2990 (taken over from *ed. pr.*). Read [γ]ύπτου α[ὐτῆς] (18), καθεῖλες (23). Grégoire dates the text V/VI. Although there is no internal evidence to support the view that the talisman may have been used to protect a vineyard, Shippee notes that Rhodes was famed for its wine production.
p.190,	*l.*3: Shippee (*ad loc.*) reminds me that Ps. 90.11-12 is quoted by Satan to Jesus (Mt. 4.6 = Lk. 4.10-11), and points out that it was used in the Office of the Dead and in apotropaic contexts. Cf. S. Eitrem, *Norsk Teol. Tid.* 24 (1923/4) 1-37. D. Duling, *HTR* 68 (1975) 239, mentions its use at Qumran. Epigraphically, it is best known in Syria, but is also attested at Kertch (Shippee). See further on this psalm D. Feissel, *BCH* 104 (1984) 571-79.
	first new paragraph: Hagg. 2.9 is quoted also in *CIJ* II.973, 974 (both from Galilee and in Hebrew; the latter is to be dated II AD). Shippee (*ad loc.*) doubts that the Jerusalem temple is in view in the example from Cilicia: the inscription refers simply to the founding of that church, and if to anything beyond it to the Universal Church.
	second last paragraph: Ps. 92.5 is also on a lintel from Deir Sem'an (*IGLS* 414). *I.Eph.* VII, 2.3522 = *CIJ* II.755; Shippee (*ad loc.*) thinks that the three young men of Daniel may be in view, since they are commonly represented in iconography.
105, p.192,	paragraph two: J.M. Robinson/A. Wouters offer an analysis of the dimensions and other physical features of the codex containing the Greek-Latin lexicon to some Pauline letters: see S. Janeras (ed.), *Miscellània Papirològica R. Roca-Puig* (Barcelona, 1987), 297-306. See further above in the present volume, p.14. Note also van Haelst, 511.
p.193,	first new paragraph: Shippee believes (*ad loc.*) that if we are to choose between Ps. 28.3 and Acts 7.2 as the source for the wording ὁ θεὸς τῆς δόξης it is almost certainly the latter, since the former is always quoted from the beginning (cf. *New Docs 1976*, 56). Only twice does this line occur in inscriptions — *CIG* IV.8939, and *SEG* 20.465, both reading ὁ θ(εὸ)ς τῆς δόξης ἐβρόντησεν. Ps. 28.3 is associated more with baptismal and Epiphany liturgies than with porticos.

110   On the rise of the synagogue in Egypt see J.G. Griffiths, *JTS* 38 (1987) 1-15.

112, p.212,   first new paragraph: R.S. Bagnall has replied to E. Wipszycka's criticism (*ZPE* 62 [1986] 173-81) of his hypothesis about the pace of conversion to Christianity in fourth-century Egypt: *ZPE* 69 (1987) 243-50. She has now written at greater length on the question, *Aeg.* 68 (1988) 117-65, including a postscript (164-65) which addresses Bagnall's rejoinder to her earlier article. Their positions remain a considerable distance apart, particularly on the question, whether it is possible to arrive at a conclusion which is not simply a general impression. Methologically, much depends on one's view whether papyrological texts lend themselves to statistical analysis for such a subject. A good deal of Wipszycka's stimulating 1988 article consists of a running religious history of IV-VI AD Egypt, based largely on the (sub-)literary sources. She draws attention to numerous 'anomalies' which torpedo the widely-held view that there is a connection between a person's social milieu and the ease or difficulty with which conversion may have occurred. While she has shown that there is much greater complexity in the process because of the ethnic mix of the country, the major differences between the cities (especially Alexandria) and the *chora*, and the range of intellectual achievement, this does not require the discarding of Bagnall's approach. The latter's initial article in *BASP* 19 (1982) 105-24 was avowedly a tentative first sounding; and a larger sample of material needs to be subjected to scrutiny in order to confirm, refine or overthrow his thesis.

113, p.214,   no.12: Solin, *ANRW* II.29.2 (1983) 726, repr. the text, reading and punctuating . . . *Secundinus, Secunda P.T.N.* . . . He suggests that the three letters indicate the *tria nomina* of Secunda's master, or perhaps stand for *Ploti T(   ) n(ostri)*.

A further certain attestation of an *archisynagogos* comes from Tarraco in Spain, conveniently repr. with references to earlier literature in Solin, *ANRW* II.29.2 (1983) 750. The very fragmentary text, in Latin and Greek, mentions someone from Kyzikos who appears to have held the office at Tarraco: . . . [- - -] ἀρχησυν[αγωγ - - -] Κυζηκο[- - -] . . . An allusion in the Latin portion of the text to the Visigoths gives a *terminus* for the date of at least V fin.

pp.219-20   The process whereby συναγωγή superseded προσευχή as the standard word for 'synagogue' naturally took some time. A dedication from Mursa in Pannonia Inferior — in Latin, and so not in Lifshitz, *Donateurs*, although he includes it in the Prolegomenon to the reprint of *CIJ* I, pp.60-61 — appears to attest the restoration of a [- - - *pro*]*seucham* [- - - *vetu*]*state* [*conlapsam a so*(?)]*lo* [- - -. The text dates from the time of Septimius Severus and Caracalla (198-211), and is repr. in Solin, *ANRW* II.29.2 (1983) 762. Was the age of the building the reason why it continued to be called a *proseuche*?

114, p.222,   *l.*6: note, by way of analogy, *I.Kalchedon* (*IK* 20; Bonn, 1980) 77, a Byzantine Christian funerary epigram for Eutropios which addresses Atropos, one of the Fates, for the sake of the pun on his name: Ἄτροπε Μοιράων, τί τὸν εὔτροπον ἥρπασας ἄνδρα (*l.*3).

p.223,   end of list 1a: add *AE* (1979) 235 (Arretium, 407), a Latin epitaph for a *puella* aged 16½, already married for 3½ years.

p.224,   list 2a: add *I.Kalchedon* 33 (= Pfuhl/Möbius I.507), a fragmentary epigram for Stratonike who is μελλογά[μ]ου (3); no age is indicated in the surviving portion of text.

116,   paragraph three: further evidence suggesting that Sabb-/Samb- names are not necessarily always Jewish is provided by *P.Princ.* 1 (1931) 1, *col.*1.13, 24; *col.*2.14; *col.*3.10; *col.*4.8, where five people called Sambas are named in a document listing individuals who pay pig-tax (Philadelphia, 24/5). Other texts in this volume relating to pig-tax attest additional instances of this name.

119, p.234,   item (d): the phrase τὸν κύριον τῶν πνευμάτων καὶ πάσης σαρκός alludes to Num. 16.22. Cf. *New Docs 1976*, **58**, which shows the flexibility of the formula. Shippee observes (*ad loc.*) that the great numbers and similarity of epitaphs in Lefebvre, *IGA* 5 which contain both the Numbers phrase and the 'bosom of Abraham' formula (cf. *New Docs 1978*, **89**) is a notable indicator of the stability of their presence in Egypt over a long period. Both occur in the Liturgy of St James (§36; *Ante-Nicene Fathers* 7.546a), while the 'bosoms' wording occurs in the *Apost. Constit.* 8.41 (*ANF* 7.497f.). These two citations occur in the context of prayers for the dead, which also contain other phrases which are present in the inscriptions.

122   G. Mussies has drawn to my attention via his recent discussion of Christian inscriptions in Palestine — in R. van den Broek et al., *Kerk en kerken in Romeins-Byzantijns Palestina. Archeologie en geschiedenis (Palaestina Antiqua* 6; Kampen, 1988), 186-211 — that the inscription for Sophia 'the second Phoibe' may be later than IV[2]. A. Alt, *Die griechischen Inschriften der Palaestina Tertia westlich der 'Araba* (Berlin, 1921) no.17 (followed by Mussies, 196-97), notes that though found on the Mount of Olives the probable provenance of the stone is Beer Sheba. Alt's version of *l*.7 of the text runs: | [ἔτ(ους)] θιτ. ὁ κύριος ὁ θεὸς | [- - - -]. I have not been able to check all the bibliography given by Alt, though this way of reading the lettering is not to be found in C. Clermont-Ganneau, *CRAI* (1903) 641, or id., *RAO* 6 (1905) 144-46, 210-11, nor in L. Cré, *Rev.Bib.* 13 (1904) 260-62; and it is unknown to Guarducci, *EG* IV.445. If correct, this version would yield the year 319, which equates to 517/8 AD. Cré's plate shows clearly ω after θιτ, however, and it is better to retain it rather than resolve it to *omikron* as Alt does.

p.240,   no.6: for a woman who may have been an elder in a Jewish community on Malta note the catacomb inscription repr. by Solin, *ANRW* II.29.2 (1983) 747 no.12: - - -] γερουσιάρχης φιλεντόλι[ος] καὶ Εὐλογία πρεσβυτήρα ἡ αὐτοῦ σύμβιος.

p.241   Further examples to add to the list include:

5. 'New Demeter' — *I.Lampsakos* (1978) 11 (after 14 AD), honorific decree on statue base for Livia, wife of Augustus, called Ἑστίαν νέαν Δήμη|τρα (2-3). Cf. no.8 below.

6. 'New Dioskouroi' — *I.Eph.* VII, 2.4337.19, sons of Drusus Caesar.

7. 'New Athamas' — *IGRR* 4.527 (Dorylaion, I), honorary decree for Tib. Claudius Philisteus, new founder of the city.

8. 'New Hera' — Loewy, *IGB* (1885, repr. 1976) 300 (Halikarnassos, II[1]), text (b): Ἰουλίαν νέαν Ἥραν | Σαβεῖναν Σεβαστήν (1-2). See also no.9 below. In *IG* VII.43 (Megara), Sabina is called 'New Demeter' (cf. no.5 above).

9. 'New Hera' — *IGRR* 4.881 (Tacina, Provincia Asia, *c*.202-03), mention of Julia Domna as Νέας Ἥρας (3). Cf. no.8 above.

10. 'New Makar' and 'New Lesbos' — L. Robert, *Opera Minora Selecta* 2 (Amsterdam, 1969) 826 discusses a coin of Lesbos originally published in 1909: on the obverse, Σέξτος νέος Μάκαρ; reverse, Ἀνδρομέδᾳ νέᾳ Λέσβῳ. Makar was the founder of Lesbos, and his wife gave her name to the island.

Several of these additional instances show that women were accorded these titles, and (as no.10 shows) not solely those from the Imperial family.

p.243,   first paragraph: O. Montevecchi provides a discussion of the term προστάτις in relation to Phoibe (Rom.16.2), in S. Janeras (ed.), *Miscellània Papirològica R. Roca-Puig* (Barcelona, 1987), 205-16, with further mention of *P.Med.Bar.* 1 (142 BC). M. Zapella, *Riv.Bibl.It.* 37 (1989) 167-71, addresses the same passage in Romans, drawing attention to the inscription in honour of Junia Theodora (Solomos, mid-I): *ed.pr.* — D.I. Pallas et al., BCH 83 (1959) 498-508 (cf. L. Robert, *REA* 62 [1960] 324-42; = *OMS* 2.840-58). R.A. Kearsley, *Ancient Society: Resources for Teachers* 15 (1985) 124-37, had already linked the Junia Theodora inscription with Phoibe to elucidate the latter's status as a benefactor, and drew attention also to several contemporaneous texts honouring Claudia Metrodora of Chios.

l.14: cf. *I.Kalchedon* (1980) 61 (n.d.) an epitaph for Urbanilla, *threpte* of Appia προφήτιδος (*l*.4). The editor takes προφῆτις here to mean that Appia is 'wife of the prophet' of Apollo Chresterios. This instance may be relevant to the methodological point noted at *New Docs 1979*, **113**, p.219 item g.

p.244,   paragraph three: another resolution of ΠΡ in *CIJ* II.1447.2 may deserve consideration, πρ(εσβύτερος). In *CIJ* II.800 = *I.Kalchedon* (1980) 75 the abbreviation ΠΡˢ is resolved as πρ(εσβύτερος) or πρ(εσβυτέρου). In *O.Leid.* (1980) 147, a receipt for weavers' tax (196 AD) ΠΡ is resolved as πρ(εσβυτέρου), 'Besarion the elder' (i.e., in age; so edd.). The same man, again with ΠΡ, figures in *O.Leid.* 148 (23/5/197).

123   On requests for healing, note the parchment Christian amulet published by W. Brashear, *Jnl of Ancient Civilizations* 3 (1988) 35-45. This text (provenance unknown, VII) refers to the Gospel story of the Stilling of the Storm (Mt. 8.26-27, etc.), and then proceeds to ask for healing of a woman (name lost) from her illness. Intercession is made through St George and Mary. Relevant to the Gospel citation here is E.A. Judge's discussion, 'The magical use of Scripture in the papyri', in E.W. Conrad/E.G. Newing (edd.), *Perspectives on Language and Text* (Festschrift F.I. Andersen; Winona Lake, 1987), 339-49.

125,   last paragraph: On the reaction against F. Cumont reference should have been made to R. MacMullen, *Paganism in the Roman Empire* (New Haven, 1981). Cumont's whole approach to ancient paganism is here brought into question, not simply his work on Mithraism. MacMullen's book is fundamentally a revisionist one (in the proper sense of that word). It has met with an ambivalent reception in some quarters of NT work, particularly regarding his thesis (both in *Paganism* and in *Christianizing the Roman Empire* [New Haven, 1984]) that miraculous demonstrations were the main if not sole factor which occasioned conversion to Christianity and other religious groups in antiquity. The view of Cumont and others, that Mithraism and Christianity were in fierce competition, is suggested not to be a balanced assessment by L.H. Martin, 'Roman Mithraism and Christianity' *Numen* 36 (1989) 2-15.

127, p.260, paragraph two: P.J. Sijpesteijn, *Tyche* 2 (1987) 171-74, notes two examples in papyrus texts of undoubtedly wealthy women called πατὴρ τῆς πόλεως. D. Feissel has also recently discussed the institution of the *pater* and provides several new references in his Appendix 1 to G. Dagron/D. Feissel, *Inscriptions de Cilicie* (Paris, 1987) 215-20. See also now C. Roueché, *Aphrodisias in Late Antiquity* (*JRS Monograph* 5; London, 1989) nos. 42-43, and her discussion at pp.77, 101.

132   L. Koenen/C. Römer have now produced a critical edition of the Mani text, *Der Kölner Mani-Kodex* (*Pap.Colon.* 14; Opladen, 1988), containing a text, apparatus, translation (with notes on the latter).

138   Some other grammars dealing with inscriptions may be noted (not all seen by me): M. Bile, *Le dialecte crétois ancien. Etude de la langue des inscriptions. Recueil des inscriptions postérieures aux IC* (*Etudes crétoises* 27; Paris, 1988); K. Hauser, *Grammatik der griechischen Inschriften Lykiens* (diss. Zurich, 1916); E. Ruesch, *Grammatik der delphischen Inschriften*, I (Berlin, 1914); J. Schlageter, *Der Wortschatz der ausserhalb Attikas gefundenen attischen Inschriften* (Strassburg, 1912); R.A. Wagner, *Quaestiones de epigrammatis Graecis ex lapidibus collectis grammaticae* (Leipzig, 1883); J. Waldis, *Sprache und Stil der grossen griechischen Inschrift vom Nemrud-Dagh in Kommagene* (*Nord-Syrien*). *Ein Beitrag zur Koine-Forschung* . . . (Heidelberg, 1920).

CORRIGENDA TO *NEW DOCS 1976-1979*

The following corrigenda affecting clarity have been noticed, which have not already been listed in previous volumes of *New Docs* (*1977*, **121**; *1978*, **113**; *1979*, **141**):

New Docs 1976

p.86,   first paragraph: the provenance of *O. Amst.* 22 is Egyptian Thebes or its vicinity. In *l.*5 of the paragraph, for '*P. Mil. Vogl.* II, 50.13 (I)' read '*P. Mil. Vogl.* II.2 (1961) 50.13 (Tebtynis, I)'. Following εἰς in the Greek text printed on that line the papyrus has the numeral μ΄ and the abbreviation for *arourai*, which the edition has resolved as (Τεσσαρακονταρούρων), 'forty acres'.

p.87,   **45**, *l.*12: for '2 Ki. 13.22' read '2 Ki. 12.22'.

p.108,   last paragraph, *l.*5: for '221-23' read '121-23'.

p.125,   paragraph below translation, *l.*5: for '2665' read '2673'.

New Docs 1977

p.23,   translation, *l.*30: for 'abcess' read 'abscess'.

p.26,   last line: for 'sumpathizers' read 'sympathizers'.

p.39,   **5**, *l.*2: for 'cntury' read 'century'.

for '*CP* (1960)' read '*CP* 55 (1960)'.

first paragraph after translation, *l.*8: for '[1978]' read '[1979]'.

p.56,   *l.*4: for 'non-Christian' read 'non-Christians'.

p.117,   first paragraph after text, *l.*6: for 'Psalms' read 'of the Psalms'.

p.144,   second new paragraph, *l.*2: for 'on' read 'of'.

p.159,   Greek text, *verso*, *l.*4: for 'τό' read 'τό-'.

*l.*5: for 'κ[ω' read 'κ[φ'.

p.177,   *l.*1 below translation: for 'her' read 'his'.

p.195,   Greek text, *l.*2: for 'ὑπὸ' read 'ὕπο'.

p.197,   **110**, second last line: for '**60**' read '**66**'.

p.208,   *l.*18: for 'became' read 'because'.

New Docs 1979

passim   After second proofs had been checked and returned to the typesetter, a keying error has resulted in the German ä being printed as W. For example, midway down p.2 'HWusle' should be read as 'Häusle'. A little lower on the same page, 'StWdte' should be read as 'Städte'.

p.20,   **5**, *l.*1 of translation: for 'god-like' read 'unmarried'.

p.43,   *l.*3 of Greek text: remove punctuation mark after βιότῳ.

p.44,   paragraph 2, *l.*11: for 'μαστιγόω' read 'μαστίζω'.

p.55,   paragraph 1, *ll.*5-6: for 'of the year 109/10' read 'to be dated between 105-109/10'.

p.81,   paragraph 2, *l.*12: for 'appeareances' read 'appearances'.

p.107,   translation, *l.*30: for '*kouretes*' read '*kouretai*'.

p.114,   paragraph below translation, *l.*14: for 'impassibility' read 'impassability'.

p.136,   **32**, third last line: for 'everday' read everyday'.

p.151,   **56**, *l.*3: for 'Rom. 2.14' read 'Rom. 12.14'.

p.164,   last line: for 'Acts 19.7' read 'Acts 19.27'.

p.188,   **104**, paragraph 2, *l*.3: for 'Θ(εός)' read 'θ(εό)ς'.

p.196   paragraph 2, *l*.5: for 'one-time student' read 'follower'.

p.230,   *ll*.1-2: W. Brashear points out to me (*per litt*., 22/9/88) that Deissmann's text has been corrected by Preisendanz, *PGM* Ostrakon 1.

p.242,   item 13, last line: for 'or' read 'of'.

p.267,   item a: for 'Hieropolis' read 'Hierapolis'.

p.276,   sub *New Docs 1976*, *l*.7: for 'p.147' read 'p.146'.

      sub *New Docs 1978*, *l*.15: for 'p.88' read 'p.89'.

p.281,   first column: for 'Acts 19.7' read 'Acts 19.27'.

      centre column: delete 'Rom. 2.14 **56**'; add 'Rom. 12.14 **56**'.

p.284,   first column: add asterisk before ἐπιλαμβάνομαι, εὐφροσύνη, and εὐχαριστέω.

      third column: s.v. λοιπόν, add **17**.

               for 'μαστιγόω' read 'μαστίζω'.

p.285,   centre column: add asterisk before Ταρσεύς.

      third column: s.v. *φίλος: for '**2**' read '**3**'.

CUMULATIVE INDEXES TO VOLUMES 1-5

These cumulative indexes to vols. 1-5 of *New Docs* have been compiled *de novo* by S.P. Swinn, and supersede the separate indexes in each of the preceding volumes. An important difference from them is that, whereas they gave a reference to an entry number in the volume, these new indexes give **references by volume and page number**. Thus, e.g., 4.83 = *New Docs 1979*, page 83, not entry **83**.

1. Biblical passages

This is a list of all references to the Bible and OT Apocrypha in *New Docs* vols. 1-5. For the OT, the book order and chapter numbers of the LXX (Rahlfs' edition) has been followed. [Note that 1, 2 Kgdms = 1, 2 Sam.; 3 Kgdms = 1 Kings. In the LXX the Hebrew Psalm 10 is incorporated into Ps. 9, and the subsequent Psalms bear numbers one less than the Hebrew Bible, down to Ps. 147, of which *vv.*1-11 count as Ps. 146, and *vv.*12-20 as Ps. 147.1-9.]

An occasional indicator '[not . . .]' after a Biblical reference corrects a misprint in one of the earlier volumes. Thus, the reference to 2 Kgdms '13.22' at vol.1 p.87 should actually read '12.22'.

2. Words

This index does not register all occurrences of words in texts printed in *New Docs*, but simply those words which have received some notice in an entry. It also includes words listed or discussed in vol.5. Page numbers in bold type indicate a more than passing reference. An asterisk (*) indicates that comment has been offered on the MM or BAGD entry, or occasionally on LSJ. New words are marked with a dagger (†). For personal names see index 4, s.v. *names*.

3. Grammar

This index provides references to all grammatical discussions of a non-lexical nature, embracing observations on orthography, phonology, syntax etc., as well as aspects of Linguistic theory.

4. Subjects

5. ECL, Patristic and Jewish Writers

6. Texts Discussed

Listed below are all texts new or old appearing in corpora and conspectus volumes which were published in 1976-1979 and referred to in the *New Docs* volume for their respective year. Of other texts, only those referred to in a more than passing manner are listed. Bold type indicates substantial discussion of a text at (or commencing at) the page indicated, or that a text from outside the given year has been reprinted. It has not been the normal practice of this review to suggest new readings or dates, but where they are offered an asterisk (*) beside the text in this index will indicate it.

909	2.100	903 (= *TAM* 5.1.490a)	3.31, 38
911, 912	2.51	910 (= *TAM* 5.1.525; cf. BE [1979]	
933	2.39	434)	3.31
937	2.14, 24	911	3.56
938	2.91	913 (= *TAM* 5.1.179a)	3.59
948a	2.**193**	914 (= *TAM* 5.1.179b)	3.14, 59
948b, 949, 950-955	2.198	917 (= *TAM* 5.1.167a)	3.92
956	2.**198**	920 (= *TAM* 5.1.167d)	3.38
987	2.123	921 (= *TAM* 5.1.168a)	3.38
996 (= *I.Tyre* 1.29b)	2.**200**; 3.169	924 (= *TAM* 5.1.168c)	3.92
997 (= *I.Tyre* 1.75, 76)	2.**148**	926	3.55
998 (= *I.Tyre* 1.149a, b)	2.199	927	3.56
1016	2.208	928	3.54
1018	2.207	929	3.56; 5.136
1021	5.138	930	3.56
1123	2.208	933	3.55
1156	2.21	934	3.92
1181	2.202	946 (cf. *I.Bithynia* III.21;	
*1238 (= Pfuhl/Möbius 783)	2.176;	*BE* [1979] 363)	3.89
	4.***237**, 238	948 (= *Homm.Vermaseren*,	
1242	2.95	3.1000-02 no.3)	3.108
1243 (cf. *BE* [1977] 23)	2.**45**	953	3.42, 79; 4.**12**
1255	2.106	954 (= *Fest.Dörner*, 2.697-99	
1260	2.50	no.6)	3.93
1262	2.10	981 (= *I.Bithynia* II.14)	3.166
1278	2.44	982 (= *I.Bithynia* III.2)	3.87
1289	2.106	986 (= *I.Bithynia* III.5)	3.108
1304 (cf. *I.Charles Univ.* 6)	2.**60**	1014 (= *Fest.Dörner*, 1.80-81,	
28 (1978) 11, 12, 48	3.85	no.SR19)	3.102
60 (= Shear, *Kallias*)	3.84	1018 (= *I.Bithynia* III.7)	3.87
89	3.84	1019 (= *I.Bithynia* III.8)	3.87
197	3.77	1020 (= *I.Bithynia* III.6)	3.43
229	3.81	1033 (= *I.Bithynia* III.12)	3.**39**
231	5.135	1037	3.**127**
233	3.31; 5.143	1054 (= *I.Bithynia* II.10)	3.91
311, 358	3.123	1060	5.136
421	3.23; 4.**110**	1070 (= *I.Bithynia* III.20)	3.42
438, 453, 465, 466, 485	3.85	1078	3.128
541	3.84	1082 (= Gibson, 32)	3.128, 129, **135**
561, 562	3.19; 5.102	1083 (= Gibson, 33)	3.128, 135
574	3.102	1084 (= Gibson, 34)	3.128, 135
714	3.85	1096 (= Gibson, 3)	3.128, 129, **133**
721 (cf. *IG* XII, 9.1179)	3.123	1097 (= Gibson, 9)	3.128, 130, 134
741	3.154	1098 (= Gibson, 10)	3.128, 134
755 *bis*	3.144	1099 (= Gibson, 11)	3.128, 129, 134
770	5.139	1100 (= Gibson, 19)	3.**128**
793 (cf. *BE* [1978] 753)	3.165	1101 (= Gibson, 16)	3.128, 134
802	3.166	1104 (= Gibson, 8)	3.128, 129, 134
826 (cf. 26.1214)	3.165; 5.136	1107 (= Gibson, 5) 3.128, **130**, 133, 134	
831	3.85	1108 (= Gibson, 7)	3.128, 134
849	3.47	1110 (= Gibson, 31)	3.42, 128, 134
853 (cf. *Fest.Dörner*, 2.489-503) 3.45		1114	3.65
857	3.54	1126 (= *NIP* IV.8)	3.**48**
863	3.165	1129 (= *NIP* IV.49)	3.93, 136
868	3.111	1144 (= *NIP* IV.48)	3.129, 136, 138
869	3.54	1148 (= *NIP* IV.47)	3.136, 137
883-86	3.52	1155 (= *NIP* IV.46)	3.136
889	5.136	1156 (= *NIP* IV.45)	3.136
890	5.135	1158 (= *NIP* IV.36)	3.37, 108
893 (= *Fest.Dörner*, 2.752-55, no.2;		1161 (= *NIP* IV.44)	3.**136**
TAM 5.1.470a)	3.**37**	1168 (= *NIP* II.5)	3.31
895 (= *TAM* 5.1.473b)	3.38	1169 (= *AE* [1978] 800; *NIP* I.11) 3.64	
899 (= *Fest.Dörner*, 2.746-52, no.1;		1174 (= *CMRDM* 1.92; *NIP* II.2) 3.28	
TAM 5.1.483a)	3.37, 92	*1194	3.31

7. Works Surveyed in Volumes 1-4

Square brackets around abbreviations in the left hand column indicate that the work was read, but no texts were selected for noting. The bold number at the end of each title indicates for which volume of *New Docs* the work was surveyed.

Actes Constantza	*Actes du VIIe Congrès international d'épigraphie grecque et latine, Constantza, 9-15 septembre 1977*, ed. D.M. Pippidi (Bucharest, 1979)	**[4]**
AE	*L'Année épigraphique 1976* (1980); *L'Année épigraphique 1977* (1981); *L'Année épigraphique 1978* (1981); *L'Année épigraphique 1979* (1982)	**[1-4]**
Anc.Maced., II	*Ancient Macedonia* II. *Papers read at the Second International Symposium held in Thessaloniki, 19-24 August 1973* (Thessaloniki, 1977)	**[2]**
Apis, III	*Apis* III. *Inscriptions, Coins and Addenda*, by G.J.F. Kater-Sibbes/M.J. Vermaseren (*EPRO*, 48; Leiden, 1977) [vol.I, *Monuments of the Hellenistic-Roman Period from Egypt*, 1975; vol.II, *Monuments from outside Egypt*, 1975]	**[2]**
Assuan	*Assuan*, by E. Bresciani/S. Pernigotti (*Biblioteca di studi antichi* 16; Pisa, 1978)	**[3]**
Bagnall/Worp, CSBE	*The Chronological Systems of Byzantine Egypt*, by R.S. Bagnall/K.A. Worp (*Studia Amstelodamensia* 8; Zutphen, 1978)	**[3]**
BCH Suppl. IV	*Etudes Delphiques* (*BCH* Suppl. vol. IV; Paris, 1977)	**[2]**
BE	*Bulletin épigraphique*, by J. and L. Robert, in *Revue des études grecques* 89 (1976) 415-595; 90 (1977) 314-448; 91 (1978) 385-510; 92 (1979) 413-541	**[1-4]**
BE Index	*Index du Bulletin épigraphique de J. et L. Robert, 1966-1973*, by J. Marcillet-Jaubert/A.-M. Vérilhac (Paris, 1979)	**[4]**
BGU	*Ägyptische Urkunden aus den staatlichen Museen zu Berlin. Griechische Urkunden* XIII. *Greek Papyri from Roman Egypt*, ed. W.M. Brashear (Berlin, 1976)	**[1]**
[*BL*]	*Berichtigungsliste der griechischen Papyrusurkunden aus Ägypten* 6, edd. E. Boswinkel/P.W. Pestman/H.-A. Rupprecht (Leiden, 1976)	**[4]**
[*BL Index*]	*A Cumulative Index to Berichtigungsliste Vols. 1-6*, by J.W. Shumaker (*TLG Publications Series* 9; Irvine, 1979)	**[4]**
Budischovsky, *Cultes isiaques*	*La diffusion des cultes isiaques autour de la mer adriatique* I. *Inscriptions et monuments*, by M.-C. Budischovsky (*EPRO* 61; Leiden, 1977)	**[2]**
Buresch, *Aus Lydien*	*Aus Lydien. Epigraphisch-geographische Reisefrüchte*, by K. Buresch (Leipzig, 1898; repr. in the series *Subsidia Epigraphica* 8; Hildesheim, 1977)	**[2]**
Carthage	*Excavations at Carthage 1975, 1976, 1977 conducted by the University of Michigan*, ed. J.H. Humphrey (5 vols., 1976-1980; [Tunis, vol.1; Ann Arbor, vols.2-5])	**[3]**
Chiat, *Synagogue Art*	*A Corpus of Synagogue Art and Architecture in Roman and Byzantine Palestine*, by M.J.S. Chiat (4 vols; Diss. Minnesota, 1979)	**[4]**
[*Ch.L.A.*]	*Chartae Latinae Antiquiores: Facsimile-Edition of the Latin Charters Prior to the Ninth Century* 10. *Germany* I. *Berlin* (*DDR*); 11. *Germany* II. *Bundesrepublik Deutschland und Deutsche Demokratische Republik*, edd. A. Bruckner/R. Marichal (Zurich, 1979)	**[4]**
Christophilopoulos, *Νομ. Ἐπιγ.*	*Νομικὰ Ἐπιγραφικά*, by A.P. Christophilopoulos (2 vols; Athens, 1977, 1979)	**[4]**
CIL III Add.	*Inscriptiones Latinae in Graecia repertae. Additamenta ad CIL III*, ed. M. Sašel-Kos (*Epigrafia e Antichità* 5, Faenza, 1979)	**[4]**
CIMAH	*Corpus Inscriptionum Medii Aevi Helvetiae. Die frühchristlichen und mittelalterlichen Inschriften der Schweiz* I. *Die Inschriften des Kantons Wallis bis 1300*, ed. C. Jörg (Freiburg, 1977)	**[2]**
CMC (ET)	*The Cologne Mani Codex* (*P.Colon. inv.nr. 4780*). *"Concerning the Origin of his body"*, trans. R. Cameron/A.J. Dewey (*SBL Early Christian Literature Series* 3, *Texts and Translations* 15; Missoula, 1979)	**[4]**
CMRDM	*Corpus Monumentorum Religionis Dei Menis* (*CMRDM*), by E.N. Lane (4 vols., *EPRO* 19; Leiden 1971-1978)	**[3]**
[Cohen, et al., *Coin-Inscriptions*]	*The Coin-Inscriptions and Epigraphical Abbreviations of Imperial Rome*, by H. Cohen/J.C. Egbert/R. Cagnat (Chicago, 1978)	**[3]**
CPR	*Corpus Papyrorum Raineri* V. *Griechische Texte* II, edd. J. Rea/ P.J. Sijpesteijn (2 vols; Vienna, 1976); VI. *Griechische Texte* III.1, edd. H. Harrauer/ S.M.E. van Lith (2 vols; Vienna, 1978); VII. *Griechische Texte* IV, edd. H. Zilliacus et al. (2 vols; Vienna, 1979)	**[1, 3, 4]**
CSIR	*Corpus Signorum Imperii Romani* (*Great Britain*) I.1. *Corbridge, Hadrian's Wall East of the North Tyne*, by E.J. Phillips (Oxford, 1977)	**[3]**
Didymos, *Eccl.*	*Didymos der Blinde, Kommentar zum Ecclesiastes* (*Tura-Papyrus*) I-VI, edd. G. Binder/M. Gronewald/J. Kramer/B. Krebber/L. Liesenborghs (*Papyrologische Texte und Abhandlungen* 9, 13, 16, 22, 24, 25, 26; Bonn, 1969-1983)	**[4]**

IGA	II. *Inscriptiones nunc Alexandriae in museo*, ed. E. Breccia (Cairo, 1911; repr. Chicago, 1978)
	III. *Inscriptiones 'Memnonii' sive Besae oraculi ad Abydum Thebaidis*, edd. P. Pedrizet/G. Lefebvre (Nancy, 1919; repr. Chicago, 1978)
	IV. *Inscriptiones nominum graecorum et aegyptiacorum aetatis romanae incisae sive scriptae in tabellis. 'Mummy Labels'*, ed. W. Spielberg (Leipzig, 1901; repr. Chicago, 1978)
	V. *Inscriptiones Christianae Aegypti*, ed. G. Lefebvre (Cairo, 1907; repr. Chicago, 1978) **[1, 3]**
[*IGAnt.*]	*Inscriptiones Graecae antiquissimae praeter Atticas in Attica repertas*, ed. H. Roehl (Berlin, 1882; repr. Chicago, 1978) **[4]**
IGB	*Inschriften griechischer Bildhauer*, by E.M. Loewy (1885; repr. Chicago, 1976) **[4]**
IGCB	*Inscriptiones Graecae Christianae veteres et Byzantinae* I. *Peloponnesus. Isthmos-Korinthos*, ed. N.A. Bees (privately printed, Athens, 1941; repr. Chicago, 1978) **[3]**
IGLR	*Inscripţiile greceşti şi latine din secolele IV-XIII descoperite in România* (= *Inscriptiones intra fines Dacoromaniae repertae graecae et latinae anno CCLXXXIV recentiores*), ed. E. Popescu (Bucharest, 1976) **[1]**
IGM	*Inscriptiones graecae metricae ex scriptoribus praeter Anthologiam collectae*, ed. Th. Preger (Leipzig 1891; repr. Chicago, 1977) **[4]**
IGUR	*Inscriptiones Graecae Urbis Romae* III, ed. L. Moretti (Rome, 1979) **[4]**
I.Kyme	*Inschriften griechischer Städte aus Kleinasien* V. *Die Inschriften von Kyme*, ed. H. Engelmann (Bonn, 1976) **[1]**
I.Lampsakos	*Inschriften griechischer Städte aus Kleinasien* VI. *Die Inschriften von Lampsakos*, ed. P. Frisch (Bonn, 1978) **[3]**
I.Magnesia Sip.	*Inschriften griechischer Städte aus Kleinasien* VIII. *Die Inschriften von Magnesia am Sipylos*, ed. T. Ihnken (Bonn, 1978) **[3]**
I.Medizin	*Inschriften der Griechen. Epigraphische Quellen zur Geschichte der antiken Medizin*, ed. G. Pfohl (Darmstadt, 1977) **[2]**
IMS	*Inscriptions de la Mésie supérieure*:
	I. *Singidunum et le nord-ouest de la province*, edd. M. Mirković/S. Dušanić (Belgrade, 1976)
	IV. *Naissus-Remesiana-Horreum Margi*, ed. P. Petrović (Belgrade, 1979) **[1, 4]**
I.Nikaia	*Inschriften griechischer Städte aus Kleinasien* IX-X.2. *Katalog der antiken Inschriften des Museums von Iznik (Nikaia)* I-II.2, ed. S. Şahin (3 vols; Bonn, 1979-1982) **[4]**
I.Pamphyl. dial.	*Le dialect grec de Pamphylie. Documents et grammaire*, by C. Brixhe (Paris, 1976) [cf. id., *Etudes d'archéologie classique* 5 (1976) 9-16, which publishes a supplement of texts, nos. 179-192] **[2]**
I.Pan	*Pan du désert*, by A. Bernand (Leiden, 1977) **[2]**
ISE	*Iscrizioni storiche ellenistiche* II, ed. L. Moretti (Florence, 1976) **[1]**
[*I.Thess.Grab.*]	*Thessalische Grabgedichte vom 6. bis zum 4. Jahrhundert v. Chr.*, ed. B. Lorenz (*Commentationes Aenipontanae* 22, *Philologie und Epigraphik* 3; Innsbruck, 1976) **[1]**
I.Tyre	*Inscriptions grecques et latines découvertes dans les fouilles de Tyr (1963-1974)* I. *Inscriptions de la nécropole*, by J.-P. Rey-Coquais (*Bull. du Musée de Beyrouth*, 29; Paris, 1977) **[2]**
I.Wadi Haggag	*The Inscriptions of Wadi Haggag, Sinai*, ed. A. Negev (*Qedem* 6; Jerusalem, 1977) **[2]**
Kenchreai	*Kenchreai, Eastern Port of Corinth* III. *The Coins*, by R.L. Hohlfelder (Leiden, 1978) **[3]**
Kenyon, *Class.Texts*	*Classical Texts from Papyri in the British Museum*, ed. F.G. Kenyon (London, 1891; repr. Milan, 1977) **[3]**
Lang, *Agora*	*The Athenian Agora* XXI. *Graffiti and Dipinti*, by M. Lang (Princeton, 1976) **[2]**
Lodi, *Enchiridion*	*Enchiridion euchologicum fontium liturgicorum*, by E. Lodi (*Bibliotheca 'Ephemerides Liturgicae', Subsidia* 15; Rome, 1979) **[4]**
MPL	*Museum Philologum Londiniense* II. *Special Papyrological Number*, ed. G. Giangrande (1977) **[2]**
MPR	*Les monuments paléochrétiens de Roumanie*, by I. Barnea (*Sussidi allo studio delle antichità cristiane* 6; The Vatican, 1977) **[2]**
Nachtergael, *Galates*	*Les Galates en Grèce et les Soteria de Delphes*, by G. Nachtergael (Brussels, 1977) **[2]**
NIP	*Nouvelles inscriptions de Phrygie*, ed. T. Drew-Bear (*Studia Amstelodamensia* 16; Zutphen, 1978) **[3]**
O.Amst.	*Ostraca in Amsterdam Collections*, ed. R.S. Bagnall, P.J. Sijpesteijn, K.A. Worp (Zutphen, 1976) **[1]**
[*O.Brüss.-Berl.²*]	*Au temps où on lisait le grec en Egypte*, edd. J. Bingen et al. (Brussels, 1977) **[2]**
O.Florida	*The Florida Ostraca. Documents from the Roman Army in Upper Egypt*, ed. R.S. Bagnall (Durham, N. Carolina, 1976) **[1]**
[*O.Lund*]	*Ostraca Lundensia. Ostraka aus der Sammlung des Instituts für Altertumskunde an der Universität zu Lund*, ed. C. Tsiparis (Lund, 1979) **[4]**
O.Medînet Mâdi	*Missione di scavi in Egitto a Medînet Mâdi. Rapporto preliminare delle campagne di scavo 1968-1969*, by E. Bresciani. *Ostraka e papiri greci da Medînet Mâdi nelle campagne 1968-1969*, by D. Foraboschi (Milan, 1976) **[2]**

[*Pap.Flor.*] *Euripide, Eretteo*, ed. P. Carrara (*Papyrologica Florentina* 3; Florence, 1977); *Demosthenis fragmenta in papyris et membranis servata*, ed. B. Hausmann (2 vols.; *Papyrologica Florentina* 4, 8; Florence, 1978, 1981) **[3]**

[Pflaum, *Narbon.*] *Les fastes de la province de Narbonnaise*, by H.-G. Pflaum (*Gallia Suppl.* 30; Paris, 1978) **[4]**

Pfohl, *Studium* *Das Studium der griechischen Epigraphik. Eine Einführung*, ed. G. Pfohl (Darmstadt, 1977) **[2]**

Pfuhl/Möbius *Die ostgriechischen Grabreliefs*, edd. E. Pfuhl/H. Möbius (2 vols, and 2 vols of plates; Mainz am Rhein 1977-1979) **[4]**

Pircher *Das Lob der Frau im vorchristlichen Grabepigramm der Griechen*, by J. Pircher with G. Pfohl (*Commentationes Aenipontanae* 26, *Philologie und Epigraphik* 4; Innsbruck 1979) **[4]**

Raffeiner, *Sklaven* *Sklaven und Freigelassene. Eine soziologische Studie auf der Grundlage des griechischen Grabepigramms*, by H. Raffeiner (*Commentationes Aenipontanae* 23, *Philologie und Epigraphik* 2; Innsbruck, 1977) **[2]**

Reilly, *Slaves* *Slaves in Ancient Greece. Slaves from Greek manumission inscriptions*, by L.C. Reilly (Chicago, 1978) **[4]**

RIS *Römische Inschriften in der Schweiz*, ed. G. Walser (3 vols; Bern, 1979, 1980) **[4]**

SB *Sammelbuch griechischer Urkunden aus Ägypten*, ed. H.-A. Rupprecht: XII, 1 (Wiesbaden, 1976); XII, 2 (Wiesbaden, 1977); [XIII. *Index zu Bd. XII* (Wiesbaden, 1979)] **[1, 2, 4]**

SEG *Supplementum Epigraphicum Graecum*, 26 (1976/77 [1979]); 27 (1977 [1980]); 28 (1978 [1982]); 29 (1979 [1982]) **[1-4]**

SGPI *Sammlung griechischer Ptolemäer-Inschriften*, by M.L. Strack; originally published as an appendix in his *Die Dynastie der Ptolemäer* (Berlin, 1897; repr. separately Chicago, 1976) **[4]**

Shear, *Kallias* *Kallias of Sphettos and the Revolt of Athens in 286 B.C.*, by T.L. Shear (*Hesperia Suppl.* 17; Princeton, 1978) **[3]**

SIA *Inscriptiones Atticae, Paraleipomena et Addenda. Supplementum Inscriptionum Atticarum* [I], II, III, ed. A.N. Oikonomides (Chicago, 1976-1979) **[1, 4]**

Speidel, *Dolichenus* *The Religion of Iuppiter Dolichenus in the Roman Army*, by M.P. Speidel (*EPRO* 73; Leiden, 1978) **[4]**

TAM *Tituli Asiae Minoris* IV. *Tituli Bithyniae* 1. *Paeninsula Bithynica praeter Calchedonem*, ed. F.K. Dörner (Vienna, 1978) **[3]**

Thorikos Test. *Thorikos. Les Testimonia*, by J. Labarbe (Ghent, 1977) **[2]**

Tibiletti, *Lettere* *Le lettere private nei papiri greci del III e IV secolo d. C. Tra paganesimo e cristianesimo*, by G. Tibiletti (*Pubblicazioni della Università Cattolica di Milano, Scienze filologiche e letteratura* 15; Milan, 1979) **[4]**

Tod, *PGE* *The Progress of Greek Epigraphy 1937-1953*, by M.N. Tod (repr. from *JHS* 54 [1939] - 75 [1955]; Chicago, 1979) **[4]**

Tsigaridas, *Κατάλογος* Κατάλογος χριστιανικῶν ἐπιγραφῶν στὰ μουσεῖα τῆς Θεσσαλονίκης, by E. Tsigaridas/K. Loverdou-Tsigarida (*Μακεδονικὴ Βιβλιοθήκη* 52; Thessaloniki, 1979) **[4]**

Tuchelt, *Denkmäler* *Frühe Denkmäler Roms in Kleinasien. Beiträge zur Überlieferung aus der Zeit der Republik und des Augustus* 1. *Roma und Promagistrate*, by K. Tuchelt (*Istanbuler Mitteilungen Beiheft* 23; Tübingen, 1979) **[4]**

[*Urk.dramat.Griechen.*]*Urkunden dramatischer Aufführungen in Griechenland*, by H.J. Mette (Berlin, 1977) **[2]**

Walbank, *Proxenies* *Athenian Proxenies in the Fifth Century B.C.*, by M.B. Walbank (Toronto, 1978) **[3]**

Wiseman, *Corinthians* *The Land of the Ancient Corinthians*, by J. Wiseman (*Studies in Mediterranean Archaeology* 50; Göteborg, 1978) **[3]**

Wistrand *The so-called Laudatio Turiae. Introduction, Text, Translation, Commentary*, by E. Wistrand (*Studia Graeca et Latina Gothoburgensia* 34; Göteborg, 1976) **[3]**

[Wouters, *Gramm.Pap.*] *The Grammatical Papyri from Graeco-Roman Egypt. Contributions to the Study of the 'Ars Grammatica' in Antiquity*, by A. Wouters (*Verhandelingen van de koninklijke Akademie voor Wetenschappen, Letteren en Schone Kunste van België, Klasse der Letteren* 41.92; Brussels, 1979) **[4]**